1001 College Scholarships 2015

By

Adam Lawrence

Thanks

First off I'd like to thank you for purchasing my book. I've very excited about it and hope that you are able to use the information to get some money to make it easier to afford your college degree. I'm always open to feedback and would love to hear from you. If you get a scholarship, have one to add to the next edition of the book or anything else drop by and see me at 1001collegescholarships.com

How to Use This Book

I have stressed over this for a long time and in the end I think that there is no simple answer. I wish that I could organize this book in a way that was best for everyone, but it is impossible. I don't know how you can organize it for each reader's individual needs. Some people are only looking for degrees for those in Rhode Island and others are looking for degrees for those studying horses. In the end the best way to list these scholarships was in alphabetical order. I know, I know, you think I'm nuts now right. No, I'm not. Don't make the mistake of going through this book one by one, it would take you forever. Instead use the indexes in the back. I've spent a lot of time making a number of indexes that will fit your specific needs. Take a look at them in the back of the book and you can see that I listed the scholarship name and scholarship number where you can find the information. This is a much faster and less stressful way to search. Good luck!

Table of Contents

(1) $1,000 "A GPA Isn't Everything" Montly Scholarship

URL:http://www.cappex.com/page/account/quickApply.jsp?scholarshipID=gp&code=HO1002-5-

Goal: To help deserving students pay for college.
Eligibility: Applicants must be in high school or college or plan to attend college in the next 12 months.
Target Student: Applicants must be in high school, college or non-traditional students
Amount: $1,000
Number of Awards: 12
Based on Financial Need: No
Deadline: Last day of each month.
Apply online only

(2) $1,000 MoolahSPOT

MoolahSpot
2713 Newlands Avenue
Belmont, CA 94002

URL:http://www.moolahspot.com/index.cfm?scholarship=1

Goal: The $1,000 MoolahSPOT Scholarship is sponsored by MoolahSPOT.com and helps students of any age pay for higher education. The scholarship is a competition based on a short essay. Family income, grades and test scores are not used in selecting a winner. The award must be used for any education-related expenses such as tuition, fees, books and room and board.

Eligibility: Any student at least 16 years or older who plans to attend, or is currently attending, college or graduate school. Students may be of any nationality and reside in any country. Students may study any major or plan to enter any career field at any accredited college or graduate school. Although applicants can be from any country, all applications must be completed in English.
Target Student: Any high school, undergraduate or graduate student.
Amount: $1,000
Number of Awards: Varies
Based on Financial Need: No
Deadline: April, August, Decemeber
Apply online only

(3) $,1500 College JumpStart Scholarship

College JumpStart Scholarship Fund
4516 B10 El Camino Real No. 325
Los Altos, CA 94022

URL: http://www.jumpstart-scholarship.net

Goal: To help students who are committed to using education to better your life and that of your family and/or community.
Eligibility: Applicants must be in 10th, 11th or 12th grade in high school or college. Scholarship open to non-traditional students. Applicants may study any major and attend any school in the US and must be legal residents of the US. The scholarship can be used for tuition, room and board, books and other educational expenses.
Target Student: High school students, College students and Non-traditional students.
Amount: $1,500
Number of Awards: 3
Based on Financial Need: No
Deadline: April and October

Apply online only

---

(4) $1,500 Scholarship Detective Launch Scholarship

Scholarship Detective

URL:http://www.scholarshipdetective.com/scholarship/index.cfm

Goal: To help students pay for college.
Eligibility: Applicants must be in high school, college or a non-traditional student and a US Citizen or permanent resident. The scholarship can be used at any college for any major.
Target Student: Applicant must be in high schoool, college or a non-traditional student.
Amount: $1,500
Number of Awards: 3
Based on Financial Need: No
Deadline: May, August, December
Apply online only

---

(5) $2,000 "No Essay" College Scholarship

URL:https://collegeprowler.com/scholarship/apply.aspx?source=sc

Goal: To help students pay for college related expenses.
Eligibility: Applicants must be in college or planning to enroll in the next 12 months. The winner is chosen by random drawing.
Target Student: High school, undergraduate, graduate or non-traditional students.
Amount: $2,000
Number of Awards: 12
Based on Financial Need: No
Deadline: Last day of each month at 11pm EST.
Apply online only.

---

(6) 100th Infantry Battalion Memorial Scholarship Fund

Hawaii Community Foundation
Scholarships
1164 Bishop Street, Suite 800
Honolulu, HI 96813

Phone: 888-731-3863
Fax: 808-521-6286
URL:http://www.hawaiicommunityfoundation.org

Goal: The scholarship's goal is to promote awareness of the accomplishments of the 100th Infantry Battalion veterans of WWII and to perpetuate its legacy of continuing service by rewarding direct descendants of the veterans who demonstrate these values and beliefs.
Eligibility: Applicant must be a full time undergraduate or graduate student at a US college or university. They must be a direct descendant of a 100th Infantry Battalion World War II veteran and demonstrate excellence in academics and community service. A minimum GPA of 3.5 is required. Students can live in any state.
Target Student: Full time college and adult students
Amount: Varies
Number of Awards: Varies
Based on Financial Need: No
Deadline: February
Application can be found online. A completed application, transcripts and two letters of recommendation are required.

---

(7) 1st Marine Division Association Scholarship

1st Marine Division Association Inc.
410 Pier View Way
Oceanside, CA 92054

Phone: 877-967-8561

Fax: 760-967-8567
Email: oldbreed@sbcglobal.net
URL:http://www.1stmarinedivisionassociation.org

Goal: To assist dependents of deceased or 100% permanently disabled veterans of service with the 1st Marine Division in furthering their education towards a bachelor's degree.
Eligibility: Limited to dependents of honorably discharged veterans, now deceased from any cause or totally and permanently disabled, who served in a unit that was part of, attached to, or operating in support of, the 1st Marine Division. Beneficiaries who marry before completion of the course, or who fail to complete an academic year for reasons other than scholastic, must reapply before benefits may be resumed.
Target Student: College students and adult students$1,750
Amount: $1,750
Number of Awards: Varies
Based on Financial Need: No
Deadline: Varies
Applications are available online

(8) A. Harry Passow Classroom Teacher Scholarship

National Association for Gifted Children
Chair Awards Committee
1707 L Street NW
Suite 550
Washington, DC 20036

Phone: 202-785-4268
Fax: 202-785-4248
Email: nagc@nagc.org
URL: http://www.nagc.org

Goal: To acknowledge teachers of gifted k-12 students.

Eligibility: Applicants must be teachers of gifted students grades K-12 who are continuing their education and who have been members of the NAGC for at least one year. The award is based on reviews from students, parents, principals and peers and the applicants admission into a graduate or certificate program in gifted education.
Target Student: Graduate and Adult students.
Amount: Varies
Number of Awards: Varies
Based on Financial Need: No
Deadline: April
Applications are available online.

(9) A.O. Putnam Memorial Scholarship

Institute of Industrial Engineers
3577 Parkway Lane
Suite 200
Norcross, GA 30092

Phone: 800-494-0460
Fax: 770-441-3295
Email: bcameron@iienet.org
URL: http://www.iienet2.org

Goal: To assist undergraduate Institute members planning on careers in management consulting.
Eligibility: Applicants must be undergraduate students enrolled in a college in the U.S., Mexico or Canada in an accredited industrial engineering program and be active members of the Institute of Industrial Engineers. Students must be nominated for this award.
Target Student: College and Adult students.
Amount: $700
Number of Awards: 1
Based on Financial Need: Yes
Deadline: November
Nomination information is available online.

(10) AAAE Foundation Scholarship

American Association of Airport
Executives
601 Madison Street, Ste 400
Alexandria, VA 22314

Phone: 703-824-0500
Fax: 703-820-1395
Email: member.services@aaae.org
URL: http://www.aaae.org

Goal: To assist aviation students.
Eligibility: Applicants must be juniors or
above enrolled in an aviation program with
a GPA of 3.0 or higher.
Target Student: College and Adult
students.
Amount: $1,000
Number of Awards: 10
Based on Financial Need: Yes
Deadline: March
Application information is available from
the schools financial aid office.

(12) AACE International Competitive Scholarships

Association for the Advancement of Cost
Engineering
Attn: Staff Director-Education
1265 Suncrest Towne Centre Drive
Morgantown, WV 26505

URL: http://www.aacei.org

Goal: To assist students in programs
related to cost engineering and cost
management.

Eligibility: Applicants must be full time
students who are enrolled in an agricultural
engineering, architechural engineering,
building construction, business
administration, chemical engineering, civil
engineering, industrial engineering,
manufacturing engineering, mechanical
engineering, mining engineering, electrical
engineering or quantity surveying.
Applicants in their final year of
undergraduate study need to be accepted at
a graduate program for full-time study for
the next academic year.
Target Student: College, Graduate and
Adult students.
Amount: $2,000 - $8,000
Number of Awards: Varies
Based on Financial Need: No
Deadline: February
Applications are available online. A
completed application and essay are
required to apply.

(13) AACT National Candy Technologists John Kitt Memorial Scholarship Program

American Association of Candy
Technologists
175 Roch Road
Glen Rock, NJ 07452

Phone: 201-652-2655
Fax: 201-652-3419
Email: aactinfo@gomc.com
URL: http://www.aactcandy.org

Goal: To assist students who have a
demonstrated interest in confectionery
technology.
Eligibility: Applicants must be
sophomores, juniors or seniors at an
accredited four-year college or university in
North America, majoring in food science,
biological science, chemical science, or a
related field with a GPA of 3.0 or higher.
Target Student: College and Adult
students.

Amount: $5,000
Number of Awards: 1
Based on Financial Need: No
Deadline: April
Applications are available online. A completed application, list of honors, awards, academic and work activities, transcript and statement of goals is required to apply.

---

(11) AAF Student ADDY Awards

American Advertising Foundation
1101 Vermont Avenue, NW
Suite 500
Washington, DC 20005

Phone: 800-999-2231
Email: crucker@aaf.org
URL: http://www.studentaddys.com

Goal: To assist students interested in advertising.
Eligibility: Applicants must be enrolled in an accredited U.S. college or university full or part-time and must submit an advertising project. The work must have been created while the student was in school or working as an intern, but not in advertising. The scholarship charges a fee, and as mentioned it is not recommended to apply to these scholarships.
Target Student: College and Adult students.
Amount: $1,000
Number of Awards: Varies
Based on Financial Need: No
Deadline: Varies
Applications are available online.

---

(15) AAGS JosephF. Dracup Scholarship Award

American Congress on Surveying and Mapping
6 Montgomery Village Avenue
Suite 403

Gaithersburg, MD 20879

Phone: 240-632-9716
Fax: 240-632-1321
Email: ilse.genovese@acsm.net
URL: http://www.acsm.net

Goal: To assist ACSM members enrolled in a four-year surveying program or program that is closely related.
Eligibility: Applicants must be ACSM members. Award preference is given to those with coursework that is significantly geared on geodetic surveying.
Target Student: College and Adult students.
Amount: $2,000
Number of Awards: Varies
Scholarship can be renewed.
Based on Financial Need: Yes
Deadline: February
Applications are available online. A completed application, personal statement, transcripts, three letters of recommendation, and proof of ACSM membership is required to apply.

---

(14) AALL Educational Scholarships

American Association of Law Libraries
105 W. Adams
Suite 3300
Chicago, IL 60604

Phone: 312-939-4764
Fax: 312-431-1097
Email: scholarships@aall.org
URL: http://www.aallnet.org

Goal: To assist students stuying to become law librarians.

Eligibility: There are five different awards. 1. Library Degree for Law School Graduates - is awarded to a law school graduate pursuing a degree at an accredited library school. 2. Library School Graduates Attending Law School - given to a library school graduate who is pursuing a degree at an accredited law school who has law library experience and no more than 36 semester hours left before finishing their law degree. 3. Library Degree for Non-Law School Graduates - given to a college graduate with law library experience and is seeking a degree involving law librarianship at an accredited library school. 4. Library School Graduates Seeking A Non-Law Degree - for library school graduates seeking degrees in fields other than law. 5. Law Librarians in Continuing Education Courses - for law librarians with a degree from an accredited law or library school who are continuing their education. Preference for all scholarships is given to AALL members, but anyone can apply. Awards 1-4 are given to those with financial need.
Target Student: Graduate and Adult students.
Amount: Varies
Number of Awards: Varies
Scholarship can be renewed.
Based on Financial Need: Yes
Deadline: April
Applications are available online, by fax, mail, phone or email.

(16) Abe Schechter Graduate Scholarship

Radio Television Digital News Association
4121 Plank Road #512
Fredericksburg, VA 22407

Phone: 202-659-6510
Fax: 202-223-4007
Email: staceys@rtdna.org
URL: http://www.rtdna.org

Goal: To acknowledge professional achievement in electronic journalism.
Eligibility: Applicants must be full-time or incoming graduate students studying any major with a career goal of working in television or radio news.
Target Student: Graduate and Adult students.
Amount: $2,000
Number of Awards: 1
Based on Financial Need: No
Deadline: May
Applications are available online.

(17) Abel Wolman Fellowship

American Water Works Association
6666 W. Quincy Avenue
Denver, CO 80235

Phone: 303-347-3201
Fax: 303-795-7603
Email: lmoody@awwa.org
URL: http://www.awwa.org

Goal: To assist doctoral students studying and researching in the area of water supply and treatment.
Eligibility: Applicants must obtain their Ph.D. withing two years of the award and be citizens of the U.S., Canada and Mexico.
Target Student: Graduate and Adult students.
Amount: Up to $25,000
Number of Awards: 1
Scholarship can be renewed.
Based on Financial Need: No
Deadline: January
Applications are available online. A completed application, transcripts, three letters of recommendation, GRE score, course of study and description of their dissertation and how it relates to water supply and treatment are required to apply.

(18) Above and Beyond Scholarship

California School Library Association
950 Glenn Drive
Suite 150
Folsom, CA 95630

Phone: 916-447-2684
Fax: 916-447-2695
Email: csla@pacbell.net
URL: http://www.csla.net

Goal: To assist library media teachers working towards advanced degrees or National Board Certification.
Eligibility: Applicants must be members of the California School Library Association and California residents planning to continue working in California in the school library profession after completion of their education. Applicants must write a 500 word essay detailing their professional goals how their additional education will help with those goals.
Target Student: Graduate and Adult students.
Amount: $1,000
Number of Awards: Varies
Based on Financial Need: No
Deadline: May
Applications are available online.

---

(19) Academic Achievement Award

American Water Works Association
6666 W. Quincy Avenue
Denver, CO 80235

Phone: 303-347-3201
Fax: 303-795-7603
Email: lmoody@awwa.org
URL: http://www.awwa.org

Goal: To acknowledge contributions in the field of public water supply.

Eligibility: Doctoral dissertations and master's theses are eligible for the award. The paper must be the work of a single author and submitted in the same year it is submitted for the degree. The applicant can major in any subject as long as their research is related to drinking water supply.
Target Student: Graduate and Adult students.
Amount: $1,500 - $3,000
Number of Awards: 4
Based on Financial Need: No
Deadline: October
Applications are available online. A completed application, one page abstract of the manuscript and letter from the major professor or department chair are required to apply.

---

(20) Academic Scholarship for High School Seniors

National Restaurant Assocation
Educational Foundation
175 W. Jackson Boulevard
Suite 1500
Chicago, IL 60604

Phone: 800-765-2122
Fax: 312-715-1010
Email: scholars@naref.org
URL: http://www.naref.org

Goal: To assist students majoring in food services.
Eligibility: Applicants must have been accepted into an accredited food service or related program and have 250 hours of restaurant or food service work experience. Applicants must submit an application, letter of recommendation and have a GPA of 2.75 or higher.
Target Student: High school students.
Amount: Varies
Number of Awards: Varies
Based on Financial Need: No
Deadline: August
Applications are available online.

(21) Academic Scholarship for Undergraduate ProStart Alumni and ManageFirst Students

National Restaurant Assocation
Educational Foundation
175 W. Jackson Boulevard
Suite 1500
Chicago, IL 60604

Phone: 800-765-2122
Fax: 312-715-1010
Email: scholars@naret.org
URL: http://www.naref.org

Goal: To assist students in restaurant and food service programs.
Eligibility: Applicants must be majoring in a restaruant or food service program. Applicants must submit a transcript, proof of 750 hours of food service related work experience and a letter of recommendation.
Target Student: College and Adult students.
Amount: $2,000
Number of Awards: Varies
Based on Financial Need: No
Deadline: March
Applications are available online.

(22) Academic Study Award

American Association of Occupational
Heath Nurses Foundation
2920 Brandywine Road
Suite 100
Atlanta, GA 30341

Phone: 770-455-7757
Fax: 770-455-7271
Email: ann@aaohn.org
URL: http://www.aaohn.org

Goal: To assist occupational and environmental health professionals with continuing their education.
Eligibility: Applicants must registered nurses who are enrolled part- or full-time in a nationally accredited bachelor's degree in nursing and have an interest in occupational and environmental health or be registered nurses in a graduate program related to occupational or environmental health as part-time or full-time students.
Target Student: College, Graduate and Adult students.
Amount: $2,500
Number of Awards: 2
Scholarhip can be renewed.
Based on Financial Need: No
Deadline: January
Applications are available online.

(23) ACEC New York Scholarship Program

American Council of Engineering
Companies of New York
6 Airline Drive
Albany, NY 12205

Phone: 518-452-8611
Fax: 518-452-1710
URL:http://www.acecny.org/scholar.html

Goal: To assist students who are planning on becoming consulting engineers.
Eligibility: Applicants must be in their third year of a four year engineering program or in their fourth year of a five year engineering program in New York State. Applicants must major in civil engineering, environmental engineering, chemical engineering, engineering techinology or surveying and plan on working and living in New York State after graduation.
Target Student: College and Adult students.
Amount: $2,500 - $5,000
Number of Awards: At least 10

Based on Financial Need: No
Deadline: December
Applications are available online. A completed application, transcript, essay and two letters of recommendation are required to apply.

---

(24) ACES Copy Editing Scholarships

American Copy Editor's Society
c/o Kathy Schenck
333 W. State Street
Milwaukee, WI 53203

Email: kschenck@journalsentinel.com
URL: http://www.copydesk.org/scholarships.htm

Goal: To assist students interested in copy editing.
Eligibility: Applicants must be college juniors, seniors or graduate students with demonstrated interest and aptitude for copy editing. Graduating students who will take a full time position or internship as a copy editor are eligible.
Target Student: College, Graduate and Adult students.
Amount: $1,000 - $2,500
Number of Awards: 5
Based on Financial Need: No
Deadline: November
Applications are available online. A completed application, list of copy editing coursework, list of copy editing experience, two letters of recommendation, copies of 5 to 10 headlines written by the applicant and a copy of a story edited by the applicant are requried to apply.

---

(25) ACI James Instruments Student Award for Research on NDT on Concrete

American Concrete Instiute ACI James Instruments Student Award
F. Dirk Heidbrink

Wiss Janney, Elstner Associates, Inc
330 Pfingsten Road
Northbrook, IL 60062

Phone: 248-848-3700
Fax: 248-848-3701
Email: fheidbrink@wje.com
URL: http://www.aci-int.org

Goal: To acknowledge research in the concrete and concrete materials field using NDT methods.
Eligibility: Applicants must submit original research on a topic related to nondestructive testingof concrete that was conducted at the undergraduate or graduate level at an accredited college or university.
Target Student: College, Graduate and Adult students.
Amount: $1,200
Number of Awards: 1
Based on Financial Need: No
Deadline: December
There is no application. To be considered a paper must be submitted.

---

(26) ACI NA Airport Commissioner's Scholarships

Airports Council International North America
1775 K Street, NW
Suite 500
Washington, DC 20006

Phone: 888-424-7767
Fax: 202-331-1362
URL: http://www.aci-na.org

Goal: To assist students pursuing careers in ariport management or administration.
Eligibility: Applicants must be undergraduate or graduate students enrolled in an airport management or airport operations program in the U.S. or Canada with a GPA of 3.0 or higher.

Target Student: High school, College, Graduate and Adult students.
Amount: Up to $2,500
Number of Awards: Up to 6
Based on Financial Need: No
Deadline: April and December
Applications are available online.

---

(27) ACI Student Fellowship Program

American Concrete Insitute Student
Fellowship Program
38800 Country Club Drive
Farmington Hills, MI 48331

Phone: 248-848-3816
Fax: 248-848-3801
Email: scholarships@concrete.org
URL: http://www.concrete.org

Goal: To encourage students to go into the concrete field.
Eligibility: Applicants must be full-time undergraduate or graduate students who are nominated by a faculty member who is a member of the ACI. Applicants must be studying engineering, construction management or a related field. Applicants can live anywhere, but must study in the U.S. or Canada.
Target Student: College, Graduate and Adult students.
Amount: Up to 10,000
Number of Awards: Varies
Scholarship can be renewed.
Based on Financial Need: No
Deadline: October
Applicants must be nomiated by an ACI member faculty.

---

(28) ACIL Scholarship

American Council of Independent
Laboratories
1629 K Street NW
Suite 400
Washington, DC 20006

Phone: 202-887-5872
Fax: 202-887-0021
Email: jallen@acil.org
URL: http://www.acil.org

Goal: To encourage students to enter the field of laboratory testing.
Eligibility: Applicants must be college juniors or higher and attending a four year college or university or graduate program in physics, chemistry, engineering, biology, or environmental science.
Target Student: College, Graduate and Adult students.
Amount: Up to $4,000
Number of Awards: Varies
Based on Financial Need: No
Deadline: April
Applications are available online. A completed application, resume, transcripts two letters of recommendation and information about other scholarships received are required to apply.

---

(29) ACJA/Lambda Alpha Epsilon Scholarship

American Criminal Justice Association
P.O. Box 601047
Sacramento, CA 95360

Phone: 916-484-6553
Fax: 916-488-2227
Email: acjalae@aol.com
URL: http://www.acjalae.org

Goal: To assist criminal justice students with educational expenses.

Eligibility: Applicants must be undergraduate or graduate students who are studying criminal justice. Applicants must be ACJA/LAE members, but they can apply for membership as they apply for the scholarship. Students must have completed two semesters or three quarters of their education and earn at least a 3.0 GPA. To apply applicants must submit and application, transcripts, letters of enrollment and a goals statement.
Target Student: Undergraduate, graduate and non-traditioanl students.
Amount: $100 to $400
Number of Awards: Up to 9
Based on Financial Need: No
Deadline: December
Applications are available by written request to the executive secretary

---

(30) ACL/NJCL National Greek Examination Scholarship

American Classical League
Miami University
Oxford, OH 45056

Phone: 513-529-7741
Fax: 513-529-7742
Email: info@aclclassics.org
URL: http://www.aclclassics.org

Goal: To assist outstanding students of Greek.
Eligibility: Applicants must be high school seniors who have earned purple or blue ribbons in the upper level National Greek Exam. Applicants must also agree to earn six units of Greek during their first year of college.
Target Student: High school students.
Amount: $1,000
Number of Awards: 1
Based on Financial Need: No
Deadline: Varies
Applications are sent to the teachers of eligible students each year.

(31) ACL/NJCL National Latin Examination Scholarships

American Classical League
Miami University
Oxford, OH 45056

Phone: 513-529-7741
Fax: 513-529-7742
Email: info@aclclassics.org
URL: http://www.aclclassics.org

Goal: To assist outstanding students of Latin.
Eligibility: Applicants must be high school seniors who have earned a gold medalon the Latin III or Latin IV National Latin Exams. Applicants must also agree to take one course in Latin or Classical Greek during each of their first two semesters of college.
Target Student: High school students.
Amount: $1,000
Number of Awards: 21
Scholarship can be renewed.
Based on Financial Need: No
Deadline: Varies
Applications are mailed to NLE gold medal winners who are high school seniors.

---

(32) ACLS Digital Innovation Fellowships

American Council of Learned Societies
633 Third Avenue
New York, NY 10017

Phone: 212-697-1505
Fax: 212-949-8058
Email: sfisher@acls.org
URL: http://www.contemplativemind.org

Goal: To assist humanities scholars working on digital projects.

Eligibility: Applicants must be students in the humanities fields and have a Ph.D. degree. A completed application, proposal, project plan, budget, bibliography, publication list, three reference letters and one institutional statement are required to apply.
Target Student: Graduate and Adult students.
Amount: Up to $85,000
Number of Awards: Up to 6
Based on Financial Need: No
Deadline: September
Applications are available online.

---

(33) ACLS Fellowships

American Council of Learned Societies
633 Third Avenue
New York, NY 10017

Phone: 212-697-1505
Fax: 212-949-8058
Email: sfisher@acls.org
URL: http://www.contemplativemind.org

Goal: To assist a scholar in the study of humanities.
Eligibility: Applicants must have a Ph.D. and at least three years since their last supported research. A completed application, proposal, bibliography, publication list, and two letters of recommendation are required to apply. Award levels are based on the applicants position (professor, associate professor, assistant professor).
Target Student: Graduate and Adult students.
Amount: Up to $65,000
Number of Awards: Varies
Based on Financial Need: No
Deadline: September
Applications are available online.

---

(34) ACOR-CAORC Fellowships

American Center of Oriental Research
656 Beacon Street, 5th Floor
Boston, MA 2215

Phone: 617-353-6571
Fax: 671-353-6575
Email: acor@bu.edu
URL: http://www.bu.edu/acor

Goal: To assist master's and pre-doctoral students researching in Jordan.
Eligibility: Applicants must be U.S. citizens and graduate studenst studying topics related to Near Eastern studies. Winners are required to engage in scholarly and cultural pursuits while working at the American Center for Oriental Research in Jordan. The fellowship lasts for two to six months and includes a stipend, research funds, room/board and transportation.
Target Student: Graduate and Adult students.
Amount: Varies
Number of Awards: Varies
Based on Financial Need: No
Deadline: February
Applications are available online.

---

(35) ACSM - AAGS - NSPS Scholarships

American Congress on Surveying and Mapping
6 Montgomery Village Avenue
Suite 403
Gaithersburg, MD 20879

Phone: 240-632-9716
Fax: 240-632-1321
Email: ilse.genovese@acsm.net
URL: http://www.acsm.net

Goal: To acknowledge students for excellence in surveying and mapping.

Eligibility: There are a number of awards available. One is for students in a two-year surveying technology program. The second is for students enrolled in graduate programs in geodetic surveying or geodesy. The third is for those enrolled in a four-year degree program in surveying or a related field. The forth is for students in a two-year or four-year surveying or related field full or part time.
Target Student: College, Graduate and Adult students.
Amount: $500 - $2,500
Number of Awards: Varies
Based on Financial Need: No
Deadline: February
Applications are available online.

(36) Actor Fund Work Program

Actor's Fund of America/Actors' Work Program
729 Seventh Avenue
11th Floor
New York, NY 10019

Phone: 800-221-7303
Fax: 212-921-4295
Email: info@actorsfund.org
URL: http://www.actorsfund.org

Goal: To support members of the entertainment industry with finding suplementary work and pursuing new careers.
Eligibility: Applicants must be members of good standing of an entertainment industry union and have a referral from the fund's social service department or another organization that is able to document entertainment industry work.
Target Student: Junior high students or younger, High school, College, Graduate and Adult students.
Amount: Varies
Number of Awards: Varies
Based on Financial Need: No
Deadline: Varies

Applicants must attend a Actors' Work Program Orientation for more information.

(37) ADAF Student Scholarship

American Dietetic Association Foundation
120 South Riverside Plaza
Suite 2000
Chicago, IL 60606

Phone: 800-877-1600
Email: education@eatright.org
URL: http://www.eatright.org

Goal: To encourage students to enter dietetic programs.
Eligibility: Applicants must be American Dietetic Association member who are in their junior or senior year of a bachelor's degree program in dietetics or in their second year in a dietetic technician program, a dietetic internship or graduate dietetic program.
Target Student: College, Graduate and Adult students.
Amount: $500 - $3,000
Number of Awards: Varies
Based on Financial Need: No
Deadline: Varies
Applications are available online.

(38) ADDC Education Trust Scholarship

Desk and Derrick Educational Trust
5153 E 51st Street
Suite 107
Tulsa, OK 74135

Phone: 918-622-1749
Fax: 918-622-1675
Email: adotulsa@swbell.net
URL: http://www.addc.org

Goal: To encourage study in the energy industry.

Eligibility: Applicants must be U.S. or Canadian citizens who have completed two years of their undergraduate program with a 3.0 or higher GPA and demonstrated financial need. Applicants must be working towards a degree in a field that is related to petroleum, energy, or allied industries and plan to work full-time in the petroleum, energy, or allied industry or research alternative fuels such as coal, electric, solar, wind hydroelectric, nuclear or ethanol.
Target Student: College and Adult students.
Amount: Varies
Number of Awards: Varies
Based on Financial Need: Yes
Deadline: April
Applications are available online.

---

(39) ADEA/Sigma Phi Alpha Linda Devore Scholarship

American Dental Education Association
1400 K Street NW
Suite 1100
Washington, DC 20005

Phone: 202-289-7201
Fax: 202-289-7204
Email: morganm@adea.org
URL: http://www.adea.org

Goal: To assist allied dental education students.
Eligibility: Applicants must be members of the American Dental Education Association and be enrolled in a dental hygiene, dental education, or public health degree program with demonstrated leadership in dental education.
Target Student: College, Graduate and Adult students.
Amount: $1,000
Number of Awards: 1
Based on Financial Need: No
Deadline: November

Applications are available online. A completed application, transcript, two letters of recommentation and personal statement are required to apply.

---

(40) Adelle and Erwin Tomash Fellowship in the History of Information Processing

Charles Babbage Institute
Center for History of Information Processing
211 Anderson Library, University of Minnesota
222 - 21st Avenue South
Minneapolis, MN 55455

Phone: 612-624-5050
Email: yostx003@tc.umn.edu
URL: http://www.cbi.umn.edu

Goal: To assist gradaute students researching the history of computing.
Eligibility: Applicants must be graduate students who have completed all of their doctoral degree requirements aside from the dissertation. Applicants must submit a curriculum vitae and a five page statement that provides justification for the research project.
Target Student: Graduate and Adult students.
Amount: $14,000
Number of Awards: 1
Based on Financial Need: No
Deadline: January
Additional information is available on the website.

---

(41) ADHA Institute Scholarship Program

American Dental Hygienists' Association
Institute for Oral Health
Scholarship Award Program
444 North Michigan Avenue
Suite 3400

Chicago, IL 60611

Phone: 312-440-8900
Email: institute@adha.net
URL: http://www.adha.org/ioh

Goal: To assist students pursuing careers in dental hypiene with educational expenses.
Eligibility: Applications should be full-time or part-time students in an accredited dental hygiene program in the U.S. with a GPA of 3.0 or higher and be completing the first year of their program. Undergraduate applicants must be members of the American Dental Hygienists' Association or the American Dental Hygienists Association and graduate students should be members of the Student American Dental Hygienists Association or the American Dental Hygienists Association with a valid hygiene license and a bachelor's degree. Applicants must have financial need unless they are applying for the merit based scholarship.
Target Student: College, Graduate and Adult students.
Amount: $1,000 - $2,000
Number of Awards: Varies
Based on Financial Need: No
Deadline: February
Applications are available online.

---

(42) Admiral Mike Boorda Scholarship Program

Navy-Marine Corps Relief Society
875 North Randolph Street Suite 225
Arlington, VA 22203

Phone: 703-696-4960
Fax: 703-696-0144
Email: education@hq.nmcrs.org
URL: http://www.nmcrs.org

Goal: To assist eligible Navy and Marine Corp members with educational expenses.

Eligibility: Applicants must be enrolled or plan to enroll as a full time, undergraduate student in a college, university, technical college or vocational insituation. Students must have a mimimum GPA of 2.0 and be active duty service members accepted into the Enlisted Commissioning Program, the Marine Englisted Commissioning Education Program or the Medical Enlisted Commissioning Program
Target Student: College and Adult students.
Amount: $500-$3,000
Number of Awards: Varies
Scholarship can be renewed
Based on Financial Need: No
Deadline: May
Applications are available online.

---

(43) Adult Studnets in Scholastic Transition

Executive Women Internatioanl
515 South 700 East
Suite 2A
Salt Lake City, UT 84102

Phone: 801-355-2800
Fax: 801-355-2852
Email: ewi@ewiconnect.com
URL: http://www.executivewomen.org

Goal: To assist adult students facing a mojor life transition.
Eligibility: Applicants may be single parents, displaced workers or individuals who are just entering the workforce.
Target Student: College and Adult students.
Amount: $2,000 - $10,000
Number of Awards: Varies
Based on Financial Need: No
Deadline: Varies by Chapter
For more information contact your local EWI Chapter.

(44) Advancing Aspirations Global Scholarship

Womenetics
99 West Paces Ferry Road NW Suite 200
Atlanta, GA 30305

Phone: 404-818-7224
Email: info@womenetics.com
URL: http://www.womenetics.com

Goal: The scholarship is designed to engage young people in pressing women's issues and to connect students who are interested in the global advancement of women with thought leaders in impactful roles.
Eligibility: Applicants must be undergraduate students and US citizens or legal residents. Applicants must write a 2,500 word essay on a given topic. The scholarship is based on the essay.
Target Student: College and Adult students.
Amount: Up to $5,000
Number of Awards: 10
Based on Financial Need: No
Deadline: July
A registration form and essay are required to apply.

---

(45) AFCEA General Emmett Paige Scholarships

Armed Forces Communications and Electronics Association
4400 Fair Lakes Court
Fairfax, VA 22033

Phone: 703-631-6149
Fax: 703-631-4693
URL: http://www.afcea.org

Goal: To assist members of the armed forces with educational expenses.

Eligibility: Merit-based scholarships of varying amounts will be awarded to persons on active duty in the uniformed military services, to honorably discharged U.S. military veterans (including Reservists and National Guard personnel), and to disabled veterans who are currently enrolled part time or full time in an eligible degree program at an accredited two- or four-year college or university in the U.S. Candidates must be majoring in the following or C4I-related fields of electrical, aerospace, systems or computer engineering; computer engineering technology; computer network systems; information systems security; computer information systems; information systems management; technology management; electronics engineering technology; computer science; physics; or mathematics.
Target Student: College and Adult students.
Amount: $2,500
Number of Awards: Varies
Based on Financial Need: No
Deadline: May
Applications are available online. Two letters of recommendation are required.

---

(46) AFCEA General John A. Wickham Scholarships

Armed Forces Communications and Electronics Association
4400 Fair Lakes Court
Fairfax, VA 22033

Phone: 703-631-6149
Fax: 703-631-4693
URL: http://www.afcea.org

Goal: To assist college sophomores and juniors who are studying electrical, computer, chemical, areospace, engineering, computer science, physics or mathematics with educational expenses.

Eligibility: Applicants must be U.S. citizens, full-time college sophomores or juniors at a four-year U.S. college or university with a 3.4 or higher GPA. Applicants must be majoring in electrical, computer, chemical, systems or aerospace engineering, computer science, computer information systems, technology management, management information systems, physics, mathematics, bioinformatics or other related majors.
Target Student: College and Adult students.
Amount: $2,000
Number of Awards: Varies
Based on Financial Need: No
Deadline: May
Applications are available online.

(47) AFCEA Ralph W. Shrader Diversity Scholarships

Armed Forces Communications and Electronics Association
4400 Fair Lakes Court
Fairfax, VA 22033

Phone: 703-631-6149
Fax: 703-631-4693
URL: http://www.afcea.org

Goal: To assist graduate students studying electrical, computer, chemical or aerospace engineering, mathematics, physics, computer science, computer technology, electronics, communications technology or engineering or information management systems.
Eligibility: Applicants must be U.S. citizens, full-time students working towards a master's degree in electrical, computer, chemical or aerospace engineering, mathematics, physics, computer science, computer technology, electronics, communication technology, communications engineering, or information management at an accredited U.S. college or university.

Target Student: Graduate and Adult students.
Amount: $3,000
Number of Awards: Varies
Based on Financial Need: No
Deadline: May
Applications are available online.

(48) AFCEA ROTC Scholarships

Armed Forces Communications and Electronics Association
4400 Fair Lakes Court
Fairfax, VA 22033

Phone: 703-631-6149
Fax: 703-631-4693
URL: http://www.afcea.org

Goal: To assist ROTC sophomores or juniors who are majoring in aerospace engineering, electronics, computer science, computer engineering, physics or mathematics.
Eligibility: Candidates must be a U.S. citizen enrolled in ROTC, be of good moral character, demonstrate academic excellence, have the potential to serve as an officer in the United States Armed Forces, and have a financial need. The AFCEA Educational Foundation ROTC scholarships are awarded to ROTC students enrolled full-time in C4I-related eligible majors. Applications must be endorsed and submitted by the ROTC Professors of Military Science, Naval Science or Aerospace Studies to the AFCEA Educational Foundation. Applicants must have a 3.0 GPA.
Target Student: College and Adult students.
Amount: $2,000
Number of Awards: Varies
Based on Financial Need: Yes
Deadline: March
Applications are available online.

(49) AFCEA Scholarship for Working Professionals

Armed Forces Communications and
Electronics Association
4400 Fair Lakes Court
Fairfax, VA 22033

Phone: 703-631-6149
Fax: 703-631-4693
URL: http://www.afcea.org

Goal: To assist students pursuing degrees in science and technology.
Eligibility: Applicants must be U.S. citizens and currently employed in the science and technology field and be undergraduate sophomores, juniors or seniors and graduate students. Applicants must be enrolled part-time at an accredited U.S. college or university studying computer science, aerospace engineering, electrical engineering, chemical engineering, systems engineering, mathematics, physics, computer information systems, technical management or a related subject with a GPA of 3.0 or higher.
Target Student: College, Graduate and Adult students.
Amount: $2,000
Number of Awards: Varies
Based on Financial Need: No
Deadline: September
Applications are available online. A completed application, transcript, and two letters of recommendation are required to apply.

(51) AFSA Academic Merit

American Foreign Service Association
(AFSA)
2101 East Street NW
Washington, DC 20037

Phone: 202-944-5504
Fax: 202-338-6820

Email: dec@afsa.org
URL: http://www.afsa.org

Goal: The AFSA Scholarship Program provides to children of Foreign Service employees: need-based, financial aid scholarships (for undergraduate study) and one-time only academic scholarships (for high school seniors).
Eligibility: Have at least one parent who is a member of the AFSA, attending or will attend a 2 or 4 year accredited college, university, community college, art school or conservatory. Applicants must have a 3.0 GPA.
Target Student: High school students
Amount: $2,000
Number of Awards: 15
Based on Financial Need: No
Deadline: March
Applications are available online. Students will also need to submit standardized test scores, an essay and two letters of recommendation.

(50) AFSA Financial Aid Scholarship

American Foreign Service Association
(AFSA)
2101 East Street NW
Washington, DC 22037

Phone: 202-944-5504
Fax: 202-338-6820
Email: dec@afsa.org
URL: http://www.afsa.org

Goal: The AFSA Scholarship Program provides to children of Foreign Service employees: need-based, financial aid scholarships (for undergraduate study) and one-time only academic scholarships (for high school seniors).

Eligibility: Have at least one parent who is a member of the AFSA, attending or will attend a 2 or 4 year accredited college, university, community college, art school or conservatory. Maintian a 2.0 GPA, complete your degree in four years and demonstrate financial need.
Target Student: High school students
Amount: $1,500 - $4,000
Number of Awards: 65
Based on Financial Need: Yes
Deadline: February
Applications are available online. Students will also need to fill out a college scholarship service profile and submit official transcripts.

---

(52) AfterCollege/AACN Nursing Scholarship Fund

American Association of Colleges of Nursing
One Dupont Circle NW
Suite 350
Washington, DC 20036

Phone: 202-463-6930
Fax: 202-785-8320
Email: anniea@aacn.nche.edu
URL: http://www.aacn.nche.edu

Goal: To assist students purusing a career in nursing.
Eligibility: Applicants must be pursuing a bachelor's, master's or doctoral program in nursing at an AACN member institution with a GPA of 3.25 or higher.
Target Student: College, Graduate and Adult students.
Amount: $2,500
Number of Awards: 8
Based on Financial Need: No
Deadline: January, April, July and October
Applications are available online.

---

(53) AGA Scholarships

Association of Government Accountants
2208 Mount Vernon Avenue
Alexandria, VA 22301

Phone: 800-242-7211
Email: rortiz@agacgfm.org
URL: http://www.agacgfm.org

Goal: To assist public financial management students.
Eligibility: Applicants must be a member or family member of the AGA and use the scholarship for full or part-time undergraduate study in a subject area related to financial management (accounting, auditing, budgeting, economics, finance, public administration etc). A completed application, essay and transcript are required to apply. There are two categories in which you may apply. One is an academic scholarship based on academic achievement and the student's potential for making a contribution to the field. The second is a community service scholarship that does not require the applicant to be an AGA member, but requires community service and service projects.
Target Student: High school, College, Graduate and Adult students.
Amount: $1,000 - $3,000
Number of Awards: 6
Based on Financial Need: No
Deadline: March
Applications are available online.

---

(54) AGC Graduate Scholarships

Associated General Contractors of America
333 John Carlyle Street
Suite 200
Alexandria, VA 22314

Phone: 703-837-5342
Fax: 703-837-5402
Email: sladef@agc.org

URL: http://www.agc.org

Goal: To assist college seniors planning to pursue a graduate degree leading to a career in construction or civil engineering.
Eligibility: Applicants must be college seniors who are enrolled in an undergraduate construction or civil engineering degree program or college graduates with a bachelor's degree in construction or civil engineering. Applicants must plan to enroll full-time in a graduate construction or civil engineering program.
Target Student: College, Graduate and Adult students.
Amount: $7,500
Number of Awards: 2
Based on Financial Need: No
Deadline: November
Applications are available online.

---

(55) AGC Undergraduate Scholarships

Associated General Contractors of America
333 John Carlyle Street
Suite 200
Alexandria, VA 22314

Phone: 703-837-5342
Fax: 703-837-5402
Email: sladef@agc.org
URL: http://www.agc.org

Goal: To assist students pursuing a degree that leads to a career in construction or civil engineering.
Eligibility: Applicants must be sophomores or juniors planning to enroll or currently enrolled in ABET or ACCE accredited construction or civil engineering program at a college or university.
Target Student: College and Adult students.
Amount: $2,500
Number of Awards: Over 100
Scholarship can be renewed.

Based on Financial Need: No
Deadline: November
Applications are available online.

---

(56) AHIMA Foundation Merit Scholarships

American Health Information Management Association Foundation
233 N. Michigan Avenue
21st Floor
Chicago, IL 60601

Phone: 312-233-1175
Email: info@ahimafoundation.org
URL: http://www.ahimafoundation.org

Goal: To assist those in health information technology or health information administration with merit scholarships.
Eligibility: Applicants must be AHIMA members with a GPA of 3.0 or higher, with at least six hours completed in health information management or health information technology with a minimum of one semester remaining in their program and currently taking six hours each semester to earn their degree. Associate's, bachelor's and master's degree programs are all eligible.
Target Student: College, Graduate and Adult students.
Amount: $1,000 - $2,500
Number of Awards: Varies
Based on Financial Need: No
Deadline: September
Applications are available online.

---

(57) AIA/AAF Minority/Disadvantaged Scholarship

American Architechtural Foundation
1799 New York Avenue NW
Washington, DC 20006

Phone: 202-626-7318
Fax: 202-626-7420

Email: info@archfoundation.org
URL: http://www.aia.org

Goal: To assist students planning to study architecture and cannot aford the program without the award.
Eligibility: Applicants must be high school seniors or college freshman who plan to study architecture at a NABB accredited school.
Target Student: High school, College and Adult students.
Amount: $3,000 - $4,000
Number of Awards: Up to 5
Scholarship can be renewed.
Based on Financial Need: Yes
Deadline: March
Applications are available online. A completed application and a letter of recommendation are required to apply.

(58) AIAA Foundation Undergraduate Scholarship Program

American Institute of Aeronautics and Astronautics
1801 Alexander Bell Drive
Suite 500
Reston, VA 20191

Phone: 800-639-AIAA
Fax: 703-264-7551
Email: stephenb@aiaa.org
URL: http://www.aiaa.org

Goal: To advance the art, science and technology of aeronautics and astronautics.
Eligibility: Applicants must be enrolled at a college or university with at least one semester or quarter completed with a GPA of 3.3 or higher. Applicants must become AIAA members before accepting the scholarhsip and must be planning to enter a career in science or engineering that is related to the technical activities of the AIAA.
Target Student: College and Adult students.

Amount: $2,000 - $2,500
Number of Awards: 30
Scholarship can be renewed.
Based on Financial Need: No
Deadline: January
Applications are available online.

(59) AICPA/Accounttemps Student Scholarship

American Institute of Certified Public Accountants
220 Leigh Farm Road
Durham, NC 27707

Phone: 919-402-4500
Fax: 919-412-4505
Email: service@aicpa.org
URL: http://www.aicpa.org

Goal: To assist AICPA student affiliate members pursuing degrees in information systems, accounting or finance.
Eligibility: Applicants must be U.S. citizens or permanent residents studying at an accredited U.S. college or university full-time and majoring in accounting, finance or information systems, completed 30 semester or 45 quarter hours of studying (with at least 6 of these being in accounting), with a GPA of 3.0 or higher. Current CPA's are not eligible.
Target Student: College, Graduate and Adult students.
Amount: $2,500
Number of Awards: Up to 5
Based on Financial Need: No
Deadline: April
Applications are available online. A completed application, transcripts, course schedule, standarized test scores for gradaute students, essay and two letters of recommendation are required to apply.

(60) Air Force ROTC ASCP

Air Force Reserve Officer Training Corp

AFROTC Admissions
551 E. Maxwell Boulevard
Maxwell AFB, AL 36112

Phone: 866-423-7682
Fax: 334-953-6167
URL: http://www.afrotc.com

Goal: Allows active duty Air Force personnel to earn a commission while completing their bachelor's degree.
Eligibility: Applicants must be active-duty Air Force personnel who are U.S citizens and under 31 and nurses are eligible up to age 47. Applicants must have at least one year of time in service and at least one year of time on station. Applicants must also be recommended by their immediate commander.
Target Student: College and Adult students.
Amount: Up to $20,310
Number of Awards: Varies
Based on Financial Need: No
Deadline: July and September
Application information is available online.

(61) Air Force ROTC High School Scholarship

Air Force Reserve Officer Training Corp
AFROTC Admissions
551 E. Maxwell Boulevard
Maxwell AFB, AL 36112

Phone: 866-423-7682
Fax: 334-953-6167
URL: http://www.afrotc.com

Goal: To help students who demonstrate a financial need and have an interest in joining the Air Force.

Eligibility: Applicants must pass the physical fitness assessment and show academic achievement or outstanding leadership skills. Three awards are available: full tuition along with most fees and books, a second that pays tuition up to $15,000 along with most fees and books and a third that pays full tuition at a college or university where tuition is less than $9,000 per year. In return for the scholarship the recipients must serve in the Air Force.
Target Student: High school students.
Amount: Up to Full tuition, books and stipend.
Number of Awards: Varies
Based on Financial Need: Yes
Deadline: December
Application information is available online.

(62) Air Force ROTC In College Program

Air Force Reserve Officer Training Corp
AFROTC Admissions
551 E. Maxwell Boulevard
Maxwell AFB, AL 36112

Phone: 866-423-7682
Fax: 334-953-6167
URL: http://www.afrotc.com

Goal: To help promote the Air Force ROTC.
Eligibility: Applicants must be U.S. citizens who have passed the Air Force Officer Qualifying Test, the Air Force ROTC Physical Fitness Test and the Department of Defense medical exam. Students must have a 2.5 GPA or higher and be in their first two years of college.
Target Student: College and adult students.
Amount: Up to $18,000
Number of Awards: Varies
Based on Financial Need: No
Deadline: December
Application information is available online.

(63) Air Force ROTC Professional Officer Course Early Release Program

Air Force Reserve Officer Training Corp
AFROTC Admissions
551 E. Maxwell Boulevard
Maxwell AFB, AL 36112

Phone: 866-423-7682
Fax: 334-953-6167
URL: http://www.afrotc.com

Goal: To help active duty Air Force personnel complete their bachelor's degree.
Eligibility: Applicants must be active-duty Air Force personnel who are U.S. citizens and under age 31 (47 if they are nurses). They must meet all testing and waiver requirements, be recommended by their commander and be withing one year of completing their bachelor's degree. Applicants must have a 2.5 GPA.
Target Student: College and adult students.
Amount: Up to $6,900
Number of Awards: Varies
Scholarship can be renewed.
Based on Financial Need: No
Deadline: October
Application information is available online.

(64) Air Force ROTC SOAR Program

Air Force Reserve Officer Training Corp
AFROTC Admissions
551 E. Maxwell Boulevard
Maxwell AFB, AL 36112

Phone: 866-423-7682
Fax: 334-953-6167
URL: http://www.afrotc.com

Goal: To allow active duty Air Force personnel the ability to earn their commission while completing their bachelor's degree.

Eligibility: Applicants must be active duty personnel who are U.S. citizens under the age of 31 (47 for nurses). They must meet all testing and waiver requirements and be recommened by their commanding officer. Students must have a minimum GPA of 2.5 or an ACT score of 24 or SAT score of 1100 or above.
Target Student: College and adult students.
Amount: Up to $24,000
Number of Awards: Varies
Scholarship can be renewed.
Based on Financial Need: No
Deadline: Varies
Application information is available online.

(65) Air Force Spouse Scholarship

Air Force Association
1501 Lee Highway
Arlington, VA 22209

Phone: 800-727-3337
Fax: 703-247-5853
Email: lcross@afa.org
URL: http://www.afa.org

Goal: To assist U.S. Air Force spouses who wish to attend undergraduate or graduate school.
Eligibility: Applicants must be the spouse of an active duty member of the U.S. Air Force, Air National Guard, or Air Force Reserve. They must be enrolled in an accredited college or university and have a GPA of 3.5 or higher. Awards are based on the strength of the application.`
Target Student: High school, College and Adult students.
Amount: $2,500
Number of Awards: Varies
Based on Financial Need: No
Deadline: April

Applications are available online. A completed application, official transcript, essay, photo, college acceptance letter for freshman only and two letters of recommendation are needed when applying.

(66) Air Traffic Control Association Scholarship Program

Air Traffic Control Association
1101 King Street
Suite 300
Alexandria, VA 22134

Phone: 703-299-2430
Fax: 703-299-2437
Email: info@atca.org
URL: http://www.atca.org

Goal: To assist students who are enrolled in courses related to aviation and full-time air traffic control employees and their children.
Eligibility: Applicants must be accepted or enrolled into a bachelor's or graduate degree program related to aviation, be full-time aviation employees doing advanced study in air traffic control or aviation or be the children of airt traffic controlers.
Target Student: High school, College, Graduate and Adult students.
Amount: Varies
Number of Awards: Varies
Based on Financial Need: No
Deadline: May
Applications are available online.

(67) Airman Memorial Foundation Scholarship Program

Air Force Sergeants Association
5211 Auth Road
Suitland, MD 20746

Phone: 301-899-3500
Fax: 301-899-8136

Email: ygreen@hqafsa.org
URL: http://www.hqafsa.org

Goal: To help dependents of Air Force enlisted personnel obtain a college degree.
Eligibility: Applicants must be dependents of Air Force enlisted personnel who are in high school or college. Applicants must have a GPA of 3.5 or higher.
Target Student: High school, College and Adult students.
Amount: Up to $2,000
Number of Awards: Varies
Based on Financial Need: No
Deadline: March
Applications are available online.

(68) AISI/AIST Foundation Premier Scholarship

Association for Iron and Steel Technology
186 Thorn Hill Road
Warrendale, PA 15086

Phone: 202-452-7143
Fax: 724-814-3001
Email: blakshminarayana@steel.org
URL: http://www.aistfoundation.org

Goal: To encourage engineering students to pursue a career in the iron and steel industry.
Eligibility: Applicants must be undergraduate sophomores attending a college or university full-time majoring in engineering with a 3.0 or higher GPA with demonstrated interest in a career in the iron and steel industry.
Target Student: College and Adult students.
Amount: $10,000
Number of Awards: 1
Scholarship can be renewed.
Based on Financial Need: No
Deadline: March

Applciations are available online. A completed application, essay, transcript and two letters of recommendation are required to apply.

---

(69) AIST Benjamin F. Fairless Scholarship

Association for Iron and Steel Technology
186 Thorn Hill Road
Warrendale, PA 15086

Phone: 202-452-7143
Fax: 724-814-3001
Email: blakshminarayana@steel.org
URL: http://www.aistfoundation.org

Goal: To honor the memory of former Chairman of the U.S. Steel Corp. Board Benjamin F. Fairless.
Eligibility: Applicants must be enrolled full-time and majoring in engineering, metallurgy or materials science at a college or university in North America with a GPA of 3.0 or higher and planning to pursue a career in the iron and steel industry.
Target Student: College, Graduate and Adult students.
Amount: $3,000
Number of Awards: 2
Based on Financial Need: No
Deadline: March
Applications are available online.

---

(70) AIST Ronald E. Lincoln Memorial Scholarship

Association for Iron and Steel Technology
186 Thorn Hill Road
Warrendale, PA 15086

Phone: 202-452-7143
Fax: 724-814-3001
Email: blakshminarayana@steel.org
URL: http://www.aistfoundation.org

Goal: To honor the memory of Ronald Lincoln as well as reward students for leadership and innovation.
Eligibility: Applicants must be full-time students at a college or university in North America majoring in engineering, metallurgy or materials science with a GPA of 3.0 or higher and plan to pursue a career in the iron and steel industry.
Target Student: College and Adult students
Amount: $3,000
Number of Awards: 2
Based on Financial Need: No
Deadline: March
Applications are available online.

---

(71) AIST Smith Graduate Scholarship

Association for Iron and Steel Technology
186 Thorn Hill Road
Warrendale, PA 15086

Phone: 202-452-7143
Fax: 724-814-3001
Email: blakshminarayana@steel.org
URL: http://www.aistfoundation.org

Goal: To assist graduate engineering students pursuing careers in metallurgy.
Eligibility: Applicants must be full-time students attending a college or university in the U.S. or Canada and be in an engineering degree program with demonstrated interest in a career in metallurgy in the iron or steel industry.
Target Student: Graduate and Adult students.
Amount: $3,000
Number of Awards: 2
Based on Financial Need: No
Deadline: March
Applications are available online.

---

(72) AIST William E. Schwabe Memorial Scholarship

Association for Iron and Steel Technology
186 Thorn Hill Road
Warrendale, PA 15086

Phone: 202-452-7143
Fax: 724-814-3001
Email: blakshminarayana@steel.org
URL: http://www.aistfoundation.org

Goal: To honor the memory of the steelmaking pioneer William E. Schwabe.
Eligibility: Applicants must be full-students at a college or university in North America majoring in engineering, metallurgy, or materials science with a GPA of 3.0 or higher and plan on a career in the iron and steel industry.
Target Student: College and Adult students.
Amount: $3,000
Number of Awards: 1
Based on Financial Need: No
Deadline: March
Applications are available online.

---

(73) AIST Willy Korf Memorial Fund

Association for Iron and Steel Technology
186 Thorn Hill Road
Warrendale, PA 15086

Phone: 202-452-7143
Fax: 724-814-3001
Email: blakshminarayana@steel.org
URL: http://www.aistfoundation.org

Goal: To honor the memory of Willy Koef and assist students purusing careers in engineering, metallurgy and materials science in the iron and steel industry.
Eligibility: Applicants must be full-time students in a college or university in North America majoring in engineering, metallurgy or materials science with a GPA of 3.0 or higher who are planning a career in the iron or steel industry.
Target Student: College and Adult students.

Amount: $3,000
Number of Awards: 3
Based on Financial Need: No
Deadline: March
Applications are available online.

---

(74) Akash Kuruvilla Memorial Scholarship

Akash Kuruvilla Memorial Scholarship Fund Inc.
P.O. Box 140900
Gainsville, FL 32614

Email: info@akmsf.com
URL: http://www.akmscholarship.com

Goal: To help continue the legacy of generosity of Akash Kuruvilla.
Eligibility: Applicants must be full-time college students at an accredited U.S. four year college or university. Applicants must demonstrate academic achievement, leadership, integrity and excellence in diversity. The award is based on the applicants character, need and ability to positivity impact their community.
Target Student: High school, College and Adult students
Amount: $1,000
Number of Awards: 2
Based on Financial Need: Yes
Deadline: June
Applications are available online. To apply you must submit an application form, essay, personal statement, letter of recommendation and resume.

---

(75) Al Neuharth Free Spirit Scholarship and Conference Program

Freedome Forum
1101 Wilson Boulevard
Arlington, VA 22209

Phone: 703-284-2814
Fax: 703-284-3529

Email: freespirit@freedomforum.org
URL:
http://www.freedomforum.org/freespirit

Goal: To assist students who are free spirits.
Eligibility: Applicants must be high school seniors planning to pursue a career in journalism and who are "free spirits" meaning that they "dream, dare and do."
Target Student: High school students.
Amount: $1,000
Number of Awards: Varies
Based on Financial Need: No
Deadline: February
Applications are available online.

---

(76) Alice T. Schafer Prize

Association of Women in Mathematics
4114 Computer and Space Sciences Building
University of Maryland
College Park, MD 20742

Phone: 301-405-7892
Fax: 301-314-9074
Email: awm@math.umd.edu
URL: http://www.awm-math.org

Goal: To assist female students studying mathematics.
Eligibility: Applicants must be female college undergraduate students who are U.S. citizens or have a school address in the U.S. and must be nominated for the award. Award selection is based on the nominee's mathematics performance and performance on mathematical competitions.
Target Student: College and Adult students.
Amount: Varies
Number of Awards: Varies
Based on Financial Need: No
Deadline: October
Applicants must be nominated.

(77) Alice W. Rooke Scholarship

National Society Daughters of the American Revolution
Committee Services Office
Attn: Scholarship Committee
1776 D Street NW
Washington, DC 20006

Phone: 202-628-1776
URL: http://www.dar.org

Goal: To assist students in becoming medical doctors.
Eligibility: Applicants must be accepted or enrolled in a graduate medical doctor program and be sponsored by their local DAR chapter.
Target Student: Graduate and Adult students.
Amount: Up to $5,000
Number of Awards: Varies
Scholarship can be renewed.
Based on Financial Need: No
Deadline: April
Applications are available by written request.

---

(78) Allied Dental Health Scholarships

American Dental Association Foundation
211 East Chicago Avenue
Chicago, IL 60611

Phone: 312-440-2763
Fax: 312-440-3526
Email: famularor@ada.org
URL: http://www.ada.org

Goal: To encourage students to pursue careers in dental assisting, dental hygiene, dentistry and dental laboratory technology.

Eligibility: Applicants must be in their final year of their dental hygiene program, entering a dental assisting program or in their final year in a dental laboratory technician program with a GPA of 3.0 or higher.
Target Student: College, Graduate and Adult students.
Amount: $1,000
Number of Awards: Varies
Based on Financial Need: No
Deadline: Varies
Applications are available from your dental school.

(79) Alpha Kappa Alpha Financial Need Scholars

Alpha Kappa Educational Advancement Foundation Inc.
5656 S. Stony Island Avenue
Chicago, IL 60637

Phone: 800-653-6528
Fax: 773-947-0277
Email: akaeaf@akaeaf.net
URL: http://www.akaeaf.org

Goal: To help undergraduate and graduate students who have a financial need and have demonstrated community service.
Eligibility: Applicants must be full time students who are at least in their sophomore year with a GPA of 2.5 or higher. Applicants must demonstrate leadership, volunteer or civic service as well as financial need. The scholarship is open to all students regardless of race and applicants do not need to be members of Alpha Kappa Alpha. The deadline for undergraduate applicants is April 15 and the deadline for graduate students is August 15.
Target Student: College and Graduate school students.
Amount: $1,000 - $3,000
Number of Awards: Varies
Based on Financial Need: Yes

Deadline: April and August
Applications are available online. To apply a completed application form, personal statement, and three letters of recommendation must be submitted.

(80) Alpha Kappa Alpha Merit Scholarship

Alpha Kappa Educational Advancement Foundation Inc.
5656 S. Stony Island Avenue
Chicago, IL 60637

Phone: 800-653-6528
Fax: 773-947-0277
Email: akaeaf@akaeaf.net
URL: http://www.akaeaf.org

Goal: To help undergraduate and graduate students who demonstrate community service and involvement.
Eligibility: Applicants must be full time students who are at least in their sophomore year with a GPA of 3.0 or higher. Applicants must demonstrate leadership, volunteer or civic service. The scholarship is open to all students regardless of race and applicants do not need to be members of Alpha Kappa Alpha. The deadline for undergraduate applicants is April 15 and the deadline for graduate students is August 15.
Target Student: College and Graduate school students.
Amount: $1,000-$3,000
Number of Awards: Varies
Based on Financial Need: No
Deadline: April and August
Applications are available online. To apply a completed application form, personal statement, and three letters of recommendation must be submitted.

(81) Alpha Mu Tau Fraternity Undergraduate Scholarships

American Society for Clinical Laboratory
Science
6701 Democracy Boulevard, Suite 300
Bethesda, MD 20817

Phone: 301-657-2768
Fax: 301-657-2909
Email: ascls@ascls.org
URL: http://www.ascls.org

Goal: To assist new professionals in
clinical laboratory science.
Eligibility: Applicants must be
undergraduate students who are U.S.
citizens or permanent residents who are
entering or in their last year of a clinical
laboratory science/medical technology, or
clinical laboratory technician/medical
laboratory techninican program accredited
by the NAACLS.
Target Student: College and Adult
students.
Amount: Up to $1,500
Number of Awards: Varies
Based on Financial Need: No
Deadline: April
Applications are available online.

---

(82) Alphonso Deal Scholarship Award

National Black Police Association
NBPA Scholarship Award
30 Kennedy Street NW
Washington, DC 20011

Phone: 202-986-2070
Fax: 202-986-0410
Email: nbpanatofc@worldnet.att.net
URL: http://www.blackpolice.org

Goal: To assist students who plan to
pursue a career in law enforcement.
Eligibility: Applicants must be high
school seniors with good moral character
and are U.S. citizens. They must have a
recommendation from their principal,
counselor, or teacher. They must attend a
two year college.

Target Student: High school students
Amount: Varies
Number of Awards: Varies
Based on Financial Need: No
Deadline: May
Applications are available online. To apply
submit your completed application,
transcripts, photo and a letter of
acceptance from the college you plan to
attend.

---

(83) AMBUCS Scholars

AMBUCS
P.O. Box 5127
High Point, NC 27262

Phone: 800-838-1845
Fax: 336-852-6830
Email: janiceb@ambucs.org
URL: http://www.ambucs.org

Goal: To help provide opportunities for
disabled individuals to become therapy
students.
Eligibility: Applicants must be
undergraduate juniors or seniors or
graduate students working towards their
master's or doctorate in physical therapy,
occupational therapy, speech language
pathology or hearing audiology. Assistant
program are not eligible for this award.
Target Student: College, Graduate and
Adult students.
Amount: $500 - $6,000
Number of Awards: Varies
Based on Financial Need: Yes
Deadline: April
Applications are available online.

---

(84) AMCA Music Scholarship

Associated Male Choruses of America
Robert H. Torborg Scholarship Chair
P.O. Box 342
Cold Spring, MN 56320

Phone: 320-685-3848
Email: scholarships@amcofa-sing.org
URL: http://www.amcofa-sing.org

Goal: To encourage students to study chorus and music studies.
Eligibility: Applicants must be full time students working towards a bachelors degree in a music-related field (preference given to vocal and choral studies) and be sponsored by a chorus of the Associated Male Choruses of America.
Target Student: College and Adult Students
Amount: $1,200
Number of Awards: Varies
Based on Financial Need: No
Deadline: March
Applications are available online.

---

(85) Amelia Earhart Fellowships

Zonta International
1211 West 22nd Street
Oak Brook, IL 60523

Phone: 630-928-1400
Fax: 630-928-1559
Email: zontaintl@zonta.org
URL: http://www.zonta.org

Goal: To assist women in science and engineering.
Eligibility: Applicants must be working towards a graduate PhD/doctoral degree in aerospace-related sciences and aerospace-related engineering.
Target Student: Graduate and Adult students.
Amount: $10,000
Number of Awards: 35
Based on Financial Need: No
Deadline: November
Applications are available online.

---

(87) American Architectural Foundation and Sir John Soane's Museum Foundation Traveling Fellowship

American Architechtural Foundation
1799 New York Avenue NW
Washington, DC 20006

Phone: 202-626-7318
Fax: 202-626-7420
Email: info@archfoundation.org
URL: http://www.aia.org

Goal: To assist graduate students in traveling to England to study the work of Sir John Soane.
Eligibility: Applicants must be enrolled in a graduate program that focuses on the history of art, architecture, decorative arts and interior design.
Target Student: Graduate and Adult students.
Amount: $5,000
Number of Awards: 2
Based on Financial Need: No
Deadline: March
Applications are available online.

---

(88) American Bar Association Essay and Writing Competition

American Bar Association
321 North Clark Street
Chicago, IL 60610

Phone: 312-988-5415
Email: legalosf@abanet.org
URL: http://www.abanet.org/lsd/

Goal: To assist and acknowledge the achievements of law students.
Eligibility: Each year the American Bar Association holds a number of essay and writing competitions for student members with topics ranging from housing and community, community development, law and aging, anti-trust and others.

Target Student: Graduate and Adult students
Amount: $2,000 + traveling expenses
Number of Awards: Varies
Based on Financial Need: No
Deadline: February
Applications are available online. The requirements vary based on the award.

---

(89) American Bar Association-Bar/Bri Scholarshisp

BAR/BRI Bar Review
ABA Scholarship Committee
111 W. Jackson Boulevard
Chicago, IL 60604

Email: abalsd@abanet.org
URL: http://www.barbri.com

Goal: To assist graduating law students who are required to take the BAR/BRI examination.
Eligibility: Applicants must be ABA Law Student Division members graduating in December or May and must use the award towards their BAR/BRI tuition. The award size is determined by the applicants financial need and the number of applicants.
Target Student: Graduate and Adult students.
Amount: Varies
Number of Awards: Varies
Based on Financial Need: No
Deadline: November and February
Applications are available online.

---

(90) American Darts Organization Memorial Scholarships

American Darts Organization
230 N. Crescent Way Suite K
Anaheim, CA 92801

Phone: 714-254-0212
Fax: 714-254-0214

Email: adooffice@aol.com
URL: http://www.adodarts.com

Goal: The American Darts Organization Memorial Scholarship Fund is established as a permanent memorial to those friends of the Sport of darts who have passed away.
Eligibility: Applicants must be ADO members and they must have been at least quarter-finalists in the ADO Youth Playoff Program. Students must be under 21 on Decemeber 1 on the year when they start college. Thye must be accepted or enrolled full time with a 2.0 GPA or higher. They must have lived in the U.S. for two years and 1 day.
Target Student: High school and college students.
Amount: $500-$1,500
Number of Awards: 8
Based on Financial Need: No
Deadline: Varies
Applications are available online.

---

(91) American Essay Contest

Fleet Reserve Association (FRA)
FRA Scholarship Administrator
125 N. West Street
Alexandria, VA 22314

Phone: 800-372-1924
Email: news-fra@fra.org
URL: http://www.fra.org

Goal: To assist and acknowledge outstanding student essayists.
Eligibility: Applicants must be in grades 7 to 12 and sponsored by a Fleet Reserve Association branch or Ladies Auxiliary unit. They must submit an essay on a topic that is selected by the scholarship sponsor. The award is based on the quality of the essay.
Target Student: Junior high and High school students.
Amount: Up to $10,000

Number of Awards: Varies
Based on Financial Need: No
Deadline: December
Instructions are available online.

---

(92) American Express Scholarship Competition

American Hotel and Lodging Educational Foundation
1201 New York Avenue NW
Suite 600
Washington, DC 20005

Phone: 202-289-3188
Fax: 202-289-3199
Email: chammond@ahlef.org
URL: http://www.ahlef.org

Goal: To assist students working towards a degree in hospitality management.
Eligibility: Applicants must be enrolled in an accredited undergraduate degree program in hospitality management. The student or their parents must be employed in the lodging industry by an American Hotel and Lodging Association member facility.
Target Student: College and Adult students.
Amount: Up to $2,000
Number of Awards: Varies
Based on Financial Need: No
Deadline: May
Applications are available online.

---

(93) American Legion Baseball Scholarship

American Legion Baseball
700 N. Pennsylvania Street
Indianapolis, IN 46204

Phone: 317-630-1249
Fax: 317-630-1369
Email: baseball@legion.org
URL: http://www.legion.org/baseball

Goal: To assist members of American Legion affiliated baseball teams cover educational expenses.
Eligibility: Applicants must be graduating high school seniors and be nominated by a head coach or team manager. One player per state will receive the scholarship. Scholarships can be used to pay for education expenses at accredited colleges and universities.
Target Student: High school students.
Amount: Varies
Number of Awards: Varies
Based on Financial Need: No
Deadline: July
Applications are available online.

---

(94) American Legion Junior Air Rifle National Championship Scholarships

American Legion
Attn: Americanism and Children and Youth Division
P.O. Box 1055
Indianapolis, IN 46206

Phone: 317-630-1249
Fax: 317-630-1369
Email: acy@legion.org
URL: http://www.legion.org

Goal: To help outstanding young marksmen and women.
Eligibility: Applicants must be 18 years old or younger. Thye must compete in the Junior Air Rifle National Championship. Winners receive a $2,500 scholarship.
Target Student: High school and Junior high school students.
Amount: $2,500
Number of Awards: 2
Based on Financial Need: No
Deadline: Varies
Applications are available from local American Legion chapters.

(95) American Legion Legacy Scholarship

American Legion
700 N. Pennsylvania Street
P.O. Box 1055
Indianapolis, IN 46206

Phone: 317-630-1202
Fax: 317-630-1223
URL: http://www.legion.org

Goal: To assist the children of U.S. military personnel who have died on active duty after September 11, 2001.
Eligibility: Applicants must be the children or adopted children of a parent who died while serving the U.S. military while on active duty after September 11, 2001. Students must be pursuing or planning to purse an undergraduate degree in the U.S.
Target Student: High school, college and adult students.
Amount: Varies
Number of Awards: Varies
Based on Financial Need: No
Deadline: April
Applications are available online.

(96) American Police Hall of Fame Educational Scholarship Fund

American Police Hall of Fame and Museum
6350 Horizon Drive
Titusville, FL 32780

Phone: 321-264-0911
Email: info@aphf.org
URL:http://www.aphf.org/scholarships.html

Goal: To assist the children of law enforcement officers who have died in the line of duty.

Eligibility: Applicants must be the children of law enforcement officers that were killed in the line of duty. They may attend a public, private or vocational school. To apply a transcript, letter of acceptance and student ID is required.
Target Student: High school, college students and adult students.
Amount: $1,500
Number of Awards: Varies
Scholarship can be renewed.
Based on Financial Need: No
Deadline: Varies
Applications are available online.

(97) American Quarter Horse Foundation Scholarship

American Quarter Horse Foundation Scholarship Program
2601 East Interstate 40
Amarillo, TX 79104

Phone: 806-378-5029
Fax: 806-376-1005
Email: foundation@aqha.org
URL: http://www.aqha.com

Goal: To develop Quarter Horse Industry professionals.
Eligibility: Applciants must have demonstrated involvement with equine related activities and be members of American Quarter Horse Association or American Quarter Horse Youth Association for at least three years.
Target Student: High school, College, Graduate and Adult students
Amount: Varies
Number of Awards: Varies
Scholarship can be renewed.
Based on Financial Need: Yes
Deadline: December
Applications are available online. A completed application, transcript, and three letters of recommendation are required to apply.

(99) American Society of Crime Laboratory Directors Scholarship Program

American Society of Crime Laboratory Directors
139K Technology Drive
Garner, NC 27529

Phone: 919-773-2600
Fax: 919-773-2602
URL: http://www.ascld.org

Goal: To assist students who are enrolled in a forensic related degree program and who are planning to pursue a career in the forensic field.
Eligibility: Applicants must be undergraduate or graduate students who are enrolled in a degree program in forensic science, forensic chemistry, or a related physical or natural science. They must be attending an accredited college and must be interested in pursuing a career in forensic science. Preference is given to applicants enrolled in a degree program that is accredited by the Forensic Science Education Program Accreditation Commission (FEPAC). The award is given based on academic achievement, achievement in forensic science courses, personal statement, level of interest in forensic science careers and a letter of recommendation.
Target Student: College, graduate and adult students.
Amount: $1,000
Number of Awards: Varies
Based on Financial Need: No
Deadline: April
Applications are available online. A completed application, transcripts, persoanal statement and one letter of recommendation are required.

(100) American Society of Travel Agents American Express Travel Undergraduate Scholarship

Tourism Cares
275 Turnpike Street
Suite 307
Canton, MA 02021

Phone: 781-821-5990
Fax: 781-821-8949
Email: scholarship@tourismcares.org
URL: http://www.tourismcares.org

Goal: To assist undergraduate freshman planning to pursue degrees in travel, tourism and hospitality.
Eligibility: Applicants must be U.S. citizens or permanent residents and graduating high school seniors at a school that has an Academy of Hospitality and Tourism program. Applicants must have a 3.0 GPA for higher and be accepted into a postsecondary school in the U.S. or Canada with the goal of studying travel, tourism, or hospitality.
Target Student: High school students.
Amount: $1,000
Number of Awards: 1
Based on Financial Need: No
Deadline: April
Applications are available online. A completed application, resume, proof of residency, transcript, essay, two letters of recommendation and proof of college acceptance are required to apply.

(101) American Society of Travel Agents Arnold Rigby Graduate Scholarship

Tourism Cares
275 Turnpike Street
Suite 307
Canton, MA 02021

Phone: 781-821-5990
Fax: 781-821-8949

Email: scholarship@tourismcares.org
URL: http://www.tourismcares.org

Goal: To assist graduate students studying travel, hospitality and tourism.
Eligibility: Applicants must be citizens or permanent residents of the U.S. or Canada who are entering or returning graduate students at a four year college or university in the U.S. or Canada. Applicants must be studying hospitality, travel or tourism and have a 3.0 GPA or higher.
Target Student: Graduate and Adult students.
Amount: $2,500
Number of Awards: 2
Based on Financial Need: No
Deadline: April
Applications are available online. A completed application, transcript, resume, proof of residency, essay and two letters of recommendation are required to apply.

(102) American Society of Travel Agents Avis Budget Group Graduate Scholarship

Tourims Cares
275 Turnpike Street
Suite 307
Canton, MA 02021

Phone: 781-821-5990
Fax: 781-821-8949
Email: scholarship@tourismcares.org
URL: http://www.tourismcares.org

Goal: To assist those studying hospitality, travel and tourism at the graduate level.
Eligibility: Applicants must be citizens or permanent residents of the U.S. or Canada who are entering or returning graduate students at a four year college or university in the U.S. or Canada. Applicants must be studying hospitality, travel or tourism and have a 3.0 GPA or higher.
Target Student: College, Graduate and Adult students.

Amount: $2,000
Number of Awards: 1
Based on Financial Need: No
Deadline: April
Applications are available online. A completed application, transcript, resume, proof of residency, essay and two letters of recommendation are required to apply.

(103) American Society of Travel Agents David J. Hallissey Memorial Undergraduate or Graduate Internship

Tourims Cares
275 Turnpike Street
Suite 307
Canton, MA 02021

Phone: 781-821-5990
Fax: 781-821-8949
Email: scholarship@tourismcares.org
URL: http://www.tourismcares.org

Goal: To assist those studying travel, tourism, and hospitality and are interested in market research.
Eligibility: Applicants can be from any country and must be enrolled at an accredited four year U.S. college or university. Applicants must be returning grading students or undergradautc sophomores, juniors or seniors. Applicants must be studying tourism, travel or hospitality, have a 3.0 or higher GPA and be interested in market research as it applies to marketing and have strong oral and written communication skills.
Target Student: College, Graduate and Adult students.
Amount: $2,000
Number of Awards: 1
Based on Financial Need: No
Deadline: April
Applications are available online. A completed application, transcript, resume, proof of residency, essay and two letters of recommendation are required to apply.

(104) American Society of Travel Agents Healy Graduate Scholarship

Tourims Cares
275 Turnpike Street
Suite 307
Canton, MA 02021

Phone: 781-821-5990
Fax: 781-821-8949
Email: scholarship@tourismcares.org
URL: http://www.tourismcares.org

Goal: To assist those studying hospitality, travel and tourism at the graduate level.
Eligibility: Applicants must be citizens or permanent residents of the U.S. or Canada who are entering or returning graduate students at a four year college or university in the U.S. or Canada. Applicants must be studying hospitality, travel or tourism and have a 3.0 GPA or higher.
Target Student: College, Graduate and Adult students.
Amount: $1,000
Number of Awards: 1
Based on Financial Need: No
Deadline: April
Applications are available online. A completed application, transcript, resume, proof of residency, essay and two letters of recommendation are required to apply.

(105) American Society of Travel Agents Holland America Line Graduate Research Scholarship

Tourims Cares
275 Turnpike Street
Suite 307
Canton, MA 02021

Phone: 781-821-5990
Fax: 781-821-8949
Email: scholarship@tourismcares.org
URL: http://www.tourismcares.org

Goal: To assist graduate students doing tourism related research.
Eligibility: Applicants must be citizens or permanent residents of the U.S. or Canada who are entering or returning graduate students at a four year college or university in the U.S. or Canada. Applicants must be conducting tourism related research and have a 3.0 or higher GPA.
Target Student: College, Gradaute and Adult students.
Amount: $4,000
Number of Awards: 1
Based on Financial Need: No
Deadline: April
Applications are available online. A completed application, transcript, resume, proof of residency, essay and two letters of recommendation are required to apply.

(106) American Society of Travel Agents Joseph R. Stone Graduate Scholarship

Tourims Cares
275 Turnpike Street
Suite 307
Canton, MA 02021

Phone: 781-821-5990
Fax: 781-821-8949
Email: scholarship@tourismcares.org
URL: http://www.tourismcares.org

Goal: To assist those studying hospitality, travel and tourism at the graduate level.
Eligibility: Applicants must be citizens or permanent residents of the U.S. or Canada who are entering or returning graduate students at a four year college or university in the U.S. or Canada. Applicants must be studying hospitality, travel or tourism and have a 3.0 GPA or higher.
Target Student: College, Gradaute and Adult students.
Amount: $2,500
Number of Awards: 3
Based on Financial Need: No

Deadline: April

Applications are available online. A completed application, transcript, resume, proof of residency, essay and two letters of recommendation are required to apply.

---

(107) American String Teachers Association National Solo Competition - Senior Division

American String Teachers Association (ASTA)
4153 Chain Bridge Road
Fairfax, VA 22030

Phone: 703-279-2113
Fax: 703-279-2114
Email: asta@astaweb.com
URL: http://www.astaweb.com

Goal: To assist outstanding musicians
Eligibility: Applicants must be ASTA members or students of professional ASTA members who are between the ages of 19-25 and play the violin, cello, bass, classical guitar or harp. Applicants may enter the competition in their home state or the state in which they are studying.
Target Student: High school, College and Graduate students.
Amount: Varies
Number of Awards: Varies
Based on Financial Need: No
Deadline: Varies

Applications are available online. A completed application and proof of birth date are required to apply.

---

(108) American Theatre Organ Society Scholarships

American Theatre Organ Society
Carlton B. Smith, Director
2175 N. Irwin Street
Indianapolis, IN 46219

Phone: 317-356-1240

Fax: 317-322-9379
Email: smith@atos.org
URL: http://www.atos.org

Goal: To provide students with the opportunity to study with professional theatre organ teachers or to further their organ performance education in college.
Eligibility: Applicants must be 13 to 27 years old on July 1 and working toward college organ performance degrees or be studying with professional organ instructors. Students' names must be submitted by their organ instructor or the school's music department head.
Target Student: Junior high students and younger, High school, College and Adult students.
Amount: Up to $1,500
Number of Awards: Varies
Based on Financial Need: No
Deadline: April

Applications are available online.

---

(109) America's First Freedom Student Competition

First Freedom Center
1321 E. Main Street
Richmond, VA 23219

Phone: 804-643-1786
Fax: 804-644-5024
Email: competition@firstfreedom.org
URL: http://www.firstfreedom.org

Goal: To assist students to examine religious freedom.
Eligibility: Applicants must be in the 9th to 12th grade in a public, private, home schooled, or distance school and living in the U.S. or its territories. American students living abroad and non-American students attending American schools and foreign-exchange students studying in the U.S. are also eligible for the scholarship.
Target Student: High school students
Amount: $2,500

Number of Awards: 2
Based on Financial Need: No
Deadline: November
Applications and required materials are listed online.

---

(110) Americoprs Vista

AmeriCorps
1201 New York Ave NW
Washington, DC 20525

Phone: 202-606-5000
Fax: 202-606-3472
Email: questions@americorps.org
URL: http://www.americorps.gov

Goal: To provide financial assistance in exchange for community service.
Eligibility: Applicants must be U.S. citizens who are at least 17 years old. They must be able to serve in a one year, full time position at a nonprofit organization or a local government agency fighting illiteracy, helping communities or health services.
Target Student: High school, college, graduate and adult students.
Amount: Up to $5,550
Number of Awards: Varies
Based on Financial Need: No
Deadline: Varies
Applications are available online.

---

(111) Americorps National Civilian Community Corps

AmeriCorps
1201 New York Ave NW
Washington, DC 20525

Phone: 202-606-5000
Fax: 202-606-3472
Email: questions@americorps.org
URL: http://www.americorps.gov

Goal: To strengthen communities and develop leaders through national and community service.
Eligibility: Applicants must be U.S. citizens between the ages of 18 and 24. Recipients must live on a AmeriCorps campus in Denver, Sacramento, Perry Point, Maryland or Vicksburg, Mississippi. Applicants must commit to 10 months of service projects that are within the region of the campus.
Target Student: High school, college, graduate and adult students.
Amount: $5,550
Number of Awards: Varies
Based on Financial Need: No
Deadline: Varies
Applications are available online.

---

(112) AMS Graduate Fellowship in the History of Science

American Meteorlogical Society
Fellowship and Scholarship Department
45 Beacon Street
Boston, MA 02108

Phone: 617-227-2416 x246
Fax: 617-742-8718
Email: dsampson@ametsoc.org
URL: http://www.ametsoc.org/ams

Goal: To assist students who are writing dissertations on the history of atmospheric or related oceanic or hydorlogic sciences.
Eligibility: Applicants must be graduate students planning on writing dissertations on the history of atmospheric or related oceanic or hydrologic sciences.
Target Student: Graduate and Adult students.
Amount: $15,000
Number of Awards: Varies
Based on Financial Need: No
Deadline: February

A cover letter with curriculum vitae, transcripts, three letters of recommendation and description of the disseratation should be mailed in.

(113) AMS Undergraduate Scholarships

American Meteorlogical Society
Fellowship and Scholarship Department
45 Beacon Street
Boston, MA 02108

Phone: 617-227-2416 x246
Fax: 617-742-8718
Email: dsampson@ametsoc.org
URL: http://www.ametsoc.org/ams

Goal: To encourage undergraduates to work towards careers in the atmospheric and related oceanic and hydrologic sciences.
Eligibility: Applicants must be full-time students who are majoring in atmospheric or related oceanic or hydrologic science and beginning their final year of undergraduate study with a 3.25 GPA or higher. The Schroeder scholarship requires finanical need, the Murphy scholarship requires interest in weather forecasting with curriculum abnd extracurricular activies teh the Crow scholarhip requires demonstrated interest in applied meteorology.
Target Student: College and Adult students
Amount: Varies
Number of Awards: Varies
Based on Financial Need: Yes for some.
Deadline: February
Applications are available online.

(114) AMS/Industry Minority Scholarships

American Meteorlogical Society
Fellowship and Scholarship Department
45 Beacon Street
Boston, MA 02108

Phone: 617-227-2416 x246
Fax: 617-742-8718
Email: dsampson@ametsoc.org
URL: http://www.ametsoc.org/ams

Goal: To assist minority students who are underrepresented in the sciences, specifically Hispanic, African American and Native American students.
Eligibility: Applicants must be minority students beginning their freshman year of college and must be planning to puruse a degree in atmospheric or related oceanic or hydrologic sciences.
Target Student: High school students.
Amount: $3,000
Number of Awards: Varies
Scholarship can be renewed.
Based on Financial Need: No
Deadline: February
Applciations are available online. A completed application, transcript, SAT scores, and letters of recommendation are required to apply.

(110) AMS/Industry/Government Graduate Fellowships

American Meteorlogical Society
Fellowship and Scholarship Department
45 Beacon Street
Boston, MA 02108

Phone: 617-227-2426 x246
Fax: 617-742-8718
Email: dsampson@ametsoc.org
URL: http://www.ametsoc.org/ams

Goal: To encourage students to pursue careers in the meteorological oceanic and hydrologic fields.
Eligibility: Applicants must be beginning their first year of graduate school in the upcoming year and be working towards advanced degrees in atmospheric and related oceanic and hydrologic sciences.

Target Student: College and Adult students
Amount: $24,000
Number of Awards: Varies
Based on Financial Need: No
Deadline: February
Applications are available online. A completed application, transcripts, references, and GRE scores are requied to apply.

(114) AMT Student Scholarship

American Medical Technologists
10700 W. Higgins Road
Rosemont, IL 60018

Phone: 800-275-1268
Fax: 847-823-0458
URL: http://www.amt1.com

Goal: To assist students interested in careers in medical technology careers.
Eligibility: Applicants must be high school graduates or current seniors planning to attend college to obtain an American Medical Technolgists certified career including medical laboratory technology, medial assisting, dental assisting, phlebotomy and office laboratory technician.
Target Student: High school students.
Amount: $500
Number of Awards: 5
Based on Financial Need: No
Deadline: April
Applications are available online.

(115) Amtrol Inc. Scholarship

American Ground Water Trust
16 Centre Street
Concord, NH 03301

Phone: 603-228-5444
Fax: 603-228-6557
URL: http://www.agwt.org

Goal: To assist high school seniors pursuing a career in ground water-related field.
Eligibility: Applicants must be high school seniors with the goal of obtaining a career in ground water management or a related field. Prior experience and research in the field is required.
Target Student: High school students.
Amount: $1,500
Number of Awards: Varies
Based on Financial Need: No
Deadline: June
Applications are available online.

(117) AMVETS National Scholarship for Entering College Freshman

AMVETS National Headquarters
4647 Forbes Boulevard
Lanham, MD 20706

Phone: 877-726-8387
Fax: 301-459-7924
Email: thilton@amvets.org
URL: http://www.amvets.org

Goal: To provide financial assistance to graduating JROTC cadets.
Eligibility: Applicants must be high school seniors with a 3.0 GPA or higher or documented extenuating circumstances. They must be US citizens and children or grandchildren of U.S. veterans. They must also show academci potential and financial need.
Target Student: High school students.
Amount: $1,000
Number of Awards: 1
Based on Financial Need: Yes
Deadline: April
Applications are available online.

(116) AMVETS National Scholarship for Veterans

AMVETS National Headquarters
4647 Forbes Boulevard
Lanham, MD 0

Phone: 877-726-8387
Fax: 301-459-7924
Email: thilton@amvets.org
URL: http://www.amvets.org

Goal: To provide assistance to veterans.
Eligibility: Applicants must be U.S. citizens and veterans who have a financial need. They must be honorably discharged or be active duty and eligible for release.
Target Student: High school, college and adult students.
Amount: $1,000
Number of Awards: 3
Based on Financial Need: Yes
Deadline: April
Applications are available online.

(118) Amy Lowell Poetry Travelling Scholarship

Choate, Hall and Stewart
Two International Place
Boston, MA 02110

Phone: 617-248-5253
Email: amylowell@choate.com
URL: http://www.amylowell.org

Goal: To assist travel abroad for American-born poets.
Eligibility: Applicants must submit an application, curriculum vitae and poetry samples. Award recipients cannot accept another scholarship during the scholarship year, must travel outside North America and should have three poems by the end of the scholarship year.
Target Student: College, Graduate and Adult students.
Amount: $52,000
Number of Awards: 1-2
Based on Financial Need: No
Deadline: October

Applications are available online.

(119) Anchor Scholarship Foundation Scholarship

Anchor Scholarship Foundation
P.O. Box 9535
Norfolk, VA 23505

Phone: 757-374-3769
Email: admin@anchorscholarship.com
URL: http://www.anchorscholarship.com

Goal: To provide financial assistance to dependents of current and former members of the Naval Surface Forces, Atlantic and Navel Surface Forces, Pacific.
Eligibility: Applicants must be high school seniors or college students planning to attend or currently attending an accredited, four year college full time and in person. Applicants must be dependents of service members who are on active duty or retired with a minimum of 6 years of service in Navel Surface Force or US Atlantic or Pacfic Fleet Support . The award is based on academics, extracurricular activities, character and all around ability and financial need.
Target Student: High school, college and adult students.
Amount: Varies
Number of Awards: Varies
Based on Financial Need: Yes
Deadline: March
Applications are available online.

(120) Angus Foundation Scholarship

American Foundation
3201 Frederick Avenue
St. Joseph, MO 64506

Phone: 816-383-5100
Fax: 816-233-9703
Email: angus@angus.org
URL: http://www.angusfoundation.org

Goal: To assist youths active in the Angus breed.

Eligibility: Applicants must have been members of the National Junior Angus Association and must be junior, regular or life members of the American Angus Association when applying and be enrolled in a two-year, four year or other accredited school with a GPA of 2.0 or higher.

Target Student: High school and college students.

Amount: $1,000 - $5,000

Number of Awards: Varies

Based on Financial Need: No

Deadline: May

Applications are available online or by written request.

---

(121) Annie's Sustainable Agriculture Scholarships

Annie's Homegrown Inc.
564 Gateway Drive
Napa, CA 94558

Phone: 800-288-1089
Email: scholarships@annies.com
URL: http://www.annies.com

Goal: To assist undergraduate and graduate students working towards degrees in sustainable foods and organic agriculture.

Eligibility: Applicants must be full-time undergraduate and graduate students currently attending a college or university in the U.S. and be working towards completing a large amount of coursework in sustainable agriculture.

Target Student: High school, College, Graduate and Adult students.

Amount: Varies

Number of Awards: Varies

Based on Financial Need: No

Deadline: Unknown

Applications are available online. A completed application, transcript, personal statement and two letters of recommendation are required to apply.

---

(122) Annual Logistics Scholarship Competition

International Society of Logistics
Chairman, Scholarships Review Committee
Logistics Education Foundation
8100 Professional Place Suite 111
Hyattsville, MD 20785

Phone: 301-459-8446
Fax: 301-459-1522
Email: solehq@sole.org
URL: http://www.sole.org

Goal: To improve the quaility and access of logistics education.

Eligibility: Applicants must be full-time undergraduate or graduate students pursing a bachelor's or master's in logistics or a logistics related major. The applicants interntion or pursuing a logistics related career, their academics, and contributions to the profession of logistics are considered.

Target Student: College, Graduate and Adult students.

Amount: $1,000

Number of Awards: Varies

Based on Financial Need: No

Deadline: May

Applications are available online.

---

(123) Annual Music Student Scholarships

School Band and Orchestra Magazine
21 Highland Circle
Suite One
Needham, MA 02494

Phone: 800-964-5150

Fax: 781-453-9389
Email:pgalileos@symphonypublishing.com
URL: http://www.sbomagazine.com

Goal: To assist music students.
Eligibility: Applicants must be public, private or home schooled students grades 4 to 12 who are music students. Five scholarships are awarded to students in grades 4 to 8 and 5 scholarships for students grades 9 to 12.
Target Student: Junior high and younger and High School students.
Amount: $1,000
Number of Awards: 10
Based on Financial Need: No
Deadline: December
Applications are available online. A completed essay, contact information, school contact information and instrument played are required to apply.

---

(124) Annual NBNA Scholarships

National Black Nurses Association
8630 Fenton Street
Suite 330
Silver Spring, MD 20910

Phone: 800-575-6298
Fax: 301-589-3223
Email: nbna@erols.com
URL: http://www.nbna.org

Goal: To encourage and assist continuing education for African American nurses and allied health professionals.
Eligibility: Applicants must be African Americans currently enrolled in nursing programs who are members of NBNA, members for a local chapter, have at least one year of school remaining, and be in good academic standing.
Target Student: College and Adult students.
Amount: $500 - $2,000
Number of Awards: Varies

Based on Financial Need: No
Deadline: April
Applications are available online. A completed application, essay, reference, transcripts, evidence of student nurse activities and demonstrated involvement in the African American community.

---

(125) ANS Graduate Scholarship

American Nuclear Society
555 North Kensington Avenue
La Grange Park, IL 60526

Phone: 800-323-3044
Email: hr@ans.org
URL: http://www.ans.org

Goal: To assist graduate students pursuing degrees in nuclear related fields full-time.
Eligibility: Applicants must be full-time students at an accredited graduate school pursuing a degree in nuclear science, nuclear engineering, or another nuclear related field.
Target Student: Graduate and Adult students
Amount: Varies
Number of Awards: Up to 29
Based on Financial Need: No
Deadline: February
Applications are available online. A completed application, transcript, recommendation letter and three reference forms must be submitted to apply.

---

(126) ANS Incoming Freshman Scholarships

American Nuclear Society
555 North Kensington Avenue
La Grange Park, IL 60526

Phone: 800-323-3044
Email: hr@ans.org
URL: http://www.ans.org

Goal: To assist high school seniors planning begin their undergraduate education and major in nuclear engineering.
Eligibility: Applicants must be graduating high school seniors who are accepted into a college or university and plan to major in nuclear engineering.
Target Student: High school students.
Amount: $1,000
Number of Awards: Up to 4
Based on Financial Need: No
Deadline: April
Applications are available online. A completed application, essay, two letters of recommendation, and transcript are required to apply.

(127) ANS Undergraduate Scholarships

American Nuclear Society
555 North Kensington Avenue
La Grange Park, IL 60526

Phone: 800-323-3044
Email: hr@ans.org
URL: http://www.ans.org

Goal: To assist undergraduate students working towards careers in the nuclear science field.
Eligibility: Applicants must be at least college sophomores who have completed at least two years and will be starting their junior or senior year and majoring in nuclear science, nuclear engineering or related field.
Target Student: College and Adult students.
Amount: Varies
Number of Awards: Up to 38
Based on Financial Need: No
Deadline: February
Applications are available online. A completed application, transcript, letters of recommendtion and three reference forms are required to apply.

(128) Antoinette Lierman Medlin Scholarship

Geological Society of America
Program Officer
Grants, Awards and Recognition
P.O. Box 9140
Boulder, CO 80301

Phone: 303-357-1028
Fax: 303-357-1070
Email: awards@geosociety.org
URL: http://www.geosociety.org

Goal: To assist full-time students who are involved in the research of coal geology.
Eligibility: Applicants must be full-time students involved in the research of coal geology in relation to origin, occurrence, geologic characteristics, and economic implications.
Target Student: Graduate and Adult students.
Amount: Varies
Number of Awards: 2
Based on Financial Need: No
Deadline: Varies
An application is not required. Applicants must send in a cover letter, letter of recommendation and proposal.

(129) AOC Scholarships

Association of Old Crows
1000 N. Payne Street
Suite 300
Alexandria, VA 22314

Phone: 703-549-1600
Fax: 703-549-2589
Email: richetti@crows.org
URL: http://www.crows.org

Goal: To assist students interested in a strong national defense with a focus on electronic warfare and information operations.

Eligibility: Applicants should contact their local AOC chapter for requirements.
Target Student: College, Graduate and Adult students.
Amount: Varies
Number of Awards: Varies
Based on Financial Need: No
Deadline: Unknown
Applications are available online.

(130) AORN Foundation Scholarship Program

Association of Perioperative Registered Nurses
2170 S. Parker Road
Suite 300
Denver, CO 80231

Phone: 800-755-2676
Email: sstokes@aorn.org
URL: http://www.aorn.org

Goal: To assist in the education of nurses.
Eligibility: Applicants must be current nursing students or AORN members who are accepted into a nursing program with a GPA of 3.0 or higher.
Target Student: College, Graduate and Adult students.
Amount: Varies
Number of Awards: Varies
Based on Financial Need: No
Deadline: June
Applications are available online.

(131) AOS Master's Scholarship Program

American Orchid Society
16700 AOS Lane
Delray Beach, FL 33446

Phone: 561-404-2000
Fax: 561-404-2045
Email: theaos@aos.org
URL: http://www.aos.org

Goal: To assist students completing a master's thesis regarding orchard education, orchidology or a related topic.
Eligibility: Applicants must be enrolled in a master's program and have a thesis focus on orchard education, applied science or orchard biology.
Target Student: Graduate and Adult students.
Amount: Varies
Number of Awards: Varies
Scholarship can be renewed.
Based on Financial Need: No
Deadline: Unknown
Applications are available online.

(132) APF/COGDOP Graduate Research Scholarships

American Psychological Association Foundation
750 First Street, NW
Washington, DC 20002

Phone: 800-374-2721
URL: http://www.apa.org/apf

Goal: To assist graduate psychology students.
Eligibility: Applicants must be students at a school whose psychology department is a member in good standing with the Council of Graduate Department of Psychology and they must be nominated by their school's department. (Each school can nominate up to 3).
Target Student: Graduate and Adult students.
Amount: $1,000 - $5,000
Number of Awards: 13
Based on Financial Need: No
Deadline: June
Applicants are nominated.

(133) APF/TOPSS Scholars Essay Competition

American Psychological Association
Foundation
750 First Street, NW
Washington, DC 20002

Phone: 800-374-2721

URL: http://www.apa.org/apf

Goal: To assist students studying
psychology.
Eligibility: Applicants must be high
school students who have or who are
taking a psychology course. Applicants
must write an essay on a sponsor specified
topic and be sponsored by a Teachers of
Psychology in Secondary Schools member.
Target Student: High school students.
Amount: $250
Number of Awards: 4
Based on Financial Need: No
Deadline: March
Application information is available online.

(134) Appaloosa Youth Association Art Contest

Appaloosa Horse Club
Appaloosa Youth Foundation Scholarship
Committee
2720 W. Pullman Road
Moscow, ID 83843

Phone: 208-882-5578
Fax: 208-882-8150
Email: acaap@appaloosa.com
URL: http://www.appaloosa.com

Goal: To give students the opportunity to
exhibit their artistic talents with
Appaloosa-themed projects.
Eligibility: Applicants must be 18 years
old and under and submit drawings,
paintings and hand built ceramics or
sculptures with an Appaloosa theme.
Target Student: Junior high and younger
and High school students.

Amount: $50 - $100
Number of Awards: 6
Based on Financial Need: No
Deadline: May
Applications are available online.

(135) Appaloosa Youth Association Essay Contest

Appaloosa Horse Club
Appaloosa Youth Foundation Scholarship
Committee
2720 W. Pullman Road
Moscow, ID 83843

Phone: 208-882-5578
Fax: 208-882-8150
Email: acaap@appaloosa.com
URL: http://www.appaloosa.com

Goal: To acknowledge students for essays
that show their love of the Appaloosa
breed.
Eligibility: Applicants must be under 18
years old and submit an essay on a sponsor
provided topic.
Target Student: Junior high and younger
and High school students.
Amount: Up to $100
Number of Awards: 6
Based on Financial Need: No
Deadline: May
Applications are available online.

(136) Appaloosa Youth Association Speech Contest

Appaloosa Horse Club
Appaloosa Youth Foundation Scholarship
Committee
2720 W. Pullman Road
Moscow, ID 83843

Phone: 208-882-5578
Fax: 208-882-8150
Email: acaap@appaloosa.com
URL: http://www.appaloosa.com

Goal: To acknowledge studetns for their speeches on Appaloosa.

Eligibility: Applicants must be under 18 years old and perform a speech on a pre-determined topic or impromptu topic.

Target Student: Junior high and younger and High school students.

Amount: $100

Number of Awards: 4

Based on Financial Need: No

Deadline: May

Applications are available online.

---

(137) Apprentice Ecologist Initiative Youth Scholarship Program

Nicodemus Wilderness Project
P.O. Box 40712
Albuquerque, NM 87186

Email: mail@wildernessproject.org
URL: http://www.wildernessproject.org

Goal: To assist ecologically focused youth.

Eligibility: Applicants must be students between 13 and 21 years old and create an environmental conservation project and complete an essay describing the experience.

Target Student: Junior high and younger, High school and College students.

Amount: $850

Number of Awards: 3

Based on Financial Need: No

Deadline: December

Application infomration is available online. A completed application, essay and photo of the project is required to apply.

---

(138) APS Minority Scholarship

American Physical Society
One Physics Ellipse
College Park, MD 20740

Phone: 301-209-3200

Fax: 301-209-0865
Email: wilson@aps.org
URL: http://www.aps.org

Goal: To assist minorities who are studying physics.

Eligibility: Applicants must be African-American, Hispanic American, or Native American U.S. citizens or permanent residents planning to major in physics.

Target Student: High school, College and Adult students.

Amount: Varies

Number of Awards: Varies
Scholarship can be renewed.

Based on Financial Need: No

Deadline: February

Applications are available online.

---

(139) ARC Welding Awards

James F. Lincoln Arc Welding Foundation
Secretary
P.O. Box 17188
Cleveland, OH 44117

URL: http://www.jflf.org

Goal: To reward applicants and applicant groups or arc welding projects.

Eligibility: Applicants must create a project in one of the following categories: home, recreational or artistic equipment, shop tool, machine or mechanical device, structure, agricultural equipment or a repair. Applicants must also write a paper regarding the creation of the project and be enrolled in a shop class at a high school, adult evening class, two-year/community college, vocational school, apprentice program, trade school, in-plant training or tech school and not be enrolled in a bachelor's or master's degree program.

Target Student: High school, College and Adult students.

Amount: Up to $1,000

Number of Awards: 95

Based on Financial Need: No

Deadline: June
Applications are available online.

---

(140) ARIT Fellowships for Research in Turkey

American Research Insitute in Turkey
3260 South Street
Philadelphia, PA 19104

Phone: 215-898-3474
Fax: 215-898-0657
Email: leinwand@sas.upenn.edu
URL: http://ccat.sas.upenn.edu/ARIT

Goal: To assist scholars in their research in Turkey.
Eligibility: Applicants must be advanced graduate students or scholars that are involved in research of ancient, medieval or modern Turkey in any field of humanities or social science. Non-U.S. applicants must be associated with a U.S. or Canadian insitution.
Target Student: Graduate and Adult students.
Amount: Varies
Number of Awards: Varies
Based on Financial Need: No
Deadline: November
Applications are available online

---

(141) Armed Services YMCA Annual Essay Contest

Armed Services YMCA
6359 Walker Lane Suite 200
Alexandria, VA 22310

Phone: 703-313-9600
Fax: 703-313-9668
Email: essaycontest@asymca.org
URL: http://www.asymca.org

Goal: To give children a chance to show their love and admiration for their military heroes.

Eligibility: Applicants must children in K-12 who are children of active duty/reserve/guard military personnel. Applicants in 8th grade and lower submit 300 word essay and those above 8th grade submit a 500 word essay on a topic that is chosen by the sponsor.
Target Student: High school, junior high and younger students.
Amount: Varies
Number of Awards: Varies
Based on Financial Need: No
Deadline: March
Applications and information available online.

---

(142) Army College Fund

U.S. Army
Building 1307
Third Avenue
Fort Knox, KY 40121

Phone: 502-626-1587
Email: brian.shalosky@usaac.army.mil
URL: http://www.hrc.army.mil

Goal: To provide assitance for Army enlisted personnel to puruse education in needed occupational specialties.
Eligibility: Applicants must be enlisted in the Army with no prior service and a high school diploma. A minimum score of 50 is required on the Armed Forces Qualification Test Battery (ASVAB). Students must be enrolled in the Montgomery G.I. Bill and must enlisted in a specified military occupational speciality. The funding for the scholarship depends on the speciality.
Target Student: High school, College and Adult students.
Amount: Varies
Number of Awards: Varies
Scholarship can be renewed
Based on Financial Need: No
Deadline: Varies

Applications are available at your local Army recruiting office.

---

(143) Army Nurse Corps Association Scholarships

Army Nurse Corps Association (ANCA)
Education Committee
P.O. Box 458
Lisbon, MD 21765

Phone: 210-650-3534
Fax: 210-650-3494
Email: education@e-anca.org
URL: http://e-anca.org

Goal: To assist nursing or nurse anesthesia students who are affiliated with or plan to become affiliated with the U.S. Army.
Eligibility: Applicants must be enrolled in a bachelor's or graduate degree program in nursing or nurse anesthesia. Applicants must be in the U.S. Army or be planning on entering, or have a parent, spouse or child who has served in the U.S. Army.
Target Student: College, Graduate and Adult students.
Amount: $3,000.00
Number of Awards: Varies
Based on Financial Need: No
Deadline: April
Applications are available online. A completed application, personal statement, official transcript, military service documentation and a recommendation from the student's academic dean.

---

(144) Army ROTC Advanced Course

U.S. Army
Building 1307
Third Avenue
Fort Knox, KY 40121

Phone: 502-626-1587
Email: brian.shalosky@usaac.army.mil
URL: http://www.hrc.army.mil

Goal: To help prepare ROTC members to serve as military officers.
Eligibility: Applicants must be in the junior year of college and have completed the ROTC Basic Course or Leader's Training Course who have committed to serve in the Army after graduation. Applicants must take an ROTC class each semester of their final two years of college as well as attend a summer leadership camp.
Target Student: College and Adult students.
Amount: Varies
Number of Awards: Varies
Scholarship can be renewed
Based on Financial Need: No
Deadline: Varies
Applications are available from your school's military department.

---

(145) Army ROTC Four-Year Scholarship Program

Headquarters
U.S. Army Cadet Command
55 Patch Road
Fort Monroe, VA 23651

Email: atccps@monroe.army.mil
URL: http://www.goarmy.com/rotc

Goal: To help develop military officers by providing funds to help eligible students pay for college.
Eligibility: Applicants must be U.S. citizens and high school seniors or graduates, or college freshman with at least four years of college remaining. Recipients must attend one of 600 collegesa and serve at a minimum of four to eight years in the Army after graduation.
Target Student: High school, College and Adult students.
Amount: Up to Full tuition.
Number of Awards: Varies
Scholarship can be renewed

Based on Financial Need: No
Deadline: January
Applications are available online.

---

(146) Army ROTC Green to Gold Scholarship Program

Headquarters
U.S. Army Cadet Command
55 Patch Road
Fort Monroe, VA 23651

Email: atccps@monroe.army.mil
URL: http://www.goarmy.com/rotc

Goal: To provide financial assistance to enlisted Army personnel.
Eligibility: Applicants must be active duty enlisted Army personnel who want to complete their bachelor's degree and obtain an officer commission. Recipients must serve in the U.S. Army, be high school graduates, have a GPA of 2.5 or above and be under 31 years old.
Target Student: College and adult students.
Amount: Varies
Number of Awards: Varies
Based on Financial Need: No
Deadline: Varies
Applications are available online.

---

(147) Arnold Sobel Endowment Fund Scholarships

Coast Guard Foundation
2100 Second Street SW
Washington, DC 20593

URL: http://www.uscg.mil

Goal: To provide educational scholarships for children of Coast Guard Members.

Eligibility: Applicants must be a dependent of an enlisted Coast Guard member or a Coast Guard Reserve member on extended active duty. Children of retired or deceased Coast Guard members are eligible.
Target Student: High school, College and Adult students.
Amount: $5,000
Number of Awards: 4
Based on Financial Need: No
Deadline: March
Applications are available online after January 2.

---

(148) ARRL Scholarship Honoring Senator Barry Goldwater, K7UGA

American Radio Relay League Foundation
225 Main Street
Newington, CT 06111

Phone: 860-594-0397
Fax: 860-594-0259
Email: foundation@arrl.org
URL: http://www.arrlf.org

Goal: To assist ham radio operators with educational expenses.
Eligibility: Applicants must have a novice ham radio license or higher and be studying for a bachelor's or graduate degree at a regionally accredited college or university.
Target Student: High school, College, Gradaute and Adult students.
Amount: $5,000
Number of Awards: 1
Based on Financial Need: No
Deadline: February
Applications are available online.

---

(149) Art Awards

Scholastic
557 Broadway
New York, NY 10012

Phone: 212-343-6100
Fax: 212-389-3939
Email: a&wgeneralinfo@scholastic.com
URL: http://www.artandwriting.org

Goal: To acknowledge America's best student artists.
Eligibility: Applicants must be in 7th through 12th grade in an American or Canadian school and submit their artwork to one of the flowing categories: art portfolio, animation, ceramics and glass, computer art, design, digital imagery, drawing, mixed media, painting, photography, photography portfolio, printmaking, sculpture or video and film.
Target Student: Junior high and younger, High school students.
Amount: Varies
Number of Awards: Varies
Based on Financial Need: No
Deadline: Varies
Applications are available online.

---

(150) ASABE Foundation Engineering Scholarship Foundation

Adminstrator
Scholarship Fund
2950 Niles Road
St. Joseph, MI 49085

Phone: 269-429-0300
Fax: 269-429-3852
URL: http://www.asabe.org

Goal: To assist members of the ASABE.
Eligibility: Applicants must have completed at least one year of undergraduate study with at least one year left and majoring in agriculturl or biological engineering at a U.S. or Canada college or university with a GPA of 2.5 or higher and demonstrated financial need.
Target Student: College and Adult students.
Amount: $1,000

Number of Awards: 1
Based on Financial Need: No
Deadline: March
Application is available online.

---

(151) ASCA/AISC Student Design Competition

Association of Collegiate Schools of Architecture
1735 New York Avenue NW
Washington, DC 20006

Phone: 202-765-2324
Fax: 202-628-0448
URL: http://www.acsa-arch.org

Goal: To assist with the innovation in architecture.
Eligibility: Applicants must be undergraduate juniors, seniors or graduate architecture students at an ACSA member school in Mexico, Canada or the U.S..
Target Student: College, Graduate and Adult students.
Amount: Up to $2,500
Number of Awards: 6
Based on Financial Need: No
Deadline: February
Applications are available online. A completed application and design project are required to apply.

---

(152) ASDSO Dam Safety Scholarships

Association of State Dam Safety Officials
450 Old Vine Street
2nd Floor
Lexington, KY 40507

Phone: 859-257-5140
Fax: 859-323-1958
Email: info@damsafety.org
URL: http://www.damsafety.org

Goal: To increase the knowledge of careers in dam safety.

Eligibility: Applicants must be full-time seniors with demonstrated interest in a career related to dam design, construction or operation and be enrolled in a civil engineering program with a GPA of 2.5 or higher and be recommended by their advisor.
Target Student: College and Adult students.
Amount: Up to $10,000
Number of Awards: Varies
Based on Financial Need: Yes
Deadline: March
Applications are available online. A completed application, essay and recommendation from advisor is required to apply.

(153) ASEV Scholarships

American Society for Enology and Viticulture
P.O. Box 1855
Davis, CA 95617

Phone: 530-753-3142
Fax: 530-753-3318
Email: society@asev.org
URL: http://www.asev.org

Goal: To support students purusing a degree in enology, viticulture or a degree focused no the basic science of the wine and grape industry.
Eligibility: Applicants must be undergraduate or graduate students beginning or enrolled in a full-time four year program in North America. Applicants must be at least juniors in the next school year with a GPA of 3.2 or higher and enrolled in a program focused on enology or viticulture or in a curriculum based on the science of the wine and grape industry.
Target Student: College, Graduate and Adult students..
Amount: Varies
Number of Awards: Varies

Based on Financial Need: No
Deadline: March
Applications are available online. A completed application, two letters of recommendation and transcripts are required.

(154) ASF Olin Fellowship

Atlantic Salmon Federation
P.O. Box 807
Calais, ME 4619

Phone: 506-529-1033
Fax: 506-529-4438
Email: asfweb@nbnet.nb.ca
URL: http://www.asf.ca

Goal: To assist with projects that are designed to solve problems with Atlantic salmon biology, management and conservation.
Eligibility: Applicants must be studying or engaged in research and management related to salmon.
Target Student: College, Graduate or Adult students.
Amount: $1,000 - $3,000
Number of Awards: Varies
Based on Financial Need: No
Deadline: March
Applications are available by mail.

(155) ASHA Youth Scholarships

American Saddlebred Horse Association Foundation
4083 Iron Works Parkway
Lexington, KY 40511

Phone: 859-259-2742 x343
Fax: 859-259-1628
URL: http://www.saddlebred.com

Goal: To assist youths who are involved with Saddlebreds.

Eligibility: Applicants must have involvement with American Saddlebred. The award is based on academic excellence, financial need, community service, and extracurricular activities.
Target Student: High school students.
Amount: $2,500 - $5,000
Number of Awards: 6
Based on Financial Need: Yes
Deadline: April
Applications are available online. A completed application and essay is required to apply.

---

(156) ASHRAE Scholarship Program

American Society of Heating, Refrigerating and Air-Conditioning Engineers
1791 Tullie Circle, NE
Atlanta, GA 30329

Phone: 404-636-8400
Fax: 404-321-5478
Email: lbenedict@ashrae.org
URL: http://www.ashrae.org

Goal: To promote education in heating, ventilating, air conditioning and refrigeration education.
Eligibility: Applicants must be full-time undergraduate students who are majoring in engineering or engineering technology or graduate students who are in a program approved by the Accreditation Board for Engineering and Technology or another ASHRAE approved accredited agency with a GPA of 3.0 or higher.
Target Student: College, Graduate and Adult students.
Amount: $3,000 - $10,000
Number of Awards: Varies
Based on Financial Need: Yes
Deadline: December
Applications are available online.

---

(157) ASLA Council of Fellows Scholarships

Landscape Architecture Foundation
818 18th Street NW
Suite 810
Washington, DC 20006

Phone: 202-331-7070
Fax: 202-331-7079
Email: scholarships@lafoundation.or
URL: http://www.lafoundation.org

Goal: To assist students who have financial need or who are from underrepresented groups who are purusing careers in landscape architecture.
Eligibility: Applicants must be U.S. citizen or permanent resident in their third to fifth year of a undergraduate degree that is approved by the Landscape Architecture Accreditation Board.
Target Student: College and Adult students.
Amount: $4,000
Number of Awards: 2
Based on Financial Need: Yes
Deadline: February
Applications are available online. A completed application, essay, financial aid information, photo and two recommendations are required to apply.

---

(158) ASM Outstanding Scholars Awards

ASM International
9639 Kinsman Road
Materials Park, OH 44073

Phone: 440-338-5151
Fax: 440-338-4634
Email: jeane.deatherage@asminternational.org
URL: http://www.asminternational.org/portal/site/www/foundation/scholarships

Goal: To acknowledge scholars in metallurgy or materials science engineering.

Eligibility: Applicants must be student members of ASM International who are majoring in metallurgy or materials science engineering, and be undergraduate juniors and seniors.
Target Student: College and Adult students.
Amount: $2,000
Number of Awards: 3
Based on Financial Need: No
Deadline: May
Applications are available online. A completed application, transcripts, two letters of recommendation, personal statement and photographs are required.

---

(160) ASME Foundation - ASME Auxiliary FIRST Clarke Scholarship

American Society of Mechanical Engineers
Three Park Avenue
New York, NY 10016

Phone: 800-843-2763
Fax: 973-882-1717
Email: infocentral@asme.org
URL: http://www.asme.org

Goal: To assist FIRST Robotics members interesting in a career in mechanical engineering or mechanical engineering technology.
Eligibility: Applicants must be high school seniors who are FIRST Robotics members and must be nominated by an ASME member, Auxiliary member or student member. Applicant must be starting their undergraduate studies not later than fall after their graduation from high school and be planning to enroll in an ABET-accredited or similiarly accredited mechanical engineering, or mechanical engineering technology degree program.
Target Student: High school students.
Amount: $5,000
Number of Awards: 8
Based on Financial Need: No
Deadline: March

Applications are available online. A completed application, resume, transcript, financial data and nomination letter are required to apply.

---

(159) ASME Foundation Scholarships

American Society of Mechanical Engineers
Three Park Avenue
New York, NY 10016

Phone: 800-843-2763
Fax: 973-882-1717
Email: infocentral@asme.org
URL: http://www.asme.org

Goal: To assist ASME members enrolled in undergraduate mechancial engineering, mechanical engineering technology or related degree program students.
Eligibility: Applicants must be ASME members must be enrolled or accepting into a ABET or simliar accredited undergraduate program in mechanical engineering, mechanical engineering technology or a related subject.
Target Student: College and Adult students.
Amount: $2,000
Number of Awards: 20
Based on Financial Need: No
Deadline: March
Applications are available online. Transcript, letters of recommendation and application must be submitted through an online program.

---

(161) ASNE Scholarship Program

American Society of Navel Engineers
1452 Duke Street
Alexandria, VA 22314

Phone: 703-836-6727
Fax: 703-836-7491
Email: dwoodbury@navalengineers.org
URL: http://www.navalengineers.org

Goal: To encourage students to enter the naval engineering field and to assist naval engineers with their advanced education.
Eligibility: Applicants must be U.S. citizens working towards a career in naval engineering. Graduate students must be members of ASNE. The award is based on academics, employment history, professional promise, recommendations and extracurriculiar activities. Finanical need can be considered.
Target Student: College, Graduate and Adult students.
Amount: $3,000 - $4,000
Number of Awards: Varies
Based on Financial Need: Yes
Deadline: February
Applications are available online or by written request.

(162) ASNT Fellowship

American Society for Nondestructive Testing
1711 Arlingate Lane
P.O. Box 28518
Columbus, OH 43228

Phone: 800-222-2768
Fax: 614-274-6899
Email: sthomas@asnt.org
URL: http://www.asnt.org

Goal: To encourage research in nondestructive testing.
Eligibility: The award is given to a college or university that is accredited by the ABET for research in nondestructive testing. One proposal per faculty member will be considered. Faculty should submit a proposal, program of study, budget, description of facilities, background of the faculty and background of the graduate student.
Target Student: Graduate and Adult students.
Amount: Up to $15,000

Number of Awards: Up to 5
Based on Financial Need: No
Deadline: October
Applications are available online.

(163) Aspiring Police Officer Scholarship

Police Officer Training
P.O. Box 2790
Turlock, CA 95380

Email: info@police-officer-training.com
URL: http://www.police-officer-training.com

Goal: To assist students pursuing careers in law enforcment.
Eligibility: Applicants must be 17 years old or above, be in college or planning to begin college in the next 12 months and be planning to pursue a career in law enforcement.
Target Student: High school, College, Graduate and Adult students.
Amount: $100
Number of Awards: 1
Based on Financial Need: No
Deadline: August
Applications are available online.

(164) Association for Women in Science Educational Awards

Association for Women in Science
1442 Duke Street
Alexandria, VA 22314

Phone: 202-326-8940
Fax: 202-326-8960
Email: awisedfd@awis.org
URL: http://www.awis.org

Goal: To assist female students studying science.

Eligibility: The undergraduate scholarship is for second and third year students planning to major in area of science. The graduate scholarship is for doctoral students admitted to cadidacy for a Ph.D. in life or physical science or engineering.
Target Student: College, Graduate and Adult students.
Amount: $1,000 - $3,000
Number of Awards: Varies
Based on Financial Need: No
Deadline: December
Applciations are available online.

(165) Association of Equipment Management Professionls Foundation Scholarship

Association of Equipment Management
Professionals
P.O. Box 1368
Glenwood Springs, CO 81602

Phone: 970-384-0510
Fax: 970-384-0512
Email: stan@aemp.org
URL: http://www.aemp.org

Goal: To assist students interested in heavy equipment management.
Eligibility: Applicants must attend a school that has a diesel technology program and have a 2.0 GPA to apply and recipients must maintain a 3.0 GPA or higher.
Target Student: High school, College, Adult students.
Amount: Up to $2,000
Number of Awards: Varies
Based on Financial Need: No
Deadline: May
Applications are available online. A completed application, transcripts and two letters of recommendation are required to apply.

(166) Association of Federal Communications Consulting Engineers Scholarships

Association of Federal Communications
Consulting Engineers
P.O. Box 19333
Washington, DC 20036

Phone: 703-780-4824
Email: secretary@afcce.org
URL: http://www.afcce.org

Goal: To assist full-time undergraduate students who are studying telecommunications or a related field at an accredited college or university.
Eligibility: Applicants must be full-time undergraduate students who are juniors or seniors majoring in a field related to radio communications consulting engineering field.
Target Student: College and Adult students.
Amount: Up to $2,500
Number of Awards: Varies
Based on Financial Need: No
Deadline: Varies
Applications are available online. A completed application, transcript, statement and sponsorship by an AFCCE member are required to apply.

(167) Association of Food and Drug Officials Scholarship Award

Association of Food and Drug Officials
2550 Kingston Road
Suite 311
York, PA 17402

Phone: 717-757-2888
Fax: 717-755-8089
Email: afdo@afdo.org
URL: http://www.afdo.org

Goal: To assist college students studying food, drug and consumer product safety.

Eligibility: Applicants must be attending an accredited college in their third or fourth year with demonstrated desire to work in a career of research, regulartory work, quality control and teaching in the food, drug and consumer safety field and have a GPA of 3.0 or higher.
Target Student: College and Adult students.
Amount: $1,500
Number of Awards: 3
Based on Financial Need: No
Deadline: February
Applications are available online.

---

(168) ASTM International Katherine and Bryant Mather Scholarship

ASTM International
100 Barr Harbor Drive
P.O. Box C700
West Conshohocken, PA 19428

Phone: 610-832-9500
Email: awards@astm.org
URL: http://www.astm.org

Goal: To assist students in degree programs related to the cement and conrete technology industry.
Eligibility: Applicants must be full-time undergraduate sophomores, seniors or graduate students enrolled in a degree program related to construction or contrete materials technology.
Target Student: College, Graduate and Adult students.
Amount: $7,500
Number of Awards: Varies
Scholarship can be renewed.
Based on Financial Need: No
Deadline: Varies
Applications are available online. A copleted application, one letter of recommendation, transcript and personal statement are required to apply.

(169) Astronaut Scholarship

Astronaut Scholarship Foundation
6225 Vectorspace Boulevard
Titusville, FL 32780

Phone: 321-269-6101
Fax: 321-264-9176
Email: linnleblanc@astronautscholarship.org
URL: http://www.astronautscholarship.org

Goal: To assist promising physical science and engineering students to ensure the United States continued leadership in science.
Eligibility: Applicants must be undergraduate sophomores, juniors or seniors or graduate students in physical science or engineering at Clemson University, Georgia Institute of Technology, Harvey Mudd College, Miami University, North Carolina A&T State University, North Carolina State University, North Dakota State University, Pennsylvania State University, Purdue University, Syracuse University, Texas A&M University, Tufts University, University of Central Florida, University of Colorado, University of Kentucky, University of Minnesota, University of Michigan, University of Okalahoma, University of Washington, or Washington University and be nominated by a faculty or staff member.
Target Student: College, Graduate and Adult students.
Amount: $10,000
Number of Awards: Varies
Based on Financial Need: No
Deadline: Varies
Applicants must be nominated.

---

(170) Atlas Shrugged Essay Contest

Ayn Rand Institute Atlas Shrugged Essay Contest

Department W
P.O. Box 57044
Irvine, CA 92619

Phone: 949-222-7044
Fax: 949-222-6550
Email: essay@aynrand.org
URL: http://www.aynrand.org

Goal: To assist college students who have an outstanding understanding of Ayn Rand's Atlas Shrugged.
Eligibility: Applicants must be college and high school seniors who will enter college in the fall. Applicants must submit an 800 to 1,600 word essay that is judged on style and content.
Target Student: High school, College and Adult students.
Amount: Up to $10,000
Number of Awards: 84
Based on Financial Need: No
Deadline: September
Applications information is available online.

---

(171) AUA Foundation Research Scholars Program

American Foundation for Urologic Disease Inc.
100 Corporate Boulevard
Linthicum, MD 21090

Phone: 410-689-3750
Fax: 410-489-3850
Email: grants@auafoundation.org
URL: http://www.urologyhealth.org

Goal: To assist young students who want to pursue a career in urologic research.
Eligibility: Applicants must be researchers in the U.S. or Canada.
Target Student: Graduate and Adult students.
Amount: Varies
Number of Awards: Varies
Based on Financial Need: No

Deadline: August
Applications are available online.

---

(172) Automotive Hall of Fame Scholarships

Automotive Hall of Fame
Award and Scholarship Programs
21400 Oakwood Boulevard
Dearborn, MI 48124

Phone: 313-240-4000
Fax: 313-240-8641
URL: http://www.automotivehalloffame.org

Goal: To assist students pursuing careers in the automotive industry.
Eligibility: Applicants must be interested in an automotive career. There are a number of scholarships available with specific requirements for each.
Target Student: High school, College and Adult students.
Amount: Varies
Number of Awards: Varies
Based on Financial Need: No
Deadline: June
Applications are available online or by mail.

---

(173) Aviation Distributors and Manufacturers Association Scholarship Program

Aviation Distributors and Manufacturers Association
100 North 20th Street
4th Floor
Philadelphia, PA 19103

Phone: 215-564-3484
Fax: 215-963-9784
Email: adma@fernley.com
URL: http://www.adma.org

Goal: To assist students planning to puruse a career in aviation.
Eligibility: Applicants must be in their third or fourth year in a four year program working towards their Bachelor of Science in aviation management or professional piloting or they must be in the second year of a A&P mechanic program. Applicants must have a 3.0 GPA or higher.
Target Student: College and Adult students.
Amount: Varies
Number of Awards: Varies
Based on Financial Need: Yes
Deadline: March
Applications are available online. A completed application, trancripts, two letters of recommendation and statement are required to apply.

(174) Aviation Insurance Association Education Foundation Scholarship

Aviation Insurance Association
400 Admiral Boulevard
Kansas City, MO 64106

Phone: 816-221-8488
Fax: 816-472-7765
Email: mandie@robstan.com
URL: http://www.aiaweb.org

Goal: To assist upper division undergradaute aviation students.
Eligibility: Applicants must be enrolled in an undergraduate aviation program that is approved by the University Aviation Association. Applicants must have a GPA of 2.5 or higher with at least 45 units completed 15 or more of which must have been aviation courses.
Target Student: College and Adult students.
Amount: $2,500
Number of Awards: 4
Based on Financial Need: No
Deadline: Varies

Applications are available online. Five sets of materials are required to apply. A completed application, statement, transcript, one letter of recommendation and any FAA certificates are required.

(175) AWSEF Scholarship

American Water Ski Educational Foundation
1251 Holly Cow Road
Polk City, FL 33868

Phone: 863-324-2472
Email: info@waterskihalloffame.com
URL: http://www.waterskihalloffame.com

Goal: To assist those involved with USA Water Ski with educational expenses.
Eligibility: Applicants must be full time undergraduate students currently attending a two year or four year college currently entering their sophomore year or beyond. Applicants must also be active members of USA Water Ski.
Target Student: College and adult students.
Amount: Up to $3,000
Number of Awards: 6
Scholarship can be renewed.
Based on Financial Need: No
Deadline: March
Applications are available online.

(176) AXA Achievement Community Scholarship

AXA Achievement Scholarship
c/o Scholarship America
One Scholarship Way
St. Peter, MN 56082

Phone: 800-537-4180
Email: axachievement@scholarshipamerica.org
URL: http://www.axa-equitable.com/axa-foundation/community-scholarships.html

Goal: To assist outstanding high school seniors.
Eligibility: Applicants must be U.S. citizens or legal residents and be high school seniors in the U.S. or Puerto Rico. They must be planning on attending a two year or four year accredited college or university in the fall following their high school graduation. They must be ambitious and driven, determined to set and reach goals and respectful of self, family and the community and able to succeed in college. The award is based on the strength of the applicant.
Target Student: High school students.
Amount: $2,000
Number of Awards: Varies
Based on Financial Need: No
Deadline: February
Applications are available online. A completed application, transcript, personal essay and one letter of recommendation are required.

---

(177) AXA Achievement Scholarships

AXA Achievement Scholarship
c/o Scholarship America
One Scholarship Way
St. Peter, MN 56082

Phone: 800-537-4180
Email: axachievement@scholarshipamerica.org
URL: http://www.axa-equitable.com/axa-foundation/AXA-achievement-scholarship.html

Goal: To assist ambitious students with educational expenses.

Eligibility: Applicants must be U.S. citizens or legal residents and be high school seniors in the U.S. or Puerto Rico. They must be planning on attending a two year or four year accredited college or university in the fall following their high school graduation. Applicants must be U.S. citizens or legal residents and be high school seniors in the U.S. or Puerto Rico. They must be planning on attending a two year or four year accredited college or university in the fall following their high school graduation. They must be ambitious and driven, determined to set and reach goals and respectful of self, family and the community and able to succeed in college. The award is based on the strength of the applicant. Only the first 10,000 applications will be accepted.
Target Student: High school students.
Amount: $10,000-$25,000
Number of Awards: 52
Based on Financial Need: No
Deadline: December
Applications are available online. A recommendation form from an adult who can attest to the student's achievement is required.

---

(178) Babe Ruth League Scholarships

Babe Ruth League Inc.
1770 Brunswick Avenue
P.O. Box 5000
Trenton, NJ 08638

URL: http://www.baberuthleague.org

Goal: To assist players in the Babe Ruth Baseball and Softball league.
Eligibility: Applicants must be members or former members of the Babe Ruth Baseball and Softball leagues. They must be high school seniors.
Target Student: High school students.
Amount: $1,000
Number of Awards: Varies
Based on Financial Need: No

Deadline: July

Applications are available online. A completed application, high school transcript and one letter of recommendation is required.

---

(179) Bachelor's Scholarships

Oncology Nursing Society
ONS Foundation
125 Enterprise Drive
Pittsburgh, PA 15275

Phone: 412-859-6100
Fax: 412-859-6163
Email: foundation@ons.org
URL: http://www.ons.org

Goal: To improve oncology nursing by assisting RN's in their education.
Eligibility: Applicants who are not registered nurses must be enrolled in an undergraduate nursing degree program in a school approved by the National League for Nursing or the Commission on Collegiate Nursing Education. They must be in the nursing component of the program and have an interest in oncology nursing and living in Ohio or West Virginia. Applicants who are registered nurses must have a high school diploma and be enrolled in an undergraduate nursing program that is approved by the National League for Nursing or the Commisison on Collegiate Nursing Education. There is a $5 application fee. It is not recommended to apply to program with a fee.
Target Student: College and Adult students.
Amount: $2,000
Number of Awards: Varies
Based on Financial Need: No
Deadline: February
Applications are available online or by email.

---

(180) Banks Family Scholarship

Foundation for Global Scholars
12050 North Pecos Street
Suite 320
Westminster, CO 80234

Phone: 303-502-7256
Email:kbrockwell@foundationforglobalscholars.org
URL:http://www.foundationforglobalscholars.org

Goal: To assist business students study abroad.
Eligibility: Applicants must be U.S. or Canadian students currently enrolled at a college or university in North America. Applicants must be able to transfer credits earned during the study abroad experience to their degree program and be business majors with an interest in entrepreneurship with a GPA of 3.0 or higher and be GlobalLinks Learning Abroad students. Winners must study abroad for one semester.
Target Student: College and Adult students.
Amount: Varies
Number of Awards: Varies
Based on Financial Need: No
Deadline: Varies
Applications are available online. A completed application, transcripts and essay are required to apply.

---

(181) Barold Scholarship

American Ground Water Trust
16 Centre Street
Concord, NH 03301

Phone: 603-228-5444
Fax: 603-228-6557
Email:
URL: http://www.agwt.org

Goal: To assist high school seniors planning to pursue careers in a field related to ground water.
Eligibility: Applicants must be high school seniors entering a four-year college or university and planning to pursue a career in a field related to ground water.
Target Student: High school students.
Amount: $2,000
Number of Awards: Varies
Based on Financial Need: No
Deadline: June
Applications are available online.

---

(182) Barry M. Goldwater Scholarship and Excellence in Education Program

Barry M. Goldwater Scholarship and Excellence in Education Foundation
6225 Brandon Avenue
Suite 315
Springfield, VA 22150

Phone: 703-756-6012
Fax: 703-756-6015
Email: goldwater@act.org
URL: http://www.act.org/goldwater

Goal: To assist college students pursuing careers as mathematicians, engineers and scientists.
Eligibility: Applicants must be full-time college sophomores or juniors who are U.S. citizens or reisdent aliens with a 3.0 GPA or higher and in the upper 25% of their class.
Target Student: College and Adult students.
Amount: Up to $7,500
Number of Awards: Up to 300
Based on Financial Need: No
Deadline: January
Each college or univeristy will nominate the students.

---

(183) Battery Division Student Research Award

Electrochemical Society
65 South Main Street
Building D
Pennington, NJ 08534

Phone: 609-737-1902
Fax: 609-737-2743
Email: awards@electrochem.org
URL: http://www.electrochem.org

Goal: To award young engineers and scientists in the field of electrochemical power sources.
Eligibility: Applicants must be enrolled in a college or university and submit a transcript, outline of the project, description of how the project relates to the field of electrochemical power sources, details of acheivement in industrial work and letters of recommednation.
Target Student: High school, College and Graduate students.
Amount: $1,000
Number of Awards: Varies
Based on Financial Need: No
Deadline: March
Applications are available online.

---

(184) BEA National Scholarships in Broadcasting

Broadcast Education Association
1771 North Street NW
Washington, DC 20036

Phone: 888-380-7222
Email: beainfo@beaweb.org
URL: http://www.beaweb.org

Goal: To assist future broadcasters with educational expenses.

Eligibility: Applicants must be college juniors or seniors, or graduate students at BEA member schools, students seeking freshman or sophomore instruction only or students who have completed BEA two-year programs at a four year college or university.
Target Student: College, Graduate and Adult students.
Amount: Varies
Number of Awards: Varies
Based on Financial Need: No
Deadline: October
Applications are available online.

---

(185) Beat the GMAT Scholarship

Beat the GMAT

Email: scholarship@beatthegmat.com
URL: http://www.beatthegmat.com

Goal: To assist members of the Beat the GMAT discussion forum.
Eligibility: Applicants must be in their final year of college or completed college and plan on attending business school. They must have a PayPal account to receive their winnings and submit the required essays.
Target Student: College and Adult students.
Amount: Varies
Number of Awards: 6
Based on Financial Need: No
Deadline: April
Applications are available online. A completed application, contact information, picture, bio, two references and two essays are required to apply.

---

(186) Beef Industry Scholarship

National Cattlemen's Foundation
9110 East Nichols Avenue
Suite 300
Centennial, CO 80112

Phone: 303-694-0305
Fax: 303-770-7745
Email: ncf@beef.org
URL: http://www.nationalcattlemensfoundation.org

Goal: To assist students purusing careers in the beef industry.
Eligibility: Applicants must be graduating high school seniors or college undergraduates planning to enroll full-time in a two- or four-year undergraduate program that is related to the beef industry. They, or their family, must be members of the National Cattlemen's Beef Association.
Target Student: High school, College and Adult students.
Amount: $1,500
Number of Awards: 10
Scholarship can be renewed.
Based on Financial Need: No
Deadline: December
Applications are available online. A completed application, letter of intent, essay and two letters of recommendations are required to apply.

---

(187) Begun Scholarship

California Library Assocation
4030 Lennane Drive
Sacramento, CA 95834

Phone: 916-779-4573
Fax: 916-419-2874
Email: info@cla-net.org
URL: http://www.cla-net.org

Goal: To assist information sciences graduate students in California schools.

Eligibility: Applicants must be California graduate students at an American Library Association accredited school who has completed their core coursework for a master's of library science or information studies degree. Winners must plan on becoming a children's or young adult librarian at a California public library and become a member of the California Library Association.
Target Student: Graduate and Adult student.
Amount: $3,000
Number of Awards: 1
Based on Financial Need: No
Deadline: May
Applications are available online.

(188) Behavioral Sciences Student Fellowship

Epilepsy Foundation
8301 Professional Drive
Landover, MD 20785

Phone: 301-459-3700
Email: researchwebsupport@efa.org
URL: http://www.epilepsyfoundation.org

Goal: To encourage students to pursue careers in the research and practice of epilepsy.
Eligibility: Applicants must be undergraduate and graduate students in the behavioral sciences, have a qualified mentor who is able to supervise the project and have a field of study related to epilepsy. The project must be in the U.S. and it should not be for a dissertation.
Target Student: College, Graduate and Adult students.
Amount: $3,000 stipend
Number of Awards: Varies
Based on Financial Need: No
Deadline: March

Application information is available online. A completed application, recommendation letter, biography, statement of intent and research plan are required to apply.

(189) Benjamin Willard Niebel Scholarship

Institute of Industrial Engineers
3577 Parkway Lane
Suite 200
Norcross, GA 30092

Phone: 800-494-0460
Fax: 770-441-3295
Email: bcameron@iienet.org
URL: http://www.iienet2.org

Goal: To assist students who are majoring in industrial engineering.
Eligibility: Applicants must be enrolled in a college or university in the U.S., Canada or Mexico full-time as undergraduate or graduate students majoring in industrial engineering and must be nominated for the award.
Target Student: College, Graduate and Adult students.
Amount: $2,000
Number of Awards: 2
Based on Financial Need: Yes
Deadline: November
Nomination information is available online.

(190) Benton-Meier Scholarships

American Psychological Association Foundation
750 First Street NE
Washington, DC 20002

Phone: 800-374-2721
URL: http://www.apa.org/apf

Goal: To assist neuropsychology graduate students with educational expenses.

Eligibility: Applicants must have demonstrated financial need and demonstrated potential for a career in neuropsychology.
Target Student: Graduate and Adult students.
Amount: $2,500
Number of Awards: 2
Based on Financial Need: Yes
Deadline: June
Application information is available online. A completed application, letter explaining their research accomplishments and financial need are required to apply.

(191) Berna Lou Cartwright Scholarship

American Society of Mechanical Engineers
Three Park Avenue
New York, NY 10016

Phone: 800-843-2763
Fax: 973-882-1717
Email: infocentral@asme.org
URL: http://www.asme.org

Goal: To assist U.S. mechanical engineering majors.
Eligibility: Applicants must be U.S. citizens who are beginning their final year of an ABET accredited undergraduate mechanical engineering program.
Target Student: College and Adult students.
Amount: $2,000
Number of Awards: 1
Based on Financial Need: Yes
Deadline: March
Applications are available online. A completed application, transcripts and three letters of recommendation are required apply.

(192) Best Buy @ 15 Scholarship Program

Best Buy Children's Foundation

7601 Penn Avenue S.
Richfield, MN 55423

Phone: 612-292-6397
Email: bestbuy@scholarshipamerica.org
URL: http://www.bestbuy-communityrelations.com/scholarship.htm

Goal: To assist high school students (grades 9-12) that will be attending a college, university or vocational school following high school.
Eligibility: Applicants must be currently in 9th to 12th grade living in the U.S. or Puerto Rico with a minimum GPA of 2.5, with demontrated commitment and involvement to community service. The award is based on academic performance and community service or work experience. School leadership can also be a consideration. Best Buy employees and/or relatives who qualify are eligible for the scholarship.
Target Student: High school students.
Amount: $1,000
Number of Awards: Up to 1,200
Based on Financial Need: No
Deadline: February
Applications are available online.

(193) Best Buy Scholarships

Best Buy Children's Foundation
7601 Penn Avenue S.
Richfield, MN 55423

Phone: 612-292-6397
Email: bestbuy@scholarshipamerica.org
URL: http://www.bestbuy-communityrelations.com/scholarship.htm

Goal: To assist students in affording college.

Eligibility: Applicants must be in high school and living in the U.S. or Puerto Rico. The students must live within 75 miles of a Best Buy store and have a minimum GPA of 2.5 and have work or community experience. They must plan to enter college as a full time student at a two year or four year college the fall after high school graduation.
Target Student: High school students.
Amount: $1,000
Number of Awards: Up to 1,200
Based on Financial Need: No
Deadline: February
Applications are available online. A completed application and transcripts are required when applying.

(194) Betsy Plank/PRSSA Scholarship

Public Relations Student Society of America
33 Maiden Lane
11th Floor
New York, NY 10038

Phone: 212-460-1474
Fax: 212-995-0757
Email: prssa@prsa.org
URL: http://www.prssa.org

Goal: To assist public relations students with educational expenses.
Eligibility: Applciants must be PRSSA members who are college juniors or seniors enrolled at in an undergraduate public relations degree program. The award is based on academics, leadership, experience and commitment ot public relations.
Target Student: College and Adult students
Amount: $1,500 - $2,000
Number of Awards: 3
Based on Financial Need: No
Deadline: June
Applications are available online.

(195) Better Choice Scholarship

Associates of Vietnam Veterans of America
8605 Cameron Street Suite 400
Silver Spring, MD 20910

Phone: 301-585-0519
Fax: 301-585-0519
Email: pvarnell@avva.org
URL: http://www.avva.org

Goal: To assist the family members of veterans.
Eligibility: Applicants must be VVA or AVVA members or their spouses, children, grandchildren, or spouses, children or grandchildren of KIA or MIA Vietnam Veterans. They must be registered at an accredited college or university and they must show a financial need with a FASFA printout.
Target Student: High school, college and adult students.
Amount: $750-$1,000
Number of Awards: Varies
Based on Financial Need: Yes
Deadline: June
Applications are available online.

(196) Big Dig Scholarship

Antique Trader
4216 Pacific Coast Highway #302
Torrance, CA 90505

Phone: 310-294-9981
Email: henryk@antiquetrader.tv
URL: http://www.antiquetrader.tv

Goal: To assist the student who has written the best essay on a specific antique item.

Eligibility: Applicants must be in their last year of high school or their first two years of college. They must write an essay on a sponsor given question that relates to antiques. Selection is based on content, originality and grammar and punctuatlity.
Target Student: High school, College and Adult students.
Amount: $3,000
Number of Awards: 1
Based on Financial Need: No
Deadline: June
Application instructions are available online.

---

(197) Bill Gove Scholarship

National Speakers Association
1500 S. Priest Drive
Attn: Scholarship Committee
Tempe, AZ 85281

Phone: 480-968-2552
Fax: 480-968-0911
URL: http://www.msaspeaker.org

Goal: To encourage the study of professional speaking.
Eligibility: Applicants must be full time college students majoring or minoring in speech.
Target Student: College, Graduate and Adult students.
Amount: $5,000
Number of Awards: 4
Based on Financial Need: No
Deadline: June
Applications are available online.

---

(198) Bill Kane Scholarship, Undergraduate

American Association for Health Education
1900 Association Drive
Reston, VA 20191

Phone: 703-476-3437
Fax: 703-476-6638
Email: aahe@aahperd.org
URL: http://www.aahperd.org/aahe

Goal: To assist health education students.
Eligibility: Applicants must be health majors with a 3.25 or higher GPA attending full-time as undergraduate sophomore, juniors or seniors.
Target Student: College and Adult students.
Amount: $1,000
Number of Awards: 1
Based on Financial Need: No
Deadline: November
Applications are available online.

---

(199) Bill Salerno, W2ONV, Memorial Scholarship

American Radio Relay League Foundation
225 Main Street
Newington, CT 06111

Phone: 860-594-0397
Fax: 860-594-0259
Email: foundation@arrl.org
URL: http://www.arrlf.org

Goal: To assist amateur radio operators with a high level of academic achievement with educational expenses.
Eligibility: Applicants must have an Amateur Radio License of any class and be currently attending a four-year college or university with a GPA of 3.7 or higher with a household income below $100,000 per year.
Target Student: High school, College and Adult students.
Amount: $1,000
Number of Awards: 2
Based on Financial Need: Yes
Deadline: February
Applications are avaiilable online.

(200) Billy Welu Scholarship

United States Bowling Congress
5301 S. 76th Street
Greendale, WI 53129

Phone: 800-514-2695 x3168
Fax:
Email: smart@bowl.com
URL: http://www.bowl.com

Goal: To assist amateur bowlers who are in college.
Eligibility: Applicants must be amateur bowlers who are currently attending college and have a minimum GPA of 2.5.
Target Student: College, graduate and adult students.
Amount: $1,000
Number of Awards: 1
Based on Financial Need: No
Deadline: Varies
Applications are available online.

(201) Biographies of Contemporary Women In Mathematics Essay Contest

Association for Women in Mathematics
4114 Computer and Space Sciences Building
University of Maryland
College Park, MD 20742

Phone: 301-405-7892
Fax: 301-314-9074
Email: awm@math.umd.edu
URL: http://www.awn-math.org

Goal: To increase the awareness of the contributions to mathematical sciences women have made.
Eligibility: Applicants must interview a women who is working in a carrer in mathematics.
Target Student: Junior high students or younger, High school, College and Adult students.
Amount: Varies

Number of Awards: At least 3
Based on Financial Need: No
Deadline: January
Applications are available online.

(202) BioQuip Undergraduate Scholarship

Entomological Society of America
10001 Derekwood Lane
Suite 100
Lanham, MD 20706

Phone: 301-7314535
Fax: 301-731-4538
Email: esa@entsoc.org
URL: http://www.entsoc.org

Goal: To assist students entering the field of entomology.
Eligibility: Applicants must have enrooled in and undergraduate entomology, zoology, biology or other related program the previous fall and completed at least 90 units when the award is presented in August.
Target Student: College and Adult students.
Amount: $2,000
Number of Awards: 1
Based on Financial Need: No
Deadline: July
Applications are available online.

(203) Black and Veatch Scholarships

Black and Veatch
11401 Lamar Avenue
Overland Park, KS 66211

Phone: 913-458-2000
Fax: 913-458-2934
URL: http://www.rmel.org

Goal: To assist students attending at specific universities, tech schools and engineering colleges.

Eligibility: For information regarding this award please contact your financial aid office.
Target Student: College and Adult students.
Amount: Varies
Number of Awards: Varies
Based on Financial Need: No
Deadline: March
Contact your finanical aid officer for application information.

---

(204) Blogging Scholarship

CollegeScholarships.org
150 Caldecott Lane #8
Oakland, CA 94618

Phone: 888-501-9050
Email: info@collegescholarships.org
URL:http://www.collegescholarships.org/our-scholarships/blogging.htm

Goal: To assist college students who blog.
Eligibility: Applicants must maintain a blog with unique and interesting blog about yourself or something that you are passionate about. Applicants must be U.S. citizens or permanent residents who are enrolled as full time students in a U.S. post secondary institution.
Target Student: College and Adult students.
Amount: Up to $10,000
Number of Awards: Varies
Based on Financial Need: No
Deadline: November
Applications are available online. An essay is required.

---

(205) BMW/SAE Engineering Scholarship

Society of Automotive Engineers International
400 Commonwealth Drive
Warrendale, PA 15096

Phone: 724-776-4841
Fax: 724-776-0790
Email: scholarship@sae.org
URL: http://www.sae.org

Goal: To assist engineering students with potential.
Eligibility: Applicants must be U.S. citizens with a 3.75 GPA or higher ranking in the 90th percentile in math and critical reading on the SAT or ACT test and be working working towards a engineering or related degree.
Target Student: College and Adult students.
Amount: $1,500
Number of Awards: 1
Scholarship can be renewed.
Based on Financial Need: No
Deadline: January
Applciations are available online. A completed application, transcript and SAT or ACT test scores are required to apply.

---

(206) Bob East Scholarship

National Press Photographers Foundation
Bob East Scholarship
Chuck Fadely
The Miami Hearld
One Heald Plaza
Miami, FL 33132

Phone: 305-376-2015
URL: http://www.nppa.org

Goal: To assist new photojournalists.
Eligibility: Applicants must be an undergraduate in the first 3.5 years of college or planning on attending graduate school.
Target Student: College, Graduate and Adult students.
Amount: $2,000
Number of Awards: 1
Based on Financial Need: No
Deadline: March

Applications are available online.

---

(207) Bob Warnicke Scholarship

National Bicylce League (NBL)
3958 Brown Park Drive Suite D
Hilliard, OH 43026

Phone: 614-777-1625
Fax: 614-777-1680
Email: administration@nbl.org
URL: http://www.nbl.org

Goal: To assist students who have participated in BMX events.
Eligibility: Applicants must be members, have a current NBL competition license or official's license and have participated in BMX racing events for at least one year. Applicants must be high school graduates who are attending or who plan to attend college full or part time.
Target Student: College, graduate and Adult students.
Amount: $1,000
Number of Awards: Varies
Based on Financial Need: No
Deadline: December
Applications are available online, by mail or by phone.

---

(208) Bobby Sox High School Senior Scholarship Program

Bobby Sox Softball
P.O. Box 5880
Buena Park, CA 90622

Phone: 714-522-1234
Fax: 714-522-6548
URL:http://www.bobbysoxsoftball.org/scholar.html

Goal: To assist players of Bobby Sox softball with educational expenses.

Eligibility: Applicants must be eighth grade girls who have at least four years of participation in Bobby Sox softball, or high school seniors who have at least five seasons of participation. A GPA of 2.0 or higher is required.
Target Student: High school students.
Amount: Up to $2,500
Number of Awards: 45
Based on Financial Need: No
Deadline: Unknown
Applications are available online. A completed application and an essay are required.

---

(209) Bodie McDowell Scholarship

Outdoor Writers Association of America
121 Hickory Street
Suite 1
Missoula, MT 59801

Phone: 406-728-7434
Fax: 406-728-7445
Email: krhoades@owaa.org
URL: http://www.owaa.org

Goal: To assist students in the outdoor communication field.
Eligibility: Applicants must be students in the outdoor communication field that includes: print, film, art or broadcasting and be in their junior or senior year of undergraduate work or graduate students.
Target Student: College, Graduate and Adult students.
Amount: $1,000 - $5,000
Number of Awards: 3 or more
Based on Financial Need: No
Deadline: March
Applications are available online.

---

(210) Bonner Scholars Program

Bonner Foundation
10 Mercer Street
Princeton, NJ 08540

Phone: 609-924-6663
Fax: 609-683-4626
Email: info@bonner.org
URL: http://www.bonner.org

Goal: To assist students participating in community service at one of 80 participating colleges.
Eligibility: Applicants must demonstrate a financial need and complete an annual service requirement.
Target Student: High school students.
Amount: Varies
Number of Awards: Varies
Based on Financial Need: Yes
Deadline: Varies
Contact the admissions department at a participating college for an application.

(211) Bound to Stay Bound Books Scholarship

Association for Library Serivce to Children
50 E. Huron Street
Chicago, IL 60611

Phone: 800-545-2433
Fax: 312-944-7671
Email: alsc@ala.org
URL: http://www.ala.org/alsc

Goal: To assist students pursuing their Master's in Library Science degree.
Eligibility: Applicants must be U.S. or Canadian citizens who are planning to puruse their MLS degree and work with children. The award is based on academics, leadership and the applicants desire to work with children.
Target Student: College, Graduate and Adult students
Amount: $7,000
Number of Awards: 4
Based on Financial Need: No
Deadline: March
Applications are avaiable online.

(212) Brian Jenneman Memorial Scholarship

Community Foundation of Louisville
Waterfront Plaza
325 West Main Street
Suite 1110
Louisville, KY 40202

Phone: 502-585-4649
Fax: 502-487-7484
Email: gails@cflouisville.org
URL: http://www.cflouisville.org

Goal: To assist U.S. students studying to become paramedics.
Eligibility: Applicants must be 18 years old or above, accepted into a paramedic training program, U.S. residents and training in the U.S.
Target Student: High school and Adult students.
Amount: Up to $1,500
Number of Awards: 4
Scholarship can be renewed.
Based on Financial Need: No
Deadline: July
Applications are available online. A completed application,transcript, and three letters of recommendation are required to apply.

(213) Bridging Scholarships for Study Abroad in Japan

Association of Teachers of Japanese
Bridging Project Clearinghouse
Campus Box 279
240 Humanities Building, University of Colorado
Boulder, CO 80309

Phone: 303-492-5487
Fax: 303-492-5856
Email: atj@colorado.edu
URL: http://www.colorado.edu/ealc/atj

Goal: To assist students with living and studying in Japan.
Eligibility: Applicants must be undergraduate, U.S. citizens enrolled in a U.S. college who are going to study in Japan for a minimum of three months during the academic year. Summer programs are not eligible.
Target Student: College and Adult students.
Amount: $2,500 - $4,000
Number of Awards: 85
Based on Financial Need: No
Deadline: October and April
Applications are available online.

---

(214) Bronlslaw Kaper Award

Los Angeles Philharmonic
Education Department
151 S. Grand Avenue
Los Angeles, CA 90012

Phone: 213-972-3454
Fax: 213-972-7650
Email: education@laphil.org
URL: http://www.laphil.org

Goal: To assist the development of young musicians.
Eligibility: Applicants must be residents of California and are required to prepare and perform a piano or string piece for competition.
Target Student: Junior high students or younger and High school students.
Amount: $500 - $2,500
Number of Awards: 4
Based on Financial Need: No
Deadline: December
Applications are available online.

---

(215) BSN Scholarship

Association of Rehabilitation Nurses
4700 W. Lake Avenue
Glenview, IL 60025

Phone: 800-229-7530
Fax: 888-458-0456
Email: gelliott@connect2amc.com
URL: http://www.rehabnurse.org

Goal: To assist nurses pursuing a bachelor's of science in nursing.
Eligibility: Applicants must be active members of ARN, enrolled in a bachelor's of science of nursing program, have completed at least one course, be currently practicing rehabilitation nursing with at least two years of experience.
Target Student: College and Adult students.
Amount: $1,500
Number of Awards: Varies
Based on Financial Need: No
Deadline: June
Applications are available online.

---

(216) Bud Glover Memorial Scholarship

Aircraft Electronics Association
4217 South Hocker
Independence, MO 64055

Phone: 816-373-6565
Fax: 816-478-3100
Email: info@aea.net
URL: http://www.aea.net

Goal: To assist students who want to pursue a career in avionics and aircraft repair.
Eligibility: Applicants must be high school seniors or college students planning to or attending a accredited college or university in an avionics or aircraft repair program.
Target Student: High school, College and Adult students.
Amount: $1,000
Number of Awards: 1
Based on Financial Need: No
Deadline: February

Applications are available by contacting the organization.

---

(217) Buddy Pelletier Surfing Foundation Scholarship

Buddy Pelletier Surfing Foundation Fund
5121 Chalk Street
Morehead City, NC 28557

Phone: 252-727-7917
Fax: 866-925-7125
Email: lynne.pelletier@bbandt.com
URL: http://buddy.pelletier.com

Goal: The scholarship has been established to support the Educational and Humanitarian needs of the East Coast surfing community and itís
youth.
Eligibility: These scholarships will be limited to members of the East Coast Surfing
community. Students of all ages are eligible. Rising Senior and Undergraduate Students or Returning Students may apply. Applicants and previous winners may reapply on a yearly basis.
Target Student: High school, College and Adult students.
Amount: $1,000
Number of Awards: Varies
Scholarship can be renewed.
Based on Financial Need: No
Deadline: June
Applications are available online. A completed application, two letters of recommendation, college or high school transcripts and essay are required.

---

(218) Buick Achievers Scholarship Program

General Motors Foundation
300 Renaissance Center
MC 482-C27-D76
Detroit, MI 48265

URL: http://www.buickachievers.com

Goal: To acknowledge college bound students who have excelled in the classroom and in their community.
Eligibility: Applicants must be high school seniors or high school graduates entering college for the first time and plan to enroll in a full-time undergraduate program at an accredited four-year school and be U.S. citizens or permanent residents. Applicants must major in a degree that focuses on science, technology, engineering or math. Some programs in marketing, design, accounting, finance and business are also eligible for the award. Applicants must have demonstrated interest in a career in the automotive or related industry. Award selction is based on financial need, work experience, education and career goals, and participation and leadership in school and community acitivities. Also considered during the selection process include being a military veteran or dependent of military personnel, minority, female or first generation college student.
Target Student: High school, College and Adult students.
Amount: Up to $25,000
Number of Awards: 100
Scholarship can be renewed.
Based on Financial Need: Yes
Deadline: March
Applications are available online.

---

(219) Burger King Scholars Program

Burger King Scholars Program
5505 Blue Lagoon Drive
Miami, FL 33126

Phone: 507-931-1682
Email: burgerkingscholars@scholarshipamerica.org
URL: http://www.bkmclamorefoundation.org/Home

Goal: To assist high school seniors who have part-time jobs with educational expenses.
Eligibility: Applicants must be high school students in the U.S., Canada, and Puerto Rico and must be U.S. or Canadian residents. Applicants must have at least a 2.5 GPA and work part time (averaging 15 hours a week unless there are extenuating circumstances), participate in community service activities, show a financial need, and plan to enroll in an accredited two or four year college, university or vocational/tech school in the fall or summer following their graduation from high school.
Target Student: High school students.
Amount: $1,000 to $50,000
Number of Awards: Varies
Based on Financial Need: Yes
Deadline: January
Applications are available online.

(220) C.B. Gambrell Undergraduate Scholarship

Institute of Industrial Engineers
3577 Parkway Lane
Suite 200
Norcross, GA 30092

Phone: 800-494-0460
Fax: 770-441-3295
Email: bcameron@iienet.org
URL: http://www.iienet2.org

Goal: To assist industrial engineering students from the U.S.
Eligibility: Applicants must be full-time undergraduate students who have completed their freshman year in an industrial engineering program. Students must be nominated for the award.
Target Student: College and Adult students.
Amount: $600
Number of Awards: 1

Based on Financial Need: No
Deadline: November
Nomination information is available online.

(221) C.I.P. Scholarship

College is Power
1025 Alameda de las Pulgas No. 215
Belmont, CA 94002

URL:http://www.collegeispower.com/scholarship.cfm

Goal: To assist college students aged 18 and over with educational expenses.
Eligibility: Applicants must be 18 an over and attending or planning ot attend a two or four year college or university in the next 12 months. Applicants must be U.S. citizens or permanent residents. Scholarship funds can be used for full or part time study in person or online.
Target Student: High school, College and Adult students.
Amount: $1,500
Number of Awards: Varies
Based on Financial Need: No
Deadline: May, August, December
Applications are available online.

(222) Cadbury Adams Community Outreach Scholarships

American Dental Hygienists' Association
Institute for Oral Health
Scholarship Award Program
444 North Michigan Avenue
Suite 3400
Chicago, IL 60611

Phone: 312-440-8900
Email: institute@adha.net
URL: http://www.adha.org/ioh

Goal: To acknowledge students who are committed to improving oral health in their community.

Eligibility: Applicants must have demonstrated financial need of at least $1,500 and completed one year in an accredited dental hygiene program. Applicants must have a demonstrated commitment to improving oral health in their communities and be active members of SADHA or ADHA.

Target Student: College and Adult students.

Amount: $1,000 - $2,000

Number of Awards: Varies

Based on Financial Need: Yes

Deadline: February

Applications are available online.

---

(223) CaGIS Scholarships

American Congress on Surveying and Mapping
6 Montgomery Village Avenue
Suite 403
Gaithersburg, MD 20879

Phone: 240-632-9716
Fax: 240-632-1321
Email: ilse.genovese@acsm.net
URL: http://www.acsm.net

Goal: To support cartography or GIScience.

Eligibility: Applicants must be full-time students in an undergraduate or graduate cartography or geographic information science degree program. The award is based on records, statements, letters of recommendation and the applicants professional activities.

Target Student: College, Graduate and Adult students

Amount: $500 - $1,000

Number of Awards: 2

Scholarship can be renewed.

Based on Financial Need: No

Deadline: January

Applications are available online. A completed application, transcripts, two letters of recommendation and a summary of professional and educational goals is required to apply.

---

(224) California - Hawaii Elks Association Vocational Grants

California-Hawaii Elks Association
5450 E. Lamona Avenue
Fresno, CA 93727

Phone: 559-222-8071
Fax: 559-222-8073
URL: http://www.chea-elks.org

Goal: To assist those purusing vocational/technical education.

Eligibility: Applicants must be U.S. citizens and residents of California or Hawaii who plan to pursue a vocational or technical program after high school. A high school diploma or equivalent is not required and students planning to transfer into a bachelor's degree program are ineligible.

Target Student: High school, College and Adult students.

Amount: $1,000

Number of Awards: 58

Scholarship can be renewed.

Based on Financial Need: No

Deadline: 3 months after the issuing of the application.

Applications are availiable online.

---

(225) Campus Safety Health and Environmental Management Association Scholarship

National Safety Council
CSHEMA, Scholarship Committee
CSHEMA Division, National Safety Council
12100 Sunset Hills Road, Suite 130
Reston, VA 20190

Phone: 703-234-4141
Fax: 703-435-4390
Email: info@cshema.org
URL: http://www.cshema.org

Goal: To encourage students to study safety.
Eligibility: Applicants must be full-time undergraduate or graduate students with at least one year left in their degree program.
Target Student: College and Adult students.
Amount: $2,000
Number of Awards: 1
Based on Financial Need: No
Deadline: March
Applications are available online.

---

(226) Canadian Section Student Award

Electrochemical Society
65 South Main Street
Building D
Pennington, NJ 08534

Phone: 609-737-1902
Fax: 609-737-2743
Email: awards@electrochem.org
URL: http://www.electrochem.org

Goal: To assist students at Canadian universities pursuing advanced degrees in electrochemical science and technology or solid state science and technology.
Eligibility: Applicants must be nominated by a faculty member of a Canadian University.
Target Student: Graduate and Adult students.
Amount: Up to $1,500
Number of Awards: 1
Based on Financial Need: No
Deadline: February

Application material is available online. The nomination should include a curriculum vitae, letter of recommendation from the nominating faculty member, outline of the proposed and completed research project witten by the student.

---

(228) Captain Caliendo College Assistance Fund Scholarship

U.S. Coast Guard Chief Petty Officers Association
5520-G Hempstead Way
Springfield, VA 22151

Phone: 703-941-0395
Fax: 703-941-0397
Email: cgcpoa@aol.com
URL: http://www.uscgcpoa.org

Goal: To assist children of CPOA/CGEA members.
Eligibility: Applicants must be dependents of a USCG CPOA/CGEA member (living or deceased) who are under 24 as of March 1 on the award year. The age limit is not applicable for disabled students.
Target Student: High school and College students.
Amount: $5,000
Number of Awards: 1
Based on Financial Need: No
Deadline: March
Applications are available online. A completed application and letter or enrollment or acceptance is required.

---

(227) Captain James J. Regan Scholarship

Explorers Learning for Life
P.O. Box 152079
Irving, TX 75015

Phone: 972-580-2433
Fax: 972-580-2137

Email: pchestnu@lflmail.org
URL:http://www.learningforlife.org/expl
oring

Goal: To assist Law Enforcement
Explorers with educational expenses.
Eligibility: Applicants must be high
school seniors or older. Applicants will
need to submit an essay along with three
letters of recommendation.
Target Student: High school, College and
Adult students.
Amount: $500
Number of Awards: 2
Based on Financial Need: No
Deadline: March
Applications are available online. Three
letters of recommendation and an essay are
required.

(229) Careers in Agriculture Scholarship Program

Winfield Solutions LLC
MS 5850
1080 Country Road F West
Shoreview, MN 55126

Phone: 800-426-8109
Email: info@winfieldsolutions.com
URL: http://www.agrisolutionsinfo.com

Goal: To assist high school seniors interest
in a career in agriculture.
Eligibility: Applicants must be high
school seniors planning to enroll in a two-
year or four-year degree program in
agriculture. Dependents of employees of
Winfield Solutions or Land O'Lakes are
ineliglble.
Target Student: High school students.
Amount: $1,000
Number of Awards: 20
Based on Financial Need: No
Deadline: February

Applications are available online. A
completed application, two character
evaluations, essay and transcripts are
required to apply.

(230) Carl A. Ross Student Paper Award

Appalachian Studies Association Carl A.
Ross Student Paper Award
William Schumann
Emory and Henry College
P.O. Box 947
Emory, VA 24327

Phone: 304-696-2904
Fax: 276-944-6170
URL: http://www.appalachianstudies.org

Goal: To assist Appalachian studies.
Eligibility: Applicants must subit a 20 to
30 page research paper on an Appalachian
related topic. The award is given out in
two categories, middle/high school and
undergraduate/graduate.
Target Student: Junior high and younger,
High school, College, Graduate and Adult
students.
Amount: $100
Number of Awards: Varies
Based on Financial Need: No
Deadline: December
To apply submit the research paper.

(231) Carole J. Streeter, KB9JBR Scholarship

American Radio Relay League Foundation
225 Main Street
Newington, CT 06111

Phone: 860-594-0397
Fax: 860-594-0259
Email: foundation@arrl.org
URL: http://www.arrlf.org

Goal: To assist students involved in amateur radio.
Eligibility: Applicants must have an amateur radio license of Technician Class or higher with preference going to those with Morse Code proficiency and studying health or healing.
Target Student: High school, College and Adult students.
Amount: $750
Number of Awards: 1
Based on Financial Need: No
Deadline: February
Applications are available online.

---

(232) Carole Simpson Scholarship

Radio Television Digital News Association
4121 Plank Road #512
Fredericksburg, VA 22407

Phone: 202-659-6510
Fax: 202-223-4007
Email: stacey@rtdna.org
URL: http://www.rtdna.org

Goal: To acknowledge achievements in electronic journalism.
Eligibility: Applicants must be full-time college sophomores or above with at least one year of school remaining. Applicants can be majoring in anything as long as their career goal is to work in television or radio news. Applicants are limited to applying for one RTNDA scholarship.
Target Student: College and Adult students.
Amount: $2,000
Number of Awards: 1
Based on Financial Need: No
Deadline: May
Applications are available online.

---

(233) Caroline H. Newhouse Scholarship Fund

Career Transition for Dancers

Caroline and Theodore Newhouse Center for Dancers
165 West 46th Street Suite 701
The Actors' Equity Building
New York, NY 10036

Phone: 212-764-0172
Fax: 212-764-0343
Email: info@careertransition.org
URL: http://www.careertransition.org

Goal: To assist dancers seeking second careers with educational expenses.
Eligibility: Applicants must show 100 weeks or more of paid employment a dancer in the U.S. over 7 years or more not under union jurisdiction with gross earnings of $56,000 or more. Choreographers and dance teachers are not eligible. There are deadlines in January, March, May, July, August and October.
Target Student: College, Graduate and Adult students.
Amount: $2,000
Number of Awards: Varies
Based on Financial Need: No
Deadline: Varies
Applicants must call to determine eligibility.

---

(234) Carson Scholars

Carson Scholars Fund
305 W. Chesapeake Avenue
Suite L-020
Towson, MD 21204

Phone: 887-773-7236
Email: caitlin@carsonscholars.org
URL: http://www.carsonscholars.org

Goal: To assist students who show academic excellence and community service.

Eligibility: Applicants must be nominated by their school. They must have a GPA of 3.75 or higher in English, reading, language arts, math, science, social studies and foreign language and be in grades 4 - 11. Applicants must attend a four year college or university after graduation and must have completed community service beyond what is required by their school.
Target Student: Junior high and younger, High school students.
Amount: $1,000
Number of Awards: Varies
Based on Financial Need: No
Deadline: January
Applications are available from the schools of those who are nominated. Only one student can be nominated per school

(235) Carville M. Akehurst Memorial Scholarship

American Nursery and Landscape Association
Horticultural Research Institute
1000 Vermont Avenue NW
Suite 300
Washington, DC 20005

Phone: 202-789-5980 x3014
Fax: 202-789-1893
Email: tjodon@anla.org
URL: http://www.anla.org

Goal: To assist undergraduate and graduate student who are planning to pursue a career in horticulture.
Eligibility: Applicants must be full-time landscaping or horticulture students at a two- or four-year accredited program and be residents of Maryland, Virginia or West Virginia.
Target Student: College, Graduate and Adult students.
Amount: $2,000
Number of Awards: 1
Scholarship can be renewed.
Based on Financial Need: No

Deadline: Unknown
Applications are available online.

(236) Castle Ink's Green Scholarship

Castle Ink
37 Wyckoff Street
Greenlawn, NY 11740

Phone: 800-399-5193
Fax: 404-460-5001
Email: scholarships@castleink.com
URL: http://www.castleink.com

Goal: To assist environmentlly concious students.
Eligibility: Applicants must be U.S. citizens or permanent residents who are high school seniors or current college students at an accredited college or university. Applicants must have a 2.5 GPA or higher. The award is based on the quality of the essay.
Target Student: High school, College, Graduate and Adult students.
Amount: $2,500
Number of Awards: 1
Based on Financial Need: No
Deadline: June
Applications are available online. A completed application and essay on one's own efforts towards conservation are required.

(237) Cavett Robert Scholarship

National Speakers Association
Attn: Scholarship Committee
1500 S. Priest Drive
Tempe, AZ 85281

Phone: 480-968-2552
Fax: 480-968-0911
URL: http://www.nsaspeaker.org

Goal: To encourage the study of professional speaking.

Eligibility: Applicants must be full-time students majoring or minoring in speech.
Target Student: College, Graduate and Adult students.
Amount: $1,000
Number of Awards: 1
Based on Financial Need: No
Deadline: June
Applications are available online.

---

(238) Cedarcrest Farms Scholarships

American Jersey Cattle Association
6486 East Main Street
Reynoldsburg, OH 43068

Phone: 614-861-3636
Fax: 614-861-8040
Email: info@usjersey.com
URL: http://www.usjersey.com

Goal: To assist American Jersey Cattle Association members who are studying dairy product marketing, large animal vetrinary science, dairy manufacturing or dairy production.
Eligibility: Applicants must be members of the AJCA with a 2.5 GPA or higher, studying dairy manufacturing, dairy production, large animcal veterinary science or dairy product manufacturing.
Target Student: College, Graduate and Adult students.
Amount: Varies
Number of Awards: Varies
Based on Financial Need: No
Deadline: July
Applications are available online. A completed application, transcript, and two letters of recommendation are required to apply.

---

(239) Centex Homes "Build Your Future" Scholarship

National Housing Endowment
1201 15th Street NW
Washington, DC 20005

Phone: 800-368-5242
Fax: 202-266-8177
Email: nhe@nahb.com
URL: http://www.nationalhousingendowment.org

Goal: To assist U.S. students who are planning to pursue a career in the building industry.
Eligibility: Applicants must be U.S. undergraduate freshmen, sophomores, or juniors enrolled full-time in a program that is related to housing (construction, civil engineering, architecture, building trades or management). Applicants must have a GPA of 2.0 or higher and at least one full academic year remaining in their degree program. Selection is based on financial need, GPA, work experience, academics, extracurricular activities and professional goals.
Target Student: College and Adult students.
Amount: Up to $3,000
Number of Awards: Varies
Scholarship can be renewed.
Based on Financial Need: Yes
Deadline: March
Applications are available online. A completed application, transcript, two letters of recommendation, personal essay, statement of finances and list of degree requirements is required to apply.

---

(240) Chain des Rotisseurs Scholarship

American Academy of Chefs
180 Center Place Way
St. Augustine, FL 32095

Phone: 800-624-9458
Fax: 904-825-4758
Email: educate@acfchefs.net
URL: http://www.acfchefs.org

Goal: To assist students in culinary arts programs.
Eligibility: Applicants must be enrolled in an accredited culinary arts or AAC-approved cunlinary traning program. Applicants must be excellent students who have completed at least one grading period.
Target Student: College and Adult students.
Amount: Varies
Number of Awards: Varies
Based on Financial Need: Yes
Deadline: May and September
Applications are available online. A completed application, transcripts, two recommendations, signed photo release, and financial aid forms are required to apply.

(241) Challenge Scholarship

National Strength and Conditioning Association Foundation
1885 Bob Johnson Drive
Colorado Springs, CO 80906

Phone: 800-815-6826
Fax: 719-632-6367
Email: nsca@nsca-lift.org
URL: http://www.nsca-lift.org

Goal: To assist NSCA members who are studying strength and conditioning.
Eligibility: Applicants must be NSCA members for one year and pursing careers in strength and conditioning. An essay must be completed that covers the applicants course of study, career goals and financial needs. The award is based on the applicants grades, experience, honors, recommendation and involvement with NCSA.
Target Student: College, Graduate and Adult students.
Amount: $1,500
Number of Awards: Varies
Based on Financial Need: Yes

Deadline: March
Applications are available with membership. A completed application and essay are needed to apply.

(242) Charles A. Ryskamp Research Fellowships

American Council of Learned Societies
633 Third Avenue
New York, NY 10017

Phone: 212-697-1505
Fax: 212-949-8058
Email: sfisher@acls.org
URL: http://www.contemplativemind.org

Goal: To assist research in the humanities.
Eligibility: The fellowships are for assist professors and associate professors without tenure. By the application deadline applicants must have completed the insitution's last reappointment review before tenure review and not yet completed their tenure review. Applicants should have a Ph.D. or equivalent and be in a tenure track position at a U.S. college or university during the fellowship.
Target Student: Graduate and Adult students
Amount: Up to $80,722
Number of Awards: Up to 12
Based on Financial Need: No
Deadline: September
Applications are available online.

(243) Charles and Lucille Family Foundation Undergraduate Scholarships

Charles and Lucille King Family Foundation
366 Madison Avenue
10th Floor
New York, NY 10017

Phone: 212-682-2913

Fax:
Email: info@kingfoundation.org
URL: http://www.kingfoundation.org

Goal: To assist film and television students with educational expenses.
Eligibility: Applicants must be undergraduate juniors and seniors who are majoring in film and television and have demonstrated academic skills, financial need and professional potention.
Target Student: College and Adult students.
Amount: Up to $3,500
Number of Awards: Varies
Scholarship can be renewed.
Based on Financial Need: Yes
Deadline: March
Applications are available online or by written request. A completed application, personal statement, transcript and three letters of recommendation are required to apply.

---

(244) Charles Clarke Cordle Memorial Scholarship

American Radio Relay League Foundation
225 Main Street
Newington, CT 06111

Phone: 860-594-0397
Fax: 860-594-0259
Email: foundation@arrl.org
URL: http://www.arrlf.org

Goal: To assist ham radio operators with their educational expenses.
Eligibility: Applicants must have a ham radio license, a GPA of 2.5 or higher, and attend school in Alabama or Georgia.
Target Student: High school, College, Graduate and Adult students.
Amount: $1,000
Number of Awards: 1
Based on Financial Need: No
Deadline: February
Applications are available online.

(245) Charles N. Fisher Memorial Scholarship

American Radio Relay League Foundation
225 Main Street
Newington, CT 06111

Phone: 860-594-0397
Fax: 860-594-0259
Email: foundation@arrl.org
URL: http://www.arrlf.org

Goal: To assist ham radio operators with their educational expenses.
Eligibility: Applicants must have a ham radio license, live in the ARRL Southwestern Division (Arizona, Los Angeles, Orange, San Diego and Santa Barbara counties) and attend a regionally accredited college or university and majoring in electronics, communications, or related.
Target Student: College, Graduate and Adult students.
Amount: $1,000
Number of Awards: 1
Based on Financial Need: No
Deadline: February
Applications are available online.

---

(246) Charles Shafae' Scholarship

Papercheck

Phone: 866-693-3348
Email: scholarships@papercheck.com
URL: http://www.papercheck.com

Goal: To assist students who have written the best essay.

Eligibility: Applicants must be legal residents of the U.S. or must have a valid student visa, as well as be enrolled, full-time, as an undergraduate student at an accredited four year college or university. Applicants must have a 3.2 GPA or higher, be in good academic standing, and write an essay on a topic selected by Papercheck.
Target Student: College and Adult students.
Amount: $500
Number of Awards: 2
Based on Financial Need: No
Deadline: May
Applications are available online. A completed application and essay are required.

(247) Charlie Logan Scholarship Program for Seaman

Seafarers International Union of North American
Ms. Lou Delma, Administrator
Seafarers Welfare Plan Scholarship Program
5201 Auth Way
Camp Springs, MD 20746

Phone: 301-899-0675
Fax: 301-899-7355
URL: http://www.seafarers.org

Goal: To assist members of the SIU.
Eligibility: Applicants must be active seaman who are high school graduates and able to receive Seafarers' Plan Benefits with two years of work credit (730 days) with an employer who makes contributions to the Seafarers' Plan on behalf of the employee before the date of application for the scholarship. The award is based on high school and equivalent scores, college transcripts and SAT/ACT scores (if any), references and autobiography. The $6,000 scholarship is for two-year programs and the $20,000 award is for four-year programs.

Target Student: College and Adult students.
Amount: $6,000-$20,000
Number of Awards: 3
Scholarship can be renewed.
Based on Financial Need: No
Deadline: April
Applications are available by written request.

(248) Charlie Wells Memorial Aviation Scholarships

Charlie Wells Memorial Scholarship Fund
P.O. Box 262
Springfield, IL 62705

Email: rog@wellsscholarship.com
URL: http://www.wellsscholarship.com

Goal: To assist students who want to pursue a career in aviation.
Eligibility: Applicants must be a resident of the U.S. or its territories and be full-time students in an aviation related program.
Target Student: College and Adult students.
Amount: Varies
Number of Awards: Varies
Based on Financial Need: No
Deadline: April
Applications are available online. A completed application, two lettes of recommendation and transcripts are required to apply.

(249) Charlotte McGuire Scholarship

American Holistic Nurses' Association
P.O. Box 2130
Flagstaff, AZ 86003

Phone: 800-278-2462
Fax: 928-526-2752
Email: info@ahna.org
URL: http://www.ahna.org

Goal: To assist nurses in undergraduate and graduate nursing programs or other graduate programs that are related to holistic nursing.
Eligibility: Applicants must be pursuing an education in holistic nursing and be an AHNA member.
Target Student: College, Graduate and Adult students.
Amount: Varies
Number of Awards: Varies
Based on Financial Need: No
Deadline: March
Applications are available online or from the AHNA headquarters.

(250) Charlotte Woods Memorial Scholarship

Transportation Clubs International Scholarships
Attn: Bill Blair
Zimmer Worldwide Logistics
15710 JFK Boulevard
Houston, TX 77032

Phone: 877-858-8627
Email: bblair@zimmerworldwide.com
URL: http://www.transportationclubsinternational.com

Goal: To assist students pursuing careers in the transportation industry.
Eligibility: Applicants must be graduating high school seniors or undergraduate college students enrolled in an accredited program in the field of transportation logistics, supply chain management, traffic management, transportation safety and/or related transportation industry operations and services and must be TCI members or dependents of members.
Target Student: High school, College and Adult students.
Amount: Variese
Number of Awards: Varies

Based on Financial Need: Need may be considered.
Deadline: May
Applications are available online.

(251) Chester Burger Scholarship for Excellence

Public Relations Student Society of America
33 Maiden Lane
11th Floor
New York, NY 10038

Phone: 212-460-1474
Fax: 212-995-0757
Email: prssa@prsa.org
URL: http://www.prssa.org

Goal: To encourage graduate students in public relations and journalism to enter the field of corporate public relations.
Eligibility: Applicants must be beginning or current graduate students at a U.S. college or university and majoring in journalism, public relations or a related field. Applicants must have an undergraduate GPA of 3.0 or greater and be interested in a career in corporate public relations.
Target Student: College, Graduate and Adult students.
Amount: $1,000
Number of Awards: 1
Based on Financial Need: No
Deadline: October
Applications are available online.

(252) Chicago RM Club Scholarship

American Radio Relay League Foundation
225 Main Street
Newington, CT 06111

Phone: 860-594-0397
Fax: 860-594-0259
Email: foundation@arrl.org

URL: http://www.arrlf.org

Goal: To assist ham radio operators with their educational expenses.
Eligibility: Applicants must have a minimum of a technician ham radio license and live in the FCC Ninth Call District (Illinois, Indiana and Wisconsin) and be students at an accredited two or four-year college or trade school.
Target Student: College and Adult students.
Amount: $500
Number of Awards: Varies
Based on Financial Need: No
Deadline: February
Applications are available onlilne.

---

(253) Chick Evans Caddie Scholarship

Western Golf Association
1 Briar Road
Golf, IL 60029

Phone: 847-724-4600
Fax: 847-724-7133
Email: evansscholars@wgaesf.com
URL:http://www.evansscholarsfoundation.com

Goal: To assist golf caddies with educational expenses.
Eligibility: Applicants must have completed their junior year of college and have a 3.0 GPA, have taken the ACT and have caddied for at least two years. Applicants must be nominated by their club and they must be a caddie at the nominating club the year they apply for the scholarship. The award is based on financial need, outstanding character, integrity and leadership.
Target Student: High school students.
Amount: Varies
Number of Awards: Varies
Scholarship can be renwed.
Based on Financial Need: Yes
Deadline: September

Applications are available from the sponsoring golf club. A completed application, high school evaluation, transcript, ACT scores, caddy evaluation, letters of recommendation, essay, parents latest federal tax return and financial aid profile are required to apply.

---

(254) Chief Master Sergeants of the Air Force Scholarship

Air Force Sergeants Association
5211 Auth Road
Suitland, MD 20746

Phone: 301-899-3500
Fax: 301-899-8136
Email: ygreen@hqafsa.org
URL: http://www.hqafsa.org

Goal: To assist dependent children of Air Force members including the Air National Guard and Air Force Reserve Command.
Eligibility: Applicants must be dependents of enlisted Air Force members on active duty or retired. Applicants must also participate in the Airman Memorial Foundation Scholarship Foundation. A GPA of 3.5 or higher is required, but extenuating circumstances are considered.
Target Student: High school, College and Adult students.
Amount: Varies
Number of Awards: Varies
Based on Financial Need: No
Deadline: March
Applications are available online.

---

(255) Chief Petty Officer Scholarship Fund

Chief Petty Officer Scholarship Fund
8401 Hampton Boulevard Suite 3
Norfolk, VA 23505

Phone: 757-233-9136
Email: cposfboard@cposf.org

URL: http://www.cposf.org

Goal: To assist the families of Chief Petty officers of the U.S. Navy.
Eligibility: Applicants must be the spouse or child of active, retired, or reserve Chief, Senior Chief or Master Chief Petty Officers in the U.S. Navy. They must be either high school graduates or have earned their GED and plan to attend or currently attend a college or university to earn their bachelors or associates degree.
Target Student: High school, College and Adult students.
Amount: Varies
Number of Awards: Varies
Based on Financial Need: No
Deadline: April
Applications are available online. A completed application, three letters of recommentation, a copy of your dependents ID card and a personal statement are required to apply.

---

(256) Christianson Grant

InterExchange Inc.
161 Sixth Avenue
New York, NY 10013

Phone: 212-924-0446
Fax: 212-924-0575
Email: grants@interexchange.org
URL:http://www.interexchange.org/content/1/en/home.html

Goal: To promote international understanding and cultural awareness.
Eligibility: Applicants must be between 18 and 28 years old and have arranged their own work abroad program.
Target Student: High school, College, Graduate and Adult students.
Amount: $2,500 - $10,000
Number of Awards: Varies
Based on Financial Need: No
Deadline: March, July, and October
Applications are available online.

(257) Chuck Reville, K3FT Memorial Scholarship

Foundation for Amateur Radio Inc.
FAR Scholarships
P.O. Box 911
Columbia, MD 21044

Phone: 410-552-2652
Fax: 410-981-5146
Email: dave.prestel@gmail.com
URL: http://www.farweb.org

Goal: To assist licensed amateur radio operators working towards a bachelors in engineering or physical science degree.
Eligibility: Applicants must be licensed radio operators enrolled full-time in an engineering or physical science bachelors degree.
Target Student: College and Adult students.
Amount: $1,000
Number of Awards: Varies
Based on Financial Need: No
Deadline: April
Applications are available online.

---

(258) Church Hill Classics "Frame My Future" Scholarship

Church Hill Classics
594 Pepper Street
Monroe, CT 06468

Phone: 800-477-9005
Fax: 203-268-2468
Email: info@diplomaframe.com
URL: http://www.framemyfuture.com

Goal: To assist students with their educational expenses.

Eligibility: Applicants must be high school seniors or eligible for graduation in the school year of the application or currently attending college. Applicants must be U.S. residents. A photograph, essay, painting or other creative entry is required and the work needs to communicate "This is How I Frame My Future." Employees of Church Hill Classics and all affiliated companies, their families and individuals from the same households are not eligible.
Target Student: High school, College and Adult students.
Amount: $1,000
Number of Awards: 5
Based on Financial Need: No
Deadline: March
Applications are available online. An entry form and piece of original art is required to apply.

---

(259) CIA Undergraduate Scholarship Program

Central Intelligence Agency
Office of Public Affairs
Washington, DC 20505

Phone: 703-482-0623
Fax: 703-482-1739
URL: http://www.cia.gov

Goal: To encourage students to work for the CIA.
Eligibility: Applicants must be high school seniors or college freshman or sophomore. High school seniors must have SAT scores of 1500 hor higher (1000 Math and Critical Reading and 500 for Writing) or 21 or higher on the ACT test, and a 3.0 or higher GPA. Applicants must have a demonstrated financial need by having a maximum family income of $70,000 for a family of four and $80,000

for a family of five or more. Applicants must meet all qualifications for employment at the CIA including passing security and medical checks. Applicants must commit to working at the CIA after completion of their degree for a period of 1.5 times the length of the sponsorship. Applicants will also work at the CIA during summers.
Target Student: High school, College and Adult students.
Amount: Annual salary including benefits and up to $18,000 for tuition.
Number of Awards: Varies
Scholarship can be renewed.
Based on Financial Need: Yes
Deadline: August-October
Applications are available online. A resume, SAT/ACT scores, family income information, FASFA report, transcripts, and two letters of recommendation are required.

---

(260) CKSF Scholarships

Common Knowledge Scholarship Foundation
P.O. Box 290361
Davie, FL 33329

Phone: 954-262-8553
Email: info@cksf.org
URL: http://cksf.org

Goal: To assist high school and college students.
Eligibility: Applicants must register with CKSF online and complete quizzes on various topics. Students must be U.S. high school students in grades 9-12 or in college.
Target Student: High school, College, Graduate and Adult students.
Amount: $250-$2,500
Number of Awards: Varies
Based on Financial Need: No
Deadline: Monthly
Applications are available online.

(261) CLA Reference Services Press Fellowship

California Library Association
4030 Lennane Drive
Sacramento, CA 95834

Phone: 916-779-4573
Fax: 946-419-2874
Email: info@cla-net.org
URL: http://www.cla-net.org

Goal: To assist college seniors and graduates who are pursing a master's degree in library science.
Eligibility: Applicants must be California residents who are enrolled in a master's degree program in library science that is approved by the Amiercan Library Association in any state. A residents from any state can apply if they are attending a school accredited by the American Library Association in California. Those selected are expected to pursue a career in reference or information service and take at least three classes about reference or information service.
Target Student: College, Graduate and Adult students.
Amount: $3,000
Number of Awards: 1
Based on Financial Need: No
Deadline: May
Applications are available online.

(262) CLA Scholarship for Minority Students in Memory of Edna Yelland

California Library Association
4030 Lennane Drive
Sacramento, CA 95834

Phone: 916-779-4573
Fax: 946-419-2874
Email: info@cla-net.org
URL: http://www.cla-net.org

Goal: To assist minority California graduate students who are working towards a degree in library or information science.
Eligibility: Applicants must be California residents who are American Indian, Afrianc American, Mexican American, Latino, Asian American, Pacific Islander or Filipino and be accepted or enrolled in an American Library Association school.
Target Student: Graduate and Adult students.
Amount: $2,500
Number of Awards: 1
Based on Financial Need: Yes
Deadline: June
Applications are available online.

(263) Clan MacBean Foundation Grant Program

Clan MacBean Foundation
441 Wadsworth Boulevard Suite 213
Denver, CO 80226

URL: http://www.clanmacbean.net

Goal: To assist those studying Scottish culture.
Eligibility: Applicants must be in a program that is related directly to Scottish culture. If the applicant is doing a project, they must pick a project that directly invovles the preservation or enhancement of Scottish culture.
Target Student: College and Adult students.
Amount: Up to $5,000
Number of Awards: Varies
Based on Financial Need: No
Deadline: May
Applications are available by written request.

(264) Clauder Competition Prize

Portland Stage Company
P.O. Box 1458
Portland, ME 04104

Email: dburson@portlandstage.com
URL: http://www.portlandstage.com

Goal: To assist playwrights.
Eligibility: Applicants must live or attend school in Connecticut, Maine, Massachusetts, New Hampshire, Rhode Island or Vermont. However, this requirement can be waived for those who have lived in New England and written material that is related to the area. Applicants must submit a full-length, never published or produced, play.
Target Student: High school, College, Graduate and Adult students.
Amount: Up to $2,500
Number of Awards: Varies
Based on Financial Need: No
Deadline: March
No application is required, simply submit your play.

---

(265) Clifford H. "Ted" Rees, Jr. Scholarship

Air Conditioning, Heating and Refrigeration Institute
Clifford H. "Ted" Rees, Jr. Scholarship Foundation
2111 Wilson Boulevard
Suite 500
Arlington, VA 22201

Phone: 703-524-8800
Fax: 703-528-3816
Email: ahri@ahrinet.org
URL: http://www.ahrinet.org

Goal: To assist students pursuing careers in heating, air-contditioning and refrigeration technology.

Eligibility: Applicants must be U.S. citizens, nationals or resident aliens planning on becoming U.S. citizens. Applicants must be enrolled in an accredited HVACR technician program and plan on becoming an entry-level commerical rerigeration technician, residential air-conditioning and heating technician after they graduate.
Target Student: College and Adult students.
Amount: Up to $2,000
Number of Awards: 15
Based on Financial Need: No
Deadline: Varies
Applications are available online. A completed application, two letters of recommendation, personal statement are required to apply.

---

(266) Clinical Research Pre-Doctoral Fellowship

American Nurses Association
8515 Georgia Avenue, Suite 400
Attn: Janet Jackson, Program Manager
Silver Springs, MD 20910

Phone: 301-628-5247
Fax: 301-628-5349
URL: http://www.nursingworld.org

Goal: To assist nurses studying minority psychiatric mental health and substance abuse with stipends and tuition assistance.
Eligibility: Applicants must be members of the ANA, have their masters, and plan to pursue a doctoral degree. Fellowships can last from three to five years.
Target Student: Graduate and Adult students.
Amount: Varies
Number of Awards: Varies
Based on Financial Need: No
Deadline: March
Applications are available online.

(267) CNF Professional Growth Scholarship

Child Nutrition Foundation
Scholarship Committee
700 S. Washington Street, Suite 300
Alexandria, VA 22314

Phone: 703-739-3900
Email: jcurtis@schoolnutrition.org
URL: http://www.schoolnutrition.org

Goal: To assist School Nutrition Association members with educational expenses.
Eligibility: Applicants must be a member of the School Nutrition Association for at least one year an be enrolled in a food service field degree program at the undergraduate or graduate level.
Target Student: College, Graduate and Adult students.
Amount: Up to $2,500
Number of Awards: Varies
Scholarship can be renewed.
Based on Financial Need: No
Deadline: April
Applications are available online.

(268) Coast Guard College Student Pre-Commissioning Initiative

U.S. Coast Guard
4200 Wilson Boulevard
Arlington, VA 22203

Phone: 877-663-1800
Fax: 703-235-1880
URL: http://www.gocoastguard.com

Goal: To develop future Coast Guard officers.

Eligibility: Applicants must be between 19 and 27 years old and be college sophomores or juniors with at least 60 college credits completed. Applicants must be enrolled in a four year degree program at an insitution approved by the Coast Guard and a minority population of at least 25%. Applicants must be U.S. citizens with a 2.5 GPA or higher and meet all the physical requirements of the Coast Guard with a minimum score of 1100 on the SAT, 23 on the ACT or 109 on the ASVAB.
Target Student: College and Adult students.
Amount: Tuition plus salary.
Number of Awards: Varies
Scholarship can be renewed.
Based on Financial Need: No
Deadline: January
Applications are available online. A completed application, physical exam, immunization record, copy of drivers license and social security card, transcripts, test results, proof of enrollment, and tuition statement are required to apply.

(269) Coca-Cola All-State Community College Academic Team

Coca-Cola Scholars Foundation
P.O. Box 442
Atlanta, GA 30301

Phone: 800-306-2653
Email: questions@coca-colascholars.org
URL: http://www.coca-colascholarsfoundation.com

Goal: To assist community college students with educational expenses.

Eligibility: Applicants must be currently enrolled at a community college and have a GPA of 3.5 or higher and be on track to earn an associates degree or bachelors degree. One student from each state will win a $2,000 scholarship, Fifty students will win a $1,500 scholarship, fifty students will win a $1,250 scholarship and fifty students will win a $1,000 scholarship.
Target Student: College and Adult students.
Amount: $1,000 to $2,000
Number of Awards: 200
Based on Financial Need: No
Deadline: December
Applications are available online. Applicants must be nominated by the schools nominator.

---

(270) Coca-Cola Scholars Program

Coca-Cola Scholars Foundation
P.O. Box 442
Atlanta, GA 30301

Phone: 800-306-2653
Email: questions@coca-colascholars.org
URL: http://www.coca-colascholarsfoundation.com

Goal: The mission of the Coca-Cola Scholars Foundation is to provide scholarship programs and alumni enrichment opportunities in support of exceptional peoples' thirst for knowledge and their desire to make a difference in the world.
Eligibility: Applicants must be high school seniors in the U.S. who will attend an accredited U.S. college or university. The award is based on character, personal merit and commitment.
Target Student: High school students.
Amount: $10,000 - $20,000
Number of Awards: 250
Scholarship can be renewed.
Based on Financial Need: No
Deadline: October

Applications are available online.

---

(271) Colgate "Bright Smiles, Bright Futures" Minority Scholarships

American Dental Hygienists' Assocaition (ADHA) Institute for Oral Health Scholarship Award Program
444 North Michigan Avenue
Suite 3400
Chicago, IL 60611

Phone: 312-440-8900
Email: institute@adha.net
URL: http://www.adha.org/ioh

Goal: To assist members of groups that are underrepresented in dental hygiene programs.
Eligibility: Applicants must be a member of a group that is underrepresented in the field of dental hygiene and have completed one year of an accredited dental hygiene curriculum. Some examples of eligible groups include African-American, Hispanic, Asian, Native American and male students. Applicants must have a demonstrated financial need of at least $1,500, be active members of SADHA or ADHA and submit a statement of their goals.
Target Student: College and Adult students.
Amount: $1,000 - $2,000
Number of Awards: Varies
Based on Financial Need: No
Deadline: February
Applications are available online.

---

(272) College Answer $1,000 Scholarship

College Answer
Sallie Mae
300 Continental Drive
Newark, DE 19714

URL: http://www.collegeanswer.com

Goal: To assist students with their educational expenses.
Eligibility: Applicants must be high school, undergraduate or graduate students and register on the CollegeAnswer website. A registered user is randomly selected in a montly drawing.
Target Student: High school, College, Graduate and Adult students
Amount: $1,000
Number of Awards: 1 per month.
Based on Financial Need: No
Deadline: Monthly
To enter the scholarship register online.

---

(273) College Photographer of the Year

National Press Photographers Foundation
College Photographer of the Year
David Rees
CPOY Director, School of Journalism,
The University of Missouri
106 Lee Hills Hall
Columbus, MO 65211

Phone: 573-882-4442
Fax: 919-383-7261
Email: jourdlr@showme.missouri.edu
URL: http://www.nppa.org

Goal: To acknowledge work in photojournalism and provide students with a place to guage their skills.
Eligibility: Applicants must be full time college students with demonstrated financial need and a portfolio.
Target Student: College and Adult students.
Amount: Varies
Number of Awards: Varies
Based on Financial Need: Yes
Deadline: Varies
Applications are available by request via email or mail.

---

(274) College Prep Scholarship for High School Juniors

QuestBridge
120 Hawthrone Avenue Suite 103
Palo Alto, CA 94301

Phone: 888-275-2054
Fax: 650-653-2516
Email: questions@questbridge.org
URL: http://www.questbridge.org

Goal: To assist low income high school juniors with admission to leading colleges.
Eligibility: Applicants must be high school juniors with an annual household income of less than $60,000.
Target Student: High school students.
Amount: Varies
Number of Awards: Varies
Based on Financial Need: Yes
Deadline: March
Applications are available online starting in February. A completed application, transcripts and one letter of recommendation is required to apply.

---

(275) College Television Awards

Academy of Television Arts and Sciences Foundation
5220 Lankershim Boulevard
North Hollywood, CA 91601

Phone: 818-754-2800
Fax: 818-761-2827
Email: collegeawards@emmys.org
URL: http://www.emmys.org

Goal: To assist college student film or video producers.

Eligibility: Applicants must produce an original film or video in one of the following: drama, comedy, music, documentary, news, magazine show, traditional or computer-generated animation, children's program or commercials. Professionals cannot be involved in the produce and applicants must be full time students who have produced their video for course credit at an American college or univeristy during the current calendar year.
Target Student: College, Graduate and Adult students.
Amount: $500 - $10,000
Number of Awards: Varies
Based on Financial Need: No
Deadline: January
Applications are available online from September 1 to January 15.

(277) College/University Excellence of Scholarship Awards

National Council for Geographic Education
Jacksonville State University
206-A Martin Hall
700 Pelham Road North
Jacksonville, AL 36265

Phone: 256-782-5293
Fax: 256-782-5336
Email: ncge@jsu.edu
URL: http://www.ncge.org

Goal: To acknowledge senior geography majors.
Eligibility: Applicants must be nomintated by their university geography department.
Target Student: College and Adult students.
Amount: Varies
Number of Awards: Varies
Based on Financial Need: No
Deadline: April

Nomination information is available online.

(276) CollegeNET Scholarship

CollegeNET Scholarship Review Committee
805 SW Broadway Suite 1600
Portland, OR 97205

Phone: 503-973-5200
Fax: 503-973-5252
Email: scholarship@collegenet.com
URL: http://www.collegenet.com

Goal: To assist college students and future college students.
Eligibility: Applicants must sign up at the website and participate in their forums. The winner is chosen by user votes on their website.
Target Student: High school, College and Adult students.
Amount: $3,000-$5,000
Number of Awards: Varies
Based on Financial Need: No
Deadline: Weekly
Applications are available online.

(278) Collegiate Inventors Competition

National Inventors Hall of Fame
221 S. Broadway
Akron, OH 44308

Phone: 330-849-6887
Email: collegiate@invent.org
URL: http://www.invent.org

Goal: To encourage students to completed degrees in science, engineering, mathematics, technology, and createive invention to stimulate an interest in technology and economic leadership.

Eligibility: Applicants must have been full-time college or university students for part of the last 12 months. Up to four students can work in a team and one of the students must meet the full-time requirement.
Target Student: College, Graduate and Adult students.
Amount: Up to $15,000
Number of Awards: Varies
Based on Financial Need: No
Deadline: Unknown
Applications are available online.

(279) Color Solutions International Textile and Apparel Design Scholarship

American Association of Textile Chemists and Colorists
1 Davis Drive
Research Triangle Park, NC 27709

Phone: 919-549-3544
Fax: 919-549-8933
URL: http://www.aatcc.org

Goal: To assist undergraduate students studying textiles and apparel.
Eligibility: Applicants must be current or incoming undergraduate students who are earning a degree in the textile arena. Applicants must be American citizens born in the U.S. and eligible for in state tuition. Award selection is based on the applicants focus on design and fashion, SAT scores, financial need, leadership experience and work experience.
Target Student: High school, College and Adult students.
Amount: $2,500
Number of Awards: 1
Scholarship can be renewed.
Based on Financial Need: Yes
Deadline: March
Applications are available online.

(280) Composites Division/Harold Giles Scholarship

Society of Plastics Engineers
13 Church Hill Road
Newtown, CT 06470

Phone: 203-775-0471
Fax: 203-775-8490
Email: info@4spe.org
URL: http://www.4spe.org

Goal: To assist undergraduate and graduate students who have an interest in the plastics industry.
Eligibility: Applicants must have an interest in the plastics industry and major in, or take classes that lead to a career in the plastics industry.
Target Student: College, Graduate and Adult students.
Amount: $1,000
Number of Awards: 1
Based on Financial Need: Yes
Deadline: February
Applications are available online.

(281) Congress Bundestag Youth Exchange Program

Congress Bundestag Youth Exchange Program

URL:http://www.usagermanyscholarship.org

Goal: To assist high school students who want to study in Germany.
Eligibility: Applicants must be U.S. citizens or permanent residents who will be between 15 and 18 years old at the beginning of the program. They must have a 3.0 GPA or higher. Selection for the award is based on academics, written and oral communication and the applicants potential and skills for adapting to a different cutlure. Prior knowledge of the German language is not required.

Target Student: High school students.
Amount: Varies
Number of Awards: Varies
Based on Financial Need: No
Deadline: Varies
Applications are available online.

---

(282) Congressional Black Caucus Spouses Cheerios Brand Health Initiative Scholarship

Congressional Black Caucus Foundation
1720 Massachusetts Avenue NW
Washington, DC 20036

Phone: 202-263-2800
Fax: 202-775-0773
Email: info@cbcfinc.org
URL: http://www.cbcfinc.org

Goal: To assist minority students studying fields realted to health.
Eligibility: Applicants do not need to be African American to apply. Applicants must attend a school or reside in a district represented by a Congressional Black Caucus member, have a 2.5 or higher GPA and be enrolled or accepted as full time undergraduate students.
Target Student: High school, College and Adult students.
Amount: Varies
Number of Awards: Varies
Based on Financial Need: No
Deadline: June
Applications are available online.

---

(283) Congressional Black Caucus Spouses Education Scholarship

Congressional Black Caucus Foundation
1720 Massachusetts Avenue NW
Washington, DC 20036

Phone: 202-263-2800
Fax: 202-775-0773
Email: info@cbcfinc.org

URL: http://www.cbcfinc.org

Goal: To assist students pursuing an undergraduate and graduate degree.
Eligibility: Applicants do not need to be African American, but must reside or attend school in a congressional district that is represented by a CBC member. Students must attend or plan to attend collge full time and must have a 2.5 GPA or above and demonstrate leadership qualities.
Target Student: High school, College, Graduate and Adult students.
Amount: Varies
Number of Awards: Varies
Based on Financial Need: No
Deadline: Varies
Applications are available online.

---

(284) Congressional Black Caucus Spouses Performing Arts Scholarship

Congressional Black Caucus Foundation
1720 Massachusetts Avenue NW
Washington, DC 20036

Phone: 202-263-2800
Fax: 202-775-0773
Email: info@cbcfine.org
URL: http://www.cbcfinc.org

Goal: To assist students who are pursuing careers in performing arts.
Eligibility: Applicants do not need to be African American, but must reside or attend school in a congressional district that is represented by a CBC member. Students must attend or plan to attend collge full time and must have a 2.5 GPA or above and demonstrate leadership qualities.
Target Student: High school, College, and Adult students.
Amount: Up to $3,000
Number of Awards: 10
Based on Financial Need: No
Deadline: April

Applications are available online.

---

(285) Congressional Black Caucus Spouses Visual Arts Scholarship

Congressional Black Caucus Foundation
1720 Massachusetts Avenue NW
Washington, DC 20036

Phone: 202-263-2800
Fax: 202-775-0773
Email: info@cbcfine.org
URL: http://www.cbcfinc.org

Goal: To assist students who are pursuing careers in visual arts.
Eligibility: Applicants do not need to be African American, but must reside or attend school in a congressional district that is represented by a CBC member. Students must attend or plan to attend collge full time and must have a 2.5 GPA or above and demonstrate leadership qualities.
Target Student: High school, College, and Adult students.
Amount: Up to $3,000
Number of Awards: 10
Based on Financial Need: No
Deadline: April
Applications are available online.

---

(286) Congressional Medal of Honor Society

Congressional Medal of Honor Society
40 Patriots Point Road
Point Pleasant, SC 29464

Phone: 843-884-8862
Fax: 843-884-8862
Email: medalhq@earthlink.net
URL: http://www.cmohs.org

Goal: To assist children of Congressional Medal of Honor recipients.

Eligibility: Applicants must be the biological or adopted children of Congressional Medal of Honor recipients or of other combat veterans if recommended by a Medal of Honor recipient.
Target Student: High school, College and Adult students.
Amount: $5,000
Number of Awards: Varies
Based on Financial Need: No
Deadline: Varies
Applications are available form the Congressional Medal of Honor Society.

---

(287) Constance Eberhardt Memorial Award, AIMS Graz Experience Scholarship and Banff Center School of Fine Arts Scholarship

National Opera Assocation
Vocal Competition
P.O. Box 60869
Canyon, TX 79016

Phone: 806-651-2857
Email: rhansen@mail.wtamu.edu
URL: http://www.noa.org

Goal: To assist young opera singers with educational expenses.
Eligibility: Applicants must be enrolled in undergraduate or graduate programs or equivalent and be between 18 and 24 years old. The applicant's teachers must be a member of the National Opera Association and selection is based on recording of two arias and a live audition of four arias for the final judging. A $20 entry fee is required. Applying to a scholarship that requires a fee is never recommended.
Target Student: High school, College, Graduate and Adult students.
Amount: $500 - $1,250
Number of Awards: Varies
Based on Financial Need: No
Deadline: October

Applications are available online.

---

(288) Corporate Leadership Scholarships

Gravure Education Foundation
1200-A Scottsville Road
Rochester, NY 14624

Phone: 315-589-8879
Fax: 585-436-7689
Email: lwshatch@gaa.org
URL: http://www.gaa.org

Goal: To assist undergraduate and graduate students working towards degrees in printing or graphic arts.
Eligibility: Applicants must be enrolled full-time at a GEF Learning Resource Center at Arizona State University, California Polytechnic State University, Clemson University, Murray State, Rochester Institute of Technology, University of Wisconsin-Stout or Western Michigan University. Applicants must be sophomore, junior, or seniors who are majoring in printing, graphic arts, graphic communications.
Target Student: College, Graduate and Adult students.
Amount: $1,500
Number of Awards: 7
Based on Financial Need: No
Deadline: April
Applications are available online.

---

(289) Corrosion Division Morris Cohen Graduate Student Award

Electrochemical Society
65 South Main Street
Building D
Pennington, NJ 8534

Phone: 609-737-1902
Fax: 609-737-2743
Email: awards@electrochem.org

URL: http://www.electrochem.org

Goal: To acknowledge graduate research in corrosion science and/or engineering.
Eligibility: Applicants must be graduate students who have completed their degree requirements within two years of the nomination deadline. The nomination must be made by the applicants research supervisor or someone familiar with the applicant's research.
Target Student: Graduate and Adult students.
Amount: $1,000 plus travel expenses.
Number of Awards: 1
Based on Financial Need: No
Deadline: December
Application materials are available online.

---

(290) Council on International Educational Exchange Scholarships

Council on International Educational Exchange
7 Custom House Street, 3rd Floor
Portland, ME 04101

Phone: 800-40-STUDY
Fax: 207-553-7699
Email: scholarships@ciee.org
URL: http://www.ciee.org

Goal: To open study abroad programs to more people and to assist CIEE Study Center members with demonstrated acadmiic skills and financial need.
Eligibility: Applicants must plan to participate in a CIEE study abroad program. Finanical need is considered for this scholarship.
Target Student: College, Graduate and Adult students.
Amount: Up to $5,000
Number of Awards: Varies
Based on Financial Need: Yes
Deadline: April and November
Applications are available online.

(291) Courtland Paul Scholarship

Landscape Architecture Foundation
818 18th Street NW
Suite 810
Washington, DC 20006

Phone: 202-331-7070
Fax: 202-331-7079
Email: scholarships@lafoundation.org
URL: http://www.lafoundation.org

Goal: To assist students majoring in landscape architecture.
Eligibility: Applicants must be U.S. citizens and undergraduate students in their final two years of a landscape architecture degree program that is accredited by the Landscape Architecture Accreditation Board. Applicants must have a 2.0 or higher GPA and demonstrated financial need.
Target Student: College and Adult students.
Amount: $5,000
Number of Awards: 1
Based on Financial Need: Yes
Deadline: February
Applications are available online. A completed application, two letters of recommendation, essay, photo and financial aid information is required to apply.

(292) CPAexcel Scholarship

CPAexcel

URL:http://www.capexcel.com/students/scholarship.html

Goal: To assist students in accounting courses.
Eligibility: Applicants must be full or part-time college juniors or seniors or graduate students taking at least one course in accounting.

Target Student: College, Graduate and Adult students.
Amount: $2,500
Number of Awards: 1
Based on Financial Need: No
Deadline: November
Applications are available online.

(293) Create Real Impact Contest

Impact Teen Drivers
Attn: Create Real Impact Contest
P.O. Box 161209
Sacramento, CA 95816

Phone: 916-733-7432
Email: info@impactteendrivers.org
URL: http://www.createrealimpact.com

Goal: To increase awareness of the danger of distracted driving.
Eligibility: Applicants must be legal U.S. residents between 15 and 22 years old. They must be enrolled full time at a secondary or post-secondary school. Each applicant must submit an original video, music, creative writing or artwork. Award selection is based on project concept, message, effectiveness and creativity. Projects must be on the topic of distracted driving, entries on drunk driving will not be accepted.
Target Student: High school, College and Graduate students.
Amount: $500
Number of Awards: Up to 20
Based on Financial Need: No
Deadline: June
Entry instructions are available online.

(294) Crest Oral-B Laboratories Dental Hygiene Scholarships

American Dental Hygienists' Association
Institute for Oral Health
Scholarship Award Program
444 North Michigan Avenue

Suite 3400
Chicago, IL 60611

Phone: 312-440-8900
Email: institute@adha.net
URL: http://www.adha.org/ioh

Goal: To assist students working towards a bachelor's degree with an interest in dental hygiene and dental hygiene education.
Eligibility: Applicants must be full-time students at an accredited college or university in the U.S., working towards a degree in dental hygiene or a related field with one year of dental hygiene courses completed. Applicants must have a minimum GPA of 3.5 in dental hygiene courses, active members in ADHA, a strong interest in dental hygiene research, promoting dental hygiene education, and demonstrated financial need of at least $1,500.
Target Student: College and Adult students.
Amount: $1,000
Number of Awards: Varies
Based on Financial Need: Yes
Deadline: February
Applications are available online starting in October.

(295) CrossLites Scholarship Contest

CrossLites
1000 Holt Avenue
1178
Winter Park, FL 32789

Phone: 407-833-3886
Email: crosslites@gmail.com
URL: http://www.crosslites.com

Goal: The CrossLites Scholarship Award was created to provide high school, undergraduate, and graduate students with a chance to learn about Dr. Charles Parker, become inspired, and win some money.

Eligibility: Applicants must be high school, undergraduate or graduate students. Students must write an essay that is between 400 and 600 words based on one of Dr. Charles Parker's quotes or messages that are listed on the website. Each school level (high school, undergraduate and graduate) have their own awards. The award is given based on the judges score (10%) and votes from website visitors (90%).
Target Student: High school, College, Graduate and Adult students.
Amount: Up to $2,000
Number of Awards: 33
Based on Financial Need: No
Deadline: December
Applications are available online. An essay, transcripts and basic contact information is required to apply.

(296) Curt Greene Memorial Scholarship

Harness Horse Youth Foundation
16575 Carey Road
Westfield, IN 46074

Phone: 317-867-5877
Fax: 317-867-5896
Email: ellen@hhyf.org
URL: http://www.hhyf.org

Goal: To assist students who are interested in harness racing.
Eligibility: Applicants must be at least a senior in high school and demonstrate financial need.
Target Student: High school, College and Adult students.
Amount: Varies
Number of Awards: Varies
Based on Financial Need: Yes
Deadline: April
Applications are availiable online. An application, essay and two letters of reference are required.

(297) D.W. Simpson Actuarial Science Scholarship

D.W. Simpson and Company
1800 Larchmont Avenue
Chicago, IL 60613

Phone: 800-837-8338
Fax: 312-951-8386
Email: actuaries@dwsimpson.com
URL:http://www.dwsimpson.com/scholar.html

Goal: To assist college students interested in a career in actuarial science.
Eligibility: Applicants must be college seniors who are majoring in actuarial science, eligible to work in the U.S. and have passed at least one actuarial examinations.
Target Student: College and Adult students.
Amount: $1,000
Number of Awards: 2
Based on Financial Need: No
Deadline: April and October
Applications are available online.

(298) DAAD/AICGS Research Fellowship Program

American Institute for Contemporary German Studies
1755 Massachusetts Avenue, NW
Suite 700
Washington, DC 20036

Phone: 202-332-9312
Fax: 202-265-9531
Email: jwindell@aicgs.org
URL: http://www.aicgs.org

Goal: To bring scholars from Germany, Europe to AICGS for research stays.
Eligibility: Applicants must have a Ph.D. or be enrolled in a Ph.D. program and hold U.S. or German citizenship.

Target Student: Graduate school and Adult students.
Amount: Up to $4,725 monthly
Number of Awards: Varies
Based on Financial Need: No
Deadline: February
Apply via email to jwindell@aicgs.org

(299) Daedalian Foundation Matching Scholarship Program

Daedalian Foundation
P.O. Box 249
Randolph AFB, TX 78148

Phone: 210-945-2113
Fax: 210-945-2112
Email: icarus2@daedalians.org
URL: http://www.daedalians.org

Goal: To assist undergraduate students who are studying to become military pilots.
Eligibility: Applicants must be rising or current undergraduate students attending a four-year institution and must have demonstrated interest in a career in military aviation. The award is based on the strength of the application.
Target Student: High school, College and Adult students.
Amount: Varies
Number of Awards: Varies
Based on Financial Need: No
Deadline: Varies
Applications are available online. A completed application and photo are requied to apply.

(300) Dairy Student Recognition Program

National Dairy Shrine
P.O. Box 1
Maribel, WI 54227

Phone: 920-863-6333
Fax: 920-863-8328

Email: info@dairyshrine.org
URL: http://www.dairyshrine.org

Goal: To acknowledge graduating college seniors pursuing careers in the dairy industry.
Eligibility: Applicants must be U.S. citizens who are planning to enter a career that is related to the dairy industry (dairy production agriculture, marketing, agricultural law, veterinary medicine, business, or environmental science).
Target Student: College and Adult students.
Amount: Up to $2,000
Number of Awards: 7
Based on Financial Need: No
Deadline: April
Applications are available online. Only two applicants per school are accepted each year.

---

(301) Dan L. Meisinger Sr. Memorial Learn to Fly Scholarship

National Air Transportation Foundation
Meisinger Scholarship
4226 King Street
Alexandria, VA 22302

Phone: 703-845-9000
Fax: 703-845-8176
URL: http://www.nata.aero

Goal: To provide a scholarship for flight training.
Eligibility: Applicants must be enrolled in an aviation program with a 3.0 GPA or higher and be residents of Kansas, Missouri, or Illinois.
Target Student: College, Graduate and Adult students.
Amount: $2,500
Number of Awards: Varies
Based on Financial Need: No
Deadline: November
Applications are available online.

---

(302) Darling International Inc, FFA Scholarship

National FFA Organizations
P.O. Box 68960
6060 FFA Drive
Indianapolis, IN 46268

Phone: 317-802-6060
Fax: 317-802-6051
Email: scholarships@ffa.org
URL: http://www.ffa.org

Goal: To assist students of land grant schools in Colorado, Iowa, Illinois, Kansas, Nebraska, and Wisconsin who are pursuing degrees in agriculture.
Eligibility: Applicants must be FFA members and high school seniors or college students who are planning to enroll or are enrolled as full-time students. One application will qualify the applicants for all FFA scholarships.
Target Student: College and Adult students.
Amount: $2,000
Number of Awards: 1
Based on Financial Need: No
Deadline: February
Applications are available online.

---

(303) Darrel Hess Community College Geography Scholarship

Association of American Geographers
(AAG) Hess Scholarship
1710 Sixteenth Street NW
Washington, DC 20009

Phone: 202-234-1450
Fax: 202-234-2744
Email: grantsawards@aag.org
URL: http://www.aag.org/cs/grants/hess

Goal: To assist geography majors.

Eligibility: Applicants must be enrolled in a U.S. junior, community, city or other two year college and have completed at least two transfer courses in geography and plan to transfer to a four-year college as a geography major.
Target Student: College and Adult students
Amount: $1,000
Number of Awards: 2
Based on Financial Need: No
Deadline: December
Applications are available online. A completed application, personal statement, two letters of recommendation and transcripts are required to apply.

(304) Dating and Relationship Psychology Scholarship

Datingadvice.com
c/o Digital Brands Inc.
15 SE 1st Avenue, Suite B
Gainesville, FL 32601

URL: http://www.datingadvice.com/scholarship

Goal: To assist psychology students planning on careers in relationship counseling.
Eligibility: Applicants must be U.S. undergraduate or graduate psychology students with a GPA of 3.5 or higher.
Target Student: College, Graduate and Adult students
Amount: $1,000
Number of Awards: 1
Based on Financial Need: No
Deadline: June
To apply, submit transcripts and the required essay by mail.

(305) Daughters of the Cincinnati Scholarship

Daughters of the Cincinnati

National Headquarters
122 East 58th Street
New York, NY 10022

Phone: 212-319-6915
URL: http://www.fdncenter.org/grantmaker/cincinnati

Goal: To assist daughters of Armed Services commissioned officers.
Eligibility: Applicants must be daughers of active duty officers in the United States Army, Navy, Air Force, Coast Guard, or Marine Corps (active, retired or deceased). Daughters of reserve officers are not eligible. Applicants must also be high school seniors.
Target Student: High school students.
Amount: Varies
Number of Awards: Varies
Scholarship can be renewed.
Based on Financial Need: No
Deadline: March
Applications are available by mailing your parents rank, branch of service and enclosinga self-addressed and stamped envelpe to the organization.

(306) David Alan Quick Scholarship

EAA Aviation Center
P.O. Box 2683
Oshkosh, WI 54903

Phone: 877-806-8902
Fax: 920-426-6865
Email: scholarships@eaa.org
URL: http://www.youngeagles.org

Goal: To assist students in aerospace or aeronautical engineering.
Eligibility: Applicants must be in their junior or senior year of college and be working towards a degree in aerospace or seronautical engineering. Applicants must be EAA members or recommended by an EAA member and be involved in activities in school and the community.

Target Student: College and Adult students.
Amount: $500
Number of Awards: 1
Scholarship can be renewed.
Based on Financial Need: No
Deadline: February
Applications are available online.

---

(307) David S. Barr Awards

Newspaper Guild - CWA
501 3rd Street NW
6th Floor
Washington, DC 20001

Phone: 202-434-7177
Fax: 202-434-1472
Email: guild@cwa-union.org
URL: http://www.newsguild.org

Goal: To assist student journalists.
Eligibility: Applicants must be high school or college students at any type of school and have published or broadcast working the past year with the goal of promoting justice or correcting an injustice.
Target Student: High school, College, Graduate and Adult students.
Amount: $500 - $1500
Number of Awards: 2
Based on Financial Need: No
Deadline: January
Applications are available online. A completed application, five copies of the work and a brief summary of the work are required to apply.

---

(308) David S. Bruce Awards for Excellence in Undergraduate Research

American Physiological Society
Education Office
9650 Rockville Pike
Bethesda, MD 20814

Phone: 301-634-7787
Fax: 301-634-7241
Email: education@the-aps.org
URL: http://www.the-aps.org

Goal: To reward undergraduate students for excellence in research in experimental biology.
Eligibility: Applicants must be enrolled as undergraduate students at the time of the meeting and application. Applicants must be authors of the abstract and working with an APS member who can confirm authorship.
Target Student: College and Adult students.
Amount: $500
Number of Awards: Varies
Based on Financial Need: No
Deadline: January
Applications are available online.

---

(309) Davidson Fellows Award

Davidson Institute for Talent Development
9665 Gateway Drive Suite B
Reno, NV 89521

Phone: 775-852-3483
Email: davidsonfellows@ditd.org
URL: http://www.davidson-institute.org

Goal: To recognize outstanding young students for their work in mathematics, service, technology, music, literature, philosophy or "outside the box."
Eligibility: Applicants must be under 18 and have completed a significant piece of work in one of the categories. Applicants must be able to attend the award ceremony, the institute will page for travel and lodging. Three moninator forms, three copies of a 15 minute DVD or VHS take and additional materials related to the work completed are required.
Target Student: Junior high and younger and High school students.

Amount: $10,000 to $50,000
Number of Awards: Varies
Based on Financial Need: No
Deadline: February
Applications are available online.

---

(310) Davis-Putter Scholarship Fund

Davis-Putter Scholarship Fund
P.O. Box 7307
New York, NY 10116

Email: information@davisputter.org
URL: http://www.davisputter.org

Goal: The Davis-Putter Scholarship Fund provides grants to students actively working for peace and justice. These need-based scholarships are awarded to those able to do academic work at the university level and who are part of the progressive movement on the campus and in the community.
Eligibility: Applicants must be undergraduate or graduate students who participate in the progressive movement, working to expand civil rights, fight against racism, homophobia and other civil injustice. Applicants must also demonstrate financial need in addition to a strong academic record.
Target Student: College, Graduate and Adult students.
Amount: Up to $10,000
Number of Awards: Varies
Based on Financial Need: Yes
Deadline: April
Applications are available online.

---

(311) Dayton Amateur Radio Association Scholarship

American Radio Relay League Foundation
225 Main Street
Newington, CT 06111

Phone: 860-594-0397

Fax: 860-594-0259
Email: foundation@arrl.org
URL: http://www.arrlf.org

Goal: To assist amateur radio operators with educational expenses.
Eligibility: Applicants must have any class of amateur radio license and be accepted or enrolled in a four-year college or university.
Target Student: High school, College or Adult students.
Amount: $1,000
Number of Awards: 4
Based on Financial Need: No
Deadline: February
Applications are available online.

---

(312) Delete Cyberbullying Scholarship Award

Delete Cyberbulling
2261 Market Street #291
San Francisco, CA 94114

Email:applications@deletecyberbullying.org
URL: http://www.deletecyberbullying.org

Goal: To encourage students to commit to deleting cyberbullying.
Eligibility: Applicants must be U.S. Citizens or permanent residents who are attending or planning to attend an accredited college or university in the U.S. for undergraduate or graduate study.
Target Student: High school, College, Graduate and Adult students.
Amount: $1,500
Number of Awards: 2
Based on Financial Need: No
Deadline: June
Applications are available online. A completed application and essay are required to apply.

---

(313) Dell Scholars Program

Michael and Susan Dell Foundation
P.O. Box 163867
Austin, TX 78716

Phone: 512-329-0799
Fax: 512-347-1744
Email: apply@dellscholars.org
URL: http://www.dellsccholars.org

Goal: To assist underprivileged high school seniors.
Eligibility: Applicants must be in an approved college readiness program and they must have a 2.4 GPA or higher. Applicants must be starting a bachelors degree in the fall immediately after their high school graduation. Students must be U.S. citizens or permanent residents and demonstrate financial need. The award is based on "individual determination to succeed," future goals, hardships that have been overcome, self motivation and financial need.
Target Student: High school students.
Amount: Varies
Number of Awards: Varies
Scholarship can be renewed.
Based on Financial Need: Yes
Deadline: January
Applications are available online.

---

(314) Delmar Cengage Learning Scholarship

Association of Surgical Technologists
6 W. Dry Creek Circle
Littleton, CO 80120

Phone: 800-637-7433
Fax: 303-694-9169
Email: kludwig@ast.org
URL: http://www.ast.org

Goal: To assist surgical technology students.

Eligibility: Applicants must currently attend or plan to attend a CAAHEP accredited program. The award is based on writing skills and academic achievement.
Target Student: College and Adult students.
Amount: $1,500
Number of Awards: 1
Based on Financial Need: No
Deadline: March
Applications are available online.

---

(315) Delta Faucet Company Scholarships

Plumbing-Heating-Cooling Contractors National Association
P.O. Box 6808
180 South Washington Street
Falls Church, VA 22046

Phone: 800-533-7694
Fax: 703-237-7442
Email: scholarships@naphcc.org
URL: http://www.phccweb.org

Goal: To increase the business and technical abilities of the plumbing-heating-cooling industry by providing scholarships to those enrolled in a related major.
Eligibility: Applicants must be students enrolled or plan to enroll in a plumbing, heating or cooling related major at an accredited four-or two-year college or university. Apprentice program students must be working full-time for a licensed plumbing or HVAC contractor who is a member of PHCC.
Target Student: High school, College and Adult students.
Amount: $2,500
Number of Awards: 6
Based on Financial Need: No
Deadline: May
Applications are available online, by phone or mail.

(316) Denny Lydic Scholarship

Transportation Clubs International
Scholarships
Attn: Bill Blair
Zimmer Worldwide Logistics
15710 JFK Boulevard
Houston, TX 77032

Phone: 877-858-8627
Email: bblair@zimmerworldwide.com
URL:http://www.transportationclubsinternational.com

Goal: To assist students in the transportation field.
Eligibility: Applicants must be graduating high school seniors or college undergraduate students who are enrolled at an accredited school in a vocational or degree program in the field of transportation logistics, supply-chain management, traffic management, transportation safety or a related field. Financial need is considered.
Target Student: High school, College and Adult students.
Amount: Varies
Number of Awards: Varies
Based on Financial Need: Yes
Deadline: May
Applications are available online.

(317) Dental Student Scholarship

American Dental Association Foundation
211 East Chicago Avenue
Chicago, IL 60611

Phone: 312-440-2763
Fax: 312-440-3526
Email: famularor@ada.org
URL: http://www.ada.org

Goal: To encourage students to pursue a career in dental hygiene, dental assisting, dentistry and dental laboratory technology.
Eligibility: Applicants must be full-time students entering their second year at an accredited dental program with a demonstrated financial need of at least $2,500 and a GPA of 3.0 or higher.
Target Student: College, Graduate and Adult students.
Amount: $1,000
Number of Awards: Varies
Based on Financial Need: Yes
Deadline: Varies
Applications are available from dental school officials. A completed application, two letters of reference and biography is required to apply.

(318) Dinah Shore Scholarship

Ladies Professional Golf Association
100 International Golf Drive
Daytona Beach, FL 32124

Phone: 386-274-6200
Fax: 386-274-1099
URL: http://www.lpga.com

Goal: To honor Dinah Shore.
Eligibility: Applicants must be female high school seniors who have been accepted for full-time study at an accredited U.S. college or university. Applicants must have played golf for the last two years, but not have played competitive collegiate golf. A GPA of 3.2 or higher is required.
Target Student: High school students.
Amount: $5,000
Number of Awards: 1
Based on Financial Need: No
Deadline: May
Applications are available online.

(319) Direction.com College Scholarship

Direction
10402 Harwin Drive

Houston, TX 77036

Phone: 713-773-3636 x1500
Fax: 281-754-4959
Email: customer_service@direction.us
URL: http://www.direction.com

Goal: To assist U.S. college students.
Eligibility: Applicants must be high school seniors or current college students. Students must submit an essay on the topic provided that is related to computers. Essay submissions are judge 50% on academic merit and 50% on creativity. Photos are recommended, but not required.
Target Student: High school, College and Adult students.
Amount: $300 to $1,000
Number of Awards: 6
Based on Financial Need: No
Deadline: May
No application is required. Applicants are to send their contact information and completed essay to information@direction.com.

(320) Discus Awards College Scholarships

Discus Awards
7101 Wisconsin Avenue Suite 750
Bethesda, MD 20814

Email: info@discusawards.com
URL: http://www.discusawards.com

Goal: To assist college bound high school students.
Eligibility: Applicants must be U.S. high school studnets who are involved or have achievements in at least three of of the following areas: academics, art, athletics, community service, faith, government, green technology, work or other achievements. The award selection is based on merit.
Target Student: High school students.

Amount: $2,000
Number of Awards: 10
Based on Financial Need: No
Deadline: Monthly
Applications are available online. A completed application and supporting documents are required to apply.

(321) Disney/ABC Television Writing Program

Disney/ABC Television Group
Talent Development and Diversity
500 South Buena Vista Street
Burbank, CA 91521

Email: abcwritingfellowship@disney.com
URL:http://www.abctalentdevelopment.com

Goal: To assist writers develop the skills needed for careers in television writing.
Eligibility: Applicants must be 21 years old or over and able to work in the U.S. legally. While professional writing experience is not required, applicants must have strong spec writing skills.
Target Student: College, Graduate and Adult students.
Amount: Salary
Number of Awards: Varies
Based on Financial Need: No
Deadline: Varies
Applications are available online. A completed application and spec script samples are required.

(322) Distinguished Service Award for Students

Society for Technical Communication
Manager of the Distinguished Community Awards Committee
7107 Paradise Park Bend
Richmond, TX 77469

Phone: 703-522-4114

Email: stc@stc.org
URL: http://www.stc.org

Goal: To assist students majoring in the area of technical communication.
Eligibility: Applicants must be full-time graduate or undergraduate students who have completed at least one year of college and have at least one year of college remaining.
Target Student: College, Graduate and Adult students.
Amount: Varies
Number of Awards: Varies
Based on Financial Need: No
Deadline: November
Applications are available online.

---

(323) Distinguished Student Scholar Award

Pi Lambda Theta
P.O. Box 6626
Bloomington, IN 47407

Phone: 800-487-3411
Fax: 812-339-3462
Email: office@pilambda.org
URL: http://www.pilambda.org

Goal: To assist education majors who have leadership potential.
Eligibility: Applicants must be sophomores or higher with demonstrated leadership skills who are majoring in education. Applicants must be nominated by an instructor or supervisor and have a GPA of 3.5 or higher. The scholarship is available in odd years only.
Target Student: College and Adult students.
Amount: $500
Number of Awards: Varies
Based on Financial Need: No
Deadline: April
Applications are available online.

---

(324) Diversity/Abroad.com Scholarship

Diversity Abroad
1731 Delaware Street
Berkeley, CA 94703

Phone: 510-982-0635
Fax: 510-647-5032
Email: feedback@diversityabroad.com
URL: http://www.diversityabroad.com

Goal: To assist minority students study abroad during the summer term.
Eligibility: Applicants must have a 2.75 GPA in a full-time undergraduate program and be U.S. citizens or legal residents. Those who receive the scholarship must enroll in a study abroad program that is sponsored by a Diversity Abroad member organization and be willing to share their experiences on Diversityabroad.com through blogs.
Target Student: College and Adult students.
Amount: $500
Number of Awards: 10
Based on Financial Need: Yes
Deadline: May and October
Applications are available online.

---

(325) Dixie Boys Baseball Scholarship Programs

Dixie Boys Baseball
P.O. Box 8263
Dothan, AL 36304

Phone: 334-793-3331
Email: jjones29@sw.rr.com
URL: http://www.dixie.org

Goal: To help high school seniors who have participated in Dixie Boys Baseball.

Eligibility: Applicants must plan on pursuing an undergraduate degree at a college or university. An application, financial statement, two letters of recommendation, proof of baseball participation, transcripts and essay are required. Award selection is based on class ranking, strong school and community leadership, and financial need.
Target Student: High school students.
Amount: $1,250
Number of Awards: 11
Based on Financial Need: Yes
Deadline: April
Applications are available online.

---

(326) Dixie Youth Scholarship Program

Dixie Youth Baseball
P.O. Box 877
Marshall, TX 75671

Phone: 903-927-2255
Email: dyb@dixie.org
URL: http://www.dixie.org

Goal: To assist high school seniors who have participated in Dixie Youth Baseball.
Eligibility: Applicants must have been registered and participated on an Dixie Youth Baseball team prior to the age of 13. Award selection is based on financial need, academic record and citizenship.
Target Student: High school students.
Amount: $2,000
Number of Awards: Varies
Based on Financial Need: Yes
Deadline: March
Contact your local, district, state or national league officials for an application. Applications can also be found online.

---

(327) DJNF Summer Internships

Dow Jones Newspaper Fund
P.O. Box 300
Princeton, NJ 08543

Phone: 609-452-2820
Fax: 609-520-5804
Email: djnf@dowjones.com
URL: http://www.dowjones.com/products-services.asp

Goal: To assist student journalists.
Eligibility: Applicants must be college students pursuing journalism careers and interested in paid summer internships. Applicants for the Multimedia, News and Sports Editing program must be juniors, seniors or graduate students and must pass a pre-qualifying copy editing test. They must also submit a resume, transcript and 500 word essay with their application. Applicants to the Business Reporting Internship program must be sophomores, juniors, seniors or graduate students and submit a resume, 3 to 5 recent articles, transcript and 500 word essay with their application. They must also pass a business reporting test.
Target Student: College, Graduate and Adult students.
Amount: Varies
Number of Awards: Varies
Based on Financial Need: No
Deadline: November
Applications are available online.

---

(328) DMI Milk Marketing Scholarship

National Dairy Shrine
P.O. Box 1
Maribel, WI 54227

Phone: 920-863-6333
Fax: 920-863-8328
Email: info@dairyshrine.org
URL: http://www.dairyshrine.org

Goal: To encourage students to pursue a career in the marketing of dairy foods.

Eligibility: Applicants must be in their second year of college or higher with a GPA of 2.5 or higher and major in dairy science, animal science, agricultural communications, agricultural education, eneral agriculture or food and nutrition.
Target Student: College and Adult students.
Amount: $1,000 - $1,500
Number of Awards: Up to 8
Based on Financial Need: No
Deadline: April
Applications are available online.

---

(329) Do Something Awards

Do Something Inc.
24-32 Union Square East
4th Floor
New York, NY 10003

Phone: 212-254-2390
Email: tacklehunger@dosomething.org
URL: http://www.dosomething.org

Goal: To assist young social entrepreneurs who are maiing a difference in their community.
Eligibility: Applicants must be under 25 and taking a leadership role in creating positve, lasting, impact on the community. Focus areas for the scholarship are health, environment and community building.
Target Student: High school, College, and Graduate students.
Amount: Varies
Number of Awards: Varies
Based on Financial Need: No
Deadline: March
Applications are available online.

---

(330) Doctoral Scholars Forgivable Loan Program

Society of Automotive Engineers
International
400 Commonwealth Drive

Warrendale, PA 15096

Phone: 724-776-4841
Fax: 724-776-0790
Email: scholarships@sae.org
URL: http://www.sae.org

Goal: To assist promising engineering graduate students to pursue careers in teaching at the college level with educational expenses.
Eligibility: Applicants must have an undergraduate degree from an engineering program and have been admitted to a doctoral program with the goal of teaching engineering at the college level.
Target Student: Graduate and Adult students.
Amount: Up to $5,000
Number of Awards: 1-2
Scholarship can be renewed.
Based on Financial Need: No
Deadline: February
Applications are available online.

---

(331) Dollars for Scholars Scholarship

Citizens' Scholarship Foundation of America
One Scholarship Way
P.O. Box 297
St. Peter, MN 56082

Phone: 800-537-4180
URL: http://www.scholarshipamerica.org

Goal: To assist and encourage students in achieving higher educational goals.
Eligibility: Applicants must be members of a local Dollars for Scholars chapter.
Target Student: High school students.
Amount: Varies
Number of Awards: Varies
Based on Financial Need: No
Deadline: Varies
Contact your local chapter for more information.

---

(332) Dolores E. Fisher Award

Mel Fisher Maritime Heritage Society and Museum
200 Greene Street
Key West, FL 33040

Phone: 305-294-2633
Email: office@melfisher.org
URL: http://www.melfisher.org

Goal: To assist female students interested in purusing a career that are ocean or marine related.
Eligibility: Applicants must be female students between 16 and 30 years old with plans to pursue a career in a ocean or marine related field.
Target Student: High school, College, Graduate and Adult students.
Amount: $1,000
Number of Awards: 1
Based on Financial Need: No
Deadline: Varies
Applications are available online. A completed application, essay, statement of career goals and three letters of recommendation are required to apply.

(333) Dolphin Scholarship

Dolphin Scholarship Foundation
5040 Virginia Beach Boulevard
Suite 104A
Virginia Beach, VA 23462

Phone: 757-671-3200
Fax: 757-671-3330
Email: info@dophinsscholarship.org
URL: http://www.dolphinscholarship.org

Goal: To assist the children of members of the Navy Submarine Force and other submarine support personnel.

Eligibility: Applicants must be the unmarried children, or step-children of Navy submariners or Navy members who served in submarine support activities and must be under 24 years old at the application deadline. The parent must have been part of the submarine force for at least 8 years or served in submarine support for 10 years or died while on active duty while in the submarine force. Children of submarines who served less than the required time due to being injured in the line of duty may still be eligible. Applicants must be studying towards a bachelors degree at a four year college.
Target Student: High school and College students.
Amount: Varies
Number of Awards: Varies
Scholarship can be renewed.
Based on Financial Need: No
Deadline: Unknown
Applications are available online.

(334) Donald F. and Mildred Topp Othmer Foundation

American Institute of Chemical Engineers
3 Park Avenue
New York, NY 10016

Phone: 212-591-7634
Fax: 212-591-8890
Email: awards@aiche.org
URL: http://www.aiche.org

Goal: To assist AIChE student members.
Eligibility: Applicants must be members of an AIChE student chapter or Chemical Engineering Club. Applicants must be nominated by their student chapter advisor.
Target Student: College, Graduate and Adult students.
Amount: $1,000
Number of Awards: 15
Based on Financial Need: No
Deadline: June

Applications are available online.

(335) Donald Groves Fund

American Numismatic Society
75 Varick Street
Floor 11
New York, NY 10013

Phone: 212-571-4470
Fax: 212-571-4479
Email: info@numismatics.org
URL: http://www.numismatics.org

Goal: To support publication in the field of early American numismatics.
Eligibility: Applicants must submit an outline for their research, research methods, along with a funding request with information about how the funds will be used. Funds can be used for travel, research and the costs of publication.
Target Student: Graduate and Adult students.
Amount: Varies
Number of Awards: Varies
Based on Financial Need: No
Deadline: Varies
Applications are available online.

(336) Donald Riebhoff Memorial Scholarship

American Radio Relay League Foundation
225 Main Street
Newington, CT 06111

Phone: 860-594-0397
Fax: 860-594-0259
Email: foundation@arrl.org
URL: http://www.arrlf.org

Goal: To assist ham radio operators with educational expenses.

Eligibility: Applicants must have a technician ham radio license or higher, be undergraduate or graduate students in international studies and be members of ARRL.
Target Student: College, Graduate and Adult students.
Amount: $1,000
Number of Awards: 1
Based on Financial Need: No
Deadline: February
Applications are available online.

(337) Doodle 4 Google

Google
1600 Amphitheatre Parkway
Mountain View, CA 94043

Phone: 650-253-0000
Fax: 650-253-0001
Email: doodle4google-team@google.com
URL:http://www.google.com/doodle4google

Goal: To develop creativity in United States school students by way of a logo contest.
Eligibility: Applicants must be elementary or secondary school students in the 50 U.S. states or Washington D.C. who have registered for the contest.
Target Student: Junior high or younger, High school students.
Amount: Up to $15,000
Number of Awards: Varies
Based on Financial Need: No
Deadline: March
Applications are available from schools that are participating.

(338) Dorothy Budnek Memorial Scholarship

Association for Radiologic and Imaging Nursing
7794 Grow Drive

Pensacola, FL 32514

Phone: 866-486-2762
Fax: 850-484-8762
Email: arin@dancyamc.com
URL: http://www.arinursing.org

Goal: To assist ARNA members in continuing their education.
Eligibility: Applicants must be active members of the American Radiological Nurses Association for at least three years, have a current nursing license, have a GPA of 2.5 or higher and be enrolled in an approved academic program.
Target Student: Graduate and Adult students.
Amount: $600
Number of Awards: 1
Based on Financial Need: No
Deadline: September
Applications are available online. A completed application, two letters of recommendation, statement of purpose, transcript, and copy of nursing license is required to apply.

---

(339) Dorothy M. and Earl S. Hoffman Award

American Vacuum Society
120 Wall Street
32nd Floor
New York, NY 10005

Phone: 212-248-0200
Fax: 212-248-0245
Email: angela@avs.org
URL: http://www.ava.org

Goal: To acknowledge excellence in continuing graduate students in the sciences and technologies related to AVS.
Eligibility: Applicants must be graduate students at an accredited college or university.
Target Student: Graduate and Adult students.

Amount: Varies
Number of Awards: 1
Based on Financial Need: No
Deadline: May
Applications are available online. A completed application, letters of recommendation, transcript and summary of research is required to apply.

---

(340) Douglas Dockery Thomas Fellowship In Garden History and Design

Landscape Architecture Foundation
818 18th Street NW
Suite 810
Washington, DC 20006

Phone: 202-331-7070
Fax: 202-331-7079
Email: scholarships@lafoundation.org
URL: http://www.lafoundation.org

Goal: To assist graduate students working on research projects that are related to garden design.
Eligibility: Applicants must be graduate students currently enrolled in a U.S. college or university. Applicants must be researching some part of garden design.
Target Student: Graduate and Adult students.
Amount: $4,000
Number of Awards: 1
Based on Financial Need: No
Deadline: February
Application information is available online. A cover letter, research proposal, budget proposal, resume and three letters of recommendation are required to apply.

---

(341) Dr. Arnita Young Boswell Scholarship

National Hook-Up of Black Women Inc.
1809 East 71st Street
Suite 205

Chicago, IL 60649

Phone: 773-667-7061
Fax: 773-667-7064
Email: nhbwdir@aol.com
URL: http://www.nhbwinc.com

Goal: To acknowledge adult students for their academic achievement.
Eligibility: Applicants must be undergraduate or graduate students. Award selection is based on academic acomplishments in addition to involvement in school and community activities along with an essay.
Target Student: College, Graduate and Adult students.
Amount: $1,000
Number of Awards: Varies
Scholarship can be renewed.
Based on Financial Need: No
Deadline: March
Applications are available by mail.

---

(342) Dr. Aura-Lee A. and James Hobbs Pittenger American History Scholarship

National Society Daughters of the American Revolution
Committee Services Office
Attn.: Scholarships
1776 D Street NW
Washington, DC 20006

Phone: 2002-628-1776
URL: http://www.dar.org

Goal: To suppor the study of American history and government.
Eligibility: Applicants must be high school seniors planning to major in American history or government. While applicants do not need to be DAR members, they must receive a letter of sponsorship from their local DAR chapter.
Target Student: High school students.
Amount: $2,000

Number of Awards: Varies
Scholarship can be renewed.
Based on Financial Need: No
Deadline: February
Applications are available by written request.

---

(343) Dr. Esther Wilkins Scholarship

American Dental Hygienists' Association
Institute for Oral Health
Scholarship Award Program
444 North Michigan Avenue
Suite 3400
Chicago, IL 60611

Phone: 312-440-8900
Email: institute@adha.net
URL: http://www.adha.org/ioh

Goal: To assist students who have completed an entry level program in dental hygiene and are working to earn an additional degree to earn a career in dental hygiene education.
Eligibility: Applicants must be full-time students at an accredited college or university in the U.S., working towards a degree in dental hygiene or a related field with one year of dental hygiene courses completed. Applicants must have a minimum GPA of 3.0 and demonstrated financial need of at least $1,500.
Target Student: College, Graduate and Adult students.
Amount: $2,000
Number of Awards: Varies
Based on Financial Need: Yes
Deadline: February
Applications are available online beginning in October. A completed application and essay are required to apply.

---

(344) Dr. Harold Kerzner Scholarship

Project Management Institute Educational Foundation

14 Campus Boulevard
Newton Square, PA 19073

Phone: 610-356-4600
Fax: 610-356-0357
Email: pmief@pmi.org
URL:http://www.pmi.org/pmief/scholar
ship/scholarship-Kerzner.asp

Goal: To assist project management students.
Eligibility: Applicants must be current or entering undergraduate or graduate students planning to major in project management.
Target Student: College and Adult students.
Amount: $7,500
Number of Awards: 4
Based on Financial Need: No
Deadline: June
Applications are available online. A completed application, resume, three letters of recommendation, two essays and transcripts are required to apply.

(345) Dr. James L. Lawson Memorial Scholarship

American Radio Relay League Foundation
225 Main Street
Newington, CT 06111

Phone: 860-594-0397
Fax: 860-594-0259
Email: foundation@arrl.org
URL: http://www.arrlf.org

Goal: To assist ham radio operators with educational expenses.

Eligibility: Applicants must have a general ham radio license or higher and be attending college or be residents of one of the New England states (Connecticut, Maine, Massachusetts, New Hampshire, Rhode Island or Vermont) or New York and be working towards a bachelors or graduate degree in electronics, communications or a related field.
Target Student: College, Graduate and Adult students.
Amount: $500
Number of Awards: 1
Based on Financial Need: No
Deadline: February
Applications are available online.

(346) Dr. Randy Pausch Scholarship Fund

Academy of Interactive Arts and Sciences
c/o Randy Pausch Scholarship
23622 Calabasas Suite 220
Calabasas, CA 91302

Phone: 818-876-0826
Fax: 818-876-0850
Email: gabriel@interactive.org
URL: http://www.interactive.org

Goal: To assist students pursuing careers in game design, development and production.
Eligibility: Applicants must be full-time students who are currently in an accredited college or university as an undergraduate or graduate student. Applicants must have a 3.3 GPA or higher and plan to enter the video game design industry.
Target Student: College, Graduate and Adult students.
Amount: $2,500
Number of Awards: 4
Based on Financial Need: No
Deadline: June

Applications are available online. A completed application, verification of enrollment, personal statement, two letters of recommendation and transcript are required to apply.

(347) Dr. Wynetta A. Frazier Sister to Sister Scholarship

National Hook-Up of Black Women Inc.
1809 East 71st Street
Suite 205
Chicago, IL 60649

Phone: 773-667-7061
Fax: 773-667-7064
Email: nhbwdir@aol.com
URL: http://www.nhbwinc.com

Goal: To assist women who are going back to school without support of family or spouse.
Eligibility: Applicants must have taken a break in their education because of employment, caring for children or because of a financial issue.
Target Student: Graduate and Adult students.
Amount: $500
Number of Awards: 2
Based on Financial Need: No
Deadline: Varies
Applications are available by mail.

(348) Dream Deferred Essay Contest on Civil Rights in the Mideast

Hands Across the Mideast Support Alliance
263 Huntington Avenue #315
Boston, MA 02115

Phone: 617-266-0080
Email: info@hamsaweb.org
URL: http://www.hamsaweb.org/essay

Goal: To acknowledge American and Middle Eastern youth who have written an outstanding essay on civil rights in the Middle East.
Eligibility: Applicants must be 25 years old or younger at the time of the entry deadline. They must reside in an Arab League nation, the U.S., Afghanistan or Iran. An essay of between 600 and 1,500 words is required on the civil rights topic given in the entry rules. The award selection is based on the strength and relevance of the essay.
Target Student: Junior high and younger, High school, College and Graduate school students.
Amount: $500 to $2,000
Number of Awards: 10
Based on Financial Need: No
Deadline: May
Applications are available online. A completed application and essay are required to apply.

(349) Dumbarton Oaks Fellowships

Dumbarton Oaks
1703 32nd Street NW
Washington, DC 20007

Phone: 202-339-6401
Fax: 202-339-6419
Email: dumbartonoaks@doaks.org
URL: http://www.doaks.org

Goal: To assist scholars of Byzantine studies, Pre-Columbian studies and a garden and landscape studies with fellowships.

Eligibility: Applicants must have a doctorate (or similar terminal degree) or have established themselves in their field and wish to pursue independent research or expect to have earned their Ph.D. before taking reisdence at Dumbarton Oaks. Fellowships are available in the following areas: Byzantine Studies, Pre-Columbian, and garden and landscape studies.
Target Student: Graduate and Adult students.
Amount: Up to $47,000 plus health benefits.
Number of Awards: Varies
Based on Financial Need: No
Deadline: November
To apply, submit ten complete, collated sets of the application letter, proposal, personal and professional data and three letters of recommendation.

(350) DuPont Challenge Science Essay Award

DuPont
The DuPont Challenge
Science Essay Awards Program, c/o
General Learning Communications
900 Skokie Boulevard, Suite 200
Northbrook, IL 60062

Phone: 847-205-3000
Fax:
Email:
URL: http://thechallenge.dupont.com

Goal: To promote the study of science.
Eligibility: Applicants must be full-time students between 7th grade and 12th grade in the U.S. and Canada. Applicants must write a 700 to 1,000 word essay about a scientific or technological development of interest to them.
Target Student: Junior high students or younger and High school students.
Amount: $200 - $5,000
Number of Awards: Varies

Based on Financial Need: No
Deadline: January
Applications are available online.

(351) Dutch and Ginger Arver Scholarship

Aircraft Electronics Association
4217 South Hocker
Independence, MO 64055

Phone: 816-373-6565
Fax: 816-478-3100
Email: info@aea.net
URL: http://www.aea.net

Goal: To assist students who are pursuing a career in avionics or aircraft repair.
Eligibility: Applicants must be high school seniors or college students who are planning or currently attend an accredited school in avionics or aircraft repair.
Target Student: High school, College or Adult students.
Amount: $1,000
Number of Awards: 1
Based on Financial Need: No
Deadline: February
Applications are available by contacting the organization.

(352) Dwight D. Gardner Scholarship

Institute of Industrial Engineers
3577 Parkway Lane
Suite 200
Norcross, GA 30092

Phone: 800-494-0460
Fax: 770-441-3295
Email: bcameron@iienet.org
URL: http://www.iienet2.org

Goal: To assist undergraduate members.

Eligibility: Applicants must be undergraduate students currently enrolled in the United States, Canada or Mexico in an accredited industrial engineering program and be active members. Students must be nominated for this award.
Target Student: College and Adult students.
Amount: $3,000
Number of Awards: 3
Based on Financial Need: Yes
Deadline: November
Nomination information is available online.

(353) E.J. Sierieja Memorial Fellowship

Institute of Industrial Engineers
3577 Parkway Lane
Suite 200
Norcross, GA 30092

Phone: 800-494-0460
Fax: 770-441-3295
Email: bcameron@iienet.org
URL: http://www.iienet2.org

Goal: To assist graduate students working on advanced studies in transportation.
Eligibility: Applicants must be full-time graduate students majoring in transportation and be active members with a GPA of 3.4 or higher. Students must be nominated for the award. The award is based on character, leadership, academics, potential service to the industrial engineering profession and financial need.
Target Student: Graduate and Adult students.
Amount: $700
Number of Awards: 1
Based on Financial Need: Yes
Deadline: November
Nomination information is available online.

(354) Earl Anthony Memorial Scholarships

United States Bowling Congress
5301 S. 76th Street
Greendale, WI 53129

Phone: 800-514-2695 x3168
Fax:
Email: smart@bowl.com
URL: http://www.bowl.com

Goal: To reward USBC members for community involvement and academic achievements.
Eligibility: Applicants must be USBC members who are high school sensiors or current college students. A GPA of 2.5 of higher is required. The award selection is based on community involvement, academic achievement and financial need.
Target Student: High school, College and Adult students.
Amount: $5,000
Number of Awards: 5
Based on Financial Need: Yes
Deadline: May
Applications are available online.

(355) Earl I. Anderson Scholarship

American Radio Relay League Foundation
225 Main Street
Newington, CT 06111

Phone: 860-594-0397
Fax: 860-594-0259
Email: foundation@arrl.org
URL: http://www.arrlf.org

Goal: To assist ham radio operators with educational expenses.
Eligibility: Applicants must be residents of Forida, Illinois, Indiana or Michigan with any level of ham radio license and be members of ARRL and majoring in electronic engineering or a related field.

Target Student: College, Graduate or Adult students.
Amount: $1,250
Number of Awards: 3
Based on Financial Need: No
Deadline: February
Applications are available online.

---

(356) Earl Nightengale Scholarship

National Speakers Association
1500 S. Priest Drive
Attn: Scholarship Committee
Tempe, AZ 85281

Phone: 480-968-2552
Fax: 480-968-0911
URL: http://www.nsaspeaker.org

Goal: To encourage the study of professional speaking.
Eligibility: Applicants must be entering full-time undergraduate juniors, seniors, or graduate students pursuing careers as professional speakers.
Target Student: College, Graduate and Adult students.
Amount: $5,000
Number of Awards: 1
Based on Financial Need: No
Deadline: June
Applications are available online.

---

(357) East Asia and Pacific Summer Institutes

National Science Foundation East Asia and Pacfic Summer Institutes
1818 N Street NW
Suite T-50
Washington, DC 20036

Phone: 866-501-2922
Email: eapsi@asee.org
URL: http://www.nsfsi.org

Goal: To develop U.S. scientists and engineers knowledgeable about the Asian and Pacific regions.
Eligibility: Applicants must be U.S. graduate students who are enrolled in a research-oriented master's or Ph.D. program or college graduates who are enrolled in a bachelor's/master's program at a U.S. college or university studying science and engineering research. The award provides a summer research experience in Australia, China, Japan, Korea, New Zealand, Singapore or Taiwan, a stipend of $5,000, airfare, living expenses and an orientation in Washington D.C.
Target Student: Graduate and Adult students.
Amount: $5,000 plus living expenses and airfare.
Number of Awards: 200
Based on Financial Need: No
Deadline: November
Applications are available online. A completed application, project description and summary, biographical information, two letters of recommendation, and supplementary documents are required to apply.

---

(358) Ecolab Scholarship Competition

American Hotel and Lodging Educational Foundation (AH&LEF)
1201 New York Avenue NW
Suite 600
Washington, DC 20005

Phone: 202-289-3188
Fax: 202-289-3199
Email: chammond@ahlef.org
URL: http://www.ahlef.org

Goal: To assist students pursuing degrees in hospitality management.
Eligibility: Applicants must be enrolled or plan to enroll full-time in a two or four-year college or university.

Target Student: High school, College or Adult students.
Amount: $1,000 - $2,000
Number of Awards: Varies
Based on Financial Need: No
Deadline: May
Applications are available online.

---

(359) Ed Bradley Scholarship

Radio Television Digital News Association
4121 Plank Road #512
Fredericksburg, VA 22407

Phone: 202-659-6510
Fax: 202-223-4007
Email: staceys@rtdna.org
URL: http://www.rtdna.org

Goal: To acknowledge achievements in electronic journalism.
Eligibility: Applicants must be full-time college sophomores or higher with at least one full academic year remaining. Applicants can be any college major, but they must have the intent to have a career in television or radio news.
Target Student: College and Adult students.
Amount: $10,000
Number of Awards: 1
Based on Financial Need: No
Deadline: May
Applications are available online.

---

(360) Edmond A. Metzger Scholarship

American Radio Relay League Foundation
225 Main Street
Newington, CT 06111

Phone: 860-594-0397
Fax: 860-594-0259
Email: foundation@@arrl.org
URL: http://www.arrlf.org

Goal: To assist ham radio operators with educational expenses.
Eligibility: Applicants must have at least a novice ham radio license and be undergraduate or graduate students in electrical engineering as well as residents of and attending college in the ARRL Central Division and be ARRL members.
Target Student: College, Graduate and Adult students.
Amount: $500
Number of Awards: 1
Based on Financial Need: No
Deadline: February
Applications are available online.

---

(361) Edna Meudt Memorial Award and the Florence Kahn Memorial Award

National Federation of State Poetry Societies
NFSPS College/University-Level Competition
N. Colwell Snell
P.O. Box 520698
Salt Lake City, UT 84152

Phone: 801-484-3113
Email: sbsenior@juno.com
URL: http://www.nfsps.com

Goal: To acknowledge the importance of poetry on the culture of the nation.
Eligibility: Appicants must be college students of any level.
Target Student: College and Adult students.
Amount: $500
Number of Awards: 2
Based on Financial Need: No
Deadline: February
Applications are available online.

---

(363) Educational Advacement Foundation Financial Needs Scholarship

Alpha Kappa Educational Advacement
Foundation Inc.
5656 S. Stony Island Avenue
Chicago, IL 60637

Phone: 800-653-6528
Fax: 773-947-0277
Email: akaeaf@akaef.net
URL: http://www.akaeaf.org

Goal: To assist students with a financial
need.
Eligibility: Applicants must be full time
college students in their sophomore year or
higher with a 2.5 GPA or higher. They
must have demonstrated community
service and a financial need.
Target Student: College, Graduate and
Adult students.
Amount: Varies
Number of Awards: Varies
Based on Financial Need: Yes
Deadline: April for Undergraduates and
August for Graduate students.
Applications are available online. A
completed application, personal statement
and three letters of recommendation are
required to apply.

(362) Educational Advacement Foundation Merit Scholarship

Alpha Kappa Educational Advacement
Foundation Inc.
5656 S. Stony Island Avenue
Chicago, IL 60637

Phone: 800-653-6528
Fax: 773-947-0277
Email: akaeaf@akaef.net
URL: http://www.akaeaf.org

Goal: To assist students for community
service and involvement.

Eligibility: Applicants must be full time
college students in their sophomore year or
higher with a 3.0 GPA or higher. They
must have demonstrated community
service.
Target Student: College, Graduate and
Adult students.
Amount: Varies
Number of Awards: Varies
Based on Financial Need: No
Deadline: April for Undergraduates and
August for Graduate students.
Applications are available online. A
completed application, personal statement
and three letters of recommendation are
required to apply.

(364) Educational Scholarship Award/George and Rosemary Murray Scholarship Award

25th Infantry Division Association (TIDA)
P.O. Box 7
Flourtown, PA 19031

URL: http://www.25thida.com

Goal: To assist the members of the 25th
Infantry Division Association and their
children and grandchildren of active and
former members of the association.
Eligibility: Applicants must be high
school seniors who are the child or
grandchild of an active association
member, the child of a member who died
during combat or an active member who
will be discharged before the end of the
award year. Applicants must be entering a
four-year college or university as a
freshman. The award selection is based on
future plans, school activities, interests,
financial status and academic achievement.
Target Student: High school students.
Amount: Up to $1,500
Number of Awards: Varies
Based on Financial Need: Yes
Deadline: February

Applications are available throughout the year in Tropic Lightening Flashes, the 25th Infantry Division Association's quarterly newsletter.

(365) Edward J. Dulls Scholarship

ASM International
9639 Kinsman Road
Materials Park, OH 44073

Phone: 440-338-5151
Fax: 440-338-4634
Email:jeane.deatherage@asminternational.org
URL:http://www.asminternational.org/portal/site/www/foundation/scholarships

Goal: To assist material science engineering students.
Eligibility: Applicants must be undergraduate juniors or seniors who are majoring in materials science engineering and be Material Advantage student members.
Target Student: College and Adult students.
Amount: $1,500
Number of Awards: 1
Scholarship can be renewed.
Based on Financial Need: No
Deadline: May
Application information is available online. A completed application, essay, transcript, photo and two letters of recommendation are required to apply.

(366) Edward J. Nell Memorial Scholarships in Journalism

Quill and Scroll Society
University of Iowa School of Journalism and Mass Communications
100 Adler Journalism Building
Iowa City, IA 52242

Phone: 319-335-3457

Fax: 319-335-3989
Email: quill-scroll@uiowa.edu
URL: http://www.uiowa.edu/~quill-sc/

Goal: To assist high school journalists improve their skills.
Eligibility: Applicants must be national winners in the Yearbook Excellence Contest or the International Witing/Photography Contest.
Target Student: High school students.
Amount: Varies
Number of Awards: Varies
Based on Financial Need: No
Deadline: May
Applications are available online.

(367) Eight and Forty Lung and Respiratory Nursing Scholarship Fund

American Legion
Attn: Americanism and Children and Youth Division
P.O. Box 1055
Indianapolis, IN 46206

Phone: 317-630-1249
Fax: 317-630-1369
Email: acy@legion.org
URL: http://www.legion.org

Goal: To assist registered nurses.
Eligibility: Applicants must plan to work full-time in hospitals, clinics or health departments in a position related to lung and respiratory control.
Target Student: College, Graduate and Adult students.
Amount: $3,000
Number of Awards: Varies
Based on Financial Need: No
Deadline: May
Applications are available by written request.

(368) Eileen J. Garrett Scholarship

Parapsychology Foundation
P.O. Box 1562
New York, NY 10021

Phone: 212-628-1550
Fax: 212-628-1559
Email: office@parapsychology.org
URL: http://www.parapsychology.org

Goal: To assist a student studying parapsychology at an accredited college or university.
Eligibility: Applicants must be undergraduate or graduate students studying parapsychology. An applicantion, writing samples about parapsycology and three references are required to apply.
Target Student: College, Graduate and Adult students.
Amount: $3,000
Number of Awards: 1
Based on Financial Need: No
Deadline: July
Applications are available online or by email.

(369) Electric Document Systems Foundation Scholarship Awards

Electronic Document Systems Foundation
1845 Precinct Line Road, Suite 212
Hurst, TX 76054

Phone: 817-849-1145
Fax: 817-849-1185
Email: info@edsf.org
URL: http://www.edsf.org

Goal: To assist students pursuing careers in document management and communication.

Eligibility: Applicants must be full-time students pursuing a career in the preparation, production, or distribution of documents. Areas of study include marketing, graphic arts, e-commerced, imaging science, printing, web authoring, electronic publishing, computer science, telecomunications or business.
Target Student: College, Graduate and Adult students.
Amount: $500 - $5,000
Number of Awards: Varies
Based on Financial Need: No
Deadline: May
Applications are available online.

(370) Elizabeth Greenshields Foundation Grants

Elizabeth Greenshields Foundation
1814 Sherbrooke Street West Suite #1
Montreal
Quebec, Canada H3H 1E4

Phone: 514-937-9225
Fax: 514-937-0141
URL: http://www.elizabethgreenshieldsfoundation.org/main.html

Goal: To develop and appreciation of painting, drawing, sculpture and graphic arts.
Eligibility: Applicants must have started, or completed training at a school of art, and/or shown through their work and future plans a commitment ot make art a lifetime career. Applicants must be in the early stages of their careers.
Target Student: High school, College, Graduate and Adult students.
Amount: CAD $15,000 - $18,000
Number of Awards: Varies
Based on Financial Need: No
Deadline: Rolling
Applications are available by phone or by writing.

(371) Elson T. Killam Memorial Scholarship

New England Water Works Association
125 Hopping Brook Road
Holliston, MA 07146

Phone: 508-893-7979
Email: tmacelhaney@preloadinc.com
URL: http://www.newwa.org

Goal: To assist civil and environmental engineering students who are members of the New England Water Works Association.
Eligibility: Applicants must be NEWWA members and enrolled in a civil or environmental engineering degree program.
Target Student: College and Adult students.
Amount: $1,500
Number of Awards: 1
Based on Financial Need: No
Deadline: April
Applications are available online. A completed application, letter of recommendation and transcripts are required to apply.

(372) ENA Foundation Undergraduate Scholarship

Emergency Nurses Association
915 Lee Street
Des Plains, IL 60016

Phone: 847-460-4100
Fax: 847-460-4004
Email: foundation@ena.org
URL: http://www.ena.org

Goal: To help promote research and education in emergency care.

Eligibility: Applicants must be nurses working towards bachelors degrees in nursing and must be ENA members for at least 12 months.
Target Student: College and Adult students.
Amount: $3,000
Number of Awards: 3
Based on Financial Need: No
Deadline: June
Applications are available online. A completed application, goals statement, references and transcript are required to apply.

(373) Engineering Undergraduate Award

American Society for Nondestructive Testing
1711 Arlingate Lane
P.O. Box 28518
Columbus, OH 43228

Phone: 800-222-2768
Fax: 614-274-6899
Email: sthomas@asnt.org
URL: http://www.asnt.org

Goal: To assist students who are studying nondestructive testing.
Eligibility: Applicants must be undergraduate students who are enrolled in an engineering program specializing in nondestructive testing.
Target Student: College and Adult students.
Amount: $3,000
Number of Awards: Up to 3
Based on Financial Need: No
Deadline: December
Applications are available online. A completed application, transcript, nomination letter, essay and three letters of recommendation are required to apply.

(374) EOD Memorial Scholarship

Explosive Ordnance Disposal (EOD)
Memorial Committee
P.O. Box 594
Niceville, FL 32588

Phone: 850-729-2401
Fax: 850-729-2401
Email: admin@eodmemorial.org
URL: http://www.eodmemorial.org

Goal: To assist those associated to Explosive Ordnance Disposal technicians.
Eligibility: Applicants must be accepted or enrolled as full-time undergraduates in a U.S. two-year, four-year or vocational school. Applicants must be family members of an active duty, guard/reserve, retired or deceased EOD tech. Award selection is based on academic achievement, community involvement and financial need.
Target Student: High school, College and Adult students.
Amount: Varies
Number of Awards: Varies
Based on Financial Need: No
Deadline: March
Applications are available online.

---

(375) Esther R. Sawyer Research Award

Institute of Internal Auditors Research Foundation
247 Maitland Avenue
Altamonte Springs, FL 32701

Phone: 407-937-1100
Fax: 407-937-1101
Email: research@theiia.org
URL: http://www.theiia.org

Goal: To assist international auditing students.

Eligibility: Applicants must be accepted or enrolled in a graduate program in internal auditing at an IIA-endorsed college or have taken undergraduate internal auditing courses at an IIA-endorsed school and are purusing a graduate degree at any school in internal auditing or business. Applicants must write an essay on a topic related to modern internal auditing.
Target Student: College, Graduate and Adult students.
Amount: Up to $5,000
Number of Awards: 1
Based on Financial Need: No
Deadline: March
Application information is available online.

---

(376) Ethnic Minority and Women's Enhancement Scholarship

National Collegiate Athletic Association
700 W. Washington Street
P.O. Box 6222
Indianapolis, IN 46206

Phone: 317-917-6222
Fax: 371-917-6888
Email: ahightower@ncaa.org
URL:
https://web1.ncaa.org/epps/exec/appform

Goal: To assist minority and female students in intercollegiate athletics with educational expenses.
Eligibility: Applicants must be planning to attend a sports administration program and plan to pursue a career in interecollegiate atheltics (coaching, traning or administration).
Target Student: College, Graduate and Adult students.
Amount: $6,000
Number of Awards: 26
Based on Financial Need: No
Deadline: December
Applications are available online.

(377) Eugene Gene Sallee, W4YFR Memorial Scholarship

American Radio Relay League Foundation
225 Main Street
Newington, CT 06111

Phone: 860-594-0397
Fax: 860-594-0289
Email: foundation@arrl.org
URL: http://www.arrlf.org

Goal: To assist students from Georgia involved in amateur radio.
Eligibility: Applicants must have an FCC amateur radio license of Tehcnician Plus or higher and have a 3.0 or higher GPA.
Target Student: High school, College and Adult students.
Amount: $500
Number of Awards: 1
Based on Financial Need: No
Deadline: February
Applications are available online.

(378) Eugene S. Kropf Scholarship

University Aviation Association Eugene S. Kroph Scholarship
Kevin R. Kuhlmann, Professor of Aviation and Aerospace Science
Metropolitan State College of Denver
Campus Box 30, P.O. Box 173362
Denver, CO 80217

Phone: 334-844-2434
Fax: 334-844-2432
URL: http://www.uaa.aero

Goal: To assist students who are studying an aviation-related curriculum.
Eligibility: Applicants must be U.S. citizens enrolled in an aviation program at a two- or four- year UAA member college or university. Applicants must have a 3.0 or higher GPA.

Target Student: College and Adult students.
Amount: $500
Number of Awards: 1
Based on Financial Need: No
Deadline: May
Applications are available online.

(379) Excellence in Engineering, Mathematics or the Sciences Scholarship

Institute for the International Education of Students
33 North LaSalle Street
15th Floor
Chicago, IL 60602

Phone: 800-995-2300
Fax: 312-944-1750
Email: info@iesabroad.org
URL: http://www.iesabroad.org

Goal: To assist students majoring in engineering, mathematics or another science.
Eligibility: Applicants must be in an IES study abroad program with a GPA of 3.3 or higher.
Target Student: College and Adult students.
Amount: Up to $3,000
Number of Awards: Varies
Based on Financial Need: No
Deadline: October
Applications are available online. A completed application, transcript, personal statement and letter of recommendation are required to apply.

(380) Excellence of Scholarship Award

National Council for Geographic Education
Jacksonville State University
206-A Martin Hall
700 Pelham Road North

Jacksonville, AL 36265

Phone: 256-782-5293
Fax: 256-782-5336
Email: ncge@jsu.edu
URL: http://www.ncge.org

Goal: To acknowledge outstandingg students of geography.
Eligibility: Applicants must be high school sensiors planning to major in geography. Applicants must be nominated by NCGE members.
Target Student: Junior high or younger and High school students.
Amount: Varies
Number of Awards: Varies
Based on Financial Need: No
Deadline: May
Nomination information is available online.

(381) Executive Women International Scholarship Program

Executive Women International
515 South 700 East
Suite 2A
Salt Lake City, UT 84102

Phone: 801-355-2800
Fax: 801-355-2852
Email: ewi@ewiconect.com
URL: http://www.executivewomen.org

Goal: To assist high school students with their educational goals.
Eligibility: Applicants must be high school juniors who are planning to pursue a four year degree at an accredited college or university.
Target Student: High school students.
Amount: $1,000-$5,000
Number of Awards: Varies
Based on Financial Need: No
Deadline: April

Applications are available by request from the local chapter of the Executive Women International.

(382) F.W. "Belch" Beichley Scholarship

American Society of Mechanical Engineers
Three Park Avenue
New York, NY 10016

Phone: 800-843-2763
Fax: 973-882-1717
Email: infocentral@asme.org
URL: http://www.asme.org

Goal: To assist mechanical engineering students.
Eligibility: Applicants must be ASME student members who are enrolled in an accredited mechanical engineering bachelors degree program. The award is available for the student's junior or senior year.
Target Student: College and Adult students.
Amount: $2,500
Number of Awards: 1
Based on Financial Need: Yes
Deadline: March
Applications are available online.

(383) FA Davis Student Awad

American Association of Medical Assistants' Endowment
20 North Wacker Drive
Suite 1575
Chicago, IL 60606

Phone: 800-228-2262
Email: info@aama-ntl.org
URL: http://www.aama-ntl.org

Goal: To acknowledge aspiring medical assistants for ad design.

Eligibility: Applicants must be enrolled in and have already completed one quarter or semester in a postsecondary medical assisting program. Applicants must create one ad that supports the medical assisting profession, the CMA credential and the AAMA.
Target Student: College, Graduate and Adult students.
Amount: $1,000
Number of Awards: 1
Based on Financial Need: No
Deadline: July
Applications are available online.

(384) FALCON - Full Year Asian Language Concentration

FALCON Program
Department of Asian Studies, Cornell University
338 Rockefeller Hall
Ithaca, NY 14853

Phone: 607-255-6457
Fax: 607-255-1345
Email: falcon@cornell.edu
URL: http://lrc.cornell.edu/falcon

Goal: To assist undergraduate and graduate students desiring long-term instruction in Chinese and Japanese.
Eligibility: The program is offered through Cornell University and students receive Cornell credit.
Target Student: College, Graduate and Adult students.
Amount: Varies
Number of Awards: Varies
Based on Financial Need: No
Deadline: March
Applications are available online.

(385) Families of Freedom Scholarship Fund

Family Travel Forum

891 Amsterdam Avenue
New York, NY 10025

Phone: 212-665-6124
Fax: 212-665-6136
Email: editorial@travelbigo.com
URL: http://www.travelbigo.com

Goal: To award college bound students who have written the best essay.
Eligibility: Applicants must be members of the Travelbigo.com online community and be between 13 and 18 years old. They must be in grades 8 to 12 and attending a U.S. or Canadian high school or junior high school (homeschools are included). They must submit an original essay about a significant travel experience that occured in the last three years and that happened when the applicant was 12 to 18 years old. The award is based on the essay's originanlity, quality of storytelling and grammar.
Target Student: Junior high and High school students.
Amount: $200 to $1,000
Number of Awards: 3
Based on Financial Need: No
Deadline: August
Application information is available online. A completed submission form and essay are required to apply.

(386) Federal Junior Duck Stamp Program and Scholarship Competition

U.S. Fish and Wildlife Service
Junior Duck Stamp Program
4401 N. Fairfax Drive
MBSP-4070
Arlington, VA 22203

Phone: 703-358-2073
Email: duckstamps@fws.gov
URL: http://www.fws.gov/juniorduck

Goal: To encourage the painting of waterfowl and learn about habitat and wildlife conservation.
Eligibility: Applicants must be in Kindergarten to 12th grade, U.S. citizens or legal residents, and submit their artwork to their local or state department.
Target Student: Junior high and younger, High school students.
Amount: $500 - $5,000
Number of Awards: Up to 100
Based on Financial Need: No
Deadline: March
Applications are available online.

---

(387) Fellowship Award

Damon Runyon Cancer Research Foundation
675 Third Avenue
25th Floor
New York, NY 10017

Phone: 212-455-0520
Fax: 212-455-0529
Email: awards@damonrunyon.org
URL: http://www.damonrunyon.org

Goal: To assist the training of postdoctoral scientists as they begin their career in research.
Eligibility: Applicants must have completed one of the following: M.D, Ph.D., M.D./Ph.D., D.D.S. or D.V.M. The award is a three year award and the research must be conducted at a university, hospital, or research institution.
Target Student: Graduate and Adult students.
Amount: $50,000-$60,000
Number of Awards: Varies
Based on Financial Need: No
Deadline: March
Applications are available online. A completed application, CV, research proposal, four letters of recommendation, biography and degree are required to apply.

(388) Fellowship in Aerospace History

American Historical Association
400 A Street SE
Washington, DC 20003

Phone: 202-544-2422
Fax: 202-544-8307
Email: info@historians.org
URL: http://www.historians.org

Goal: To assist students with funding for research related to aerospace history.
Eligibility: Applicants must have a doctorate in history or a related field or be enrolled ina doctorate program with all the coursework completed.
Target Student: Graduate and Adult students.
Amount: $20,000
Number of Awards: At least 1
Based on Financial Need: No
Deadline: March
Applications are available online.

---

(389) Fellowships for Regular Program in Greece

American School of Classical Studies at Athens
6-8 Charlton Street
Princeton, NJ 08540

Phone: 609-683-0800
Fax: 608-683-0800
Email: ascsa@ascsa.org
URL: http://www.ascsa.edu.gr

Goal: To allow graduate students from North American colleges to study the classics and related fields (literature, art, history, archaeology, philosophy of Greece and the Greek World).

Eligibility: Applicants must have completed one to two years of graduate study and be working towards and advanced degree in classical and ancient Mediterranean studies or a related field and taken exams in ancient Greek language, history and literature or archaeology. Applicants must also be able to read French, German, ancient Greek and Latin.
Target Student: Graduate and Adult students.
Amount: $11,500 plus housing, board and other fees.
Number of Awards: Up to 13
Based on Financial Need: No
Deadline: January
Applications are available online.

(390) Fellowships/Grants to Study in Scandinavia

American-Scandinavian Foundation
58 Park Avenue
New York, NY 10016

Phone: 212-879-9779
Email: grants@amscan.org
URL: http://www.amscan.org

Goal: To develop research projects related to Scandinavia.
Eligibility: Applicants must have completed their undergraduate studies and have a research or project requiring a stay in Scandinavia. Some language skills are required.
Target Student: Graduate and Adult students.
Amount: $5,000 - $23,000
Number of Awards: Varies
Scholarship can be renewed.
Based on Financial Need: No
Deadline: November
Applications are available online and by written request.

(391) Ferrous Metallurgy Education Today

Association for Iron and Steel Technology
186 Thorn Hill Road
Warrendale, PA 15086

Phone: 202-452-7143
Fax: 724-814-3001
Email: blakshminarayana@steel.org
URL: http://www.aistfoundation.org

Goal: To increase the number of students studying metallurgy and materials science and to encourage them to pursue careers in the iron and steel industry.
Eligibility: Applicants must be college juniors majoring in mettallurgy or materials science at a university in North America and have demonstrated interest in a career in the iron and steel industry with a 3.0 or higher GPA.
Target Student: College and Adult students.
Amount: $5,000
Number of Awards: 10
Scholarship can be renewed.
Based on Financial Need: No
Deadline: March
Applications are available online.

(392) FFTA Scholarship Competition

Flexographic Technical Association
900 Marconi Avenue
Ronkonkoma, NY 11779

Phone: 631-737-6020
Fax: 631-737-6813
Email: education@flexography.org
URL: http://www.flexography.org

Goal: To develop the flexography industry.

Eligibility: Applicants must be high school seniors planning to attend a college or university or currently enrolled in a college or university with a course of study in flexography and have demonstrated interest in careers in flexography. Applicants must have a GPA of 3.0 or high with skills in graphic communications.
Target Student: High school, College, and Adult students.
Amount: $3,000
Number of Awards: Varies
Scholarship can be renewed.
Based on Financial Need: No
Deadline: March
Applications are available online.

(393) Finlandia Foundation National Student Scholarships Program

Finlandia Foundation
470 W. Walnut Street
Pasadena, CA 91103

Phone: 626-795-2081
Fax: 626-795-6533
Email: ffnoffice@mac.com
URL: http://www.finlandiafoundation.org

Goal: To assist undergraduate and graduate students in Finland and the U.S. in research related to Finnish culture and society.
Eligibility: Applicants must be full time undergraduate or graduate students in the U.S. or Finland who are planning to research Finnish culture in the U.S. Applicants must be sophomores in college or higher and have a GPA of 3.0 or higher. The applicants course of study, financial need, and citizenship are considered when applying.
Target Student: College, Graduate and Adult students.
Amount: Varies
Number of Awards: Varies
Based on Financial Need: Yes
Deadline: February

Applications are available online.

(394) First Cavalry Division Association Scholarship

Foundation of the First Cavalry Division Association
Alumni Of the First Team
302 North Main Street
Copperas Cove, TX 76522

Phone: 254-547-6537
Email: firstcav@1cda.org
URL: http://www.1cda.org

Goal: To assist children of the First Cavalry Division members who have become disabled or who died while serving.
Eligibility: Applicants must be First Cavalry Division troopers who have become totally disabled while serving in the division or active duty members, spouses or children. Applicants can also be the dependents of First Cavalry members who have died while serving.
Target Student: High school, College and Adult students.
Amount: Up to $1,200
Number of Awards: Varies
Based on Financial Need: No
Deadline: Varies
Application information is available by request.

(395) FiSCA Scholarship

Financial Service Centers of America
Attn: FiSCA Scholarship Program
Court Plaza South, East Wing
21 Main Street 1st Floor, P.O. Box 647
Hackensack, NJ 07602

Phone: 201-487-0412
Fax: 201-487-3954
Email: info@fisca.org
URL: http://www.fisca.org

Goal: To assist high school seniors from areas served by FiSCA.
Eligibility: Applicants must be high school seniors. The selection of the award is based on leadership, academic achievement and financial need.
Target Student: High school students.
Amount: At least $2,000
Number of Awards: At least 2
Based on Financial Need: Yes
Deadline: April
Applications are available online.

---

(396) Fisher Broadcasting Scholarships for Minorities

Fisher Communications Inc.
100 4th Avenue N.
Suite 440
Seatle, WA 98109

Phone: 206-404-7000
Email: info@fsci.com
URL: http://www.fsci.com

Goal: To encourage minority students to pursue a career in broadcasting.
Eligibility: Applicants must be college sophomores who are enrolled in broadcasting, marketing or journalism related degrees at a college or technical school. Applicants must be non-white with a 2.5 GPA or higher. Residents outside of Washington, Oregon, Idaho and Montana must attend a college in one of the listed states. Residents of one of these states can attend school and use the award at any school.
Target Student: College and Adult students.
Amount: Varies
Number of Awards: 3
Based on Financial Need: No
Deadline: May
Applications are available online.

(397) Florence C. and Robert H. Lister Fellowship

Crow Canyon Archeological Center
23390 Road K
Cortez, CO 81321

Phone: 800-422-8975
Email: schoolprograms@crowcanyon.org
URL: http://www.crowcanyon.org

Goal: To assist graduate students studying the archeology of American Indian cultures of the Southwest.
Eligibility: Applicants must be enrolled in a North America Ph.D. program with projects based on archaeological, ethnoarchaeological or paleoenvironmental research in the soutwestern U.S. and Northern Mexico.
Target Student: Graduate and Adult students.
Amount: $7,000
Number of Awards: 1
Based on Financial Need: No
Deadline: Varies
Applications are available online.

---

(398) Foundation for Global Scholars General Scholarship

Foundation for Global Scholars
12050 North Pecos Street
Suite 320
Westminster, CO 80234

Phone: 303-502-7256
Email:kbrockwell@foundationforglobalscholars.org
URL:http://www.foundationforglobalscholars.org

Goal: To assist college students from North America study abroad.

Eligibility: Applicants must be U.S. or Canadian students who area at a North American college or university. Applicants must be enrolled in a degree program that will allow for international study and transfer credits to be applied towards the degree.
Target Student: College and Adult students.
Amount: $500 to $1,500
Number of Awards: Varies
Based on Financial Need: No
Deadline: Varies
Applications are available online. A completed application, transcripts and essay are required to apply.

---

(399) Foundation for Neonatal Research and Education Scholarships

Foundation for Neonatal Research and Education
200 East Holly Avenue
Box 56
Ptman, NJ 8071

Phone: 856-256-2343
Fax: 856-589-7463
Email: fnre@ajj.com
URL: http://www.inurse.com/fnre

Goal: To assist practicing neonatal nurses who are pursuing additional education by way of an undergraduate or graduate degree in nursing.
Eligibility: Applicants must be accepted into a Bachelor of Science in Nursing, Master of Science in Nursing, or doctoral degree in nursing or Master's or post Master's nursing program in Business Management or Nursing Administration. Applicants must have a 3.0 or higher GPA and involved in neonatal nursing at the professional level.
Target Student: College, Graduate and Adult students.
Amount: Varies
Number of Awards: Varies

Based on Financial Need: No
Deadline: May
Applications are available online. A completed application, resume, personal statement, verification of enrollement, transcripts and three evaluation letters are required to apply.

---

(400) Foundation for Surgical Technology Advanced Education/Medical Mission Scholarship

Association of Surgical Technologists
6 W. Dry Creek Circle
Littleton, CO 80120

Phone: 800-637-7433
Fax: 303-694-9169
Email: kludwig@ast.org
URL: http://www.ast.org

Goal: To assist practioners with continuing education or medical missionary work.
Eligibility: Applicants must be active AST members.
Target Student: College, Graduate and Adult students.
Amount: Varies
Number of Awards: Varies
Based on Financial Need: No
Deadline: December
Applications are available online. An application, documented educational program or missionary work and two letters of recommendation are requried to apply.

---

(401) Foundation for Surgical Technology Scholarships

Association of Surgical Technologists
6 W. Dry Creek Circle
Littleton, CO 80120

Phone: 800-637-7433

Fax: 303-694-9169
Email: kludwig@ast.org
URL: http://www.ast.org

Goal: To assist surgical technology students with continuing education.
Eligibility: Applicants must be enrolled in an accredited surgical technology program with a GPA of 3.0 or higher and be eligible to take the Certified Surgical Technologist exam that is sponsored by the National Board of Surgical Technology and Surgical Assisting.
Target Student: College and Adult students.
Amount: Varies
Number of Awards: Varies
Based on Financial Need: No
Deadline: March
Applications are available online. A completed application, transcripts, essay and letters of recommendation are required to apply.

(402) Foundation of the National Student Nurses' Association Career Mobility Scholarships

Natoinal Student Nurses' Association
45 Main Street
Suite 606
Brooklyn, NY 11201

Phone: 718-210-0705
Fax: 718-797-1186
Email: nsna@nsna.org
URL: http://www.nsna.org

Goal: To assist pre-nursing and nursing students enrolled in LPN to RN, RN to BSN and RN to MSN programs.
Eligibility: Applicants must be pre-nursing or nursing students working on a LPN ot RN, RN to BSN or RN to MSN degree.
Target Student: College, Graduate and Adult students.
Amount: $1,000 - $2,500

Number of Awards: Varies
Based on Financial Need: No
Deadline: January
Applications are available online.

(403) Foundation of the National Student Nurses' Association Specialty Scholarship

National Student Nurses' Association
45 Main Street
Suite 606
Brooklyn, NY 11201

Phone: 718-210-0750
Fax: 718-797-1186
Email: nsna@nsna.org
URL: http://www.nsna.org

Goal: To assist nursing students pursuing careers in specialized areas.
Eligibility: Applicants must be nursing students who are interested in focusing on a specialized area of practice.
Target Student: College and Adult students.
Amount: $2,000
Number of Awards: Varies
Based on Financial Need: No
Deadline: January
Applications are available online.

(404) Fountainhead Essay Contest

Ayn Rand Institute Fountainhead Essay Contest
Department W
P.O. Box 57044
Irvine, CA 92619

Phone: 949-222-6550
Fax: 949-222-6558
Email: essay@aynrand.org
URL: http://www.aynrand.org

Goal: To awknowledge high school students who've demonstrated an understanding of Ayn Rand's novel The Fountainhead.

Eligibility: Applicants must be high school juniors or senios and submit an essay that is 800 to 1,600 words. The winning essayist must show an outstanding understanding of the philosophic and psychological meaning of The Fountainhead.

Target Student: High school students.

Amount: $50 - $10,000

Number of Awards: 236

Based on Financial Need: No

Deadline: April

Applications are available online.

---

(405) FOWA Scholarship for Outdoor Communications

Florida Outdoor Writers Association
24 NW 33rd Court
Suite A
Gainsville, FL 32706

Phone: 352-284-1763
Email: execdir@fowa.org
URL: http://www.fowa.org

Goal: To assist students who plan to go into the field of outdoor communications.

Eligibility: Applicants must be students at a college or university in Florida or a student from any school whose application has been endorsed by a FOWA member or faculty advisor. Applicant must have a career goal that includes communicating love and appreciation for hunting, fishing or other outdoor activities. Selection for this award is based on an essay, faculty advisor or FOWA member recommendation, scholarship, and extracurricular activities.

Target Student: High school, College and Adult students.

Amount: $500-$1,000

Number of Awards: Varies

Based on Financial Need: No
Deadline: May

Applications are available online. To apply applicants must submit a cover page, essay, resume and letter of recommendation.

---

(406) Frances M. Schwartz Fellowship

American Numismatic Society
75 Varick Street
Floor 11
New York, NY 10013

Phone: 212-571-4479
Fax: 212-571-4479
Email: info@numismatics.org
URL: http://www.numismatics.org

Goal: To provide fellowships to support the study of numismatics and museum methodology at the American Numismatic Society.

Eligibility: Applicants must have a B.A. or equivalent.

Target Student: Graduate and Adult students.

Amount: Up to $2,000

Number of Awards: Varies

Based on Financial Need: No

Deadline: March

Applications are available online or by mail.

---

(407) Francis Walton Memorial Scholarship

American Radio Relay League Foundation
225 Main Street
Newington, CT 06111

Phone: 860-594-0397
Fax: 860-594-0259
Email: foundation@arrl.org
URL: http://www.arrlf.org

Goal: To assist ham radio operators with their education expenses.

Eligibility: Applicants must be certified at five words per minute, be residents of the ARRI Central Division (Illinois, Indiana, or Wisconsin) and pursue a bachelor's or graduate degree at a regioinally accredited college or university.
Target Student: High school, College, Graduate or Adult students.
Amount: $500
Number of Awards: 1
Based on Financial Need: No
Deadline: February
Applications are available online and must be mailed in.

---

(408) Francis X. Crowley Scholarship

New England Water Works Association
125 Hopping Brook Road
Holliston, MA 01746

Phone: 508-893-7979
Email: tmacelhaney@preloadinc.com
URL: http://www.newwa.org

Goal: To assist students studying civil enginnering, environmental engineering and business management.
Eligibility: Applicants must be student members New England Water Works Association and be civil engineering, environmental engineering or business management majors.
Target Student: College and Adult students
Amount: $3,000
Number of Awards: 1
Based on Financial Need: No
Deadline: April
Applications are available online. A completed application, essay, transcripts and letter of recommendation are required to apply.

---

(409) Frank and Brennie Morgan Prize for Outstanding Research in Mathematics by an Undergraduate Student

American Mathematical Society and Mathematical Association of America
Dr. Martha J. Siegel, MAA Secretary
Mathematics Department, Towson University
339 Yr, 8000 York Road
Towson, MD 21252

Phone: 410-704-2980
Email: siegel@towson.edu
URL: http://www.ams.org

Goal: To reward an undergraduate student for research in mathematics.
Eligibility: Applicants must be undergraduate students at a college or university in the U.S., Mexico, or Canada and be nominated for the award.
Target Student: College and Adult students.
Amount: $1,200
Number of Awards: 1
Based on Financial Need: No
Deadline: June
Nomination information is available by email.

---

(410) Frank and Dorothy Miller ASME Auxiliary Scholarships

American Society of Mechanical Engineers
Three Park Avenue
New York, NY 10016

Phone: 800-843-2763
Fax: 973-882-1717
Email: info@central@asme.org
URL: http://www.asme.org

Goal: To assist U.S. mechanical engineering and mechanical engineering technology undergraduate students.

Eligibility: Applicants must be U.S. citizens, residents of North Carolina, undergraduate sophomores, juniors or seniors enrolled in an ABET-accredited or equivalent mechanical engineering, mechanical engineering technology or related program at a U.S. college or university. Applicants must be ASME student members.
Target Student: College and Adult students.
Amount: $2,000
Number of Awards: Up to 2
Based on Financial Need: No
Deadline: March
Applications are available through the ASME online scholarship system.

---

(411) Frank Lanza Memorial Scholarship

Phi Theta Kappa Honor Society
1625 Eastover Drive
Jackson, MS 39211

Phone: 601-984-3504
Fax: 601-984-3548
Email: scholarship.programs@ptk.org
URL: http://www.ptk.org

Goal: To assist students with financial need who are working towards associate's degrees in emergency medical services, registered nursing or respiratory care.
Eligibility: Applicants must be enrolled in an associates degree program in respiratory care, emergency medical services or registered nursing at a regionally accredited community or junior college. Applicants must have a GPA of 3.0 or higher, have no disciplinary actions at school or a criminal record, completed more than 50 percent of their program and have demonstrated financial need.
Target Student: College and Adult students.
Amount: $1,000
Number of Awards: Up to 25

Based on Financial Need: Yes
Deadline: October
Applications are available online. A completed application, financial aid information and other supporting documents are required to apply.

---

(412) Frank M. Coda Scholarship

American Society of Heating, Refrigerating and Air-Conditioning Engineers
1791 Tullie Circle, NE
Atlanta, GA 30329

Phone: 404-636-8400
Fax: 404-321-5478
Email: lbenedict@ashrae.org
URL: http://www.ashrae.org

Goal: To assist undergraduate students working towards a career in heating, ventilation, air-conditioning and refrigeration.
Eligibility: Applicants must be current or beginning full-time undergraduate students enrolled in a bachelor's of science, bachelor's of engineering or pre-engineering degree and preparing for a career in HVACR. The applicant must be attending a school with a ASHRAE student branch, accredited by ABET or accredited by a non-U.S. agency that has a Memorandum of Understanding with ABET or the Washington Accord. Applicants must have a 3.0 GPA or higher and be in the top 30% of their class.
Target Student: High school, College and Adult students.
Amount: $5,000
Number of Awards: 1
Scholarship can be renewed.
Based on Financial Need: No
Deadline: December
Applications are available online. A completed application, transcripts or proof of enrollment, and two letters of recommendation are required.

---

(413) Frank Newman Leadership Award

Campus Compact
45 Temple Place
Boston, MA 02111

Phone: 617-357-1881
Email: campus@compact.org
URL: http://www.compact.org

Goal: To provide assistance and oppotunties for civic mentoring for students with financial need.
Eligibility: Applicants must attend one of 1,000 Campus Compact member schools and be nominated by the Campus Compact member president. Selection is based on students with demonstrated leadership and interest in civic responsibility.
Target Student: College and Adult students.
Amount: Varies
Number of Awards: Varies
Based on Financial Need: No
Deadline: February
Must be nominated by the Campus Compact member president.

(414) Frank Sarli Memorial Scholarship

National Court Reporters Association
8224 Old Courthouse Road
Vienna, VA 22182

Phone: 800-272-6272
Email: dgaede@ncrahq.org
URL: http://www.ncraonline.org

Goal: To assist court reporting professionals.
Eligibility: Applicants must be in good standing at an approved court reporting school with a GPA of 3.5 or higher and members of the NCRA.

Target Student: College and Adult students
Amount: Varies
Number of Awards: Varies
Based on Financial Need: No
Deadline: February
Applications are available online.

(415) Fraternal Order of Eagles Memorial Foundation

Fraternal Order of Eagles
1623 Gateway Circle S.
Crove City, OH 43123

Phone: 614-883-2200
Fax: 614-883-2201
Email: assistance@foe.com
URL: http://www.foe.com

Goal: To assist the children of Eagles with educational expenses.
Eligibility: Applicants must be the children of Eagles who have died while serving in the military or in the commission of their employment. A 2.0 GPA or higher is required.
Target Student: High school, College and Graduate students.
Amount: $30,000
Number of Awards: Varies
Scholarship can be renewable.
Based on Financial Need: No
Deadline: Varies
Eligible juniors in high school will be send a form and eligible high school seniors will be mailed a scholarship application.

(416) Fred M. Young, Sr./SAE Engineering Scholarship

Society of Automotive Engineers International
400 Commonwealth Drive
Warrendale, PA 15096

Phone: 724-776-4841

Fax: 724-776-0790
Email: scholarships@sae.org
URL: http://www.sae.org

Goal: To assist high school seniors planning to do their undergraduate degree in engineering.
Eligibility: Applicants must be U.S. citizens, high school seniors, have GPA of 3.75 or higher, have SAT or ACT scores that are in the 90th percentile or higher and plan to enroll in an ABET-accredited undergraduate program.
Target Student: High school students.
Amount: $1,000
Number of Awards: 1
Scholarship can be renewed.
Based on Financial Need: No
Deadline: January
Applications are available online. A completed application, transcripts and SAT/ACT test scores are required to apply.

---

(417) Fred R. McDaniel Memorial Scholarship

American Radio Relay League Foundation
225 Main Street
Newington, CT 06111

Phone: 860-594-0397
Fax: 860-594-0259
Email: foundation@arrl.org
URL: http://www.arrlf.org

Goal: To assist ham radio operatorrs with their educational expenses.
Eligibility: Applicants must have a general ham radio license or higher, be residents of and attend a post-secondary school in the FCC Fifth Call District (Texas, Oklahoma, Arkansas, Louisiana, Mississippi or New Mexico) and be majoring in a degree in electronics, communications or a related field.
Target Student: College, Graduate and Adult students.

Amount: $500
Number of Awards: 1
Based on Financial Need: No
Deadline: February
Applications are available online but they must be mailed in.

---

(418) Frederic G. Melcher Scholarship

Association for Library Service to Children
50 E. Huron Street
Chicago, IL 60611

Phone: 800-545-2433
Fax: 312-944-7671
Email: alsc@ala.org
URL: http://www.ala.org/alsc

Goal: To assist students who are pursuing a career in children's literature.
Eligibility: Applicants must be U.S. or Canadian citizens, have the goal of pursing an MLS degree, and plan to work as a children's librarian.
Target Student: College, Graduate and Adult students.
Amount: $6,000
Number of Awards: 2
Based on Financial Need: No
Deadline: March
Applications are available online.

---

(419) Frederick Burkhardt Residential Fellowships for Recently Tenured Scholars

American Council of Learned Societies
633 Third Avenue
New York, NY 10017

Phone: 212-697-1505
Fax: 212-949-8058
Email: sfisher@acls.org
URL: http://www.contemplativemind.org

Goal: To assist scholars who are researching in the humanities field.

Eligibility: Applicants must be recently tenured humanists and must be employed at a U.S. degree-granting institutions during their fellowship.
Target Student: Graduate and Adult students.
Amount: $75,000
Number of Awards: Up to 9
Based on Financial Need: No
Deadline: September
Applications are available online. A completed application, a proposal, a bibliography, a publication list, three letters of recommendation and one institutional statement are required to apply.

---

(420) Freedom of Speech PSA Contest

National Association of Broadcasters
1771 N. Street NW
Washington, DC 20036

Phone: 202-429-5428
Email: nab@nab.org
URL: http://www.nab.org

Goal: To acknowledge part-time and full-time undergraduate and graduate students who can effectively show what freedom of speech means to them and what it plays in the world today in a 30-second public service announcement.
Eligibility: Applicants must be part time or full-time undergraduate or graduate students currently attending a college, university or community college.
Applicants must create a 30 second public service announcement and answer the question, "What does freedom of speech mean to me?" The award is based on the quality of the submission.
Target Student: College, Graduate and Adult students.
Amount: $2,000 to $3,000
Number of Awards: 7
Based on Financial Need: No
Deadline: April
Applications are available online.

(421) Freshman and Sophmore Scholarships

Institute of Food Technologists
525 W. Van Buren
Suite 1000
Chicago, IL 60607

Phone: 312-782-8424
Email: ejplummer@ift.org
URL: http://www.ift.org

Goal: To assist young food scientists who are planning to work in industry, government or academia.
Eligibility: Applicants for the scholarship must be high school seniors or graduates who are outstanding academically and plan to enter college for the first time in an approved food science program.
Applicants for the sophomore scholarship must be oustanding freshman with a GPA of 2.5 or higher in an approved food science/technology program.
Target Student: High school, College and Adult students.
Amount: $1,000
Number of Awards: 32
Based on Financial Need: No
Deadline: March
Applications are available online.

---

(422) Freshman Undergraduate Scholarship

American Meteorological Society
Fellowship and Scholarship Department
45 Beacon Street
Boston, MA 02108

Phone: 617-227-2426 x246
Fax: 617-742-8718
Email: dsampson@ametsoc.org
URL: http://www.ametsoc.org/ams

Goal: To assist high school students pursuing careers in atmospheric and related oceanic and hydrologic sciences.

Eligibility: Applicants must be full-time freshman in the fall following their graduation from high school and major in atmospheric or related oceanic and hydrolgic sciences.

Target Student: High school students.

Amount: $2,500

Number of Awards: Varies
Scholarship can be renewed.

Based on Financial Need: No

Deadline: February
Applications are available online. A completed application, transcript, letter of recommendation and SAT score is required to apply.

---

(423) From Failure to Promise Essay Contest

From Failure to Promise
P.O. Box 352
Olympia Fields, IL 60461

Phone: 708-252-4380
Email: drcmoorer@gmail.com
URL: http://www.fromfailuretopromise.com

Goal: To assist college students.

Eligibility: Applicants must be high school seniors, undergraduate or graduate students who are planning to enroll or enrolled in a U.S. college or university. A GPA of 3.0 or higher is required and applicants must submit an essay about how the book, "From Failure to Promise: An Uncommon Path to Professoriate" has impacted their pursuit of success. The award is based on the essay's orginality, presentation and the quality of the research.

Target Student: High school, College, Graduate and Adult students.

Amount: $500 to $1,500

Number of Awards: 3

Based on Financial Need: No

Deadline: July
Applications are available online. A completed application, transcripts and essay are required.

---

(424) FSF Scholarship Program

Funeral Service Foundation
13625 Bishop's Drive
Brookfield, WI 53005

Phone: 877-402-5900
Fax: 262-789-6977
Email: kbuenger@funeralservicefoundation.org
URL: http://www.funeralservicefoundation.org

Goal: To assist students who are working in the funeral services industry.

Eligibility: Applicants must be undergraduate students who are enrolled in funeral services programs.

Target Student: College and Adult students.

Amount: Varies

Number of Awards: Varies

Based on Financial Need: No

Deadline: Varies
Applications are available online.

---

(425) Fulbright Grants

U.S. Department of State
Officer of Academic Exchange Programs,
Bureau of Educatioanl and Cultural Affairs
U.S. Department of State SA-44
301 4th Street SW, Room 234
Washington, DV 20547

Phone: 202-619-4360
Fax: 202-401-5914
Email: academic@state.gov
URL: http://fulbright.state.gov

Goal: To increase the understanding of people in the United States and people from other countries.
Eligibility:
Target Student: Graduate and Adult students.
Amount: Varies
Number of Awards: Varies
Based on Financial Need: No
Deadline: October
Applications are available online.

---

(426) Fund for American Studies Internships

Fund for American Studies
1706 New Hampshire Avenue NW
Washington, DC 20009

Phone: 800-741-6964
Email: admissions@tfas.org
URL: http://www.dcinternships.org

Goal: To assist student's attending one of the Fund's internship programs.
Eligibility: Each program includes classes, an internship and special events. There are school year and summer programs. Students take classes at Georgetown University and live in Washington, DC. Programs are available in economic systems, political journalism, business and government, philanthropy and international institutes.
Target Student: College and Adult students.
Amount: Vaires
Number of Awards: Varies
Based on Financial Need: No
Deadline: Varies
Applications are available online.

---

(427) Future Engineers Scholarship

Kelly Engineering Resources
999 West Big Beaver Road
Troy, MI 48084

Phone: 248-362-4444
Email: kfirst@kellyservices.com
URL: http://www.kellyengineering.us

Goal: To assist engineering students.
Eligibility: Applicants must be U.S. citizens, or resident aliens, full-time junior or senior students enrolled or accepted into an engineering progra with a 3.0 or higher GPA.
Target Student: College and Adult students.
Amount: $5,000
Number of Awards: 1
Based on Financial Need: No
Deadline: October
Applciations are available online. A completed application, essay, transcript, and two letters of recommendation are required to apply.

---

(428) Future Teacher Scholarship

Journalism Education Association Future Teacher Scholarship
Kansas State University
103 Kedzie Hall
Manhattan, KS 66506

Phone: 330-672-8297
Email: cbowen@kent.edu
URL: http://www.jea.org

Goal: To assist upper level and master's students who are planning to teach scholastic journalism.
Eligibility: Applicants must be majoring in education and focusing on teaching scholastic journalism at the secondary school level.
Target Student: College, Graduate and Adult students.
Amount: $1,000
Number of Awards: Up to 3
Based on Financial Need: No
Deadline: October
Application information is available online.

(429) Gabe A. Harti Scholarship

Air Traffic Control Association
1101 King Street
Suite 300
Alexandria, VA 22134

Phone: 703-299-2430
Fax: 703-299-2437
Email: info@atca.org
URL: http://www.atca.org

Goal: To assist air traffic control students.
Eligibility: Applicants must be enrolled or plan to enroll in a two-year or four-year program in air traffic control as either a part-time or full-time student.
Target Student: High school, College and Adult students.
Amount: Varies
Number of Awards: Varies
Based on Financial Need: No
Deadline: May
Applications are available online. A completed application, transcript, essay and two letters of recommendation are required to apply.

(430) Gaige Fund Award

Amiercan Society of Ichthyologists and Herpetologists
Maureen Donnelly, Secretary
Department of Biological Sciences, Florida International University
11200 SW 8th Street
Miami, FL 33199

Phone: 305-348-1235
Fax: 305-348-1986
Email: asih@fiu.edu
URL: http://www.asih.org

Goal: To assist young herpetologists.

Eligibility: Applicants must be ASIH members studying for an advanced degree. The award can be used for travel, fieldwork, museum or laboratory study or other activities to enhance their career.
Target Student: Graduate and Adult students.
Amount: $400-$1,000
Number of Awards: Varies
Based on Financial Need: No
Deadline: March
Applications are available by email or by written request.

(431) Gamma Theta Upsilon-Geographical Honor Society

Gamma Theta Upsilon
Dr. Donald Zeigler
Old Dominion University
1181 University Dr.
Virginia Beach, VA 23453

URL: http://www.gammathetaupsilon.org

Goal: To develop geography knowledge by assisting college and graduate students with their educational expenses.
Eligibility: Applicants must be initiated by a Gamma Theta Upsilon chapter.
Target Student: College, Graduate and Adult students.
Amount: $1,000
Number of Awards: 5
Based on Financial Need: No
Deadline: June
Applications are available online.

(432) Garland Duncan Scholarships

American Society of Mechanical Engineers
Three Park Avenue
New York, NY 10016

Phone: 800-843-2763
Fax: 973-882-1717
Email: infocentral@asme.org

URL: http://www.asme.org

Goal: To assist mechanical engineering students.
Eligibility: Applicants must be ASME student members enrolled in an eligible accredited bachelor's degree in mechanical engineering and be college juniors or seniors.
Target Student: College and Adult students.
Amount: $5,000
Number of Awards: 2
Based on Financial Need: No
Deadline: March
Applications are available online.

---

(433) Garmin Scholarship

Aircraft Electronics Assocaition
4217 South Hocker
Independence, MO 64055

Phone: 816-373-6565
Fax: 816-478-3100
Email: info@aea.net
URL: http://www.aea.net

Goal: To assist students wanting to pursue a career in avionics and aircraft repair.
Eligibility: Applicants must be high school seniors or college students planning to or attending an accredited school in avionics or aircraft repair.
Target Student: High school, College and Adult students.
Amount: $2,000
Number of Awards: Varies
Based on Financial Need: No
Deadline: February
Applications are available online.

---

(434) Gary Wagner, K3OMI Scholarship

American Radio Relay League Foundation
225 Main Street

Newington, CT 06111

Phone: 860-594-0397
Fax: 860-594-0259
Email: foundation@arrl.org
URL: http://www.arrlf.org

Goal: To assist engineering students who are involved in amateur radio.
Eligibility: Applicants must have a Novice amateur radio license or higher and be pursuing a bachelor's degree in any field of enginerring. Applicants must be a resident of North Carolina, Virginia, West Virginia, Maryland, or Tennessee. Those with demonstrated financial need are given preference.
Target Student: High school, College and Adult students.
Amount: $1,000
Number of Awards: 1
Based on Financial Need: Yes
Deadline: February
Applications are avaialble online.

---

(435) Gary Yoshimura Scholarship

Public Relations Students Society of America
33 Maiden Lane
11th Floor
New York, NY 10038

Phone: 212-460-1474
Fax: 212-995-0757
Email: prssa@prsa.org
URL: http://www.prssa.org

Goal: To assist public relations students with their educational expenses.
Eligibility: Applicants must be PRSSA members who have a 3.0 or higher GPA and be pursuing a degree in the field of public relations.
Target Student: College, Graduate and Adult students.
Amount: $2,400
Number of Awards: 1

Based on Financial Need: Yes
Deadline: January
Applications are available online. Applicants need to submit a completed application, essay, and statement of financial need to apply.

(436) GAT Wings to the Future Management Scholarship

Women in Aviation, International
Morningstar Airport
3647 State Route 503 South
West Alexandria, OH 45381

Phone: 937-839-4647
Fax: 937-839-4645
Email: dwallace@wai.org
URL: http://wai.org

Goal: To assist female students of aviation business and management.
Eligibility:
Target Student: College and Adult students.
Amount: $2,500
Number of Awards: 1
Based on Financial Need: No
Deadline: November
Applications are available online. A completed application, essay, resume, copies of all available medical and aviation certificates and three letters of recommendation are required to apply.

(437) GBT Student Support Program

National Radio Astronomy Observatory
NRAO Headquarters
520 Edgemont Road
Charlottesville, VA 22903

Phone: 434-296-0211
Fax: 434-296-0278
Email: info@nrao.edu
URL: http://www.nrao.edu

Goal: To help support student research at the Robert C. Byrd Green Bank Telescope.
Eligibility: Applicants must submit a preliminary funding proposal form. If the form is accepted they will be contacted for the next steps.
Target Student: College, Graduate, and Adult students.
Amount: Up to $35,000
Number of Awards: Varies
Based on Financial Need: No
Deadline: Varies
Applciations are available online.

(438) GCSAA Scholars Competition

Golf Course Superintendents Association of America
GCSAA Career Development Department
1421 Research Park Drive
Lawrence, KS 66049

Phone: 800-472-7878
Fax: 785-832-3643
Email: mbrhelp@gcsaa.org
URL: http://www.gcsaa.org

Goal: To assist students preparing for a career in gold course management.
Eligibility: Applicants must be GCSAA members and undergraduate students enrolled in an accredited turf management or related degree program. Applicants must have completed at least one year or 24 semester credited in toward their degree program.
Target Student: College and Adult students.
Amount: $500 - $6,000
Number of Awards: Varies
Based on Financial Need: No
Deadline: June
Applications are available online. A completed application, essay, transcript and report from the applicants academic advisor and gold course superintendent are required to apply.

(439) GCSAA Student Essay Contest

Golf Course Superintendents Association of America
GCSAA Career Development Department
1421 Research Park Drive
Lawrence, KS 66049

Phone: 800-472-7878
Fax: 785-832-3643
Email: mbrhelp@gcsaa.org
URL: http://www.gcsaa.org

Goal: To assist students pursuing a degree in golf course management.
Eligibility: Applicants must be undergraduate or graduate students pursuing degrees in turfgrass science, agronomy or any other golf course related management field and be GCSAA members.
Target Student: College, Graduate and Adult students
Amount: $1,000 - $2,000
Number of Awards: Up to 3
Based on Financial Need: No
Deadline: March
Applications are available by contacting Pam Smith at 800-472-7878 x3678

(440) GED Jump Start Scholarship

Child Nutrition Foundation
Scholarship Committee
700 S. Washington St.
Suite 300
Alexandria, VA 22314

Phone: 703-739-3900
Email: jcurtis@schoolnutrition.org
URL: http://www.schoolnutrition.org

Goal: To assist School Nutrition Association members earn their GED.

Eligibility: Applicants must be members of the School Nutrition Association who do not have a GED or high school diploma and plan to earn their GED within a year of receiving the scholarship award.
Target Student: College and Adult students.
Amount: $200
Number of Awards: Varies
Based on Financial Need: No
Deadline: Accepted throughout the year. Applications are available online.

(441) GEF Resource Center Scholarships

Gravure Education Foundation
1200-A Scottsville Road
Rochester, NY 14624

Phone: 315-589-8879
Fax: 585-436-7689
Email: lwshatch@gaa.org
URL: http://www.gaa.org

Goal: To assist undergraduate and graduate students who are majoring in graphic arts, graphic communications and printing.
Eligibility: Applicants must be enrolled at a GEF Learning Resource Center at: Arizona State University, California Polytechnic State University, Clemson University, Murray State University, Rochester Institute of Technology, University of Wisconsin-Stout or Western Michigan University.
Target Student: College, Graduate and Adult students.
Amount: Varies
Number of Awards: 9
Based on Financial Need: No
Deadline: April
Applications are available online.

(442) Gen and Kelly Tanabe Student Scholarship

2713 Newlands Avenue
Belmont, CA 94002

Phone: 650-618-2221
Email: tanabe@gmail.com
URL:http://www.genkellyscholarship.com

Goal: To assist high school, college and graduate students with their educational expenses.
Eligibility: Applicants must be high school, college or graduate students who are legal U.S. residents. Students can attend any college and study any major.
Target Student: High school, College, Graduate and Adult students.
Amount: $1,000
Number of Awards: Varies
Based on Financial Need: No
Deadline: July and December
Applications are available online.

(443) Gene Carte Student Paper Competition

American Society of Criminology Gene Carte Student Paper Competition
Nancy Rodriguez
Department of Criminology and Criminal Justice, Arizona State University West
4701 W. Thunderbird Road
Glendale, AZ 85306

Phone: 602-543-6601
Fax: 602-543-6658
Email: nancy.rodriguez@asu.edu
URL: http://www.asc41.com

Goal: To acknowledge outstanding student work in criminology.

Eligibility: Applicants must be full-time graduate or undergraduate students. The scholarship requries that the applicant writes on a criminology topic and must be submitted with a letter from the dean or department chair. Specific instructions regarding the paper are on the website.
Target Student: College, Graduate and Adult students.
Amount: $200 to $1,000
Number of Awards: Up to 3
Based on Financial Need: No
Deadline: April
There is no formal application. The paper must be mailed in.

(444) Gene Haas Foundation Machining Technology Scholarship

Society of Manufacturing Engineers
Education Foundation
One SME Drive
P.O. Box 930
Dearborn, MI 48121

Phone: 313-425-3300
Fax: 313-425-3411
Email: foundation@sme.org
URL: http://www.smeef.org

Goal: To assist students who are planning or pursuing degrees in manufacturing engineering, manufacturing engineering technology or a related subject.
Eligibility: Applicants must be U.S. or Canadian residents, graduating high school seniors or undergraduate students, enrolled or planning to enroll in an associate's or bachelor's degree in manufacturing engineering, manufacturing engineering technology or a related field. Applicants must have attended the Caeers in Technology event at the most recent EASTEC exposition.
Target Student: High school, College and Adult students.
Amount: Varies
Number of Awards: Varies

Based on Financial Need: No
Deadline: July
Applicantions are available online. A completed application, essay, resume, two letters of recommendation and transcript are required to apply.

(445) General Fund Scholarships

American Radio Relay League Foundation
225 Main Street
Newington, CT 06111

Phone: 860-594-0397
Fax: 860-594-0259
Email: foundation@arrl.org
URL: http://www.arrlf.org

Goal: To assist ham radio operators with educational expenses.
Eligibility: Applicants must have any level of a ham radio license.
Target Student: High school, College, Graduate and Adult students.
Amount: $2,000
Number of Awards: Varies
Based on Financial Need: No
Deadline: February
Applications are available online.

(446) General Henry H. Arnold Edcuation Grant Program

Air Force Aid Society Inc.
Education Assistance Department
241 18th Street S. Suite 202
Arlington, VA 22202

Phone: 800-429-9475
Fax: 703-607-3022
URL: http://www.afas.org

Goal: To assist Air Force members and their families reach their academic goals.

Eligibility: Applicants must be a dependent child of an Air Force member, spouses of active duty members or surviving spouses of Air Force members who died while on active duty, or in retired status. Students must be high school seniors or college students enrolled as full-time undergraduate students for the following school year with a GPA of 2.0 or higher.
Target Student: High school, College and Adult students.
Amount: $2,000
Number of Awards: Varies
Scholarship can be renewed.
Based on Financial Need: No
Deadline: March
Applications are available online.

(447) General Heritage and Culture Grants

Sons of Norway Foundation
1455 West Lake Street
Minneapolis, MN 55408

Phone: 800-945-8851
Fax: 612-827-0658
Email: foundation@sofn.com
URL: http://www.sofn.com

Goal: To protect and develop an understanding of Norwegian heritage.
Eligibility: Appicants can be individuals, groups or organizations with the goal of preservation of Norwegian heritage.
Target Student: High school, College and Adult students.
Amount: Up to $3,000
Number of Awards: Varies
Based on Financial Need: No
Deadline: April
Applications are available online.

(448) General James H. Doolittle Scholarship

Communities Foundation of Texas
5500 Caruth Haven Lane
Dallas, TX 75225

Phone: 214-750-4222
Email: info@cftexas.org
URL: http://www.cftexas.org

Goal: To assist aeronautical engineering and aerospace science students.
Eligibility: Applicants mus tbe undergraduate juniors, seniors or graduate students enrolled in an aerospace science or areonautical engineering degree program.
Target Student: College, Graduate and Adult students.
Amount: Up to $5,000
Number of Awards: Varies
Based on Financial Need: No
Deadline: May
Applications are available online.

(449) GeoEye Foundation Award for the Application of High Resolution Digital Satellite Imagery

American Society for Photogrammetry and Remote Sensing
The Imaging and Geospatial Information Society
5410 Grosvenor Lane
Suite 210
Bethesda, MD 20814

Phone: 301-493-0290 x101
Fax: 301-493-0208
Email: scholarships@asprs.org
URL: http://www.asprs.org

Goal: To assist education in remote sensing and encourage the development of applications of high-resolution digital satellite imagery for applied research by undergraduate or graduate students.

Eligibility: Applciants must be full-time graduate or undergraduate students at an accredited college or university with the needed image processing facilities.
Target Student: College, Graduate and Adult students.
Amount: Up to $20,000 in imagery.
Number of Awards: Varies
Based on Financial Need: No
Deadline: October
Applications are available online.

(450) George A. Hall / Harold F. Mayfield Award

Wilson Ornithological Society
Dr. Robert B. Payne
Museum of Zoology, University of Michigan
1109 Gedes Avenue
Ann Arbor, MI 48109

Email: rbpayne@umich.edu
URL: http://www.wilsonsociety.org

Goal: To assist those who are doing avian research.
Eligibility: Applicants must be independent researchers who don't have access to funds from colleges, universities or government agencies and must be non-professionals conducting avian research. Applicants must be able to present their research at the Wilson Ornithological Society annual meeting.
Target Student: High school, College, Graduate and Adult students.
Amount: $1,000
Number of Awards: 1
Based on Financial Need: No
Deadline: February
Applications are available online.

(451) George A. Roberts Scholarships

ASM International
9639 Kinsman Road

Materials Park, OH 44073

Phone: 440-338-5151
Fax: 440-338-4634
Email:jeane.deatherage@asminternational.org
URL:http://www.asminternational.org/portal/site/www/foundation/scholarships/

Goal: To assist students interested in pursuing a career in the metallurgy or materials engineering field.
Eligibility: Applicants must be ASM International student members who plan to major in metallurgy or materials science engineering. Applicants must be juniors or seniors at a university with a bachelor's degree program in science and engineering in North America.
Target Student: College and Adult students.
Amount: $6,000
Number of Awards: Up to 7
Based on Financial Need: Yes
Deadline: May
Applications are available online. A completed application, transcripts, two letters of recommendation, personal statement, photographs, and contact information for the financial aid office are required to apply.

---

(452) George A. Strait Minority Scholarship

American Association of Law Libraries
105 W. Adams
Suite 3300
Chicago, IL 60604

Phone: 312-939-4764
Fax: 312-431-1097
Email: scholarships@aall.org
URL: http://www.allnet.org

Goal: To encourage minority students to pursue a career as a law librarian.

Eligibility: Applicants must be a member of a minority group as defined by the U.S. government, purusing a degree at an accredited law school or library school and intend to pursue a career as a law librarian. Applicants must have demonstrated financial need and at least one quarter or semester reamining in their degree program after reciving the scholarship.
Target Student: Graduate and Adult students.
Amount: Varies
Number of Awards: Varies
Scholarship can be renewed.
Based on Financial Need: Yes
Deadline: April
Applicants are available online, mail, fax, phone or email.

---

(453) George and Viola Hoffman Award

Association of American Geographers (AAG) Hoffman Scholarship
Frostburg State University
101 Braddock Road
c/o George White
Frostburg, MD 21532

Phone: 301-687-4000
Email: gwhite@frostgurg.edu
URL: http://www.aag.org

Goal: To assist with graduate research in Eastern Europe.
Eligibility: Applicants must complete research in pursuit of a master's thesis or a doctoral dissertation on a geographical subject in Eastern Europe which includes East Central and Southeast Europe from Poland south to Romania, Bulgaria and the former Yugoslavia. The topic of research can be historical or contemporary.
Target Student: Graduate and Adult students.
Amount: $350 - $500
Number of Awards: Varies
Based on Financial Need: No

Deadline: November
Application material is available online. To apply applicants must submit a letter describing professional achievements and the goals as well as a letter of support from a sponsoring faculty member.

(454) GE-Reagan Foundation Scholarship Program

Ronald Reagan Presiential Foundation
40 Presidential Drive Suite 200
Simi Valley, CA 93065

Phone: 507-931-1682
Email: ge-reagan@scholarshipamerica.org
URL:http://www.scholarshipamerica.org/ge-reagan

Goal: To acknowledge students who show leadership, drive, integrity and citizenship.
Eligibility: Applicants must be female members of Women in Aviation International who are enrolled in an accredited aviation business or aviation management program full-time with a GPA of 3.0 or higher.
Target Student: High school students.
Amount: $10,000
Number of Awards: Up to 20
Scholarship can be renewed.
Based on Financial Need: Yes
Deadline: January
Applications are available online. Applications will not be accepted once 25,000 applications are accepted.

(455) German Studies Research Grant

German Academic Exchange Service
DAAD
871 UN Plaza
New York, NY 10017

Phone: 212-758-3223
Fax: 212-755-5780
Email: thomanck@daad.org

URL: http://www.daad.org

Goal: To encourage the research in all aspects of current and contemporary German affairs.
Eligibility: Applicants must be junior or senior undegraduates pursuing a major or minor in German studies or graduate or Ph.D. students in the humanities or social sciences working towards a certificate in German studies or dissertation on a current German topic. Applicants must have completed two years of college German, a minimum of three courses in German studies and be nominated by their department.
Target Student: College, Graduate and Adult students.
Amount: $1,500 - $2,500
Number of Awards: Up to 5
Based on Financial Need: No
Deadline: May and November
Applications are available online. To apply applicants must submit completed applications, resumes, project descriptions, budget reports, list of the German courses completed, two letters of recommendation and a language evaluation form.

(456) Gertrude Cox Scholarship For Women in Statistics

American Statistical Association
Dr. Amita Manatunga, Gertrude Cox Scholarship Committee Chair
Department of Biostatistics, Emory University
1518 Clifton Road NE #374
Atlanta, GA 30322

Phone: 404-727-1370
Fax: 404-727-1370
Email: amanatu@sph.emory.edu
URL: http://www.amstat.org

Goal: To encourage women to pursue a career in statistics.

Eligibility: Applicants must be women who are full-time students in a graduate level statistics program.
Target Student: Graduate and Adult students.
Amount: $2,000
Number of Awards: Varies
Based on Financial Need: No
Deadline: April
Applications are available online.

---

(457) Gift for Life Scholarship

United States Bowling Congress
5301 S. 76th Street
Greendale, WI 53129

Phone: 800-514-2695 x3168
Email: smart@bowl.com
URL: http://www.bowl.com

Goal: To assist high school students who have a financial need.
Eligibility: Applicants must be USBC Youth members who are in grades 9-12. Students must have a GPA of 2.0 or higher and a financial need. Two of the awards each year are reserved for children of fire department, emergency rescue or police personnel.
Target Student: High school students.
Amount: $1,000
Number of Awards: 12
Based on Financial Need: Yes
Deadline: April
Applications are available online.

---

(458) Gilbreth Memorial Fellowship

Institute of Industrial Engineers
3577 Parkway Lane
Suite 200
Norcross, GA 30092

Phone: 800-494-0460
Fax: 770-441-3295
Email: bcameron@iienet.org

URL: http://www.iienet2.org

Goal: To assist graduate student institute members.
Eligibility: Applicants must be graduate students at a school in the U.S., Canada or Mexico, majoring in industrial engineering or its equivalent. Applicants must be nominated for the award.
Target Student: Graduate and Adult students.
Amount: $3,000
Number of Awards: 2
Based on Financial Need: Yes
Deadline: November
Nomination forms are available online.

---

(459) Giles Sutherland Rich Memorial Scholarship

Federal Circuit Bar Association
1620 I Street NW
Suite 900
Washington, DC 20006

Phone: 202-466-3923
Fax: 202-833-1061
URL: http://www.fedcirbar.org

Goal: To assist law students with promise and demonstrated financial need.
Eligibility: Applicants must be undergraduate or graduate law students with demonstrated academic ability and financial need.
Target Student: College, Graduate and Adult students.
Amount: $10,000
Number of Awards: 1
Based on Financial Need: Yes
Deadline: April
To apply applicants must submit a one page statement the describes their finanical need, as well as their interest in law and what qualifications for the award. They must also submit a transcript and curriculum vitae.

(460) Gilman International Scholarship

Institute of International Education
Gilman Scholarship Program
1800 West Loop South, Suite 250
Houston, TX 77027

Phone: 832-369-3484
Fax:
Email: gilman@iie.org
URL:
http://www.iie.org/programs/gilman-scholarship-program

Goal: To assist students who have demonstrated financial need study abroad.
Eligibility: Applicants must be currently enrolled at a two-year or four-year college and recipients of a Pell Grant. Students who receive the award must study abroad for a minimum of four weeks in any country that is not on the Travel Warning List or Cuba.
Target Student: College and Adult students.
Amount: $5,000
Number of Awards: Varies
Based on Financial Need: Yes
Deadline: March and October
Applications are available online.

(461) Giuliano Mazzetti Scholarship

Society of Manufacturing Engineers
Education Foundation
One SME Drive
P.O. Box 930
Dearborn, MI 48121

Phone: 313-425-3300
Fax: 313-425-3411
Email: foundation@sme.org
URL: http://www.smeef.org

Goal: To assist undergraduate students studying manufacturing engineering and technology.

Eligibility: Applicants must be full-time undergraduate students in the U.S. or Canada who have completed at least 30 or more credit hours, have a GPA of 3.0 or higher, studying and planning to pursue a career in manufacturing engineering, technology or a related subject
Target Student: College and Adult students.
Amount: Varies
Number of Awards: Varies
Based on Financial Need: No
Deadline: February
Applications are available online. A completed application, resume, transcript, two letters of recommendation and personal statement are required to apply.

(462) Gladys Anderson Emerson Scholarship

Iota Sigma Pi
Professor Kathyrn A. Thomasson, Iota Sigma Pi Director for Student Awards
University of North Dakota, Department of Chemistry
P.O. Box 9024
Grand Forks, ND 58202

Phone: 701-777-3199
Fax: 701-777-2331
Email: kthomasson@chem.und.edu
URL: http://www.iotasigmapi.info

Goal: To acknowlege achievements by women in the chemistry and biochemistry fields.
Eligibility: Applicants must be female juniors or higher at an accredited college or university and nominated by a member of Iota Sigma Pi.
Target Student: College, Graduate and Adult students.
Amount: $2,000
Number of Awards: Up to 2
Based on Financial Need: No
Deadline: February
Applications are available online.

(463) Glenn Miller Scholarship Competition

Glenn Miller Birthplace Society
107 East Main Street
P.O. Box 61
Clarinda, IA 51632

Phone: 712-542-2461
Email: gmbs@heartland.net
URL: http://www.glenmiller.org

Goal: To remember Glen Miller by awarding future muscians.
Eligibility: Scholarships will be awarded to graduating high seniors and first year college students who intend to
make music a central part of their future. Those who have entered as high school seniors are eligible
to compete again as college freshmen, unless they have been previous first place winners.
Target Student: High school, College and Adult students.
Amount: $1,000 - $4,000
Number of Awards: 6
Based on Financial Need: No
Deadline: March
Applications are available online.

(464) Global Citizen Awards

EF Educational Tours
EF Center Boston
One Education Street
Cambridge, MA 02141

Phone: 617-619-1300
Fax: 800-318-3732
Email: marisa.talbot@ef.com
URL: http://www.eftours.com

Goal: To assist students to examine social responsibility in the new global economy.

Eligibility: Applicants must be college bound high school sophomores or juniors in the U.S. or Canada who have been nominated by their schools. Applicants must write an essay on a topic about global citizenship.
Target Student: High school students.
Amount: Educational Tour Expenses
Number of Awards: Varies
Based on Financial Need: No
Deadline: February
Applications are available online.

(465) GNC Nutritional Research Grant

National Strength and Conditioning Association Foundation
1885 Bob Johnson Drive
Colorado Springs, CO 80906

Phone: 800-815-6826
Fax: 719-632-6367
Email: nsca@nsca-life.org
URL: http://www.nsca-lift.org

Goal: To help fund nutrition research.
Eligibility: Applicants for student research grants must have Graduate student status during the term of the grant to be considered for funding. At the time of application, student applicants must be a good-standing Member of the NSCA before submitting their grant application and all faculty co-investigators or applicants must have maintained concurrent NSCA Membership for a period of at least one year prior to the March 15th grant application deadline, as verified by the NSCA Membership Department. Applicants are not eligible to receive more than one grant in any given year, but are eligible to receive up to two awards in each grant category over their

career. Two or more grant applications with similar titles and methodology submitted by investigators affiliated with the same research laboratory will be disqualified. Members of the NSCA Foundation Board of Directors, members of the Grant Review Committee, and members of the NSCA Board of Directors are ineligible to receive grant awards during their term of service. In addition, NSCA employees and their families are ineligible to receive financial awards.
Target Student: Graduate school and Adult students.
Amount: $2,500
Number of Awards: 1
Based on Financial Need: No
Deadline: March
Applications are available with a membership.

---

(466) Go! Study Abroad Scholarship

Go! Overseas Study Abroad Scholarship
2680 Bancroft Way
Berkeley, CA 94704

Phone: 415-796-6456
Email: scholarship@gooverseas.com
URL: http://www.gooverseas.com/study-abroad/

Goal: To assist students who have been accepted into a study abroad program.
Eligibility: Applicants must be current college or graduate students who are entering into a study abroad program in the upcoming year.
Target Student: College, Graduate and Adult students.
Amount: $1,000
Number of Awards: Varies
Based on Financial Need: No
Deadline: September
Applications are available online. A completed application and an essay are required to apply.

(467) Go! Volunteer Abroad Scholarship

Go! Overseas Study Abroad Scholarship
2680 Bancroft Way
Berkeley, CA 94704

Phone: 415-796-6456
Email: volunteerscholarship@gooverseas.com
URL: http://www.go-volunteerabroad.com/volunteer-abroad-scholarship

Goal: To assist those who have been accepted into a volunteer abroad thinking.
Eligibility: Applicants must be accepted into a volunteer abroad program.
Target Student: College, Graduate and Adult students.
Amount: $1,000
Number of Awards: Varies
Based on Financial Need: No
Deadline: September
Applications are available online. A completed application and an essay are required to apply.

---

(468) Golden Gate Restaurant Association Scholarship

Golden Gate Restaurant Association Scholarship Foundation
120 Montgomery Street
Suite 1280
San Francisco, CA 94104

Phone: 415-781-5348
Fax: 415-781-3925
Email: ggra@ggra.org
URL: http://www.ggra.org

Goal: To assist students who are pursuing careers in the food/restaurant industry.
Eligibility: Applicants must be California residents and be pursuing a major in food service.

Target Student: High school, College and Adult students.
Amount: $1,000 - $6,500
Number of Awards: Varies
Based on Financial Need: No
Deadline: April
Applications are available online or by mail.

(469) Graduate Fellowships

Institute of Food Technologists
525 W. Van Buren
Suite 1000
Chicago, IL 60607

Phone: 312-782-8424
Email: ejplummer@ift.org
URL: http://www.ift.org

Goal: To acknowledge graduate research in food science or technology.
Eligibility: Applicants must be graduate students working towards an M.S. and/or Ph.D. when the fellowship begins and should be researching in an area of food science or technology.
Target Student: Graduate and Adult students.
Amount: $500 - $5,000
Number of Awards: 40
Based on Financial Need: No
Deadline: Varies
Applications are available online.

(470) Graduate Research Award

American Vacuum Society
120 Wall Street
32nd Floor
New York, NY 10005

Phone: 212-248-0200
Fax: 212-248-0245
Email: angela@avs.org
URL: http://www.avs.org

Goal: To assist graduate studies in the science and technologies that are related to AVS.
Eligibility: Applicants must be graduate students at an accredited college or university.
Target Student: Graduate and Adult students.
Amount: Varies
Number of Awards: 10
Based on Financial Need: No
Deadline: May
Applications are available online. A completed application, research summaries, transcript and letters of recommendation are required to apply.

(471) Graduate Research Fellowship Program

National Science Foundation Graduate Research Fellowship
Operations Center
Suite T-50
1818 N Street, NW
Washington, DC 20036

Phone: 866-NSF-GRFP
Email: info@nsfgrfp.org
URL: http://www.fastlane.nsf.gov/grfp

Goal: To assist graduate students in science and engineering.
Eligibility: Applicants must be full-time students who have not yet competed 12 months of graduate study and be U.S. citizens, nationals or permanent residents. Fields of study open for this award are interdisciplinary sciences, geosciences, psychology, social sciences, life sciences, chemistry, physics, astronomy and engineering.
Target Student: Graduate and Adult students.
Amount: $42,000
Number of Awards: 2,000
Based on Financial Need: No
Deadline: November

Applications are available online. A completed application, transcript and three letters of recommendation are required to apply.

(472) Graduate Research Grant - Master and Doctoral

National Strength and Conditioning Association Foundation
1885 Bob Johnson Drive
Colorado Springs, CO 80906

Phone: 800-815-6826
Fax: 719-632-6367
Email: nsca@nsca-lift.org
URL: http://www.nsca-lift.org

Goal: To support research in strength and conditioning.
Eligibility: This grant program funds Graduate research in strength and conditioning that is consistent with the mission of the NSCA. Graduate Research Grants are awarded at the Masters and Doctoral level and require that a Graduate faculty member serve as co-investigator. Please indicate clearly which Graduate research grant is being applied for (Masters or Doctoral). Masters Student Research Grant proposals are not to exceed $7,500 (indirect costs, travel, and salary are NOT SUPPORTED). Eligible candidates must be actively pursuing their Master's degree at the time of application. Doctoral Student Research Grant proposals are not to exceed $15,000 (indirect costs, travel, and salary are NOT SUPPORTED). Eligible candidates must be actively pursuing their Doctoral degree at the time of application, which may include ABD status.
Target Student: Graduate and Adult students
Amount: $5,000 to $10,000
Number of Awards: Varies
Based on Financial Need: No
Deadline: March

Applications are available with membership.

(474) Graduate Scholarship

Jack Kent Cooke Foundation
44325 Woodridge Parkway
Lansdowne, VA 20176

Phone: 800-498-6478
Fax: 703-723-8030
Email: jkc-g@act.org
URL: http://www.jkcf.org

Goal: To assist students how have academic merit and financial need attend graduate school.
Eligibility: Applicants must be college seniors and recent graduates with financial need who will pursue a graduate or professional degree in the visual arts, performing arts, or creative writing. To be eligible, candidates must be nominated by the faculty representative at their undergraduate institution. Applicants must be nominated by the Jack Kent Cooke Foundation faculty representatives at their institutions and must be recipients of Jack Kent Cooke Foundation undergraduate awards. Award selection is based on academic achievement and unmet financial need. A GPA of 3.5 of higher is required.
Target Student: College, Graduate and Adult students.
Amount: $50,000
Number of Awards: Varies
Scholarship can be renewed
Based on Financial Need: Yes
Deadline: January
Applications are available online.

(475) Graduate Scholarships Program

Society of Naval Architects and Marine Engineers
601 Pavonia Avenue
Jersey City, NJ 7306

Phone: 201-798-4800
Fax: 201-798-4975
Email: efaustino@sname.org
URL: http://www.sname.org

Goal: To assist students pursuing a master's degree in a subject related to the marine industry.
Eligibility: Applicants must be Society of Naval Architects and Marine Engineers and be working towards a master's degree in ocean engineering, marine engineering, naval architecture, or another related subject.
Target Student: Graduate and Adult students.
Amount: $20,000
Number of Awards: Varies
Based on Financial Need: No
Deadline: February
Applications are available online. A completed application, standardized test scores, transcripts, and three letters of recommendation are required to apply.

(473) Graduate Student Research Grants

Geological Society of America
Program Officer
Grants, Awards, and Recognition
P.O. Box 9140
Boulder, CO 80301

Phone: 303-357-1028
Fax: 303-357-1070
Email: awards@geosociety.org
URL: http://www.geosociety.org

Goal: To assist geological science students with their thesis and/or dissertation.
Eligibility: Applicants must be enrolled in a graduate geological science graduate program at an institution in the U.S., Canada, Mexico or Central America and be members of the GSA- Geological Society of America

Target Student: Graduate and Adult students.
Amount: Up to $2,500
Number of Awards: Varies
Based on Financial Need: No
Deadline: February
Applications are available online.

(476) Graduate Student Scholarship

American Speech-Language-Hearing Foundation
2200 Research Boulevard
Rockville, MD 20850

Phone: 301-296-8700
Email: foundation@asha.org
URL: http://www.ashfoundation.org

Goal: To assist graduate students in communication sciences and disorders.
Eligibility: Applicants must be full-time graduate students in the U.S. studying communication sciences and disorders in a program accredited by the Council on Academic Accreditation for Audiology and Speech Pathology, however doctoral programs do not need to be accredited.
Target Student: Graduate and Adult students.
Amount: $5,000
Number of Awards: Up to 7
Based on Financial Need: No
Deadline: Unknown
Applications are available online.

(477) Graduate Summer Student Research Assistantship

Astronomy Observatory
NRAO Headquarters
520 Edgemont Road
Charlottesville, VA 22903

Phone: 434-296-0211
Fax: 434-296-0278
Email: info@nrao.edu

URL: http://www.nrao.edu

Goal: To give graduate students performing astronomical research the opportunity to use National Radio Astronomy Observatory sites.
Eligibility: Applicants must be first or second year graduate students interested in performing astronomical research.
Target Student: Graduate and Adult students.
Amount: Up to $672 per week plus travel expenses.
Number of Awards: Varies
Based on Financial Need: No
Deadline: February
Applications are available online.

---

(478) Gravure Publishing Council Scholarship

Gravure Education Foundation
1200-A Scottsville Road
Rochester, NY 14624

Phone: 315-589-8879
Fax: 585-436-7689
Email: lwshatch@gaa.org
URL: http://www.gaa.org

Goal: To assist undergraduate students enter the printing industry.
Eligibility: Applicants must be undergraduates, juniors or higher, who are majoring in printing, graphic arts, or graphic ocmmunications.
Target Student: College and Adult students.
Amount: $1,500
Number of Awards: 1
Based on Financial Need: No
Deadline: April
Applications are available online.

---

(479) Green Mountain Water Environment Association Scholarship

Vermont Student Assistance Corporation Scholarships
10 East Allen Street
P.O. Box 2000
Winooski, VT 05404

Phone: 888-253-4819
Fax: 802-654-3765
Email: info@vsac.org
URL: http://www.vsac.org

Goal: To assist students pursuing a degree in an environmental related subject.
Eligibility: Applicants must be full-time undergraduate students enrolled in a school eligible to receive Title V funds. Applicants must have a 3.0 or higher GPA, studying a field related to environmental studies, be active in community service and have demonstrated financial need.
Target Student: College and Adult students.
Amount: $1,000
Number of Awards: 1
Based on Financial Need: Yes
Deadline: March
Applications are available online. A completed application, essay, transcript and letter of recommendation are required to apply.

---

(480) Green/Sustainable Design Scholarship

International Furnishings and Design Association
150 South Warner Road
Suite 156
King of Prussia, PA 19406

Phone: 610-535-6422
Fax: 610-535-6423
Email: merrymabbettinc@comcast.net
URL:
http://www.ifdaef.org/scholarships.php

Goal: To assist interior design students interested in green/sustainable design.

Eligibility: Applicants must be undergraduate students enrolled in an interior design or related degree. Applicants must have demonstrated interest in eco-friendly design and green/sustainable design.
Target Student: College and Adult students.
Amount: $1,500
Number of Awards: 1
Based on Financial Need: No
Deadline: March
Applications are available online. A completed application form, transcript, essay, two design work examples and one letter recommendation letter are required to apply.

---

(481) Grotto Scholarships

DeMolay Foundation
10200 NW Ambassador Drive
Kansas City, MO 64153

Phone: 800-336-6529
Fax: 816-891-9062
Email: demolay@demolay.org
URL: http://www.demolay.org

Goal: To assist medical students.
Eligibility: Applicants must be enrolled in a dental, medical or pre-medical program at an accredited college or university and do not need to be active DeMolay members.
Target Student: College, Graduate and Adult students.
Amount: $1,500
Number of Awards: Varies
Based on Financial Need: No
Deadline: April
Applications are available online.

---

(482) H.P. Milligan Aviation Scholarship

EAA Aviation Center

P.O. Box 2683
Oshkosh, WI 54903

Phone: 877-806-8902
Fax: 920-426-6865
Email: scholarships@eaa.org
URL: http://www.youngeagles.org

Goal: To assist students studying aviation.
Eligibility: Applicants must be enrolled in an accredited college, aviation academy or tech school studying aviation, involved in school and community and be an EAA member or be recommended by an EAA member.
Target Student: High school, College and Adult students.
Amount: $500
Number of Awards: 1
Scholarship can be renewed.
Based on Financial Need: No
Deadline: February
Applications are available online.

---

(483) Hanscom Air Force Base Spouses' Club Scholarship

Hanscom Officer's Spouses' Club
P.O. Box 557
Bedford, MA 01730

Phone: 781-538-5361
Email: scholarship@hanscomsc.org
URL: http://www.hanscomsc.org

Goal: To asist dependents of past and present military members.
Eligibility: Applicants must be children or spouses of retired, deceased or current active duty members of the military. They must have a valid military ID and reside within 60 miles of Hanscom Air Force Base.
Target Student: High school and Adult students.
Amount: Varies
Number of Awards: Varies
Based on Financial Need: No

Deadline: March
Applications are available online.

---

(484) Hansen Scholarship

EAA Aviation Center
P.O. Box 2683
Oshkosh, WI 54903

Phone: 877-806-8902
Fax: 920-426-6865
Email: scholarships@eaa.org
URL: http://www.youngeagles.org

Goal: To help support excellence in those studying technologies and the skills needed in aviation.
Eligibility: Applicants must be enrolled in an accredited college or univserity working towards a degree in aerospace engineering or aeronautical engineering and involved in school and community activities. Financial need must be considered.
Target Student: College, Graduate and Adult students.
Amount: $1,000
Number of Awards: Varies
Scholarship can be renewed.
Based on Financial Need: No
Deadline: Februrary
Applciations are available online.

---

(485) Harlequin Dance Scholarship

American Harlequin Corporation
Dance Scholarship Program
1531 Glen Avenue
Moorestown, NJ 08057

Phone: 800-642-6440
Fax: 856-231-4403
Email: dance@harlequinfloors.com
URL: http://www.harlequinfloors.com

Goal: To assist dance students with educational expenses.

Eligibility: Applicants must be U.S. or Canadian citizens who are between 15 and 21 years old. Award is selected by a random drawing.
Target Student: High school and College students.
Amount: Varies
Number of Awards: Varies
Based on Financial Need: No
Deadline: November
Applications are available online.

---

(486) Harness Racing Scholarship

Harnes Horse Youth Foundation
16575 Carey Road
Westfield, IN 46074

Phone: 317-867-5877
Fax: 317-867-5896
Email: ellen@hhyf.org
URL: http://www.hhyf.org

Goal: To increase awareness of harness racing.
Eligibility: Applicants must be pursuing a career in horse racing, show academic achievements, have experience with horses and harness racing and show financial need. Applicants must be at least a high school senior and under the age of 25.
Target Student: High school, College and Graduate students.
Amount: Varies
Number of Awards: Varies
Based on Financial Need: Yes
Deadline: April
Applications are available by mail.

---

(487) Harness Tracks of America Scholarship Fund

Harness Tracks of America
4640 E. Sunrise
Suite 200
Tucson, AZ 85718

Phone: 520-529-2525
Fax: 520-529-3235
Email: info@harnesstracks.com
URL: http://www.harnesstracks.com

Goal: To assist students involved in harness racing.
Eligibility: Applicants must have a parent or parents involved in harness racing and must be a part of the buiness with demonstrated merit and financial need.
Target Student: Junior high and younger, High school, College and Adult students.
Amount: $5,000
Number of Awards: 5
Based on Financial Need: Yes
Deadline: May
Applications are available by telephone request.

(488) Harold and Inge Marcus Scholarship

Institute of Industrial Engineers
3577 Parkway Lane
Suite 200
Norcross, GA 30092

Phone: 800-494-0460
Fax: 770-441-3295
Email: bcameron@iienet.org
URL: http://www.iienet2.org

Goal: To assist engineering students who are members of the Institute of Industrial Engineers.
Eligibility: Applicants must be undergraduate and graduate industrial engineering students who have been nominated for the award by the industrial engineering deparment head. Students must be full-time students, active IIE members with a 3.4 GPA or higher.
Target Student: College and Adult students.
Amount: $1,000
Number of Awards: 1
Based on Financial Need: Yes

Deadline: February
Applications are mailed to those who are nominated.

(489) Harold Bettinger Scholarship

American Floral Endowment
1601 Duke Street
Alexandria, VA 22314

Phone: 703-838-5211
Fax: 703-838-5212
Email: afe@endowment.org
URL: http://www.endowment.org

Goal: To assist horticulture students planning on careers in a horticulture related business.
Eligibility: Applicants must be U.S. or Canadian citizens or residents, graduate students or undergraduate sophomores or above, with a GPA of 2.0 or higher. Applicants must be horticulture students planning to major or minor in business or marketing and plan on pursuing a career in horticulture business field.
Target Student: College, Graduate and Adult students.
Amount: Varies
Number of Awards: Varies
Based on Financial Need: No
Deadline: May
Applications are available online. A completed application, two letters of recommendation, a transcript and a personal statement.

(490) Harrell Family Fellowship

American Center of Oriental Research
656 Beacon Street, 5th Floor
Boston, MA 02215

Phone: 617-353-6571
Fax: 617-353-6575
Email: acor@bu.edu
URL: http://www.bu.edu/acor

Goal: To assist a graduate student with the cost of an archaeological project in Jordan.
Eligibility: Applicants must be graduate students in a recognized academic program.
Target Student: Graduate and Adult students.
Amount: $1,800
Number of Awards: 1
Based on Financial Need: No
Deadline: February
Applications are available online.

(491) Harry A. Applegate Scholarship

DECA Inc.
1908 Association Drive
Reston, VA 20191

Phone: 703-860-5000
Fax: 703-860-4013
Email: kathy_onion@deca.org
URL: http://www.deca.org

Goal: To assist current and active members of DECA.
Eligibility: Applicants must be full time students in a two or four year program studing marketing, entrepreneurship, or management.
Target Student: High school, College and Adult students.
Amount: Varies
Number of Awards: Varies
Based on Financial Need: No
Deadline: Check with your state advsior.
Applications are available online. To apply applicants must submit an application, transcripts, test scores, a statement of club participation, proof of leadership outside of DECA, proof of membership and three letters of recommendation. The award is not based on financial need, however a statement of financial need can be provided for review.

(492) Harry J. Harwick Scholarship

Medical Group Management Association
104 Inverness Terrace East
Englewood, CO 80112

Phone: 877-275-6462
Email: acmpe@mgma.com
URL: http://www.mgma.com

Goal: To assist undergraduate and graduate students of public health, health care management, health care administration, and related areas of medical practice management.
Eligibility: Applicants must be enrolled in an undergraduate or graduate degree program in health care management, public health, health care administration, or a related practice management subject.
Target Student: College, Graduate and Adult students.
Amount: Varies
Number of Awards: Varies
Based on Financial Need: No
Deadline: May
Applications are available online.

(493) Harry S. Truman Research Grant

Harry S. Truman Library Institute for National and International Affairs
Grants Administrator
500 W. U.S. Highway 24
Independence, MO 64050

Phone: 816-268-8248
Fax: 816-268-8299
Email: lisa.sullivan@nara.gov
URL: http:://www.trumanlibrary.org

Goal: To promote the Truman Library as a research center.

Eligibility: Applicants must be completing advanced research, graduate and post-doctoral students are encouraged to apply. Preference is given to those doing research in public policy, foreign policy and issues that have a high chance of being published. Applicants can receive up to two research grants in a five year period.
Target Student: Graduate and Adult students.
Amount: Up to $2,500
Number of Awards: Varies
Based on Financial Need: No
Deadline: April and October
Applications are available online.

(494) HAS Research Grants

Herb Society of America
Attn: Research Grant
9019 Kirtland Chardon Road
Kirtland, OH 44094

Phone: 440-256-0514
Fax: 440-256-0541
Email: herbs@herbsociety.org
URL: http://www.herbsociety.org

Goal: To help educate about herbs and assist with contributions to the fields of horticulture, science, literature, history, art and/or economics.
Eligibility: Applicants must have a proposed program into the scientific, academic or artistic investigation of herbal plants.
Target Student: College, Graduate and Adult students.
Amount: Up to $5,000
Number of Awards: Varies by year
Based on Financial Need: No
Deadline: January
Applications are available online or by written request.

(495) Hawaii Association of Broadcasters Scholarship

Hawaii Association of Broadcasters Inc.
P.O. Box 22112
Honolulu, HI 96823

Phone: 808-599-1455
Fax: 808-599-7784
Email: stephanieuyeda@hawaii.rr.com
URL: http://www.hawaiibroadcasters.com

Goal: To assist students who are purusing a career in broadcasting.
Eligibility: Applicants must be high school seniors or undergraduate students attending an accredited two or four year college or university full time in the U.S. Applicants must have a 2.75 GPA or higher and intend to work in Hawaii after completing their education.
Target Student: High school, College and Adult students.
Amount: Varies
Number of Awards: Varies
Based on Financial Need: No
Deadline: Unknown
Applicants are avaialble online. A completed application, letter of recommendation and transcript are required to apply.

(496) Hayek Fund for Scholars

Insitute for Humane Studies at George Mason University
3301 N. Fairfax Drive Suite 440
Arlington, VA 22201

Phone: 800-697-8799
Fax: 703-993-4890
Email: his@gmu.edu
URL: http://www.theihs.org

Goal: To assist graduate students and untenured facult with support for career-enchancing activities.

Eligibility: Applicants must be graduate students or untenured faculty or graduate students and must submit a letter explaining how participation will advance their career and how their knowledge of classical liberal tradition will be expanded. Applicants must also present an itemized expense list, resume and paper abstract that they will present.
Target Student: Graduate and Adult students.
Amount: Up to $750
Number of Awards: Varies
Based on Financial Need: No
Deadline: Rolling
There are no application forms.

---

(497) Health Careers Scholarships

International Order of the King's
Daughters and Sons
Director
P.O. Box 1040
Chautauqua, NY 14722

URL: http://www.iokds.org

Goal: To assist students who are interested in careers in healthcare.
Eligibility: Applicants must be full-time students purusing a career in medicine, dentistry, nursing, pharmacy, physical or occupational therapy or medical technologies. R.N. students and those who are working towards becoming an M.D. or D.D.S. must have completed at least one year of schooling. All others must be in their third year of school. Pre-med students are not eligilble.
Target Student: College, Graduate and Adult students.
Amount: $1,000
Number of Awards: Varies
Based on Financial Need: No
Deadline: April
Applications are available by mail.

(498) Health Resources and Services Administration-Bureau of Health Professions Scholarships for Disadvantaged Students

United States Public Health Service
Health Resources and Services
Administration
5600 Fishers Lane
Rockville, MD 20857

URL: http://bhpr.hrsa.gov/dsa

Goal: To assist students from disadvantaged backgrounds pursuing careers related to health.
Eligibility: Applicants must be full-time students, with demonstrated financial need, from a disadvantaged background, studying in a health field (medicine, nursing, veterinary medicine, dentistry, pharmacy, etc) and be U.S. citizens or permanent residents.
Target Student: High school, College, Graduate and Adult students.
Amount: Up to $15,000
Number of Awards: Varies
Based on Financial Need: Yes
Deadline: June
Applications are available from participating schools.

---

(499) Health Sciences Student Fellowship

Epilepsy Foundation
8301 Professional Place
Landover, MD 20785

Phone: 301-459-3700
Email: researchwebsupport@efa.org
URL: http://www.epilepsyfoundation.org

Goal: To encourage students to go into a career in epilepsy in research or practice.

Eligibility: Applicants must be enrolled in medical school, a doctoral program or other graduate program, have an epilepsy-related study, have a qualified mentor to supervise the project and have access to a lab. The project must be in the U.S. and not for the students dissertation.
Target Student: Graduate and Adult students.
Amount: $3,000
Number of Awards: Varies
Based on Financial Need: No
Deadline: March
Applications are available online.

---

(500) Henry Adams Scholarship

American Society of Heathing, Refrigerating and Air-Conditioning Engineers
1791 Tullie Circle, NE
Atlanta, GA 30329

Phone: 404-321-5478
Email: lbenedict@ashrae.org
URL: http://www.ashrae.org

Goal: To assist undergraduate students working towards careers in the heating, ventilation, air-conditioning and refrigeration industry.
Eligibility: Applicants must be undergraduate engineering or pre-engineering at an accredited ABET school or a non-U.S. school that has a Memorandum of Understanding with ABET or a school that hosts a student branch of the American Society of Heating, Refrigerating and Air-Conditioning Engineers. Applicants must have a 3.0 GPA or higher and be ranked in the top 30 percent of their class.
Target Student: College and Adult students.
Amount: $3,000
Number of Awards: 1
Scholarship can be renewed.
Based on Financial Need: No

Deadline: December
Applications are available online. A completed application, transcript and one letter of recommendation are required to apply.

---

(501) Henry Belin du Pont Dissertation Fellowship

Hagley Museum and Library
Center for the History of Business, Technology and Society
P.O. Box 3630
Wilmington, DE 19807

Phone: 302-655-2400
Fax: 302-658-3188
URL: http://www.hagley.org

Goal: To provide fellowships for doctoral students doing their dissertation research.
Eligibility: Applicants must be doctoral students who have already completed their courses and are doing their dissertation research. Applicants research topics should involve historical questions and should relate to the collection in the Hagley Library. Fellows recieve housing, office space, and a computer.
Target Student: Graduate and Adult students.
Amount: $6,500 plus housing.
Number of Awards: Varies
Based on Financial Need: No
Deadline: November
Applications are available online.

---

(502) Henry Luce Foundation/ACLS Dissertation Fellowships in American Art

American Council of Learned Societies (ACLS)
633 Third Avenue
New York, NY 10017

Phone: 212-697-1505

Fax: 212-949-8058
Email: sfisher@acls.org
URL: http://www.contemplativemind.org

Goal: To assist Ph.D. cadidates working on a disseration on art history.
Eligibility: Applicants must be Ph.D. candidates in art history deparments working on a disseratation on American visual arts history. Before taking the fellowship applicants must have met all degree requirements aside from the dissertation.
Target Student: Graduate and Adult students.
Amount: $25,000
Number of Awards: 10
Based on Financial Need: No
Deadline: November
Applications are available online. A completed application, proposal, bibliography, three letters of recommendation, and transcript are required to apply.

(503) Herbert Hoover Presidential Library Association Travel Grant Program

Herbert Hoover Presidential Library Association
P.O. Box 696
West Branch, IA 52358

Phone: 800-828-0475
Fax: 319-643-2391
Email:scholarship@hooverassociation.org
URL: http://www.hooverassociation.org

Goal: To assist individuals performing research at the Herbert Hoover Presidential Library in West Branch, IA.
Eligibility: Applicants must be current graduate students, post-doctoral scholars or independent researchers. Applicants must check to be sure that the libraries contents meet their needs before applying.

Target Student: Graduate and Adult students.
Amount: $500 - $1,500
Number of Awards: Varies
Based on Financial Need: No
Deadline: March
Applications are available online.

(504) Herbert Levy Memorial Scholarship

Society of Physics Students
One Physics Ellipse
College Park, MD 20740

Phone: 301-209-3007
Fax: 301-209-0839
Email: sps@aip.org
URL:http://www.spsnational.org/programs/scholarships/

Goal: To assist physics students with educational expenses.
Eligibility: Applicants must be physics majors, members of SPS and demonstrated financial need.
Target Student: College and Adult students.
Amount: $2,000
Number of Awards: 1
Based on Financial Need: No
Deadline: February
Applications are available online or from an SPS Chapter.

(505) Hertz Foundation's Graduate Fellowship Award

Fannie and John Hertz Foundation
2456 Research Drive
Livermore, CA 94550

Phone: 925-373-1642
Fax: 925-373-6329
Email: askhertz@hertzfoundation.org
URL: http://www.hertzfoundation.com

Goal: To asisst graduate students in applied physical and engineering sciences.
Eligibility: Applicants must be college seniors who are planning to pursue or graduate students pursuing a Ph.D. in applied physical and engineering sciences or modern biology which applies the physical sciences. Applicants must attend one of the foundation's approved schools.
Target Student: College, Graduate and Adult students.
Amount: Up to full tuition.
Number of Awards: Varies
Scholarhsip can be renewed.
Based on Financial Need: No
Deadline: October
Applications are available online, by email or phone.

---

(506) High School Sholarship

National Strength and Conditioning
Association Foundation
1885 Bob Johnson Drive
Colorado Springs, CO 80906

Phone: 800-815-6826
Fax: 719-632-6367
Email: nsca@nsca-lift.org
URL: http://www.nsca-lift.org

Goal: To assist graduating high school students who are beginning college study in the field of strength and conditioning.
Eligibility: Applicants must be high school seniors who are planning to pursue a degree in strength and conditioning and how have a GPA of 3.0 or above. Applicants must be NSCA member and can apply at the time of submitting an application for the scholarship. The award is based on grades, courses, experience, honors, recommendations and involment with NSCA.
Target Student: High school students.
Amount: $1,500
Number of Awards: Varies
Based on Financial Need: No

Deadline: March
Applications are available by contacting the NSCA.

---

(507) HIMSS Foundation Scholarship

Healthcare Information and Management
Systems Society
230 E. Ohio Street
Suite 500
Chicago, IL 60611

Phone: 312-664-4467
Fax: 312-664-6143
URL: http://www.himss.org

Goal: To assist healthcare information and management systems students with educational expenses.
Eligibility: Applicants must be HIMSS members studying healthcare information and management systems.
Target Student: College and Adult students.
Amount: $5,000
Number of Awards: 8
Based on Financial Need: No
Deadline: October
Application information is available online.

---

(508) Holly Cornell Scholarship

American Water Works Association
6666 W. Quincy Avenue
Denver, CO 80235

Phone: 303-664-4467
Fax: 312-664-6143
Email: lmoody@awwa.org
URL: http://www.awwa.org

Goal: To assist female and/or minority students working towards a master's degree in the field of water supply and treatment.

Eligibility: Applicants must be females and/or minoritites who have been accepted or currently enrolled in a master's degree program in the field of water supply and treatement.
Target Student: Graduate and Adult students.
Amount: $7,500
Number of Awards: 1
Based on Financial Need: No
Deadline: January
Applications are available online. A completed application, transcripts, GRE scores, statements, course of study, and three letters of recommendation are required to apply.

---

(509) Holocaust Remembrance Project Essay Contest

Holland and Knight Charitable Foundation
P.O. Box 2877
Tampa, FL 33601

Phone: 866-HK-CARES
Email: holocaust@hklaw.com
URL: http://holocaust.hklaw.com

Goal: To acknowledge high school students who have written an essay about the Holocaust.
Eligibility: Aplicants must be 19 years old or younger and currently enrolled in grades 9 to 12. Applicants must submit an essay about the Holocaust and the scholarships entry form.
Target Student: High school students.
Amount: Up to $5,000
Number of Awards: Varies
Based on Financial Need: No
Deadline: April
Applications and essays are submitted online.

---

(510) Hooper Memorial Scholarship

Transportation Clubs International Scholarships
Attn: Bill Blair
Zimmer Worldwide Logistics
15710 JFK Boulevard
Houston, TX 77032

Phone: 877-858-8627
Email: bblair@zimmerworldwide.com
URL: http://www.transportationclubsinternational.com

Goal: To assist students wanting to enter the transportation industry.
Eligibility: Applicants must be graduating high school seniors or college undergraduate students at an accredited school in a vocational or degree program in the field of transportation, logistics, supply-chain management, traffic management, transportation safety and/or a related field. Financial need is considered.
Target Student: High school, College and Adult students.
Amount: Varies
Number of Awards: Varies
Based on Financial Need: No
Deadline: May
Applications are available online.

---

(511) Horace Mann Scholarship

Horace Mann Insurance Companies
1 Horace Mann Plaza
Springfield, IL 62715

Phone: 800-999-1030
URL: http://www.horacemann.com

Goal: To assist public and private K-12 educators.

Eligibility: Applicants must be an educator who is currently employed by a U.S. public or private school. The applicant must have at least two years of teaching experience and plan on enrolling in a two or four year college or university. The award is based on an essay and school and community activities. Residents of Hawaii, New Jersey and New York are not eligible.
Target Student: College and Adult students.
Amount: $1,000 - $5,000
Number of Awards: 35
Based on Financial Need: No
Deadline: Varies
Applications are available online.

(512) Horatio Alger Association Scholarship Program

Horatio Alger Association
Attn: Scholarship Department
99 Canel Center Plaza
Alexandria, VA 22314

Phone: 703-684-9444
Fax: 703-684-9445
Email: association@horatioalger.com
URL: http://www.horatioalger.com

Goal: To assist students who are pursuing a bachelors degree who have demonstrated financial need, academic achievement, community service and integrity.
Eligibility: Applicants must be entering college by the fall after their graduation from high school. They must also demonstrate financial need ($50,000 or less per family) and be invovled in community and extracurricular activities. A GPA of 2.0 or higher is required.
Target Student: High school students.
Amount: $20,000
Number of Awards: 104
Based on Financial Need: Yes
Deadline: October
Applications are available online.

(513) Horizon - LSG Sky Chefs' International Management Award

International Flight Services Association
1100 Johnson Ferry Road
Suite 300
Atlanta, GA 30342

Phone: 404-252-3663
Fax: 404-252-0774
Email: cellery@kellencompany.com
URL: http://www.ifsanet.com/default.asp x?tabid=170

Goal: To assist onboard services and catering professionals with continuing education expenses.
Eligibility: Applicants must be currently employed as an onboard or catering professional who are middle or upper management. Applicants must be planning to enroll in leadership development courses to further their careers. Applicants must be proficient in two or more langauges and must have two or more years of international experience in the industry.
Target Student: College, Graduate and Adult students.
Amount: $4,500
Number of Awards: Varies
Based on Financial Need: No
Deadline: May
Applications are available online. A completed application, resume, essay and two letters of recommendation are required to apply.

(514) HORIZONS Foundation Scholarship

Women in Defense
HORIZONS FOUNDATION
c/o National Defense Industrial Association
2111 Wilson Boulevard, Suite 400

Arlington, VA 22201

Phone: 703-247-2552
Fax: 703-527-6945
Email: jcasey@ndia.org
URL: http://wid.ndia.org

Goal: To encourage women to enter careers related to national security and to help women already employed in national security to develop their career.
Eligibility: Applicants must be full or part-time female students in their junior year or higher at an accredited college or university. Applicants must have demonstrated interest in a national security career, a GPA of 3.25 or higher with demonstrated financial need. Preference is given to applicants in security studies, military history, government relations, engineering, computer science, physics, mathematics, business, law, international relations, political science or economics.
Target Student: College, Graduate and Adult students.
Amount: Varies
Number of Awards: Varies
Based on Financial Need: Yes
Deadline: July
Applications are available online.

(515) HSMAI Foundation Scholarship

Hospitality Sales and Marketing Association International
1760 Old Meadow Road #500
McLean, VA 22102

Phone: 703-506-2010
Email: info@hsmai.org
URL: http://www.hsmai.org

Goal: To assist students who are pursuing a career in hospitality sales or marketing.
Eligibility: Applicants must be full or part-time undergraduate or graduate students pursuing a career in hospitality sales or marketing.

Target Student: College, Graduate and Adult students.
Amount: Varies
Number of Awards: Varies
Based on Financial Need: No
Deadline: June
Applications are available online.

(516) Humane Studies Fellowships

Institute for Humane Studies at George Mason University
3301 N. Fairfax Drive Suite 440
Arlington, VA 22201

Phone: 800-697-8799
Fax: 703-993-4890
Email: his@gmu.edu
URL: http://www.theihs.org

Goal: To assist students who are interested in classical liberal tradition or individual rights.
Eligibility: Applicants must be graduate students who are relating their work to the humanities (even if the core discipline falls outside the humanities) and dedicated to advancing the ideas of liberty through research and teaching. Students can be enrolled at any school.
Target Student: Graduate students.
Amount: $2,000 to $15,000
Number of Awards: Varies
Scholarship can be renewable.
Based on Financial Need: No
Deadline: December
Applications are available online.

(517) Huntington Fellowships

Huntington Library, Art Collections and Botanical Gardens
1151 Oxford Road
San Marino, CA 91108

Phone: 626-405-2194
Fax: 626-449-5703

Email: cpowell@huntington.org
URL: http://www.huntington.org

Goal: To provide fellowships to doctoral students in British and American history, literature, art history and the history of science and medicine.
Eligibility: Applicants must have a Ph.D. or be doctoral candidates working on their dissertation. A cover sheet, project description, curriculum vitae and three letters of recommendation are required to apply.
Target Student: Gradaute and Adult students.
Amount: $2,500 - $12,500
Number of Awards: More than 100
Based on Financial Need: No
Deadline: December
Application information is available online.

(518) Huntington-British Academy Fellowships for Study in Great Britain

Huntington Library, Art Collections and Botanical Gardens
1151 Oxford Road
San Marino, CA 91108

Phone: 626-405-2194
Fax: 626-449-5703
Email: cpowell@huntington.org
URL: http://www.huntington.org

Goal: To provide exchange fellowships to research British and American history, art history, literature, and the history of science and medicine.
Eligibility: Applicants must have a Ph.D. or equivalent. To apply applicants must submit a cover sheet, project description, curriculum vitae and three letters of recommendation.
Target Student: Graduate and Adult students.
Amount: Varies
Number of Awards: Varies
Based on Financial Need: No

Deadline: December
Application information is available online.

(519) IACI/NUI Visting Fellowship in Irish Studies

Irish-American Cultural Institute (IACI)
An Foras Cultuir Gael-Mheircheanach
1 Lackawanna Place
Morristown, NJ 07960

Phone: 973-605-1991
Fax: 973-605-8875
URL: http://www.iaci-usa.org

Goal: To provide fellowships to Irish students so they can spend one semester studying at the University of Ireland-Galway.
Eligibility: Applicants are required to submit a description of how they will use the fellowship will be used as well as a curriculum vitae with a list of publications.
Target Student: Graduate and Adult students.
Amount: $4,000
Number of Awards: Varies
Based on Financial Need: No
Deadline: December
Applications are available online.

(520) IAFC Foundation Scholarship

International Association of Fire Chiefs Foundation
4025 Fair Ridge Drive
Fairfax, VA 22033

Fax: 571-344-5410
Email: iafcfoun@msn.com
URL: http://www.iafcf.org

Goal: To assist students pursuing degrees in fire sciences.

Eligibility: Applicants must be active members of the IAFC with at least three volunteer work, two years of paid work or a combination of paid and volunteer work of three years with a federal, state, county or city fire department. Preference for the award is given to those with need, desire and initiative.
Target Student: College, Graduate and Adult students.
Amount: Varies
Number of Awards: Varies
Based on Financial Need: No
Deadline: June
Applications are available online.

(521) IDSA Undergraduate Scholarships

Industrial Designers Society of America
45195 Business Court Suite 250
Dulles, VA 20166

Phone: 703-707-6000
Fax: 703-787-8501
Email: idsa@idsa.org
URL: http://www.idsa.org

Goal: To assist industrial design students complete their education.
Eligibility: Applicants must be enrolled, full-time, in an IDSA-program and be in their next to last year of the program and have a GPA of 3.0 or higher and be members of an IDSA Student Chapter.
Target Student: College and Adult students.
Amount: $1,500
Number of Awards: 1
Based on Financial Need: No
Deadline: May
Applications are available online. To apply a letter of intent, transcript and 20 visual examples of their work must be submitted.

(522) IEEE President's Scholarship

Institute of Electrical and Electronics Engineers
445 Hoes Lane
Piscataway, NJ 08854

Phone: 732-562-3860
Email: supportieee@ieee.org
URL: http://www.ieee.org/scholarships

Goal: To acknowledge a student for a project related to electrical engineering, electronics engineering, computer science or other IEEE fields of interest.
Eligibility: Applicants must be student members who use engineering, science and computing to solve a problem.
Target Student: High school students.
Amount: $10,000
Number of Awards: Varies
Scholarship can be renewed.
Based on Financial Need: No
Deadline: may
Contact the organization for additional information.

(523) IEHA Scholarship

International Executive Housekeepers Association Education Foundation
1001 Eastwind Drive
Suite 301
Westerville, OH 43081

Phone: 800-200-6342
Fax: 614-895-1248
Email: excel@ieha.org
URL: http://www.ieha.org

Goal: To assist IEHA members working towards their undergraduate or associates's degree or IEHA certification.
Eligibility: Applicants must submit a 2,000 word paper about an issue in the housekeeping industry. A panel of judges will select the winner who will be published.
Target Student: College and Adult students.

Amount: Up to $800
Number of Awards: Varies
Based on Financial Need: No
Deadline: January
Applications are available online.

(524) IFDA Leaders Commemorative Scholarship

International Furnishings and Design Association
150 South Warner Road
Suite 156
King of Prussia, PA 19406

Phone: 610-535-6422
Fax: 610-535-6423
Email: merrymabbettinc@comcast.net
URL:http://www.ifdaef.org/scholarships.php

Goal: To assist interior design students.
Eligibility: Applicants must be full-time undergraduate students at an accredited college or university and be majoring in interior design or related field.
Target Student: College and Adult students.
Amount: $1,500
Number of Awards: 1
Based on Financial Need: No
Deadline: March
Applications are available online. A completed application, essay, one letter of recommendation and design examples are required to apply.

(525) IFDA Student Member Scholarship

International Furnishings and Design Association
150 South Warner Road
Suite 156
King of Prussia, PA 19406

Phone: 610-535-6422

Fax: 610-535-6423
Email: merrymabbettinc@comcast.net
URL:http://www.ifdaef.org/scholarships.php

Goal: To assist interior design students who are IFDA members.
Eligibility: Applicants must be full-time undergraduate students who are attending an accredited school who are majoring in interior design or related field.
Target Student: Colelge and Adult students.
Amount: $2,500
Number of Awards: 1
Based on Financial Need: No
Deadline: March
Applications are available online. A completed application, personal statement, two letters of recommendation and work samples are required to apply.

(526) IFEC Scholarships Award

International Foodservice Editorial Council
P.O. Box 491
Hyde Park, NY 12538

Phone: 845-229-6973
Email: ifec@ifeconline.com
URL: http://www.ifeconline.com

Goal: To assist those interested in foodservice and communication arts.
Eligibility: Applicants must be enrolled in a post-secondary, degree program and must show training, skill and interest in the foodservice industry and communication arts. Majors that are eligible for the award are: culinary arts, hotel/restaurant/hospitality management, dietetics, nutrition, food sciience/technology, journalism, public relations, mass communication, English, broadcast journalism, marketing, photography, graphic arts and related studies.

Target Student: College, Graduate and Adult students.
Amount: $500 - $4,000
Number of Awards: 4-8
Based on Financial Need: No
Deadline: March
Applications are available online.

---

(527) IFSEA Worthy Goal Scholarship

International Food Service Executives Association
Joseph Quagliano
8824 Stancrest Drive
Las Vegas, NV 89134

Phone: 502-589-3602
URL: http://www.ifsea.com

Goal: To assist students receive food service management training after high school.
Eligibility: Applicants must be enrolled or accepted at a college as a full-time student studying a food service major. Applicants must submit a financial statement, personal statement, list of work experience, list of professional experience, transcripts, letters of recommendation and a statement that describes how the scholarship would help them reach their goals.
Target Student: High school, College, Graduate and Adult students.
Amount: $250 - $1,500
Number of Awards: Varies
Scholarship can be renewed.
Based on Financial Need: Yes
Deadline: February
Applications are avaialble online.

---

(528) IIE Council of Fellows Undergraduate Scholarship

Institute of Industrial Engineers
3577 Parkway Lane
Suite 200
Norcross, GA 30092

Phone: 800-494-0460
Fax: 770-441-3295
Email: bcameron@iienet.org
URL: http://www.iienet2.org

Goal: To assist undergraduate student members.
Eligibility: Applicants must be full-time undergraduate students enrolled ina college in the U.S., Canada or Mexico with an accredited industrial engineering program, major in industrial engineering and be active members. Applicants can apply without being nominated. Finanical need is considered.
Target Student: College and Adult students.
Amount: $1,000
Number of Awards: 1-Jan
Based on Financial Need: No
Deadline: November
Applications are available online.

---

(529) Illustrators of the Future

L. Ron Hubbard
P.O. Box 3190
Los Angeles, CA 90078

Phone: 323-466-3310
Fax:
Email: contests@authorserviceinc.com
URL: http://www.writersofthefuture.com

Goal: To discover and eventually publish aspiring amateur illustrators.
Eligibility: Applicants must have published no more than three black and white story illustrations or more than one color painting in the national media.
Target Student: High school, College, Graduate and Adult students.
Amount: $500 - $5,000
Number of Awards: 3 each quarter and one grand prize a year
Based on Financial Need: No

Deadline: December 31, March 31, June 30 and September 30
There is no application. Applicants must submit three original illustrations done in black and white with three different themes.

(530) IMA Memorial Education Fund Scholarship

Institute of Management Accountants
10 Paragon Drive
Montvale, NJ 07645

Phone: 800-638-4427
Email: students@imanet.org
URL: http://www.imanet.org

Goal: To assist students studying fields related to management accounting.
Eligibility: Applicants must be part or full-time undergraduate or graduate students, have a GPA of 2.8 or higher, be IMA student members and declare which four or five year management accounting, financial management or information technology related program they are planning to pursue as a career. Advanced degree students must pass one part of the CMA/CFM certification.
Target Student: College, Graduate and Adult students.
Amount: $1,000-$2,500
Number of Awards: Varies
Based on Financial Need: No
Deadline: February
Applications are available online.

(531) Imagine America High School Scholarship Program

Imagine America Foundation
1101 Connecticut Avenue NW
Suite 901
Washington, DC 20036

Phone: 202-336-6800

Fax: 202-408-8102
Email: scholarships@imagine-america.org
URL: http://www.imagine-america.org

Goal: To assist high school seniors in pursuing a postsecondary education.
Eligibility: Applicants must have a GPA of 2.5 or higher, have demonstrated financial need, and demonstrated community service in their senior year.
Target Student: High school students.
Amount: $1,000
Number of Awards: Varies
Based on Financial Need: Yes
Deadline: December
Applications are available online.

(532) Imagine America Promise

Imagine America Foundation
1101 Connecticut Avenue NW
Suite 901
Washington, DC 20036

Phone: 202-336-6800
Fax: 202-408-8102
Email: scholarships@imagine-america.org
URL: http://www.imagine-america.org

Goal: To further assist those who have won the Imagine America high school scholarship.
Eligibility: Applicants must be Imagine America high school scholarship, currently enrolled in college, applicants graduation date must be after December 31, have a GPA of 3.5 of higher, must have a 95% or higher attendance record and must obtain a written recommendation from the faculty/administrator representative of the college and be nominated by a participating college.
Target Student: College and Adult students.
Amount: $500
Number of Awards: Varies
Based on Financial Need: No
Deadline: Varies

Nomination forms are available online.

(533) IMCEA Scholarships

International Military Community Executives Association
1530 Dunwoody Village Parkway Suite 203
Atlants, GA 30338

Phone: 770-396-2101
Fax: 770-396-2198
Email: imcea@imcea.com
URL: http://www.imcea.com

Goal: To assist high school students and military welfare and recreation professionals with educational expenses.
Eligibility: The scholarship is open to IMCEA members in good standing enrolled in college or dependent family members who are graduating from high school or currently enrolled in high school. Applicants must provide an overview of their activities, honors and awards as well as include an essay on a provided topic.
Target Student: High school, College, Graduate and Adult students.
Amount: $1,000
Number of Awards: 2
Based on Financial Need: No
Deadline: May
Applications are available online.

(534) Incoming Freshman Scholarship

American Hotle and Lodging Educational Foundation
1201 New York Avenue NW
Suite 600
Washington, DC 20005

Phone: 202-289-3188
Fax: 202-289-3199
Email: chammond@ahlef.org
URL: http://www.ahlef.org

Goal: To acknowledge high school students interested in hospitality related programs.
Eligibility: Applicants must be graduating seniors who are planning to attend a post-secondary school, be a U.S. citizen, and have a GPA of 2.0 or better. Preference is given to those that have completed the two year Lodging Management Program in high school.
Target Student: High school students.
Amount: $1,000 - $2,000
Number of Awards: Varies
Based on Financial Need: No
Deadline: May
Applications are available online.

(535) Indianhead Division Scholarships

Second Indianhead Division Association
P.O. Box 460
Buda, TX 78610

Phone: 512-295-5324
Email: warriorvet@verizon.net
URL: http://www.2ida.org

Goal: To asisst the children and grandchildren of veterans from the Second Indianhead Division Association.
Eligibility: Applicants parents or grandparents must have been members of the association for three years or more, or they must have been killed while serving.
Target Student: High school, College and Adult students.
Amount: Varies
Number of Awards: Varies
Scholarship can be renewed.
Based on Financial Need: No
Deadline: June
Applications can be requested by phone.

(536) Industrial Electrolysis and Electrochemical Engineering Division H.H. Dow Memorial Student Award

Electrochemical Society
65 South Main Street
Building D
Pennington, NJ 8534

Phone: 609-737-1902
Fax: 609-737-2743
Email: awards@electrochem.org
URL: http://www.electrochem.org

Goal: To acknowledge young engineers and scientists in the fields of electrochemical engineering and applied electrochemistry.
Eligibility: Applicants must be accepted or enrolled in a graduate program and complete a research project related to electrochemical engineering or applied electrochemistry.
Target Student: Graduate and Adult students.
Amount: $1,000
Number of Awards: Varies
Based on Financial Need: No
Deadline: September
Application information is available online.

(537) Intel Science Talent Search

Intel Corporation and Science Service
Society for Science and the Public
1719 North Street NW
Washington, DC 20036

Phone: 202-785-2255
Fax: 202-785-1243
Email: sciedu@sciserv.org
URL: http://www.societyforscience.org/sts

Goal: To acknowledge excellence in science among the youth of the nation and encourage the use of science.
Eligibility: Applicants must be high school seniors in the U.S. or one of it's territories and complete an entrance exam and completed a research project.
Target Student: High school students.

Amount: $7,500 - $100,000
Number of Awards: 40
Based on Financial Need: No
Deadline: Varies
Applications are available online.

(538) International Association of Fire Chiefs Foundation Fire Explorer Scholarships

Explorers Learning for Life
P.O. Box 152079
Irving, TX 75015

Phone: 972-580-2433
Fax: 972-580-2137
Email: pchestnu@lflmail.org
URL: http://www.learningforlife.org/exploring

Goal: To asisst students who are pursuing careers in fire science.
Eligibility: Applicants must be high school seniors, active fire service Explorers and members of a fire department. Three letters of recommendation and an essay are required.
Target Student: High school students.
Amount: $500
Number of Awards: Varies
Based on Financial Need: No
Deadline: June
Applications are available online.

(539) International Gas Turbine Institute Scholarship

American Society of Merchant Engineers
Three Park Avenue
New York, NY 10016

Phone: 800-843-2763
Fax: 973-882-1717
Email: infocentral@asme.org
URL: http://www.asme.org

Goal: To assist American Society of Mechanical Engineers student members who are interested in the gas turbine industry.
Eligibility: Applicants must be student members of ASME, enrolled in an accredited undergraduate or graduate program in mechanical engineering or aerospace engineering and interested in turbomachinery, gas turbine or propulsion industry.
Target Student: College, Graduate and Adult students.
Amount: $5,000
Number of Awards: 1
Based on Financial Need: No
Deadline: March
Applications are available online. An electronic application, transcript, statement and one or two letters of recommendation are required to apply.

(540) International Junior Competition

Gina Bachauer International Piano Foundation
138 W. Broadway, Suite 220
Salt Lake City, UT 84101

Phone: 801-297-4250
Fax: 801-521-9202
Email: info@bachauer.com
URL: http://www.bachauer.com

Goal: To aknowledge piano prodigies from ages 11 to 13.
Eligibility: Applicants must perform a 20 minute and 30 minute program of solo music at a competition in Salt Lake City. Housing is provided, but transportation is the responsibility of the applicant.
Target Student: Junior high and younger.
Amount: Up to $7,000
Number of Awards: 6
Based on Financial Need: No
Deadline: The compeition is in June every 4 years.
Applications are available online.

(541) International Scholarships

American Institute for Foreign Study
AIFS College Division
River Plaza
9 W. Broad Street
Stamford, CT 06902

Phone: 800-727-2437
Fax: 203-399-5597
Email: info@aifs.com
URL: http://www.aifsabroad.com

Goal: To encourage international understanding through study abroad opportunities.
Eligibility: Applicants must be current undergraduate students with a GPA of 3.0 or higher with demonstrated leadership and involved in extra-curricular activities that are focused on multi-cultural or international issues.
Target Student: College and Adult students.
Amount: $1,000
Number of Awards: 40
Based on Financial Need: No
Deadline: April and September
Applications are available online. To apply a completed application and a 1,000 word essay is required to apply.

(542) International Student Scholarship

American Speech-Language-Hearing Foundation
2200 Research Boulevard
Rockville, MD 20850

Phone: 301-296-8700
Email: foundation@asha.org
URL: http://www.ashfoundation.org

Goal: To assist an international graduate student in communication sciences and disorders.

Eligibility: Applicants must be full-time students in a U.S. accredited Master's degree program or accredited or unaccredited doctoral program in speech, language and hearing.
Target Student: Graduate and Adult students.
Amount: $5,000
Number of Awards: 1
Based on Financial Need: No
Deadline: Unknown
Applications are available online.

(543) International Trumpet Guild Confeerence Scholarship

International Trumpet Guild
John Irish, Department of Music
Angelo State University
ASU Station #10906
San Angelo, TX 76909

Email:confscholarships@trumpetguild.org
URL: http://www.trumpetguild.org

Goal: To assist trumpet players.
Eligibility: Applicants must be students, ITG members, and record their audition onto a tape or CD.
Target Student: Junior high and younger, High school, College, Graduate and Adult students.
Amount: Varies
Number of Awards: Varies
Based on Financial Need: No
Deadline: February
Applications are available online.

(544) IRARC Memorial Joseph P. Rubiano WA4MMD Scholarship

American Radio Relay League Foundation
225 Main Street
Newington, CT 06111

Phone: 860-594-0397
Fax: 860-597-0259

Email: foundation@arrl.org
URL: http://www.arrlf.org

Goal: To assist amateur radio operators seeking undergraduate degrees or electronic technician certification.
Eligibility: Applicants must have an active Amateur Radio License in any class and be studying at an accredited institution with a GPA of 2.5 or higher. Preference is given to Brevard County, Florida residents with need and lower GPAs.
Target Student: High school, College and Adult students.
Amount: $750
Number of Awards: Varies
Based on Financial Need: No
Deadline: February
Aplications are available online.

(545) Irene and Daisy MacGregor Memorial Scholarship

National SocietyDaughters of the American Revolution
Committee Services Office
Attn: Scholarships
1776 D Street NW
Washington, DC 20006

Phone: 202-628-1776
URL: http://www.dar.org

Goal: To assist students in becoming medical doctors.
Eligibility: Applicants must be accepted or enrolled in a graduate program to become a medical doctor. Those who are pursuing a graduate psychiatric nursing degree at a medical school are also eligible. Preference for the award is given to females and applicants do not need to be affiliated with the DAR.
Target Student: Graduate and Adult students.
Amount: Varies
Number of Awards: Varies
Scholarship can be renewed.

Based on Financial Need: No
Deadline: April
Applications are available by written request.

---

(546) Irene Ryan Acting Scholarships

John F. Kennedy Center for the
Performing Arts
2700 F Street NW
Washington, DC 20566

Phone: 800-444-1324
URL: http://www.kennedy-center.org/education/actf/actfira.html

Goal: To assist student performers.
Eligibility: Applicants must be undergraduate or graduate who have appeared in an associate or participating production of the Kennedy Center American College Theater Festival. Applicants must be nominated by their school and perform an audition in the competition.
Target Student: College, Graduate and Adult students.
Amount: Up to $2,500
Number of Awards: 19
Based on Financial Need: No
Deadline: Varies
Applications are available through your sponsor.

---

(547) Irene Woodall Graduate Scholarship

American Dental Hygienists' Association
Insitute for Oral Health
Scholarship Award Program
444 North Michigan Avenue
Suite 3400
Chicago, IL 60611

Phone: 312-440-8900
Email: institute@adha.net
URL: http://www.adha.org/ioh

Goal: To assist students working towards a master's degree in dental hygiene.
Eligibility: Applicants must be full-time students at an accredited college or university in the U.S. working towards a master's in dental hygiene or a related field, must have completed at least one year of dental hygiene courses, have a 3.5 GPA or higher and demonstrated financial need of $1,500 or more.
Target Student: College, Graduate and Adult students.
Amount: $1,000 - $2,000
Number of Awards: 1
Based on Financial Need: Yes
Deadline: February
Applications are available beginning in October.

---

(548) IRF Fellowship Program

International Road Federation
Madison Place
500 Montgomery Street
5th Floor
Alexandria, VA 22314

Phone: 703-535-1001
Fax: 703-535-1007
Email: info@internationalroadfederation.org
URL: http://www.irfnet.org

Goal: To provide fellowships for graduate study in a field related to transportation.
Eligibility: Applicants must have demonstrated leadership in the highway industry in finance, administration, planning, design, construction, operations or maintenance. Applicants must also have between 3 and 15 years of work experience, a bachelor's in a transportation related field and a commitment to study full-time for nine months.
Target Student: Graduate and Adult students.
Amount: Varies

Number of Awards: Varies
Based on Financial Need: No
Deadline: Varies
Application information is available online.

---

(549) ISFA College Scholarship

Insurance Scholarship Foundation of America
14286-19 Beach Boulevard
Suite 3300
Jacksonville, FL 32250

Phone: 904-821-7188
Email: foundation@inssfa.org
URL: http://www.inssfa.org

Goal: To promote studies in the insurance industry.
Eligibility: Applicants must be majoring in insurance, risk management or actuarial science, have completed two insurance or risk management related courses, be attending a college or university, be completing or completed their second year with a GPA of 3.0 or higher and be a NAIW Student Member.
Target Student: College, Graduate and Adult students.
Amount: $500 - $5,000
Number of Awards: Varies
Based on Financial Need: No
Deadline: March and October
Application information is available online

---

(550) ISIA Education Foundation Scholarship

Ice Skating Institute of America Education Foundation
17120 N. Dallas Parkway Suite 140
Dallas, TX 75248

Phone: 972-735-8800
Fax: 972-735-8815
URL: http://www.skateisi.com

Goal: To assist skaters in athletic and educational achievements.
Eligibility: Applicants must have completed at least three years of high school and have a GPA of 3.0 or higher in the last two years and enroll as full-time undergraduate students. Applicants must have been Ice Skating Institute members and participated in ISI Recreational Skater Program for a minimum of four years and participated in ISI competition classes within the last two years with 240 hours of verified service with 120 volunteered.
Target Student: High school, College and Adult students.
Amount: $4,000
Number of Awards: Varies
Based on Financial Need: No
Deadline: March
Applications are available online. A completed application, two evaluations and essay are required to apply.

---

(551) J. Franklin Jameson Fellowship in American History

American Historical Association
400 A Street SE
Washington, DC 20003

Phone: 202-544-2422
Fax: 202-544-8307
Email: info@historians.org
URL: http://www.historians.org

Goal: To support one semester of research at the Library of Congress.
Eligibility: Applicants must hold a Ph.D. or equivalent, must have earned a degree within the last seven years, and may not have published a book length historical work. The research project should focus on American history.
Target Student: Graduate and Adult students.
Amount: $5,000
Number of Awards: Varies
Based on Financial Need: No

Deadline: March
Applications are available online.

---

(552) Jack Horkheimer Award

Astonomical League
7241 Jarboe
Kansas City, MO 64114

Phone: 816-444-4878
Email: carroll-iorg@kc.rr.com
URL: http://www.astroleague.org

Goal: To assist young Astronomical
League members.
Eligibility: Applicants must be
Astronomical League members under 19
when they apply.
Target Student: Junior high or younger
and High school students.
Amount: Up to $1,000 plus travel
expenses.
Number of Awards: 3
Based on Financial Need: No
Deadline: March
Applications are available online.

---

(553) Jack Kinnaman Scholarship

National Education Association
NEA-Retired, Room 410
1201 16th Street NW
Washington, DC 20036

Phone: 202-822-7149
URL: http://www.nea.org

Goal: To honor the memory of Jack
Kinnaman, NEA-retired vice president and
former advisory council member.

Eligibility: Applicants must be NEA
student members, major in education and
havea minimum 2.5 GPA. To apply
applicants must submit an essay describing
their NEA activties, a paragraph about
their financial need, two letters of
recommendation and a copy of their
transcript.
Target Student: College and Adult
students.
Amount: $2,000
Number of Awards: 1
Based on Financial Need: Yes
Deadline: April
Applications are available online.

---

(554) James A. Turner, Jr. Memorial Scholarship

American Welding Society Foundation
550 NW LeJeune Road
Miami, FL 33126

Phone: 800-443-9353
Email: info@aws.org
URL: http://www.aws.org

Goal: To assist those interested in a career
in management in welding store operations
or distributorship.
Eligibility: Applicants must be a full time
student pursuing a bachelor's in business at
a four year college. Applicants must plan
to enter management careers in welding
store operations or distributorships, be
high school gradautes, be at least 18 years
old and be employed a minimum o f10
hours per week at a welding
distributorship.
Target Student: College and Adult
students.
Amount: $3,500
Number of Awards: 1
Based on Financial Need: No
Deadline: February
Applications are available online.

(555) James M. and Virginia M. Smyth Scholarship

Community Foundation for Greater
Atlanta Inc.
50 Hurt Plaza Suite 449
Atlanta, GA 30303

Phone: 404-688-5525
Fax: 404-688-3060
Email: info@cfgreateratlanta.org
URL: http://www.cfgreateratlanta.org

Goal: To assist students who are planning to purse undergraduate degrees.
Eligibility: Applicants must have a 3.0 GPA, must have community service experience and plan to pursue a degree in arts, sciences, music, ministry or human services. Applicants from Georgia, Illinois, Oklahoma, Texas, Tennessee, Missouri and Mississippi are given preference. Applicants must demonstrate financial need.
Target Student: High school, College and Adult students.
Amount: $2,000
Number of Awards: 12-15
Scholarship can be renewed.
Based on Financial Need: Yes
Deadline: March
Applications are available online.

(556) Jane Delano Student Nurse Scholarship

American Red Cross
National Headquarters
2025 E Street NW
Washington, DC 20006

Phone: 202-303-5000
Email: littlefieldv@usa.redcross.org
URL: http://www.redcross.org

Goal: To assist Red Cross volunteers attending nursing school.
Eligibility: Applicants must be enrolled in an accredited nursing school, completed at least one academic year of college when they apply and must have volunterred with a Red Cross unit at least once within the last five years.
Target Student: College, Graduate and Adult students.
Amount: $3,000
Number of Awards: 3
Based on Financial Need: No
Deadline: June
Applications are available online. A completed application, essay, endorsement from a Red Cross unit and nursing school dean or chair are required to apply.

(557) Jane M. Klausman Women in Business Scholarship Fund

Zonta International
1211 West 22nd Street
Oak Brook, IL 60523

Phone: 630-928-1400
Fax: 630-928-1559
Email: zontaintl@zonta.org
URL: http://www.zonta.org

Goal: To assist female business management majors overcome gender barriers.
Eligibility: Applicants must be eligible to begin their junior or senior year in an undergraduate degree program at an accredited college when the scholarship is received. Applicants must have an outstanding academic record and show intent to complete a business program.
Target Student: College and Adult students.
Amount: $1,000 - $5,000
Number of Awards: Varies
Based on Financial Need: No
Deadline: July
Applications are avaialble online or from your local Zonta club.

(558) Japan-IMF Scholarship Program for Advanced Studies

Institute of International Education
1400 K Street NW
Washington, DC 20005

Phone: 202-326-7672
Fax: 202-326-7835
Email: boren@iie.org
URL: http://www.iie.org

Goal: To assist Japanese nationals working towards a Ph.D. in macroeconomics and related fields.
Eligibility: Applicants must be admitted to a school outside of Japan that has a strong doctoral program in macroeconomics and finish their Ph.D. by age 34. The scholarship covers expenses for two years of graduate study. Recipients must not receive other income or scholarships during the two years. They are also expected to apply for employement with the IMF after completion of their degree.
Target Student: College and Adult students.
Amount: Tuition plus travel expenses and a paid internship
Number of Awards: Up to 7
Scholarship can be renewed.
Based on Financial Need: No
Deadline: January
Applications are available online. A completed application, personal statement, transcript, GRE, TOEFL/IELTS score, copy of the application to the doctoral program and two letters of recommendation are required to apply.

(559) Jean Cebik Memorial Scholarship

American Radio Relay League Foundation
225 Main Street
Newington, CT 06111

Phone: 860-594-0397
Fax: 860-394-0259
Email: foundation@arrl.org
URL: http://www.arrlf.org

Goal: To assist amateur radio operators with educational expenses.
Eligibility: Applicants must hold a Technician Class Amateur Radio License or higher and they must be attending a four year college or university.
Target Student: High school, College and Adult students.
Amount: $1,000
Number of Awards: 1
Based on Financial Need: No
Deadline: February
Applications are available online.

(560) Jean Theodore Lacordaire Prize

Coleopterists Society
Anthony I. Cognato, Chair
Texas A&M University
College State, TX 77845

Phone: 979-458-0404
Email: a.cognato@tamu.edu
URL: http://www.coleopsoc.org

Goal: To acknowledge the work of coleopterists.
Eligibility: Applicants must be graduate students who have had their papers nominated for the competition. The paper must be about coleoptera systematics or bilogy and published in a journal or book.
Target Student: Graduate and Adult students.
Amount: $300
Number of Awards: 1
Based on Financial Need: No
Deadline: March
Application information is available online.

(561) Jeanne S. Chall Research Fellowship

International Reading Association
The Jeanne S. Chall Research Fellowship
Division of Research and Policy
800 Barksdale Road P.O. Box 8139
Neward, DE 19714

Phone: 302-731-1600
Fax: 302-731-1057
URL: http://www.reading.org

Goal: To assist those working on dissertations in reading.
Eligibility: Appplicants must be members of the International Reading Association and be doctoral students who are working towrads, or planning a dissertation on reading, beginning reading, readability, reading difficulty, stages of reading development, the relation of vocabulary to reading and disgnosing and teaching adults and limiting reading ability.
Target Student: Graduate and Adult students.
Amount: $6,000
Number of Awards: 1
Based on Financial Need: No
Deadline: November
Applications are available online.

(562) Jennifer C. Groot Fellowship

American Center of Oriental Research
656 Beacon Street, 5th Floor
Boston, MA 02215

Phone: 617-353-6571
Fax: 617-353-6575
Email: acor@bu.edu
URL: http://www.bu.edu/acor

Goal: To assist students with the expenses of an archaeological project.

Eligibility: Applicants must be U.S. or Canadian citizens, undergraduate or graduate students with little to no archaeologial field experience. Award winners will travel to Jordan for the project.
Target Student: College, Graduate and Adult students.
Amount: $1,800
Number of Awards: At least 2
Based on Financial Need: No
Deadline: February
Applications are available online, but must be mailed in.

(563) Jessica King Scholarship

Association for International Practical Training
10400 Little Patuxent Parkway
Suite 250
Columbia, MD 21044

Phone: 410-997-2200
Fax: 410-992-3924
Email: aipt@aipt.org
URL: http://www.aipt.org

Goal: To assist students in the international hospitality field.
Eligibility: Applicants must be between the ages of 18 and 35 years old, have a degree in the hospitality industry and be fluent in the host country's language. Applicants must also have been offered and overseas postion and be in an AIPT sponsored program.
Target Student: College, Graduate and Adult students.
Amount: Up to $2,000
Number of Awards: Varies
Based on Financial Need: No
Deadline: Accepted throughout the year.
Applications are available online.

(564) Jewell Hilton Bonner Scholarship

Navy League Foundation
2300 Wilson Boulevard
Arlington, VA 22201

Phone: 800-356-5760
Fax: 703-528-2333
Email: lhuycke@navyleague.org
URL: http://www.navyleague.org

Goal: To assist the dependents and descendants of sea personnel.
Eligibility: Applicants must be dependents or descendants of active, reserve, retired or honorably discharged members of the U.S. Navy, Coast Guard, U.S. Flag Merchant Marine, Marine Corps, or U.S. Navel Sea Cadet Corps. Applicants must be high school seniors who plan to enroll in the fall following their high school graduation.
Target Student: High school students.
Amount: $2,500
Number of Awards: 1
Based on Financial Need: No
Deadline: March
Applications are available online.

(565) Jimmy A. Young Memorial Education Recognition Award

American Association for Respiratory Care
9425 North MacArthur Boulevard
Suite 100
Irving, TX 75063

Phone: 972-243-2272
Fax: 972-484-2720
Email: info@aarc.org
URL: http://www.aarc.org

Goal: To acknowledge outstanding minority students in respiratory care programs.
Eligibility: Applicants must be enrolled in an accredited respiratory care program with a 3.0 GPA or higher and submit a paper on respiratory care.

Target Student: College, Graduate and Adult students.
Amount: Up to $1,000
Number of Awards: 1
Based on Financial Need: No
Deadline: June
Applications are available online.

(566) Joe Foss Institute Essay Scholarship Program

Joe Foss Institute
14415 North 73rd Street Suite 109
Scottsdale, AZ 85260

Phone: 480-348-0316
Email: scholarship@joefoss.com
URL: http://www.joefoss.com

Goal: To encourage applicants to befriend and apprciate military veterans.
Eligibility: Applicants must be U.S. citzens and be high school students or recent high school graduates. They must spend time with and interview a veteran and submit an essay on the experience. The award is based on essay creativity, clarity and grammar.
Target Student: High school students.
Amount: $250 to $5,000
Number of Awards: 3
Based on Financial Need: No
Deadline: October
Instructions are available online. A cover sheet and completed 1,500 essay are required.

(567) Joe Francis Haircare Scholarship Program

Joe Francis Haircare Scholarship Foundation
P.O. Box 50625
Minneapolis, MN 55405

Phone: 651-769-1757
Fax: 651-459-8371

URL: http://www.joefrancis.com

Goal: To assist barber and cosmetology students with educational expenses.
Eligibility: Applicants must be sponsored by a fully accredited and recognized barber or cosmetology school, a licensed salon owner or manager, a full-service distributor or a member of the International Chain Association, Beauty and Barber Supply Institute, Cosmetology Advancement Foundation or National Cosmetology Association. Applicants must be enrolled in a cosmetology school or planning to enroll in or after August. The award is based on financial need, motivation and character.
Target Student: High school, College and Adult students.
Amount: $1,000
Number of Awards: Varies
Based on Financial Need: Yes
Deadline: June
Applications are available online.

---

(568) Joe Perdue Scholarship

Club Foundation
1733 King Street
Alexandria, VA 22314

Phone: 703-739-9500
Fax: 703-739-0124
Email: schaverr@clubfoundation.org
URL: http://www.clubfoundation.org

Goal: To assist students who are working towards careers in private club management.
Eligibility: Applicants must be pursuing managerial careers in the private club industry, have a GPA of 2.5 or higher, have completed their freshman year of college and be enrolled as a full-time student for the following year.
Target Student: College and Adult students.
Amount: Varies

Number of Awards: Varies
Based on Financial Need: No
Deadline: May
Applications are available online. A completed application, essay and letters of recommendation are required to apply.

---

(569) Joel Polsky Academic Achievement Award

American Society of Interior Designers Educational Foundation Inc.
608 Massachusetts Avenue, NE
Washington, DC 20002

Phone: 202-546-3480
Fax: 202-546-3240
URL: http://www.asid.org

Goal: To acknowledge a student's interior design project.
Eligibility: Applicants must be undergraduate or graduate students in interior design.
Target Student: College, Graduate and Adult students.
Amount: $5,000
Number of Awards: 1
Based on Financial Need: No
Deadline: March
Applications are available online. To apply applicants must submit a completed application and a project on interior design.

---

(570) Johansen International Competition for Young String Players

Friday Morning Music Club Inc.
801 K Street, NW
Washington, DC 20001

Phone: 202-333-2075
Email: johansencomp@fmmc.org
URL: http://www.fmmc.org

Goal: To assist young musicians.

Eligibility: Applicants must be between 13 and 17 years old and play the violin, viola or cello. Applicants are required to pay a $75 application fee and play five pieces for the competition. It is not recommended to pay for scholarships, but some are included here.
Target Student: Junior high and younger and High school students.
Amount: $5,000-$10,000
Number of Awards: 9
Based on Financial Need: No
Deadline: December
Applications are available online.

---

(571) John and Elsa Gracik Scholarships

American Society of Mechanical Engineers
Three Park Avenue
New York, NY 10016

Phone: 800-843-2763
Fax: 973-882-1717
Email: infocentral@asme.org
URL: http://www.asme.org

Goal: To assist students studying mechanical engineering.
Eligibility: Applicants must be ASME student members, U.S. citizens, and enrolled in an accredited bachelor's degree in mechanical engineering.
Target Student: College and Adult students.
Amount: $2,000
Number of Awards: Up to 15
Based on Financial Need: Yes
Deadline: March
Applications are available online.

---

(572) John and Muriel Landis Scholarship

American Nuclear Society
55 North Kensington Avenue
La Grange Park, IL 60526

Phone: 800-323-3044
Fax: 708-352-0499
Email: hr@ans.org
URL: http://www.ans.org

Goal: To assist disadvantaged students seeking careers in a nuclear related field.
Eligibility: Applicants must be undergraduate or graduate students who are enrolled or planning to enroll in a U.S. college or university and planning a career in nuclear science, nuclear engineering, or another nuclear-related field. Applicants must have above average financial need.
Target Student: High school, College, Graduate and Adult students.
Amount: Varies
Number of Awards: Up to 9
Based on Financial Need: Yes
Deadline: February
Applications are available online. A completed application, transcript, three letters of recommendation and sponsor forms are required to apply.

---

(573) John Bayliss Radio Scholarship

John Bayliss Broadcast Foundation
171 17th Street
Pacific Grove, CA 93950

Phone: 212-424-6410
Email: cbutrum@baylissfoundation.org
URL:http://www.beaweb.org@bayliss.html

Goal: To assist students pursuing careers in radio with their educational expenses.
Eligibility: Applicants must be attending an institution of higher learning in the U.S., have a GPA of 3.0 or higher, and be entering their junior or senior year and be working towards a degree in the radio industry.
Target Student: College and Adult students.
Amount: $5,000

Number of Awards: Varies
Based on Financial Need: No
Deadline: Unknown
Applications are available online. A completed application, resume, transcript, essay and three letters of recommendation are required to apply.

---

(574) John D. Graham Scholarship

Public Relations Student Society of America
33 Maiden Lane
11th Floor
New York, NY 10038

Phone: 212-460-1474
Fax: 212-995-0757
Email: prssa@prsa.org
URL: http://www.prssa.org

Goal: To assist journalism and public relations students.
Eligibility: Applicants must be undergraduate seniors currently enrolled in journalism or public relations degree program. Award selection is based on academic merit, leadership, work experience, career goals and writing ability.
Target Student: College and Adult students.
Amount: $1,000 - $3,000
Number of Awards: 3
Based on Financial Need: No
Deadline: June
Applications are available online. A completed application, resume and one letter of recommendation are required to apply.

---

(575) John F. and Anna Lee Stacey Scholarship Fund for Art Education

John F. and Anna Lee Stacey Scholarship Fund
1700 N.E. 63rd Street
Oklahoma City, OK 73111

Phone: 405-478-2250
Fax: 405-478-4714
Email: emuno@nationalcowboymuseum.org
URL: http://www.nationalcowboymuseum.org

Goal: To assist young people entering the field of art.
Eligibility: Applicants must be between 18 and 35 years old. Applicants are required to submit up to 10 pieces of art in digital form with a letter that describes the artists plans and goals.
Target Student: High school, College, Graduate and Adult students.
Amount: $5,000
Number of Awards: Varies
Based on Financial Need: No
Deadline: February
Applications are available online.

---

(576) John F. Duffy Scholarship

California Peace Officers' Memorial Foundation
P.O. Box 2437
Fair Oaks, CA 95628

Email: cpomf@camemorial.org
URL: http://www.camemorial.org

Goal: To assist family members of California peace officers who have died in the line of duty.
Eligibility: Applicants must be spouses, children or stepchildren peace officers who died in the line of duty and are enrolled in the California memorial monument. Applicants must take at least 6 quarter or 8 semester units per term and have a 2.5 GPA for higher.
Target Student: High school, College, Graduate and Adult students.
Amount: $4,000
Number of Awards: Varies
Based on Financial Need: No

Deadline: June
Applications are available online.

---

(577) John F. Kennedy Profile in Courage Essay Contest

John F. Kennedy Library Foundation
Columbia Point
Boston, MA 2125

Phone: 617-514-1649
Email: profiles@nara.gov
URL: http://www.jfkcontest.org

Goal: To encourage students to research and write about John F. Kennedy.
Eligibility: Applicants must be in grades 9 to 12 and write an essay about the political courage of a U.S. elected official who served during or after 1956. Each essay must contain source citations. Applicants must register online before sending in their essay and have a nominating teacher review the essay. The scholarship winner and their teacher will be invited to the Kennedy Library for acceptance of the award and the teacher will recieve a grant.
Target Student: High school students.
Amount: $500 - $10,000
Number of Awards: Up to 7
Based on Financial Need: No
Deadline: January
Applications are available online.

---

(578) John Foster Memorial College Scholarship

Kansas Peace Officers Association
1620 S.W. Tyler
Topeka, KS 66612

Phone: 785-296-8200
Email: kpoa@kpoa.org
URL: http://www.kacp.cc

Goal: To assist the children of Kansas law enforcement officers.

Eligibility: Applicants must be the child of a full-time, active Kansas law enfrocement officer. They must be attending an accredited college or univeresity in Kansas and taking at least 12 units per semester.
Target Student: High school, College and Adult Studnts.
Amount: $3,000
Number of Awards: Varies
Based on Financial Need: No
Deadline: April
Applications are available online.

---

(579) John Henry Comstock Graduate Student Awards

Entomological Society of America
10001 Derekwood Lane
Suite 100
Lanham, MD 20706

Phone: 301-731-4535
Fax: 301-731-4538
Email: esa@entsoc.org
URL: http://www.entsoc.org

Goal: To encourage graduate students who are interested in entomology to attend the Entomological Society of America annual meeting.
Eligibility: Applicants must be graduate students as well as ESA members.
Target Student: Graduate and Adult students.
Amount: Travel expenses plus $100
Number of Awards: 6
Based on Financial Need: No
Deadline: August
Applications are available online.

---

(580) John J. McKetta Scholarship

American Institute of Chemical Engineers
Three Park Avenue
New York, NY 10016

Phone: 212-591-7634
Fax: 212-591-8890
Email: awards@aiche.org
URL: http://www.aiche.org

Goal: To assist chemical engineering students.
Eligibility: Applicants must be undergraduate juniors or seniors majoring in chemical engineering and planning a career in the chemical engineering process industry. Applicants must be attending an ABET accredited school in the U.S., Canada, or Mexico with a GPA of 3.0 or higher. Preference is given to members of AIChE.
Target Student: College and Adult students.
Amount: $5,000
Number of Awards: 1
Based on Financial Need: No
Deadline: June
Applications are available online.

---

(581) John Jowdy Scholarship

Columbia 300
P.O. Box 746
Hopkinsville, KY 42241

Phone: 800-531-5920
Email: columbiainfo@columbia300.com
URL: http://www.columbia300.com

Goal: To assist high school seniors who are involved in bowling.
Eligibility: Applicants must submit an essay and two letters of recommendation. The award can be renewed, but students will need to maintain a 3.0 GPA.
Target Student: High school students.
Amount: $500
Number of Awards: 1
Scholarship can be renewed.
Based on Financial Need: No
Deadline: April
Applications are available online.

---

(582) John L. Imhoff Scholarship

Institute of Industrial Engineers
3577 Parkway Lane
Suite 200
Norcross, GA 30092

Phone: 800-494-0460
Fax: 770-441-3295
Email: bcameron@iienet.org
URL: http://www.iienet2.org

Goal: To acknowledge students who have contributed to the development of industrial engineering by improving international understanding.
Eligibility: Applicants must be working towards a bachelor's of science, master's or doctorate in an accredited IE program with at least two years of school remaining. Students must be nominated for this award.
Target Student: College, Graduate and Adult students.
Amount: $1,000
Number of Awards: At least 1
Based on Financial Need: No
Deadline: November
Application information is available online.

---

(583) John Lennon Scholarship Competition

BMI Foundation Inc.
320 W. 57th Street
New York, NY 10019

Phone: 212-586-2000
Email: info@bmifoundation.org
URL: http://www.bmifoundation.org

Goal: To acknowledge and assist talented young songwriters.
Eligibility: Applicants must be between 15 and 25 years old and compose an original song for submission.

Target Student: Junior high and younger, High school, College and Graduate students.
Amount: $5,000 -$10,000
Number of Awards: 3
Based on Financial Need: No
Deadline: April
Applications are submitted by eligible organizations. The BMI Foundation website has a list of organizations that can apply.

---

(584) John M. Haniak Scholarship

ASM International
9639 Kinsman Road
Materials Park, OH 44073

Phone: 440-338-5151
Fax: 440-338-4634
Email:jeane.deatherage@asminternational.org
URL:http://www.asminternational.org/portal/site/www/foundation/scholarships/

Goal: To assist undergraduate students majoring in materials science and engineering.
Eligibility: Applicants must be Material Advantage student members of ASM, juniors or senior undergraduate students majoring in materials science or engineering.
Target Student: College and Adult students.
Amount: $1,500
Number of Awards: 1
Scholarship can be renewed.
Based on Financial Need: Financial need is considered.
Deadline: May
Applications are available online. A completed application, transcripts, essay, photo and up to two letters of recommendation are required to apply.

---

(585) John Mabry Forestry Scholarship

Railway Tie Association
115 Commerce Drive
Suite C
Fayetteville, GA 30214

Phone: 770-460-5553
Fax: 770-460-5573
Email: ties@rta.org
URL: http://www.rta.org

Goal: To assist forestry school students.
Eligibility: Applicants must be enrolled in an accredited forestry program at a postsecondary school. Applicants must be in the second year of a two year program or the third year of a four year program. The award is based on academics, career goals, leadership and financial need.
Target Student: College and Adult students.
Amount: Varies
Number of Awards: Varies
Based on Financial Need: Yes
Deadline: June
Applications are available online.

---

(586) John O. Crane Memorial Fellowship

Institute of Current World Affairs
Steven Butler, Executive Director
4545 42nd Street, NW
Suite 311
Washington, DC 20016

Phone: 202-364-4068
Fax: 202-364-0498
Email: apply@icwa.org
URL: http://www.icwa.org

Goal: To assit in study abroad opportunities in Central Europe, Eastern Europe and the Middle East.

Eligibility: Applicants mus be under 36 years of age and be fluent in the native language of the country where they are to study. Applicants must propose an independent research project that would be done in Central Europe, Eastern Europe or the Middle East.
Target Student: High school, College, Graduate and Adult students.
Amount: Full Support
Number of Awards: Varies
Based on Financial Need: No
Deadline: August
Application information is available online. A completed application and resume are required as an initial step.

(587) John R. Johnson Memorial Scholarship Endowment

American Association of Law Libraries
105 W. Adams
Suite 3300
Chicago, IL 60604

Phone: 312-939-4764
Fax: 312-431-1097
Email: scholarships@aall.org
URL: http://www.allnet.org

Goal: To encourage future and current law librarians in memory of John Johnson.
Eligibility: Applicants who apply for any of the AALL scholarships become automatically eligible to receive this award without submitting a separate application. Applicants must intend to have careers as law librarians. Preference is give to AALL members, but non-members can apply.
Target Student: Graduate and Adult students.
Amount: Varies
Number of Awards: Varies
Scholarship can be renewed.
Based on Financial Need: No
Deadline: Unknown
Application information is available online, by mail, phone, fax or email.

(588) John S. Marshall Memorial Scholarship

American Institute of Mining, Metallurgical and Petroleum Engineers
9956 West Remington Place
Unit A10
Suite 364
Littleton, CO 80128

Phone: 303-325-5185
Fax: 888-702-0049
Email: aime@aimehq.org
URL: http://www.aimehq.org

Goal: To assist students of mining engineering.
Eligibility: Applicants must be undergraduate juniors or seniors enrolled in an ABET accredited mining engineering degree program full-time, student members of the Society of Mining, Metallurgy and Exploration, planning to pursue a career in the mining industry and have demonstrated financial need.
Target Student: College and Adult students.
Amount: Varies
Number of Awards: Varies
Based on Financial Need: Yes
Deadline: June
Applications are available online. A completed application and two letters of recommendation are required to apply.

(589) John S.W. Fargher Scholarship

Institute of Industrial Engineers
3577 Parkway Lane
Suite 200
Norcross, GA 30092

Phone: 800-494-0460
Fax: 770-441-3295
Email: bcameron@iienet.org
URL: http://www.iienet2.org

Goal: To acknowledge graduate students in industrial engineering with demonstrated leadership.
Eligibility: Applicants must be full-time graduate students with at least one year remaining in their degree program and be enrolled in a college in the U.S. with an accredited industrial engineering program and students must be nominated for this award.
Target Student: Graduate and Adult students.
Amount: $1,000
Number of Awards: 1
Based on Financial Need: No
Deadline: September
Nomination information is available online.

(590) John V. Wehausen Graduate Scholarship

Society of Naval Architects and Marine Engineers
601 Pavonia Avenue
Jersey City, NJ 07306

Phone: 201-798-4800
Fax: 201-798-4975
Email: efaustino@sname.org
URL: http://www.sname.org

Goal: To assist students working towards master's degrees in marine related subjects.
Eligibility: Applicants must be Society of Naval Architects and Marine Engineers members, or members of another respected marine society. Applicants must be working towards a degree in naval architecture, ocean engineering, marine engineering, or another marine related subject.
Target Student: Graduate and Adult students.
Amount: Up to $6,000
Number of Awards: Varies
Based on Financial Need: No

Deadline: February
Application information is available online. A completed application, transcript and three letters of recommendation are required to apply.

(591) John Wright Memorial Scholarship

Tree Research and Education Endowment Fund
552 S. Washington Street
Suite 109
Naperville, IL 60540

Phone: 630-369-8300
Fax: 630-369-8382
Email: treefund@treefund.org
URL: http://www.treefund.org

Goal: To assist undergraduate and technical college students who are working towards careers in commercial arboriculture.
Eligibility: Applicants must be high school seniors who are entering college or community college or returning college students working towards a first associate's or bachelor's degree at a U.S. college or university, have a 3.0 or higher GPA, and planning to enter the arboriculture industry.
Target Student: High school, College and Adult students.
Amount: $2,000
Number of Awards: 1
Based on Financial Need: No
Deadline: May
Applications are available online.

(592) Johnny Davis Memorial Scholarship

Aircraft Electronics Association
4217 South Hocker
Independence, MO 64055

Phone: 816-373-6565
Fax: 816-478-3100
Email: info@aea.net
URL: http://www.aea.net

Goal: To assist avionics and aircraft repair students.
Eligibility: Applicants must be high school seniors or college students attending or planning to attend an accredited avionics or aircraft repair program.
Target Student: High school, College and Adult students.
Amount: $1,000
Number of Awards: 1
Based on Financial Need: No
Deadline: February
Applications are by contacting the sponsor.

(593) Jolly Green Meomorial Scholarship

Jolly Green Association
P.O. Box 965
O'Fallon, IL 62269

Email: bill6100@aol.com
URL:http://www.jollygreen.org/jolly_green_memorial_scholarship.htm

Goal: To assist dependents of present and former Air Force Combat Rescue, or resuce support members.
Eligibility: Applicants must be must have demonstrated an aptitude for college level study and be eligible for admission to a college or university.
Target Student: High school students.
Amount: Varies
Number of Awards: Varies
Based on Financial Need: No
Deadline: April
Applications are available by mail or email.

(594) Jon C Ladda Memorial Foundation Scholarship

Jon C. Ladds Memorial Foundation
P.O. Box 55
Unionville, CT 06085

Email: info@jonladda.org
URL: http://www.jonladda.org

Goal: To assist the children of Naval Academy graduates and Navy members who have died or become disabled while serving on active duty.
Eligibility: Applicants must be the children of Naval Academy graduates or Navy members who served in the submarine service. The Navy member or graduate must have died while on active duty or have 100% disability and be medically retired. The applicant must also be accepted and enrolled in a college or university.
Target Student: High school, College and Adult students.
Amount: Varies
Number of Awards: Varies
Scholarship can be renewed.
Based on Financial Need: No
Deadline: March
Applications are available by mail.

(595) Jonathan Jasper Wright Award

National Association of Blacks in Criminal Justice
North Carolina Central University
P.O. Box 19788
Durham, NC 27707

Phone: 919-683-1801
Fax: 919-683-1903
Email: office@nabcj.org
URL: http://www.nabcj.org

Goal: To award leadership at the regional and state level in the area of criminal justice.

Eligibility: Applicants must be affecting change or acting as a conduit for change in the area of criminal justice. The person needs to be nominated by a member of the NABCJ.
Target Student: College, Graduate and Adult students.
Amount: Varies
Number of Awards: 1
Based on Financial Need: No
Deadline: May
Applications for nomination are available online.

(596) Joseph C. Johnson Memorial Grant

American Society of Certified Engineering Technician
P.O. Box 1536
Brandon, MS 39043

Phone: 601-824-8991
Email: general-manager@ascet.org
URL: http://www.ascet.org

Goal: To assist engineering technology students.
Eligibility: Applicants must be U.S. citizens or legal citizens of the country they live in, have a 3.0 or higher GPA, be a student, certified, regular, registered or associate member of the American Society of Certified Engineering Technicians and be part- or full-time students in an engineering technology program. Students in four-year programs who apply in their third year can recieve the award for their fourth year. Students in a two-year program should apply in their first year to recieve the award in their second year.
Target Student: College and Adult students.
Amount: $750
Number of Awards: 1
Based on Financial Need: No
Deadline: Varies
Applications are available online.

(597) Joseph Frasca Excellence in Aviation Scholarship

University Aviation Association
David NewMyer
College of Applied Sciences and Arts,
Southern Illinois University Carbondale
1365 Douglas Drive, Room 126
Carbondale, IL 62901

Phone: 618-453-8898
Fax: 618-453-7286
Email: newmyer@siu.edu
URL: http://www.uaa.aero

Goal: To encourage applicants to reach the highest level of achievement in aviation studies.
Eligibility: Applicants must be juniors o seniors with a 3.0 or higher GPA and enrolled at a UAA member college or university. Applicants must be a member of an aviation organization, involved in aviation activities with demonstrated interest interest in aviation and demonstrated interest in aaviation maintenance or flight.
Target Student: College and Adult students.
Amount: $2,000
Number of Awards: 2
Based on Financial Need: No
Deadline: April
Applications are available online.

(598) Joseph M. Parish Memorial Grant

American Society of Certified Engineering Technicians
P.O. Box 1536
Brandon, MS 39043

Phone: 601-824-8991
Email: general-manager@ascet.org
URL: http://www.ascet.org

Goal: To assist engineering technology students.
Eligibility: Applicants must be U.S. citizens or legal residents of the country where they live, have a 3.0 GPA or higher, be student members of the American Society of Certified Engineering Technicians and be full-time students in an engineering program. Applicants must have demonstrated financial need.
Target Student: College and Adult students.
Amount: $500
Number of Awards: 1
Scholarship can be renewed.
Based on Financial Need: Yes
Deadline: April
Applications are available online.

---

(599) Joseph P. and Helen T. Cribbins Scholarship

Association of the United States Army
2425 Wilson Boulevard
Arlington, VA 22201

Phone: 800-336-4570
Email: ausa-info@ausa.org
URL: http://www.ausa.org

Goal: To assist U.S. Army soldiers pursuing degrees in engineering or related subjects.
Eligibility: Applicants must be active duty or honorably discharged enlisted member of the U.S. Army, Army Reserve or National Guard. Applicant must be enrolled or accepted at an accredited college or university and plan on majoring in engineering or a related subject.
Target Student: High school, College or Adult students.
Amount: $2,000
Number of Awards: Varies
Based on Financial Need: No
Deadline: July

Applications are available online. A completed application, two letters of recommendation, autobiography, transcripts, a course of study outline, certificates from other training courses and a copy of form DD-214 are required to apply.

---

(600) Joseph S. Rumbaugh Historical Oration Contest

National Society of the Sons of the American Revolution
1000 S. Fourth Street
Louisville, KY 40203

Phone: 502-589-1776
Email: contests@sar.org
URL: http://www.sar.org

Goal: To encourage students to learn about the Revolutionary War and its impact on America.
Eligibility: Applicants must prepare a five to six minute speech on an aspect of the Revolutionary War. The contest is open to high school students who are sophomores or above.
Target Student: High school students.
Amount: $200 - $3,000
Number of Awards: Varies
Based on Financial Need: No
Deadline: June
Applications are available online from local chapters of Sons of the American Revolution.

---

(601) Josephine De Karman Fellowship

Josephine De Karman Fellowship Trust
P.O. Box 3389
San Dimas, CA 91773

Phone: 909-592-0607
Email: info@dekarman.org
URL: http://www.dekarman.org

Goal: To acknowledge students who show academic achievement.

Eligibility: Only candidates for the PhD who will defend their dissertation by June 2015 and undergraduates entering their senior year (will receive bachelors degree in June 2015) are eligible for consideration. Postdoctoral and masters degree students are not eligible for consideration. Special consideration will be given to applicants in the Humanities.

Target Student: Graduate students.
Amount: $14,000 to $22,000
Number of Awards: At least 10
Based on Financial Need: No
Deadline: January

Applications are available online.

---

(602) JTG Scholarship in Scientific and Technical Translation or Interpretation

American Translators Association
225 Reinekers Lane
Suite 590
Alexandria, VA 22314

Phone: 703-683-6100
Fax: 703-683-6122
Email: ata@atanet.org
URL: http://www.atanet.org

Goal: To assist students pursuing careers in the field of translation and interpretation.

Eligibility: Applicants must be enrolled or planning to enroll in a degree program (graduate or undergraduate) in scientific and technical translation or interpretation. Applicants must be enrolled full-time, have a GPA of 3.0 or higher with a GPA of 3.5 in translation and interpretation courses, and have completed one year of college.

Target Student: College, Graduate and Adult students.
Amount: $2,500
Number of Awards: 1
Based on Financial Need: No
Deadline: June

Applications are available online.

---

(603) Judith Haupt Member's Child Scholarship

Navy Wives Clubs of America
P.O. Box 54022
NSA Mid-South
Millington, TN 38053

Phone: 866-511-6922
Email:scholarships@navywivesclubsofamerica.org
URL:http://www.navywivesclubsofamerica.org

Goal: To assist those who are the adult children of members of the Navy Wives Clubs of America.

Eligibility: Applicants must be college students who are the adult children of NWCA members. They must be accepted into college by the scholarship application due date and cannot carry a military ID.

Target Student: High school, College and Adult students.
Amount: Varies
Number of Awards: Varies
Based on Financial Need: No
Deadline: May

Applications are available online. A completed application and official transcripts are required.

---

(604) Julius and Esther Stulberg International String Competition

Julius and Esther Stulberg Compeition Inc.
359 S. Kalamazoo Mall #14
Kalamazoo, MI 49007

Phone: 269-343-2776
Email: stulbergcomp@yahoo.com
URL: http://www.stulberg.org

Goal: To assist young musicians.

Eligibility: Applicants must be 19 years old or younger and play the violin, viola, cellor or double bass and perform a Bach piece and a solo at the compeitition.
Target Student: Junior high and younger and High school students.
Amount: Up to $5,000
Number of Awards: 4
Based on Financial Need: No
Deadline: January
Applications are available online. A completed application, audition CD and proof of age are required to apply.

(605) Junior and Senior Scholarships

Institute of Food Technologists
525 W. Van Buren
Suite 1000
Chicago, IL 60607

Phone: 312-782-8424
Email: ejplummer@ift.org
URL: http://www.ift.org

Goal: To encourage undergraduate students in food science and technology.
Eligibility: Applicants must be college sophomores, juniors or seniors in an approved program in food science and technology.
Target Student: College and Adult students.
Amount: $500 - $2,500
Number of Awards: 43
Based on Financial Need: No
Deadline: Varies
Applications are available online.

(606) Junior Composers Award

National Federation of Music Clubs Junior Composers Award
Karen Greenhalgh
8261 San Juan Range Road
Littleton, CO 80127

Phone: 317-882-4003
Fax: 317-882-4019
Email: kgreenhalgh2@aol.com
URL: http://www.nfmc-music.org

Goal: To assist young music composers.
Eligibility: There are four age groups for the scholarship, 9 and under, 10-12, 13-15 and 16-18. Applicants must be a member of the National Federation of Music Clubs. An entry fee of $1.25 plus a state fee are required to apply. As mentioned, scholarships that chage a fee are never recommened.
Target Student: Junior high and younger and High school students.
Amount: $50 - $200
Number of Awards: Varies
Based on Financial Need: No
Deadline: February
Applications are available online.

(608) Junior Fellowships

Dumbarton Oaks
1703 32nd Street NW
Washington, DC 20007

Phone: 202-339-6401
Fax: 202-339-6419
Email: dumbartonoaks@doaks.org
URL: http://www.doaks.org

Goal: To assist scholars studying Byzantine, Pre-Columbian and garden and landscapes with fellowships.
Eligibility: Applicants must have met all initial requirements for a Ph.D. and be willing to work on their dissertation or final project at Dumbarton Oaks at the time of their applications. The award is based on the applicants scholarly ability, preparation and the value of the project to Dumbarton Oaks.
Target Student: Graduate and Adult students.
Amount: Up to $47,000
Number of Awards: Varies

Based on Financial Need: No
Deadline: November
Applicants must submit ten copies of the application letter, proposal, personal and professsional data along with three letters of recommendation and official transcript.

(607) Junior Felowships

American Institute of Indian Studies
1130 E. 59th Street
Chicago, IL 60637

Phone: 773-702-7638
Email: aiis@uchicago.edu
URL: http://www.indiastudies.org

Goal: To assist doctoral canadiates at U.S. universities who want to travel to India to do their dissertation research on Indian aspects of their discipline.
Eligibility: Applicants must be doctoral candidates at a U.S. university. The award lasts for 11 months and junior fellows are associated with Indian universities and research mentors.
Target Student: Graduate and Adult students.
Amount: Varies
Number of Awards: Varies
Based on Financial Need: No
Deadline: July
Applications are available online or by mail.

(609) Junior Scholarship Program

American Kennel Club
260 Madison Avenue
New York, NY 10016

Phone: 212-696-8200
URL: http://www.akc.org

Goal: To assist students involved with AKC purebred dogs.

Eligibility: Applicants must be under 18 years old with an AKC registered purebred dog. Award selction is based on involvement with AKC registered dogs, financial need and academics.
Target Student: Junior high and younger and High school students.
Amount: Varies
Number of Awards: Varies
Based on Financial Need: Yes
Deadline: February
Applications are available online.

(610) K.K. Wang Scholarship

Society of Plastics Engineers
13 Church Hill Road
Newtown, CT 06470

Phone: 203-775-0471
Fax: 203-775-8490
Email: info@4spe.org
URL: http://www.4spe.org

Goal: To assist students with injection molding and computer aided engineering experience.
Eligibility: Applicants must be enrolled full-time with professional and academic experience in computer-aided engineering and injection molding. Applicants must have taken courses related to plastics and have professional interest in the plastics/polymer industry.
Target Student: College and Adult students.
Amount: $2,000
Number of Awards: 1
Based on Financial Need: No
Deadline: February
Applications are available online. A completed application, resume, list of extracurricular activities, transcripts and three letters of recommendation are required online.

(611) K2TEO Martin J. Green, Sr. Memorial Scholarship

American Radio Relay League Foundation
225 Main Street
Newington, CT 06111

Phone: 860-594-0397
Fax: 860-594-0259
Email: foundation@arrl.org
URL: http://www.arrlf.org

Goal: To assist amateur radio operators with their educational expenses.
Eligibility: Applicants must have a general class or higher amateur radio license. Preference is given to students from ham families.
Target Student: High school, College, Graduate and Adult students.
Amount: $1,000
Number of Awards: 1
Based on Financial Need: No
Deadline: February
Applications are available online.

(612) Karen O'Neil Memorial Scholarship

Emergency Nurses Association
915 Lee Street
Des Plaines, IL 60016

Phone: 847-460-4100
Fax: 847-460-4004
Email: foundation@ena.org
URL: http://www.ena.org

Goal: To encourage students to pursue advanced degrees in emergency nursing.
Eligibility: Applicants must be nurses who are pursuing an advanced degrees and be ENA members for at least 12 months before applying.
Target Student: Graduate and Adult students.
Amount: $3,000
Number of Awards: 1

Based on Financial Need: No
Deadline: June
Applications are available online.

(613) Karla Girts Memorial Community Outreach Scholarship

American Dental Hygienists' Association
Institute for Oral Health
Scholarship Award Program
444 North Michigan Avenue
Suite 3400
Chicago, IL 60611

Phone: 312-440-8900
Email: institute@adha.net
URL: http://www.adha.org/ioh

Goal: To assist undergraduate students working towards degree completion in dental hygiene and committed to work with the geriatric population.
Eligibility: Applicants must be full-time students at an accredited college or university in the U.S. pursuing an associates or bachelor's degree in dental hygiene or related field and committed to working with the geriatric population. Applications must have demonstrated financial need of $1,500 or more, a 3.0 GPA or higher and completed at least one year of school.
Target Student: College, Graduate and Adult students.
Amount: $1,000 - $2,000
Number of Awards: Varies
Based on Financial Need: Yes
Deadline: February
Applications are available online.

(614) Kathem F. Gruber Scholarship Program

Blinded Veterans Association
477 H. Street NW
Washington, DC 20001

Phone: 202-371-8880
Email: bva@bva.org
URL: http://www.bva.org

Goal: To assist the spouses and children of blind veterans with college expenses.
Eligibility: Applicants must be the spouse or child of a blind veterans and are accepted or enrolled in a college or university.
Target Student: High school, College, Graduate and Adult students.
Amount: $2,000
Number of Awards: 6
Based on Financial Need: No
Deadline: April
Contact the Blinded Veterans Association for an application.

---

(615) Kenneth Andrew Roe Scholarship

American Society of Mechanical Engineers
Three Park Avenue
New York, NY 10016

Phone: 800-843-2763
Fax: 973-882-1717
Email: infocentral@asme.org
URL: http://www.asme.org

Goal: To assist students who are studying mechanical engineering.
Eligibility: Applicants must be ASME student members, enrolled in an ABET accredited mechanical engineering bachelor's degree program, U.S. citizens and a North American resident.
Target Student: College and Adult students.
Amount: $12,500
Number of Awards: 1
Based on Financial Need: No
Deadline: March
Applications are available online.

---

(616) King Olav V Norwegian-American Heritage Fund

Sons of Norway Foundation
1455 West Lake Foundation
Minneapolis, MN 55408

Phone: 800-945-8851
Fax: 612-827-0658
Email: foundation@sofn.com
URL: http://www.sofn.com

Goal: To encourage and educational exchange between the U.S. and Norway.
Eligibility: Applicants must be 18 years old or older, Americans and be willing to study Norwegian heritage or modern Norway at the college level. The award is based on GPA, participation in community and school activities, educational and career goals, work experience and references.
Target Student: High school, College and Adult students.
Amount: $1,000 - $1,500
Number of Awards: Varies
Based on Financial Need: No
Deadline: March
Applications are available online.

---

(617) Kit C. King Graduate Scholarship Fund

National Press Photographers Association
Kit C. King Graduate Scholarship Fund
Scott R. Sines
Managing Editor, Memphis Commerical-Appeal
495 Union Avenue
Memphis, TN 38103

Phone: 901-529-5843
Fax:
Email: sines@commercialappeal.com
URL: http://www.nppa.org

Goal: To assist photojournalism students.

Eligibility: Applicants must provide a portfolio, be working towards an advanced degree in journalism with a focus in photojournalism and demonstrate financial need. Applicants can apply to any NPPA scholarship, but they can only win one award.
Target Student: Graduate and Adult students.
Amount: $1,000
Number of Awards: 1
Based on Financial Need: Yes
Deadline: March
Applications are available online.

(618) Klussendorf Scholarship

National Dairy Shrine
P.O. Box 1
Maribel, WI 54227

Phone: 920-863-6333
Fax: 920-863-8328
Email: info@dairyshrine.org
URL: http://www.dairyshrine.org

Goal: To assist students in the field of dairy husbandry.
Eligibility: Applicants must be first, second, or third year college students at a two or four year university planning to enter the dair field and majoring in dairy husbandry.
Target Student: College and Adult students.
Amount: $2,000
Number of Awards: 6
Based on Financial Need: No
Deadline: April
Applications are available online.

(619) Kohl's Kids Who Care Scholarship

Kohls Corporation
N56 W17000 Ridgewood Drive
Menomonee Falls, WI 53051

Phone: 262-703-7000
Fax: 262-703-7115
Email: community.relations@kohls.com
URL:http://www.kohlscorporation.com/communityrelations/scholarship/index.asp

Goal: To reward young people for their contributions to their community.
Eligibility: Applicants must be nominated by a parent, educators, or community members. There is a category for kids ages 6 - 12 and another for kids ages 13-18. Applicants must not have graduated from high school.
Target Student: Junior high students or younger, High school students.
Amount: Up to $10,000
Number of Awards: At least 2,100
Based on Financial Need: No
Deadline: March
Applications are available at Kohl's stores and online.

(620) KOR Memorial Scholarship

Klingon Language Institute
P.O. Box 634
Flourtown, PA 19031

URL: http://www.kli.org/scholarship

Goal: To develop language study.
Eligibility: Applicants must be full-tme undergraduate or graduate students working towards a degree in the field of language study. Applicants must be nominated by the chair, head or dean of the department by a nominating letter. Two additional faculty letters of recommendtation, a personal statement and resume are required.
Target Student: College, Graduate and Adult students.
Amount: $500
Number of Awards: 1
Based on Financial Need: No
Deadline: June

Applicant apply through a nomination letter.

(621) Kymanox's James J. Davis Memorial Scholarship for Students Studying Abroad

Kymanox
Attn: Scholarship Administrator
2220 Sedwick Road Suite 20`1
Durham, NC 27713

Phone: 847-433-2200
Fax: 610-471-5101
URL:http://www.kymanox.com/scholarship

Goal: To assist students interested in studying abroad.
Eligibility: Applicants must be U.S. citizens or permanent residents who are planning to study at an accredited program for at least eight weeks. Strong preference is given to those with financial need. Preference is given to those studying in non-English speaking countries and to those who are majoring in engineering, math or science.
Target Student: High school, College, Graduate and Adult students.
Amount: $1,000
Number of Awards: 1
Based on Financial Need: Yes
Deadline: March
Applications are available online. A completed application, acceptance letter for a study aboard program, essay and financial need verification form are required to apply.

(622) L. Phil Wicker Scholarship

American Radio Relay League Foundation
225 Main Street
Newington, CT 06111

Phone: 860-594-0397

Fax: 860-594-0259
Email: foundation@arrl.org
URL: http://www.arrlf.org

Goal: To assist ham radio operators with their educational expenses.
Eligibility: Applicants must have at least a general ham radio license, be undergraduate or graduate students in electronics, communications or a related field and be a resident of or attending school in the ARRL Roanoke Division (North Carolina, South Carolina, Virginia and West Virginia).
Target Student: College, Graduate and Adult students.
Amount: $500
Number of Awards: 1
Based on Financial Need: No
Deadline: February
Applications are available online.

(623) La Fra Scholarship

Ladies Auxiliary of the Fleet Reserve Association
3750 Silver Bluff Blvd #2206
Orange Park, FL 32065

Phone: 904-406-9285
Email: mserfra@fra.org
URL: http://www.la-fra.org

Goal: To assist the children and grandchildren of FRA and LA FRA members.
Eligibility: Applicants must have a father or grandfather who was in the Marine Corps, Coast Guard, Navy, Fleet Reserve, Coast Guard Reserves or Fleet Marine Corps Reserve.
Target Student: High school, College and Adult students.
Amount: Varies
Number of Awards: Varies
Based on Financial Need: No
Deadline: Unknown
Applications are available online.

(624) Landscape Forms Design for People Scholarship

Landscape Architecture Foundation
818 18th Street NW
Suite 810
Washington, DC 20006

Phone: 202-331-7070
Fax: 202-331-7079
Email: scholarships@lafoundation.org
URL: http://www.lafoundation.org

Goal: To assist landscape architecture students.
Eligibility: Applicants must be full-time undergraduate students enrolled in a landscape architecture degree program by an accredited Landscape Architectural Accreditation Board and applicants must be in the final year of their program.
Target Student: College and Adult students.
Amount: $3,000
Number of Awards: 1
Based on Financial Need: No
Deadline: February
Applications are available online. A completed application, essay, work samples, and two letters of recommendation are required to apply.

(625) Larry Williams Photography and AYA Photo Contest

Appaloosa Horse Club
Appaloosa Youth Foundation Scholarship Committee
2720 W. Pullman Rd
Moscow, ID 83843

Phone: 208-882-5578
Fax: 208-882-8150
Email: acaap@appaloosa.com
URL: http://www.appaloosa.com

Goal: To assist students who have a love of Appaloosa and share it through photography.
Eligibility: Applicants must submit multiple photos in their division (13 and under, 14 to 18 and 4H/FFA youths 18 and under).
Target Student: Junior high and younger and High school students.
Amount: Up to $100
Number of Awards: 9
Based on Financial Need: No
Deadline: May
Applications are available online.

(626) Larson Aquatic Research Support

American Water Works Association
6666 W. Quincy Avenue
Denver, CO 80235

Phone: 303-347-6201
Fax: 303-795-7603
Email: lmoody@awwa.org
URL: http://www.awwa.org

Goal: To assist doctoral and master's students who are interested in corrosion control, treatment and distribution of domestic and industrial water supplies, aquatic chemistry and environmental chemistry.
Eligibility: Applicants must be working towards a master's or doctoral degree at a college or university in Canada, Guam, Puerto Rico, Mexico or the U.S. The master's grant is for $5,000 and the doctoral grant is $7,000.
Target Student: Graduate and Adult students.
Amount: $5,000 - $7,000
Number of Awards: 2
Based on Financial Need: No
Deadline: January
Applications are available online. A completed application, three letters of recommendation, transcript, GRE score and course of study are required to apply.

(627) Laurel Fund

Educational Foundation for Women in Accounting
P.O. Box 1925
Southeastern, PA 19399

Phone: 610-407-9229
Fax: 610-644-3713
Email: info@efwa.org
URL: http://www.efwa.org

Goal: To assist women pursuing advanced degrees in accounting.
Eligibility: Applicants must be women pursuing a Ph.D. in accounting. The award is based on scholarship, service and financial need. Applicants must have completed their comprehensive exams before the previous fall semester.
Target Student: Graduate and Adult students.
Amount: Up to $5,000
Number of Awards: Varies
Based on Financial Need: Yes
Deadline: May
Applications are available online.

(628) Lawrence E. and Thelma J. Norrie Memorial Scholarship

Foundation for Amateur Radio Inc.
FAR Scholarships
P.O. Box 911
Columbia, MD 21044

Phone: 410-552-2652
Fax: 410-981-5146
Email: dave.prestel@gmail.com
URL: http://www.farweb.org

Goal: To assist amateur radio operators who are pursuing or planning to pursue a postsecondary education.

Eligibility: Applicants must be U.S. residents who hold an amateur radio license and are accepted or enrolled at an accredited postsecondary school as full-time students.
Target Student: College, Graduate and Adult students.
Amount: $2,500
Number of Awards: Varies
Based on Financial Need: No
Deadline: April
Applications are available online.

(629) Lawrence G. Foster Award for Excellence in Public Relations

Public Relations Student Society of America
33 Maiden Lane
11th Floor
New York, NY 10038

Phone: 212-460-1474
Fax: 212-995-0757
Email: prssa@prsa.org
URL: http://www.prssa.org

Goal: To assist public relations students.
Eligibility: Applicants must be undergraduate students who are majoring in public relations and pursuing a career in public relations and PRSSA members.
Target Student: College and Adult students.
Amount: $1,500
Number of Awards: 1
Based on Financial Need: No
Deadline: June
Applications are available online. A completed application and essay are required to apply.

(630) Lawrence Ginocchio Aviation Scholarship

National Business Aviation Association
1200 18th Street NW

Suite 4000
Washington, DC 20036

Phone: 202-783-9250
Fax: 202-331-8364
Email: info@nbaa.org
URL: http://www.nbaa.org

Goal: To assist undergraduate aviation students.
Eligibility: Applicants must be undergraduate sophomores, juniors or seniors with a 3.0 or higher GPA and enrolled at a National Business Aviation Association member school. Applicants must have demonstrated honor, selflessness and helping others through business aviation activities.
Target Student: College and Adult students.
Amount: $4,500
Number of Awards: 5
Based on Financial Need: No
Deadline: July
Applications are available online. A completed application, transcripts, resume, essay, and two letters of recommendation are required to apply.

(631) Leaders and Achievers Scholarship Program

Comcast
1500 Market Street
Philadelphia, PA 19102

Phone: 800-266-2278
URL: http://www.comcast.com

Goal: To assist graduating high school seniors who take leadership roles in their school and help improve their community with service.

Eligibility: Applicants must be high school seniors with a GPA of 2.8 or above, be nominated by their principal or guidance counselor and attend school in a Comcast community. The website has a list of eligible communities broken down by state. Employees and family of Comcast and it's affiliates are not eligible.
Target Student: High school students.
Amount: $1,000
Number of Awards: Varies
Based on Financial Need: No
Deadline: Unknown
Applications are available from the principal or counselor who gave the nomination.

(632) Learning and Leadership Grants

NEA Foundation
1201 16th Street NW
Suite 416
Washington, DC 20036

Phone: 202-822-7840
Fax: 202-822-7779
Email: info-neafoundation@list.nea.org
URL: http://www.neafoundation.org

Goal: To assist public school teachers, public education support professionals and faculty and staff in public institutions of higher education with professional development opportunities.
Eligibility: Applicants must be current public school teachers in grades K-12, public school support personel, or faculty and staff at a public higher education institution. The professional development activity must improve practice, curriculum and student achievement.
Target Student: Graduate and Adult students.
Amount: $2,000
Number of Awards: Varies
Based on Financial Need: No
Deadline: February, June and October
Applications are available online.

(633) Lee S. Evans Scholarship

National Housing Endowment
1201 15th Street NW
Washington, DC 20005

Phone: 800-368-5242
Fax: 202-266-8177
Email: nhe@nahb.com
URL: http://www.nationalhousingendowment.org

Goal: To assist students who are pursuing careers in residential construction management.
Eligibility: Applicants must be full-time undergraduate and graduate students who have completed at least one semester of coursework at the time of application and have at least one year of study remaining. (Fifth year seniors are not eligible) Applicants must show a demonstrated interest in a career in residential construction and preference is given to National Association of Home Builders student members. Award selection is based on financial need, work experience, extracurricular activities, academics and recommendations.
Target Student: College, Graduate and Adult students.
Amount: Up to $5,000
Number of Awards: Varies
Scholarship can be renewed.
Based on Financial Need: Yes
Deadline: October
Applications are available online. A completed application, transcripts, outline of degree program and two letters of recommendations are required to apply.

(634) Lee Tarbox Memorial Scholarship

Aircraft Electronics Association
4217 South Hocker
Independence, MO 64055

Phone: 816-373-6565
Fax: 816-478-3100
Email: info@aea.net
URL: http://www.aea.net

Goal: To assist avionics and aircraft repair students.
Eligibility: Applicants must be high school seniors or college students planning or attending an accredited school in avionics or aircraft repair program.
Target Student: High school, College and Adult students.
Amount: $2,500
Number of Awards: 1
Based on Financial Need: No
Deadline: February
Applications are available by contacting the sponsor.

(635) Legal Opportunity Scholarship Fund

American Bar Association
321 North Clark Street
Chicago, IL 60610

Phone: 312-988-5415
Email: legalosf@abanet.org
URL: http://www.abanet.org/lsd/

Goal: To assist first year law students.
Eligibility: Applicants must be U.S. citizens or permanent residents, entering their first year of law school during the year of application, and have a cummulative undergraduate GPA of 2.5 of higher.
Target Student: College, Graduate and Adult students.
Amount: $5,000
Number of Awards: 20
Scholarship can be renwed.
Based on Financial Need: No
Deadline: March

Applications are available online. A completed application, personal statement, transcripts and two letters of recommendation are a required to apply.

(636) Len Assante Scholarship Fund

National Ground Water Association
601 Dempsey Road
Westerville, OH 43081

Phone: 800-551-7379
Fax: 614-898-7786
Email: ngwa@ngwa.org
URL: http://www.ngwa.org

Goal: To assist students in the ground water industry and related fields.
Eligibility: Applicants must be high school graduates or college students in associate degree programs, with a 2.5 GPA or higher and studying fields related to ground water including geology, hydrology, hydrogeology, environmental sciences, microbiology or well drilling.
Target Student: High school, College or Adult students.
Amount: Varies
Number of Awards: Varies
Based on Financial Need: No
Deadline: January
Applications are available by email or mail.

(637) Letters About Literature Contest

Letters About Literature
P.O. Box 5308
Woodbridge, VA 22194

Email:programdirector@lettersaboutliterature.org
URL:http://www.lettersaboutliterature.org

Goal: To encourage young students to read.

Eligibility: Applicants must be legal U.S. residents in grades 4 through 12 and be at least nine years old by the September 1 that precedes the award deadline. Each applicant must submit a personal letter to an author about how the author's work impacted them.
Target Student: Junior high and younger, High school students.
Amount: $100 to $500
Number of Awards: 18
Based on Financial Need: No
Deadline: January
Entry instructions are available online. A letter and entry coupon are required to apply.

(638) Lewis A. Kingsley Foundation Scholarship

Navel Sea Cadet Corps
2300 Wilson Boulevard
Arlington, VA 22201

Phone: 800-356-5760
Email: alewis@seacadets.org
URL: http://www.seacadets.org

Goal: To assist Sea Cadets with educational expenses.
Eligibility: Applicants must be former Sea Cadets who are attending college full-time in their sophomore year or higher. They must be employed with an income of $5,000 a year or higher with a 2.0 GPA or greater.
Target Student: College and Adult students.
Amount: Varies
Number of Awards: Varies
Based on Financial Need: No
Deadline: March
Applications are available online. A completed application, one to two page personal statement, a letter of recommendation and resume are responsible.

(639) Lewis C. Hoffman Scholarship

American Ceramic Society
600 North Cleveland Avenue
Suite 210
Westerville, OH 43082

Phone: 866-721-3322
Fax: 301-206-9789
Email: customerservice@ceramics.org
URL: http://www.ceramics.org

Goal: To assist undergraduate students studying ceramics and materials science and engineering.
Eligibility: Applicants must be undergraduate students who will have completed 70 or more semester or equivalent quarter units at the time the award is disbursed.
Target Student: College and Adult students.
Amount: $2,000
Number of Awards: 1
Based on Financial Need: No
Deadline: July
Award does not require an application. To apply submit an essay, letter of recommendation and list of extracurricular activities.

(640) Liberty Mutual Safety Research Fellowship

American Society of Safety Engineers
1800 East Oakron Street
Des Plaines, IL 60018

Phone: 847-699-2929
Fax: 847-768-3434
Email: mgoranson@asse.org
URL: http://www.asse.org

Goal: To establish a fellowship to promote safety research.

Eligibility: Applicants must be U.S. citizens with a Ph.D. or working towards their Ph.D. or masters. Award recipients spend six weeks during the summer at Liberty Mutual Research Center and write an outline or article about their research for a grant to continue their research.
Target Student: Graduate and Adult students.
Amount: Up to $9,500
Number of Awards: Varies
Based on Financial Need: No
Deadline: February
Applications are available online.

(641) Life Lessons Essay Contest

Life and Health Insurance Foundation for Education
1655 N. Fort Myer Drive Suite 610
Arlington, VA 22209

Phone: 202-464-5000
Fax: 202-464-5011
Email: info@lifehappens.org
URL: http://www.lifehappens.org

Goal: To assist students who have been affected financially and emotionally from the death of a parent.
Eligibility: Applicants must submit a 500 word essay or a three minute video that describes the impact of losing a parent.
Target Student: High school, College and Adult students.
Amount: $10,000
Number of Awards: 59
Based on Financial Need: No
Deadline: March
Applications are available online.

(642) Light Metals Division Scholarship

The Minerals, Metals and Materials Society
184 Thorn Hill Road
Warrendale, PA 15086

Phone: 724-776-9000
Fax: 724-776-3770
Email: students@tms.org
URL: http://www.tms.org

Goal: To assist undergraduate metallurgical engineering or materials science and engineering majors.
Eligibility: Applicants must be full-time undergraduate sophomores or juniors majoring in metallurgical engineering or materials science and engineering and student members of The Minerals, Metals and Materials Society.
Target Student: College and Adult students.
Amount: $4,000
Number of Awards: 3
Based on Financial Need: No
Deadline: March
Applications are available online. A completed application, transcripts, statement and three letters of recommendation are required to apply.

(643) Lions International Peace Poster Contest

Lions Clubs International
300 W. 22nd Street
Oak Brook, IL 60523

Phone: 630-571-5466
Email: pr@lionsclubs.org
URL: http://www.lionsclubs.org

Goal: To acknowledge creative children.
Eligibility: Applicants must be 11 - 13 years old at the deadline and be sponsored by a local Lions Club. Entries are judged at the local, district, multi-district and international level.
Target Student: Junior high and younger.
Amount: $500 - $5,000
Number of Awards: 24
Based on Financial Need: No
Deadline: November

Applications are available from the Lion's Club.

(644) Lisa Zaken Award for Excellence

Institute of Industrial Engineers
3577 Parkway Lane
Suite 200
Norcross, GA 30092

Phone: 800-494-0460
Fax: 770-441-3295
Email: bcameron@iienet.org
URL: http://www.iienet2.org

Goal: To acknowledge scholarly activities and leadership that is related to the industrial engineering profession.
Eligibility: Applicants must be undergraduate or graduate students who have at least one year remaining in their degree program, majoring in industrial engineering and be IIE active members. Students must be nominated for this award.
Target Student: College, Graduate and Adult students.
Amount: $700
Number of Awards: 1
Based on Financial Need: No
Deadline: November
Applications are available online.

(645) Litherland Scholarship

International Technology and Engineering Educators
Association Foundation for Technology and Engineering Educators
1914 Association Drive
Suite 201
Reston, VA 20191

Phone: 703-860-2100
Fax: 703-860-0353
Email: iteea@iteea.org
URL: http://www.iteaconnect.org

Goal: To assist undergraduate students working towards a career in teaching technology.

Eligibility: Applicants must be member of ITEA , have a minimum GPA of 2.5 and be undergraduate students majoring in technology education teacher preparation.

Target Student: College and Adult students.

Amount: $1,000

Number of Awards: 1

Based on Financial Need: No

Deadline: December

Applications are available online.

(646) Lockheed Martin/HENAAC Scholars Program

Great Minds in STEM
3900 Whiteside Street
Los Angeles, CA 90063

Phone: 323-262-0997

Fax: 323-262-0946

Email: jcano@greatmindsinstem.org

URL: http://www.greatmindsinstem.org

Goal: To assist computer science and engineering students.

Eligibility: Applicants must be U.S. citizens or permanent residents, full-time students majoring in computer science or aerospace, electrical, mechancial, software or systems engineering with a 3.0 GPA or higher. Applicants can be from any ethnicity but must have demonstrated leadership in the Hispanic community.

Target Student: College, Graduate and Adult students.

Amount: Varies

Number of Awards: Varies
Scholarship can be renewed.

Based on Financial Need: No

Deadline: April

Applications are available online. A completed application, transcript, essay, resume and letters of recommendation are required to apply.

(647) Lois Britt Park Industry Memorial Scholarship Program

National Park Producers Council
122 C Street, NW
Suite 875
Washington, DC 20001

Phone: 202-347-3600

Fax: 202-347-5265

Email: wrigleyj@nppc.org

URL: http://www.nppc.org

Goal: To assist students who are preparing for a career in the pork industry.

Eligibility: Applicants must be college juniors and student members of SAE who are majoring in engineering and support SAE.

Target Student: College and Adult students.

Amount: $2,500

Number of Awards: 4

Based on Financial Need: No

Deadline: January

Applications are available online. A cover letter, information sheet, essay and two letters of recommendation are required to apply.

(648) Long-Term Member Sponsored Scholarship

Society of Automotive Engineers International
400 Commonwealth Drive
Warrendale, PA 15096

Phone: 724-776-4841

Fax: 724-776-0790

Email: scholarships@sae.org

URL: http://www.sae.org

Goal: To acknowledge SAE student members and actively supports SAE or its activities.
Eligibility:
Target Student: College and Adult students.
Amount: $1,000
Number of Awards: Varies
Based on Financial Need: No
Deadline: February
Applications are available online.

(649) Lotte Lenya Competition for Singers

Kurt Well Foundation for Music
7 East 20th Street
3rd Floor
New York, NY 10003

Phone: 212-505-5240
Fax: 212-353-9663
Email: kwfinfo@dwf.org
URL: http://www.kwf.org

Goal: To acknowledge oustanding performance in music theater.
Eligibility: Applicants must be between 19 and 32 years old and perform four selections at a regional competition. Applicants can submit a video of themselves performing the songs if they cannot attend the compeition.
Target Student: High school, College, Graduate and Adult students.
Amount: $500 - $15,000
Number of Awards: Varies
Based on Financial Need: No
Deadline: January
Applications are available online.

(650) Lou and Carole Prato Sports Reporting Scholarship

Radio Television Digital News Association
4121 Plank Road #512
Fredericksburg, VA 22407

Phone: 202-659-6510
Fax: 202-223-4007
Email: staceys@rtdna.org
URL: http://www.rtdna.org

Goal: To assist students pursuing a career as a sports reporter for radio or television.
Eligibility: Applicants must be full time college sophomores or higher with at least one full academic year remaining. Applicants can be majoring in any subject, but must have the career goal of a sports reporter for television or radio. Applicants may only apply for one RTNDA scholarship.
Target Student: College and Adult students.
Amount: $1,000
Number of Awards: 1
Based on Financial Need: No
Deadline: May
Applications are available online.

(651) Lou Hochberg Awards

Orgone Biophysical Research Laboratory
P.O. Box 1148
Ashland, OR 97520

Phone: 541-522-0118
Fax: 541-522-0118
Email: info@orgonelab.org
URL: http://www.orgonelab.org

Goal: The Orgone Biophysical Research Lab has many scholarships for students, scholars and jounalists.
Eligibility: The Lou Hochberg Awards are awarded to wining theses and dissertations, university and college essays, high school essays, and published articles that focus on Reich's sociological work.
Target Student: High school, College, Graduate and Adult students.
Amount: $500 - $1,500
Number of Awards: 5

Based on Financial Need: No
Deadline: May and December
Each award has its own instructions and information is available online.

---

(652) Louis Agassiz Fuertes Award

Wilson Ornithological Society
Dr. Robert B. Payne
Museum of Zoology, University of Michigan
1109 Gedes Avenue
Ann Arbor, MI 48109

Email: rbpayne@umich.edu
URL: http://www.wilsonsociety.org

Goal: To assist ornithologists' research.
Eligibility: Applicants must be students or young professionals conducting avian research and willing to present their research at the Wilson Ornithological Society annual conference.
Target Student: High school, College, Graduate and Adult students.
Amount: $2,500
Number of Awards: Up to 2
Based on Financial Need: No
Deadline: February
Applications are available online.

---

(653) Love Your Body Poster Contest

National Organization for Women Foundation
LYB Poster Contest
1100 H Street, NW
Suite 300
Washington, DC 20005

URL: http://www.nowfoundation.org

Goal: To acknowledge those who create posters encouraging women to love their bodies.

Eligibility: Applicants my be students at any level or non-students from any country. Applicants must create a poster that challenges the stereotypical, limiting and negative portrayals of women in the media.
Target Student: Junior high and younger, High school, College, Graduate and Adult students.
Amount: Varies
Number of Awards: 4
Based on Financial Need: No
Deadline: December
Application information is available online.

---

(654) Lowell Gaylor Memorial Scholarship

Aircraft Electronics Association
4217 South Hocker
Independence, MO 64055

Phone: 816-373-6565
Fax: 816-478-3100
Email: info@aea.net
URL: http://www.aea.net

Goal: To assist students of avionics and aircraft repair.
Eligibility: Applicants must be high school or college students planning to or attending an accredited school in avionics or aircraft repair.
Target Student: High school, College and Adult students.
Amount: $1,000
Number of Awards: 1
Based on Financial Need: No
Deadline: February
Applications are available by contacting the sponsor.

---

(655) Lowell H. and Dorothy Loving Undergraduate Scholarship

American Congress on Surveying and Mapping

6 Montgomery Village Avenue
Suite 403
Gaithersburg, MD 20879

Phone: 240-632-9716
Fax: 240-632-1321
Email: ilse.genovese@acsm.net
URL: http://www.acsm.net

Goal: To assist undergraduate students in surveying and mapping.
Eligibility: Applicants must be members of the American Congress on Surveying and Mapping, undergraduate juniors or seniors majoring in surveying and mapping at a four-year college in the U.S. Applicants must have coursework in two or more of the following: spatial measurement, systems analysis and design, land surveying, photogrammetry and remote sensing or geometic geodesy.
Target Student: College and Adult students.
Amount: $2,500
Number of Awards: 1
Scholarship can be renewed.
Based on Financial Need: Yes
Deadline: February
Applications are available online. A completed application, proof of ACSM membership, personal statement, transcript and three letters of recommendation are required to apply.

---

(656) LTG and Mrs. Joseph M. Heiser Scholarship

U.S. Army Ordnance Corps Association
P.O. Box 377
Aberdeen Proving Ground, MD 21005

Phone: 410-272-8540
Fax: 410-272-8425
URL:http://www.usaocaweb.org/scholarships.htm

Goal: To honor and remember LTG Joseph M. Heiser.

Eligibility: Applicants must be active or reserve Ordinance soliders or OCA members and their immediate family. Each applicant must write two essays. The first is a 300 to 500 word essay about the their educational and career goals. The second is a 1,000 to 1,500 word essay on lifelong learning as it applies to the U.S. Army Ordnance Corps.
Target Student: High school, College and Adult students.
Amount: Varies
Number of Awards: Varies
Based on Financial Need: No
Deadline: June
Applications are available online.

---

(657) LTK Engineering Services Scholarship

Conference of Minority Transportation Officials
818 18th Street NW
Suite 850
Washington, DC 20006

Phone: 202-530-0551
Fax: 202-530-0617
Email: comto@comto.org
URL: http://www.comto.org

Goal: To assist students majoring in engineering or other technical fields that are related to transportation.
Eligibility: Applicants must be COMTO members or willing to join within 30 days of receiving the scholarship. Applicants must have a 3.0 GPA or above, in their junior or senior year of college or graduate school and enrolled in at least 12 credits per semester.
Target Student: College, Graduate and Adult students.
Amount: $6,000
Number of Awards: Varies
Based on Financial Need: No
Deadline: April
Applications are available online.

(658) Luci S. Williams Houston Scholarship

Bay Area Black Journalists Association
1714 Franklin Street
#100-260
Oakland, CA 94612

Phone: 510-464-1000
Email: info@babja.org
URL: http://babja.org

Goal: To assist aspiring photojournalists.
Eligibility: Applicants must be studying photojournalism and may be enrolled at any college in the U.S.
Target Student: College and Adult students.
Amount: $2,500
Number of Awards: 1
Based on Financial Need: No
Deadline: June
Applications are available online. A completed application, transcript, resume, work samples, essay and three letters of recommendation are required to apply.

(659) Lucille and Charles A. Wert Scholarship

ASM International
9639 Kinsman Road
Materials Park, OH 44073

Phone: 440-338-5151
Fax: 440-338-4634
Email:jeane.deatherage@asminternational.org
URL:http://www.asminternational.org/portal/site/www/foundation/scholarships

Goal: To assist undergraduate Material Advantage student members with demonstrated financial need.

Eligibility: Applicants must be undergraduate juniors or seniors at a college or university in North America and be Material Advantage student members. Award preference is given to those pursuing a bachelor's degree in metallurgy or materials science engineering. Applicants must have demonstrated financial need.
Target Student: College and Adult students.
Amount: Up to $10,000
Number of Awards: 1
Scholarship can be renewed.
Based on Financial Need: Yes
Deadline: May
Applications are available online. A completed application, photo, personal statement and two letters of recommendation are required to apply.

(660) LULAC General Awards

League of United Latin American Citizens
2000 L Street NW Suite 610
Washington, DC 20036

Phone: 202-835-9646
Fax: 202-835-9685
Email: scholarships@lnesc.org
URL: http://www.lnesc.org

Goal: To assist students who are working towards a degree.
Eligibility: Applicants can be of any ethnic background. Students must be U.S. citizens or legal residents, enrolled or applied to a two or four-year college, university or graduate school. While grades and academic achievement can be considered, the main focus of the award is motivation, sincerity and integrity shown through the interview and the essay.
Target Student: High school, College, Graduate and Adult students.
Amount: $250 to $1,000
Number of Awards: Varies
Based on Financial Need: No

Deadline: March
Applications are available online.

---

(661) LULAC Honors Awards

League of United Latin American Citizens
2000 L Street NW Suite 610
Washington, DC 20036

Phone: 202-835-9646
Fax: 202-835-9685
Email: scholarships@lnesc.org
URL: http://www.lnesc.org

Goal: To assist students in all levels of
higher education.
Eligibility: Applicants can be of any
ethnicity. Applicants must be U.S. Citizens
or legal residents, with a GPA of 3.25 or
higher and have applied to or enrolled at a
college, university or graduate school.
Applicants who are entering freshman
must have an ACT score of 23 or higher or
an SAT score of 1000 or higher.
Target Student: High school, College,
Graduate and Adult students.
Amount: $250 to $2,000
Number of Awards: Varies
Based on Financial Need: No
Deadline: March
Applications are available online.

---

(662) LULAC National Scholastic Achievement Awards

League of United Latin American Citizens
2000 L Street NW Suite 610
Washington, DC 20036

Phone: 202-835-9646
Fax: 202-835-9685
Email: scholarships@lnesc.org
URL: http://www.lnesc.org

Goal: To assist students who are attending
colleges, universities or graduate schools.

Eligibility: Applicants can be of any
ethnicity. Applicants must be U.S. citizens
or legal residents and have applied or
enrolled in any college, university or
graduate school. Students must have a 3.5
GPA or higher and entering freshman
must have an ACT score of 29 or higher or
an SAT score of 1350 or higher. A local
(state) LULAC Council in the applicants
state is required to apply.
Target Student: College, Graduate, and
Adult students.
Amount: Up to $2,000
Number of Awards: Varies
Based on Financial Need: No
Deadline: March
Applications are available online.

---

(663) Lyndon B. Johnson Foundation Grants-in-Aid Research

Lyndon B. Johnson Foundation
2313 Red River Street
Austin, TX 78705

Phone: 515-478-7829
Fax: 512-478-9104
Email: webmaster@lbjlib.utexas.edu
URL: http://www.lbjlibrary.org

Goal: To assist with expenses related to
research at the Lyndon B. Johnson
Foundation Library.
Eligibility: Applicants must start by
contacting the library to determine if their
research topic is appropriate for study at
the facility. Applicants must also estimate
the amount of the grant before making a
request.
Target Student: College and Adult
students.
Amount: $500 - $2,500
Number of Awards: Varies
Based on Financial Need: No
Deadline: March and September
Applications are available online.

---

(664) Madeline Pickett Cogswell Nursing Scholarship

National Society Daughters of the
American Revolution
Committee Services Office
Attn: Scholarships
1776 D Street NW
Washington, DC 20006

Phone: 202-628-1776
URL: http://www.dar.org

Goal: To assist nursing students.
Eligibility: Applicants must plan to attend
or attend an accedited school of nursing.
Applicants must be members, descendants
of members or eligible for membership in
NSDAR.
Target Student: High school, College and
Adult students.
Amount: $1,000
Number of Awards: Varies
Based on Financial Need: No
Deadline: February
Applications are available by written
request.

(665) Maley/FTE Scholarship

International Technology and Engineering
Educators Association
Foundation for Technology and
Engineering Educators
1914 Association Drive
Suite 201
Reston, VA 20191

Phone: 703-860-2100
Fax: 703-860-0353
Email: iteea@iteea.org
URL: http://www.iteaconnect.org

Goal: To assist technology education
teachers.

Eligibility: Applicants must be ITEA
members who plan to pursue or continue
graduate study. Applicants must provide
plans for their graduate study, description
of need, college transcripts and three
letters of recommendation.
Target Student: College, Graduate and
Adult students.
Amount: $1,000
Number of Awards: Varies
Based on Financial Need: Yes
Deadline: December
Aplication information is available online.

(666) Mandell and Lester Rosenblatt Undergraduate Scholarship

Society of Naval Architects and Marine
Engineers
601 Pavonia Avenue
Jersey City, NJ 07306

Phone: 201-798-4800
Fax: 201-798-4975
Email: efaustino@sname.org
URL: http://www.sname.org

Goal: To assist college undergraduates
studying fields in the marine industry.
Eligibility: Applicants must be U.S.
Canadian or international college students
who are working towards a degree in naval
architecture, marine engineering, ocean
engineering, or fields related to the marine
industry and members of the SNAME.
Target Student: College and Adult
students.
Amount: Up to $6,000
Number of Awards: Varies
Scholarship can be renewed.
Based on Financial Need: No
Deadline: June
Applications are available online.

(667) Marine Corps League Scholarships

Marine Corps League
P.O. Box 3070
Merrifield, VA 22116

Phone: 800-625-1775
Fax: 703-207-0047
URL: http://www.mcleague.org

Goal: To assist spouses and dependants of Marine Corps League members with educational expenses.
Eligibility: Applicants must be Marine Corp League or Auxillary members in good standing, their spouses and their children, or Marines who died while on active duty or who were honorably discharged.
Target Student: High school, College and Adult students.
Amount: Varies
Number of Awards: Varies
Based on Financial Need: No
Deadline: July
Applications are available online.

(668) Marine Corps League Scholarships

Marine Corps Scholarship Foundation
P.O. Box 3008
Princeton, NJ 08543

Phone: 800-292-7777
Fax: 609-452-2259
Email: mcsfnj@mcsf.org
URL: http://www.marine-scholars.org

Goal: To assist the children of U.S. Marines and former Marines with their educational expenses.

Eligibility: Applicants must be children of a active duty or reserve U.S. Marine, U.S. Marine who has received an Honorable Discharge, Medical Discharge or was killed while serving in the U.S. Marine Corps, and active duty or reserve U.S. Navy Corpsman who is or has served with the U.S. Marine Corps and has recieved an Honorable Discharge, Medical Discharge or was killed while serving the U.S. Navy. Applicants can also be grandchildren of a U.S. Marine who served in the 4th or 6th Marine Division during World War II and is a member of their association or a U.S. Marine who served in the 531 Gray Ghost Squadron and is a member of that association. Applicants must be high school graduates or undergraduate students and a income limit does apply and students must have a 2.0 GPA or higher.
Target Student: College and Adult students.
Amount: Varies
Number of Awards: Varies
Based on Financial Need: Yes
Deadline: March
Applications are available online.

(669) Markley Scholarship

National Association for Campus Activities
13 Harbison Way
Columbia, SC 29212

Phone: 803-732-6222
Fax: 803-749-1047
Email: info@naca.org
URL: http://www.naca.org

Goal: To assist undergraduate and graduate students who have made exceptional contributions in student activities.

Eligibility: Applicants must attend a college in the former NACA South Central Region (AR, LA, NM, OK, TX). They must also be enrolled as juniors, seniors or graduate students at a four-year college or university or a sophomore at a two-year college or university with a GPA of 2.5 or above.
Target Student: College, Graduate and Adult students.
Amount: Varies
Number of Awards: 2
Based on Financial Need: No
Deadline: September
Applications are available online.

(670) Marliave Fund

Association of Engineering Geologists Foundation Marliave Fund
Paul Santi, Department of Geology and Geological Engineering
Colorado School of Mines
Berthoud Hall
Golden, CO 80401

Phone: 303-273-3108
Email: psanti@mines.edu
URL: http://www.aegfoundation.org

Goal: To acknowledge students in engineering geology and geological engineering.
Eligibility: Applicants must be seniors or graduate students in a college program directly applicable to geological engineering and be Association of Engineering Geologist members.
Target Student: College, Graduate and Adult students.
Amount: Varies
Number of Awards: 1
Based on Financial Need: No
Deadline: February
Applications are available online.

(671) Marsh College Scholarship

Insurance Scholarship Foundation of America
14286-19 Beach Boulevard
Suite 353
Jacksonville, FL 32250

Phone: 904-821-7188
Email: foundation@inssfa.org
URL: http://www.inssfa.org

Goal: To assist actuarial science, risk management, and insurance students.
Eligibility: Applicants must be undergraduate or graduate students majoring or minoring in actuarial science, risk management or insurance. Applicants must be seeking bachelor's, master's or doctoral degree, have completed at least one year of college and have completed at least two, three credit courses in actuarial science, risk management or insurance. Applicants must have a GPA of 3.0 or higher.
Target Student: College, Graduate and Adult students.
Amount: $500 - $5,000
Number of Awards: Varies
Based on Financial Need: No
Deadline: March and October
Applications are available online.

(672) Marsh Scholarship Fund

Eastern Surfing Association
P.O. Box 321
Ormond Beach, FL 32175

Phone: 386-672-4905
Email: scholastics@surfesa.org
URL: http://surfesa.org

Goal: To assist students surfers of the Eastern Surfing Association.

Eligibility: Applicants must be current ESA members. To apply applicants must submit transcripts, a letter of recommendation, purpose letter and a completed application.
Target Student: College, Graduate and Adult students.
Amount: Varies
Number of Awards: 8
Based on Financial Need: No
Deadline: May
Applications are available online and by mail.

(673) Marshall E. McCullough Scholarship

National Dairy Shrine
P.O. Box 1
Maribel, WI 54227

Phone: 920-863-6333
Fax: 920-863-8328
Email: info@dairyshrine.org
URL: http://www.dairyshrine.org

Goal: To assist students who are planning careers in agricultural related communication.
Eligibility: Applicants must be high school seniors who are planning to begin a four-year degree in dairy or animal sciences with a communications emphasis or agricultural journalism with an emphasis in dairy or animal science and plan on working in the dair industry.
Target Student: High school students.
Amount: $1,000 - $2,500
Number of Awards: 2
Based on Financial Need: No
Deadline: April
Applications are available online.

(674) Marshall Memorial Fellowship

German Marshall Fund of the United States

1744 R. Stree NW
Washington, DC 20009

Phone: 202-683-2650
Fax: 202-265-1662
Email: info@gmfus.org
URL: http://www.gmfus.org

Goal: To assist future community leaders so they can travel in Europe and explore its societies, institutions and people.
Eligibility: Applicants must be nomitated by a leader in their community or in their professional field. Applicants must be between 28 and 40 years old with demonstrated achievement in their profession, civic involvement and leadership. Applicants must be U.S. citizens or permanent residents of one of countries listed on the scholarships webpage. Applicants should have little to no experience traveling in Europe. Winners will visit five to six cities and meet with policy makers, professionals and community leaders.
Target Student: College, Graduate and Adult students.
Amount: Varies
Number of Awards: 100+
Based on Financial Need: No
Deadline: June
Applications are available online.

(675) Marshall Scholar

Marshal Aid Commemoration Commission

Email: info@marshallscholarship.org
URL: http://www.marshallscholarship.org

Goal: To assist students with academic achievements to study in the United Kingdom and learn about its culture, society and academic values.

Eligibility: Applicants must be U.S. citizens working towards a bachelors degree with a GPA of 3.7 or higher. Studnets apply in one of eight regions in the U.S.
Target Student: College and Adult students.
Amount: Varies
Number of Awards: 40
Based on Financial Need: No
Deadline: October
Applications can be obtained by contacting the regional center listed on the scholarship website.

---

(676) Marvin Mundel Memorial Scholarship

Institute of Industrial Engineers
3577 Parkway Lane
Suite 200
Norcross, GA 30092

Phone: 800-494-0460
Fax: 770-441-3295
Email: bcameron@iienet.org
URL: http://www.iienet2.org

Goal: To assist undergraduate students with an interest in work measurement and methods engineering.
Eligibility: Applicants must be full-time undergraduate students in the U.S., Canada, or Mexico in an industrial engineering program majoring in industrial engineering.
Target Student: College and Adult students.
Amount: $1,000
Number of Awards: 2
Based on Financial Need: Yes
Deadline: November
Nomination information is available online.

---

(677) Mary Church Terrell Award

National Association of Blacks in Criminal Justice
North Carolina Central University
P.O. Box 19788
Durham, NC 27707

Phone: 919-683-1801
Fax: 919-683-1903
Email: office@nabcj.org
URL: http://www.nabcj.org

Goal: This award is for activism and positive change in the field of criminal justice at the city and state level.
Eligibility: Applicants must be nominated by a member of the NABCJ. The award is given to a student who has developed relationships with churches, courts, councils and assemblies.
Target Student: College, Graduate and Adult students.
Amount: Varies
Number of Awards: Varies
Based on Financial Need: No
Deadline: May
Nomination applications are available online.

---

(678) Mary Lou Brown Scholarship

American Radio Relay League Foundation
225 Main Street
Newington, CT 06111

Phone: 860-594-0397
Fax: 860-594-0259
Email: foundation@arrl.org
URL: http://www.arrlf.org

Goal: To assist ham radio operators with continuing their education.

Eligibility: Applicants must have a general ham radio license or higher, a GPA of 3.0 or higher, demonstrated interest in promoting the Amateur Radio Service and be residents of the ARRL Northwest Division (Alaska, Idaho, Montana, Oregon or Washington) and be working towards a bachelor's or graduate degree.
Target Student: High school, College, Graduate and Adult students.
Amount: $2,500
Number of Awards: Varies
Based on Financial Need: No
Deadline: February
Applications are available online. Completed applications must be submitted by mail.

(679) Mary Opal Walanin Scholarship

National Gerontological Nursing Association
7794 Grow Drive
Pensacola, FL 32514

Phone: 800-723-0560
Fax: 850-484-8762
Email: ngna@puetzamc.com
URL: http://www.ngna.org

Goal: To acknowledge gerontology and geriatric nursing undergraduate and graduate students.
Eligibility: The undergraduate scholarship requires applicants to be full or part time nursing students in an accredited U.S. nursing school and plan to work in gerontology or geriatric settings. The graduate scholarships require applicants to be nursing students majoring in gerontology or geriatric nursing at an accredited U.S. nursing program.
Target Student: College Graduate and Adult students.
Amount: $500
Number of Awards: 2
Based on Financial Need: No
Deadline: June

Applications are available online.

(680) Mary Paolozzi Member's Scholarship

Navy Wives Clubs of America
P.O. Box 54022
NSA Mid-South
Millington, TN 38053

Phone: 866-511-6922
Email:scholarships@navywivesclubsofamerica.org
URL:http://www.navywivesclubsofamerica.org

Goal: To assist students who are members of the Navy Wives Clubs of America.
Eligibility: Applicants must be accepted into a college by the application deadline. The award is based on academic merit and financial need.
Target Student: High school, College and Adult students.
Amount: Varies
Number of Awards: Varies
Based on Financial Need: Yes
Deadline: May
Applications are available online. A completed application, transcript and tax forms are required.

(681) Mary Rhein Memorial Scholarship

Mu Alpha Theta
c/o University of Oklahoma
601 Elm Avenue
Room 1102
Norman, OK 73019

Phone: 405-325-4489
Fax: 405-325-7184
Email: matheta@ou.edu
URL: http://www.mualphatheta.org

Goal: To assist graduating high school seniors who are active Mu Alpha Theta members.

Eligibility: Applicants must be graduating high school seniors who are outstanding in mathematics and active Mu Alpha Theta members who have participated at local, regional or national mathematics competitions and plan on purusing a career in mathematics.

Target Student: High school students.

Amount: $5,000

Number of Awards: 1

Based on Financial Need: No

Deadline: March

Applications are available online. A completed application, essay, transcript and three letters of recommendation are required to apply.

(682) Masonic-Range Science Scholarship

Society for Range Management
10030 W. 27th Avenue
Wheat Ridge, CO 80215

Phone: 303-986-3309
Fax: 303-986-3892
Email: vtrujillo@rangelands.org
URL: http://www.rangelands.org

Goal: To assist a high school senior, college freshman or college sophomore who is majoring in range science or related field.

Eligibility: Applicants must be sponsored by a Society for Range Management, National Association of Conservation Districts, or Soil and Water Conservation Society member.

Target Student: High school, College and Adult students.

Amount: Varies

Number of Awards: Varies

Based on Financial Need: No

Deadline: December

Applications are available online.

(684) Materials Processing and Manufacturing Division Scholarship

The Minerals, Metals and Materials Society
184 Thorn Hill Road
Warrendale, PA 15086

Phone: 724-776-9000
Fax: 724-776-3770
Email: students@tms.org
URL: http://www.tms.org

Goal: To assist undergraduate student members of TMS majoring in metallurgical engineering or materials science and engineering.

Eligibility: Applicants must be full-time undergraduate sophomores or juniors whose degree is focused on the integration of process control technology into manufacturing, materials technology research or the manufacturing process.

Target Student: College and Adult students.

Amount: $2,500

Number of Awards: 2

Based on Financial Need: No

Deadline: March

Applications are available online. A completed application, statement, transcripts and three letters of recommendation are required to apply.

(685) Matthew H. Parry Memorial Scholarship

Project Management Institute Educational Foundation
14 Campus Boulevard
Newton Square, PA 19073

Phone: 610-356-4600
Fax: 610-456-0357
Email: pmief@pmi.org
URL: http://www.pmief.org

Goal: To assist students interested in purusing a career in project management.
Eligibility: Applicants must be undergraduate students enrolled in a degree-granting program. Applicants must have an interest in a career in project management.
Target Student: College and Adult students.
Amount: $2,000
Number of Awards: Varies
Based on Financial Need: No
Deadline: Varies
Applications are available online. A completed application, transcript, resume, two essays and three letters of recommendation are required to apply.

---

(686) Mattie J.T. Stepanek Caregiving Scholarship

Rosalynn Carter Institute for Caregiving
800 GSW Drive
Georgia Southwestern State University
Americus, GA 31709

Phone: 229-928-1234
Fax: 229-931-2663
URL: http://www.rosalynncarter.org

Goal: To assist caregivers who are improving their skills through continued education.
Eligibility: Applicants must be family, professional or paraprofessional caregivers and enrolled or planning to enroll in a college that will help them gain additional skills in caregiving.
Target Student: High school, College, Graduate and Adult students.
Amount: $2,500
Number of Awards: 4
Based on Financial Need: No
Deadline: May
Applications are available online.

---

(683) Maurice B. Cohill, Jr. Young Investigator Award

National Center for Juvenile Justice
3700 South Water Street Suite 200
Pittsburgh, PA 15203

Phone: 412-227-6950
Fax: 412-227-6955
Email: ncjj@ncjj.org
URL: http://www.ncjj.org

Goal: To assist young people who are interested in law and justice research.
Eligibility: Applicants must be U.S. high school juniors or seniors or youth in placement facilities who will be attending a college, university or trade school after graduation or completing a GED. They must complete a research paper on a topic relating to juvenile crime, law, public policy, delinquency, courts, law data analysis or probation. Selection is based on the overall strength of the paper.
Target Student: High school students.
Amount: Up to $500
Number of Awards: 4
Based on Financial Need: No
Deadline: May
Applications are available online. A completed application, cover sheet, research paper and abstract are required to apply.

---

(687) McNeil Consumer Health Rural and Underserved Scholarship

National Association of Pediatric Nurse Practitioners
20 Brace Road
Suite 200
Cherry Hill, NJ 08034

Phone: 856-857-9700
Fax: 856-857-1600
Email: info@napnap.org
URL: http://www.napnap.org

Goal: To improve the care provided by pediatric nurse practitioners.
Eligibility: Applicants must be enrolled full-time in a PNP master's degree program and plan to work in a rural area for two years after graduation. Applicants must be a registered nurse with one year of experience in pediatrics, be NAPNAP members and have demonstrated financial need.
Target Student: Graduate and Adult students.
Amount: Varies
Number of Awards: Varies
Based on Financial Need: Yes
Deadline: June
Applications are available online.

---

(688) Medal of Honor AFCEA ROTC Scholarships

Armed Forces Communications and Electronics Association
4400 Fair Lakes Court
Fairfax, VA 22033

Phone: 703-631-6149
Fax: 703-631-4693
URL: http://www.afcea.org

Goal: To assist students who are members of the ROTC and committed to serving the United States armed forces.
Eligibility: Applicants must be enrolled in college full time in their sophomore or junior year. Applicants must have at least a 3.0 GPA.
Target Student: College and Adult students.
Amount: $4,000
Number of Awards: 4
Based on Financial Need: No
Deadline: March
Applications are available online.

---

(689) Medger Evers Award

National Association of Blacks in Criminal Justice
North Carolina Central University
P.O. Box 19788
Durham, NC 27707

Phone: 919-683-1801
Fax: 919-683-1903
Email: office@nabcj.org
URL: http://www.nabcj.org

Goal: To reward efforts to ensure that all people receive equal justice under the law.
Eligibility: This award is to honor slain civil rights leaders. Nominators should be members of NABCJ.
Target Student: College, Graduate and Adult students.
Amount: Varies
Number of Awards: 1
Based on Financial Need: No
Deadline: May
Nomination applications are available online.

---

(690) Media Fellows Program

Washington Media Scholars Foundation
815 Slaters Lane
Suite 201
Alexandria, VA 22314

Phone: 703-299-4399
Email: kara.watt@mediascholars.org
URL: http://www.mediascholars.org

Goal: To assist students planning careers in public policy advertising.

Eligibility: Applicants must be full-time undergraduate students, rising juniors and seniors who are currently enrolled in a strategic public policy advertising industry. Majors eligible for the award include, but are not limited to: mass communications, journalism, political science, and business marketing. Applicants must have a 3.0 GPA or higher, a proven interest in strategic media planning and demonstrated financial need.
Target Student: College and Adult students.
Amount: $5,000
Number of Awards: Up to 12
Based on Financial Need: Yes
Deadline: July
Applications are available online. A completed application, essay, letter of recommendation and a phone interview are required to apply.

(691) Mediacom World Class Scholarship Program

Mediacom
3737 Westown Parkway Suite A
West Des Moines, LA 50266

Email: scholarships@mediacomcc.com
URL: http://www.mediacomworldclass.com

Goal: To assist students in Mediacom service areas.
Eligibility: Applicants must be graduating high school seniors. Children of Mediacom employees are not eligible, and applicants must live in an area that is served by Mediacom.
Target Student: High school students.
Amount: $1,000
Number of Awards: Varies
Based on Financial Need: No
Deadline: February

Applications are available online. A completed application, essay, transcripts and two reference forms are needed to apply.

(692) Medical Student Summer Research Training in Aging Program

American Federation for Aging Research
70 West 40th Street
11th Floor
New York, NY 10018

Phone: 212-703-9977
Fax: 212-997-0330
Email: grants@afar.org
URL: http://www.afar.org

Goal: To assist early medical students with an interest in geriatric medicine with an opportunity to work under the top experts in the field.
Eligibility: Applicants must be osteopathic or allopathic students who have completed at least one year of medical school at a U.S. school and have a faculty sponsor.
Target Student: Graduate and Adult students.
Amount: $3,496 - $5,244
Number of Awards: 130
Based on Financial Need: No
Deadline: January
Applications are available online.

(693) Medtronic Physio-Control Advanced Nursing Practice Scholarship

Emergency Nurses Association
915 Lee Street
Des Plaines, IL 60016

Phone: 847-460-4100
Fax: 847-460-4100
Email: foundation@ena.org
URL: http://www.ena.org

Goal: To assist nurses working towards advanced training to become clinical nurse specialists or nurse practitioners.
Eligibility: Applicants must be nurses who are working towards advanced clinical practice degrees to become a clinical nurse specialists or nurse practitioner. Applicants must have been ENA members for at least 12 months before applying.
Target Student: Graduate and Adult students.
Amount: $3,000
Number of Awards: 2
Based on Financial Need: No
Deadline: June
Applications are available online.

---

(694) Melvin R. Green Scholarships

American Society of Mechanical Engineers
Three Park Avenue
New York, NY 10016

Phone: 800-843-2763
Fax: 973-882-1717
Email: infocentral@asme.org
URL: http://www.asme.org

Goal: To assist mechanical engineering students.
Eligibility: Applicants must be ASME student members with oustanding character and integrity. Applicants must be enrolled in an eligible accredited bachelor's degree in mechanical engineering and be college juniors and seniors.
Target Student: College and Adult students.
Amount: $4,000
Number of Awards: Up to 2
Based on Financial Need: No
Deadline: March
Applications are available online.

---

(695) Members-at-Large Reentry Award

Iota Sigma Pi
Dr. Joanne Bedlek-Anslow, MAL Coordinator
Camden High School, Science
1022 Ehrenclou Drive
Camden, SC 29020

URL: http://www.iotasigmapi.info

Goal: To acknowledge the potential in chemistry and related fields for women undergraduate and graduate students who have been out of school for at least three years.
Eligibility: Applicants must be female undergraduate or graduate students at an accredited school, a member of Iota Sigma Pi and nominated by a faculty member.
Target Student: College, Graduate and Adult students.
Amount: $1,500
Number of Awards: 1
Based on Financial Need: No
Deadline: February
Application information is available online.

---

(696) Memorial Scholarship Fund

Third Marine Division Association
MFySgt. James G. Kyser, USMC
15727 Vista Drive
Dumfries, VA 22025

Phone: 352-726-2767
Email: scholarship@caltrap.org
URL: http://www.caltrap.com

Goal: To assist veterans and their families.
Eligibility: Applicants must be the children of Marines who served with the Third Marine Division or in support of the Third Division and have been members of the Third Marine Division Association for at least two years.

Target Student: High school and College students.
Amount: Varies
Number of Awards: Varies
Scholarship can be renewed.
Based on Financial Need: No
Deadline: April
Applications are available by written request after September 1.

---

(697) Mensa Education and Research Foundation Scholarship Program

Mensa Education and Research Foundation
1229 Corporate Drive West
Arlington, TX 76006

Phone: 817-607-5577
Fax: 817-649-5232
Email: info@mensafoundation.org
URL: http://www.mensafoundation.org

Goal: To assist students with higher education expenses.
Eligibility: Applicants do not need to be members of Mensa, but they must be residents of a participating Mensa Group area. They must also be enrolled in a degree program at an accredited U.S. college or university in the year after the application.
Target Student: High school, College and Adult students.
Amount: Varies
Number of Awards: Varies
Based on Financial Need: No
Deadline: January
Applications are available online starting in September. A completed application and essay are required to apply.

---

(698) Metro Scholarship

American Association of Textile Chemists and Colorists
1 Davis Drive

Research Triangle Park, NC 27709

Phone: 919-549-3544
Fax: 919-549-8933
URL: http://www.aatcc.org

Goal: To assist undergraduate students studying textiles.
Eligibility: Applicants must be U.S. citizens and undergraduates who are studying an area related to textiles. Applicants must attend a college in New England, New York or New Jersey with a AATCC chapter.
Target Student: College and Adult students.
Amount: $1,000 - $2,750
Number of Awards: Varies
Scholarship can be renewed.
Based on Financial Need: No
Deadline: March
Applications are available online. A completed application, personal statement, and transcripts are required to apply.

---

(699) Metro Youth Football Association Scholarship

Metro Youth Football Association
P.O. Box 2171
Cedar Rapids, IA 52406

Phone: 319-393-8696
Email: info@metroyouthfootball.com
URL: http://www.metroyouthfootball.com

Goal: To assist participants of Metro Youth Tackle Football who are college-bound.
Eligibility: Applicants must be graduating high school seniors who are current or former Metro Youth Tackle Football participants. They must be current high school football players with a GPA of 2.5 or higher with plans to attend college.
Target Student: High school students.
Amount: $500 to $2,000

Number of Awards: 3
Based on Financial Need: No
Deadline: June
Applications are available online. A completed application, essay and one letter of recommendation are required.

---

(700) Metropolitan Opera National Council Auditions

Metropolitan Opera
Lincoln Center
New York, NY 10023

Phone: 212-870-4515
Fax: 212-870-7648
Email: ncouncil@metropera.org
URL:http://www.metroperafamily.org/metropera/auditions/national

Goal: To find young talent for the Metropolitan Opera.
Eligibility: Applicants must be U.S. or Canadian citizens who are between 20 and 30 years old and have musical training and background and potentional in opera and be able to sing in more than one langauge. There is an application fee of $30 and we do not recommend applying to scholarships that require a fee.
Target Student: High school, College, Graduate and Adult students.
Amount: $1,500 - $15,000
Number of Awards: Varies
Based on Financial Need: No
Deadline: Varies
Applications are available online.

---

(701) MG James Ursano Scholarship Fund

Army Emergency Relief
200 Stovall Street Rm. 5N13
Alexandria, VA 22332

Phone: 703-428-0035
Fax: 703-325-7183

Email: education@aerhq.org
URL: http://www.aerhq.org

Goal: To assist the children of Army families with educational expenses.
Eligibility: Applicants must be the dependent, unmarried and under 22, children of Army members. Applicants must be registered with the Defense Eligibility Enrollment Reporting System, have a GPA of 2.0 or greater and be enrolled or pending acceptance as full time students in a post-secondary educational institution. Awards are based on financial need.
Target Student: High school and College students.
Amount: Varies
Number of Awards: Varies
Scholarship can be renewed.
Based on Financial Need: Yes
Deadline: April
Applications are available online and by mail.

---

(702) MGMA Midwest Section Scholarship

Medical Group Management Association
104 Inverness Terrace East
Englewood, CO 80112

Phone: 877-275-6462
Email: acmpe@mgma.com
URL: http://www.mgma.com

Goal: To assist MGMA Midwest Section members purusing degrees related to medical practice management.
Eligibility: Applicants must be members of the Medical Group Management Association and residents of one of the

MGMA Midwest Section states (Illinois, Indiana, Iowa, Michigan, Minnesota, Nebraska, North Dakota, Ohio, South Dakota, or Wisconsin). Applicants must be undergraduate or graduate students enrolled in a medical practice management degree program.
Target Student: College, Graduate and Adult students.
Amount: Varies
Number of Awards: Varies
Based on Financial Need: No
Deadline: May
Applications are available online.

(703) MGMA Western Section Scholarship

Medical Group Management Association
104 Inverness Terrace East
Englewood, CO 80112

Phone: 877-275-6462
Email: acmpe@mgma.com
URL: http://www.mgma.com

Goal: To assist MGMA Western Section members purusing degrees related to medical practice management.
Eligibility: Applicants must be members of the Medical Group Management Association and residents of one of the MGMA Western Section states (Alaska, Arizona, California, Colorado, Hawaii, Idaho, Montana, Nevada, New Mexico, Oregon, Utah, Washington or Wyoming). Applicants must be undergraduate or graduate students enrolled in a medical practice management degree program.
Target Student: College, Graduate and Adult students.
Amount: Varies
Number of Awards: Varies
Based on Financial Need: No
Deadline: May
Applications are available online.

(704) Michael Kidger Memorial Scholarship

International Society for Optical Engineering
P.O. Box 10
Bellingham, WA 98227

Phone: 360-685-5452
Fax: 360-647-1445
Email: scholarships@spie.org
URL: http://www.spie.org

Goal: To assist students in the optial design field.
Eligibility: Applicants must be in the optial design field with one year remaining in their program.
Target Student: College and Adult students.
Amount: $5,000
Number of Awards: 1
Based on Financial Need: No
Deadline: March
Applications are available online.

(705) Microsoft Tuition Scholarships

Microsoft Corporation
One Microsoft Way
Redmond, WA 98052

Phone: 800-642-7676
Fax: 425-936-7329
Email: scholars@microsoft.com
URL: http://www.microsoft.com/college

Goal: To assist undergraduate students with an interest in the software industry and committed to leadership.
Eligibility: Applicants must be full-time students in an undegraduate computer science (or related) program. Award recipients complete a salaried internship at Microsoft in Washington. Special scholarships are available for women, minorities and those with disabilities.

Target Student: College and Adult students.
Amount: Up to full tuition.
Number of Awards: Varies
Based on Financial Need: No
Deadline: February
Applications are available online.

---

(706) Mid-Continent Instrument Scholarship

Aircraft Electronics Association
4217 South Hocker
Independence, MO 64055

Phone: 816-373-6565
Fax: 816-478-3100
Email: info@aea.net
URL: http://www.aea.net

Goal: To assist students who want to pursue a career in avionics or aircraft repair.
Eligibility: Applicants must be high school seniors or college students planning to or attending an accredited school in avionics or aircraft repair.
Target Student: High school, College and Adult students.
Amount: $1,000
Number of Awards: 1
Based on Financial Need: No
Deadline: February
Applications are available by contacting the sponsor.

---

(707) Mike Carr Student Paper Competition

League of World War I Aviation Historians
909 Pine Street
Yankton, SD 57078

Email: otf-membership@overthefront.com
URL: http://www.overthefront.com

Goal: To encourage the study of World War I-era aviation.
Eligibility: Applicants must be high school, undergraduate or graduate students enrolled at an accredited school.
Applicants are required to submit an essay about some aspect of aviation during the World War I era.
Target Student: High school, College and Graduate students.
Amount: $200 - $500
Number of Awards: Up to 6
Based on Financial Need: No
Deadline: May
Application information is available online.

---

(708) Mike Nash Memorial Scholarship Fund

Vietnam Veterans of America
8605 Cameron Street Suite 400
Silver Spring, MD 20910

Phone: 800-882-1316
Email: finance@vva.org
URL: http://www.vva.org

Goal: To assist Vietnam veterans, their widows and their children.
Eligibility: Applicants must be Vietnam Veterans of America members, their spouses, children, stepchildren, grandchildren or spouses, children, stepchildren, or grandchildren of Vietnam veterans who are deceased, MIA or KIA. Applicants must enroll at least half time at an accredited school.
Target Student: High school, College and Adult students.
Amount: Varies
Number of Awards: Varies
Based on Financial Need: No
Deadline: May
Applications are available online.

---

(709) Military Award Program

Imagine America Foundation
1101 Connecticut Avenue NW Suite 901
Washington, DC 20036

Phone: 202-336-6800
Fax: 202-408-8102
Email: scholarships@imagine-america.org
URL: http://www.imagine-america.org

Goal: To assist those who have served in the military.
Eligibility: Applicants must be enrolling in a participating college and be active duty, reservist, honorably discharged or retired veterans. They must have financial need, not be a receipient of another Imagine America scholarships and be likely to enroll and be succesful in their post secondary education.
Target Student: College, Graduate and Adult students.
Amount: $1,000
Number of Awards: Varies
Based on Financial Need: Yes
Deadline: June
Applications are available online.

(710) Military Officers' Benevolent Corporation Scholarships

Military Officers' Benevolent Corporation
1010 American Eagle Boulevard Box 301
Sun City Center, FL 33573

Phone: 813-634-4675
Fax: 813-633-2412
Email: president@mobe-online.org
URL: http://www.mobe-online.org

Goal: To assist the children and grandchildren of military members and others who have served their country.

Eligibility: Applicants must be the children or grandchildren of current or former military members, federal employees GS-7 or higher, foreign service officers (FSO-8 and below) or honorably discharged or retired foreign military officers of Allied Nations living in the U.S. Applicants must be high school seniors, recommended by their principal, have an ACT score of 21 or higher, SAT score of 900 or higher (two part) or 1350 or higher (three part. A GPA of 3.0 or higher is required.
Target Student: High school students.
Amount: $500 to $3,000
Number of Awards: 16
Scholarship can be renwed.
Based on Financial Need: No
Deadline: March
Applications are available online.

(711) Military Order of the Purple Heart Scholarship

Military Order of the Purple Heart
MOPH National Headquarters
5413-B Backlick Road
Attn: Scholarship
Springfield, VA 22151

Phone: 703-642-5360
Fax: 703-642-2054
Email: scholarship@purpleheart.org
URL: http://www.purpleheart.org

Goal: To award outstanding achievements.
Eligibility: Applicants must be a member of the Military Order of the Purple Heart, or a child, step-child, grandchild or great grandchild of a member of the MOPH or a veteran killed in action or a veteran who died of injuries who did not have the

opportunity to join the MOPH. Applicants must be U.S. citizens, high school seniors or graduates, have a GPA of 2.75 or greater and enrolled in a college or university full time. A $15 dollar application fee is required. It is not recommended by me or by any other reputable organization to pay a fee when applying for a scholarship. The only reason that this sholarship is included here is because the organization is reputable.
Target Student: High school, College, Graduate and Adult students.
Amount: $3,000
Number of Awards: Varies
Based on Financial Need: No
Deadline: February
Applications are available online. A completed application, essay and application fee are required to apply.

(712) Milton F. Lunch Research Fellowship

National Society of Professional Engineers
1420 King Street
Alexandria, VA 22314

Phone: 703-684-2885
Fax: 703-836-4875
Email: memserv@nspe.org
URL: http://www.nspe.org

Goal: To honor the memory of NSPE general counsel Milton F. Lunch.
Eligibility: Applicants must be U.S. citizens working towards a career and in an undergraduate or graduate degree program in engineering, architecture, construction or law with a 3.0 or higher GPA.
Target Student: College, Graduate and Adult students.
Amount: $8,000
Number of Awards: 1
Based on Financial Need: No
Deadline: January
Applications are available online.

(713) Minorities and Women Educational Scholarship

Appraisal Institute
550 W. Van Buren Street
Suite 1000
Chicago, IL 60607

Phone: 312-335-4100
Fax: 312-335-4400
Email: wwoodburn@appraisalinstitute.org
URL: http://www.appraisalinstitute.org

Goal: To assist minorty and women college students earn their degrees in real estate appraisal or realated fields.
Eligibility: Applicants must be women or American Indians, Alaska Natives, Asians, Afriacn Americans, Hispanics, or Latinos, Native Hawaiians or other Pacific Islanders. Applicants must be part- or full-time students working toward their degree and taking real estate courses with a GPA of 2.5 or higher and demonstrated financial need.
Target Student: College and Adult students.
Amount: $1,000
Number of Awards: Varies
Based on Financial Need: Yes
Deadline: April
Application information is available online.

(714) Minority Dental Student Scholarship

American Dental Association Foundation
211 East Chicago Avenue
Chicago, IL 60611

Phone: 312-440-2763
Fax: 312-440-3526
Email: famularor@ada.org
URL: http://www.ada.org

Goal: To encourage minority students to pursue degrees in dental hygiene, dental assisting, dentistry and dental laboratory technology.

Eligibility: Applicants must be African Americans, Hispanic, or Native American, full-time students beginning their second year in an accredited dental program. Applicants must have demonstrated financial need of at least $2,500.

Target Student: College and Adult students.

Amount: $1,000

Number of Awards: 1

Based on Financial Need: Yes

Deadline: Varies

Applications are available from the dental school.

---

(715) Minority Fellowship Program

American Sociological Association
Minority Fellowship Program
1430 K Street NW
Suite 600
Washington, DC 20005

Phone: 202-383-9005
Fax: 202-638-0882
Email: minority.affairs@asanet.org
URL: http://www.asanet.org

Goal: To assist pre-doctoral students in sociology with educational expenses.

Eligibility: Applicants may be new or continuing graduating students in sociology in a Ph.D. program. Students must be members of an underrepresented minority group in the U.S. (African American, Latino, Asian/Pacific Islander, or American Indian/Alaska Natives). Applicants must also be U.S. citizens, non-citizen nationals or have been lawfully admitted to the U.S. for permanent residence. The fellowship is for 12 months and is renewable for three years.

Target Student: Graduate and Adult students.

Amount: $18,000

Number of Awards: Varies

Scholarship is renewable.

Based on Financial Need: No

Deadline: January

Applications are available online.

---

(716) Minority Scholarship Program

Fredrikson and Byron, P.A.
200 S. Sixth Street
Suite 4000
Minneapolis, MN 55402

Phone: 612-492-7000
Fax: 612-792-7077
Email: market@fredlaw.com
URL: http://www.fredlaw.com

Goal: To assist law students from diverse backgrounds with educational expenses.

Eligibility: A completed application form, writing sample, two letters of recommendation, law school transcript, undergraduate transcript, and resume are required to apply. Along with the financial award, winners are invited to serve as summer associates with the firm.

Target Student: Graduate and Adult students.

Amount: $10,000

Number of Awards: 1

Based on Financial Need: No

Deadline: March

Applications are available online.

---

(717) Minority Student Scholarship

American Speech-Language-Hearing Foundation
2200 Research Boulevard
Rockville, MD 20850

Phone: 301-296-8700
Email: foundation@asha.org
URL: http://www.ashfoundation.org

Goal: To assist minority graduate students studying communication sciences and disorders.
Eligibility: Applicants should be full-time minority graduate students. Doctoral programs do not need to be accredited, but master's degree programs must be accredited by the Council on Academic Accreditation for Audiology and Speech Pathology.
Target Student: Graduate and Adult students.
Amount: $5,000
Number of Awards: 1
Based on Financial Need: No
Deadline: Unknown
Applications are available online.

(718) MLA Scholarship

Medical Library Association
65 East Wacker Place
Suite 1900
Chicago, IL 60601

Phone: 800-545-2433 x4276
Fax: 312-419-8950
Email: spectrum@ala.org
URL: http://www.mlanet.org

Goal: To assist a student at an ALA accredited library school with finishing their degree.
Eligibility: Applicants must be U.S. or Canadian citizens or permanent residents entering or less than half-way through as accredited graduate school program in a relevant field to library science.
Target Student: Graduate and Adult students.
Amount: Up to $5,000
Number of Awards: 1
Based on Financial Need: No
Deadline: December
Applications are available online.

(719) MLA Scholarship for Minority Students

Medical Library Association
65 East Wacker Place
Suite 1900
Chicago, IL 60601

Phone: 800-545-2433 x4276
Fax: 312-419-8950
Email: spectrum@ala.org
URL: http://www.mlanet.org

Goal: To assist minority students entering or attending graduate library school.
Eligibility: Applicants must be U.S. or Canadian citizens or permanent residents and African-American, Hispanic, Asian, Native American, or Pacific Islander and be beginning or currently attending an ALA accredited library school and be no more than halfway through their program.
Target Student: Graduate and Adult students.
Amount: Up to $5,000
Number of Awards: 1
Based on Financial Need: No
Deadline: December
Applications are available online.

(720) MLA/NLM Spectrum Scholarship

Medical Library Association
65 East Wacker Place
Suite 1900
Chicago, IL 60601

Phone: 800-545-2433 x4276
Fax: 312-419-8950
Email: spectrum@ala.org
URL: http://www.mlanet.org

Goal: To assist minority students to in becoming health sciences information professionals.

Eligibility: Applicants must be American Indian/Alaska Native, Asian, Black/African American, Hispanic/Lation, or Native Hawaiian/Other Pacific Islander who are attending accredited library schools and are studying relevant to library science planning to enter the health sciences information field.
Target Student: College, Graduate and Adult students.
Amount: Varies
Number of Awards: Varies
Based on Financial Need: No
Deadline: March
Applications are available online.

---

(721) MOAA Base/Post Scholarships

Military Officers Association of America
201 N. Washington Street
Alexandria, VA 22314

Phone: 800-234-6622
Email: msc@moaa.org
URL: http://www.moaa.org

Goal: To assist children of active duty military members with educational expenses.
Eligibility: Applicants must be the dependent of an active duty military member and be under the age of 24. The award is selected at random.
Target Student: High school and College students.
Amount: $1,000
Number of Awards: 25
Based on Financial Need: No
Deadline: March
Applications are available online.

---

(722) Montgomery GI Bill - Active Duty

Department of Veterans Affairs
Veterans Benefits Administration
810 Vermont Avenue NW
Washington, DC 20420

Phone: 888-442-4551
URL: http://www.gibill.va.gov

Goal: To assist veterans with educational expenses.
Eligibility: Applicants must have an honorable dischange and high school diploma and meet service requirements. The GI Bill provides 36 months of educational benefits for college, technical, vocational courses, correspondence courses, apprenticeship/job training, flight training, high tech training, licensing and certification tests and some entrace examinations.
Target Student: College, Graduate and Adult students.
Amount: Varies
Number of Awards: Varies
Based on Financial Need: No
Deadline: None
Applications are available online.

---

(723) Montgomery GI Bill - Selected Reserve

Department of Veterans Affairs
Veterans Benefits Administration
810 Vermont Avenue NW
Washington, DC 20420

Phone: 888-442-4551
URL: http://www.gibill.va.gov

Goal: To assist members of the U.S. military selected reserve.
Eligibility: Applicants must have a six year commitment ot the Selected Reserve after June 30, 1985. Applicants must have completed their basic military training, met the requirements for their high school

diploma or equivalency and may use the funds for degree programs, certificates, correspondence courses, training, independent study programs, apprenticeship and vocational flight training programs.
Target Student: High school, College, Graduate and Adult students.
Amount: Varies
Number of Awards: Varies
Scholarship can be renewed.
Based on Financial Need: No
Deadline: Varies
Applications are available online.

(724) Montgomery GI Bill - Tuition Assistance Top-Up

Department of Veterans Affairs
Veterans Benefits Administration
810 Vermont Avenue NW
Washington, DC 20420

Phone: 888-442-4551
URL: http://www.gibill.va.gov

Goal: To assist students who are receiving tuition assistance from the military that doesn't cover the full cost of tuition.
Eligibility: Applicants must be eligible for the Montgomery GI Bill - Active Duty benefit and they must also have served on active duty for at least two years.
Target Student: College, Graduate and Adult students.
Amount: Varies
Number of Awards: Varies
Scholarship can be renewed.
Based on Financial Need: No
Deadline: Varies
Applications are available online. For more infomration contact your education services officer or education counselor.

(725) Morton B. Duggan, Jr. Memorial Education Recognition Award

American Association for Respiratory Care
9425 North MacArthur Boulevard
Suite 100
Irving, TX 75063

Phone: 972-243-2272
Fax: 972-484-2720
Email: info@aarc.org
URL: http://www.aarc.org

Goal: To acknowledge students in respiratory care programs.
Eligibility: Applicants must be enrolled in an accredited respiratory care program with a 3.0 GPA or higher.
Target Student: College, Graduate and Adult students.
Amount: Up to $1,000
Number of Awards: 1
Based on Financial Need: No
Deadline: June
Applications are available online.

(726) Morton Gould Young Composer Award

ASCAP
One Lincoln Plaza
New York, NY 10023

Phone: 212-621-6219
URL: http://www.ascapfoundation.org

Goal: To assist young composers.
Eligibility: Applicants must be composers under 30 on January 1 of the current year who are U.S. citizens, permanent residents, or enrolled with a student visa.
Target Student: Junior high and younger, High school, College, Graduate and Adult students.
Amount: Varies
Number of Awards: Varies
Based on Financial Need: No
Deadline: February
Applications are available online.

(727) Most Valuable Student Scholarships

Elks National Foundation Headquarters
2750 North Lakeview Avenue
Chicago, IL 60614

Phone: 773-755-4732
Fax: 773-755-4733
Email: scholarship@elks.org
URL: http://www.elks.org

Goal: To assist high school seniors with financial need and demonstrated scholarship and leadership.
Eligibility: Applicants must be high school seniors who are U.S. citizens and are planning to puruse a four-year degree on a full time basis at a U.S. college or university.
Target Student: High school students.
Amount: $1,000 to $15,000
Number of Awards: 500
Scholarship can be renewed.
Based on Financial Need: Yes
Deadline: December
To apply contact your local Elks association.

(728) Myrtle and Earl Walker Scholarship

Society of Manufacturing Engineers
Education Foundation
One SME Drive
P.O. Box 930
Dearborn, MI 48121

Phone: 313-425-330
Fax: 313-425-3411
Email: foundation@sme.org
URL: http://www.smeef.org

Goal: To assist manufacturing engineering and technology undergraduate students.

Eligibility: Applicants must be full-time undergraduate students studying manufacturing engineering or technology at an accredited school in the U.S. or Canada. Applicants must have a GPA of 3.0 or higher and completed at least 15 or more credit hours. Applicants must plan to pursue a career in manufacturing engineering or technology.
Target Student: College and Adult students.
Amount: Varies
Number of Awards: Varies
Based on Financial Need: No
Deadline: February
Applications are available online. A completed application, statement, transcripts, resume and two letters of recommendation are required to apply.

(729) NABF Scholarship Program

National Amateur Baseball Federation
Awards Committee Chairman
P.O. Box 705
Bowie, MD 20718

Phone: 301-464-5460
Fax: 301-352-0214
Email: nabf1914@aol.com
URL: http://www.nabf.com

Goal: To assist students involved with the federation with educational expenses.
Eligibility: Applicants must be enrolled in an accredited college or university, must have participated in a federation event and must be sponsored by a member association.
Target Student: College and Adult students.
Amount: $1,000
Number of Awards: Varies
Based on Financial Need: Yes
Deadline: Varies
Applications are available online.

(730) NACA East Coast Graduate Student Scholarship

National Association for Campus Activities
13 Harbison Way
Columbia, SC 29212

Phone: 803-732-6222
Fax: 803-749-1047
Email: info@naca.org
URL: http://www.naca.org

Goal: To assist graduate students attending a college or university on the East Coast.
Eligibility: Applicants must be enrolled in master's or doctorate degree programs in student personnel services or a related field, be attending school in Washington, DC, Delaware, Maryland, New Jersey, New York or Eastern Pennsylvania and be involved in campus activities along with planning ot pursue a career in campus activities.
Target Student: Graduate and Adult students.
Amount: Varies
Number of Awards: 2
Based on Financial Need: No
Deadline: May
Applications are available online.

(731) NACA Regional Council Student Leader Scholarships

National Association for Campus Activities
13 Harbison Way
Columbia, SC 29212

Phone: 803-732-6222
Fax: 803-749-1047
Email: info@naca.org
URL: http://www.naca.org

Goal: To assist students in NACA's regions with educational expenses.

Eligibility: Applicants must be undergraduate students in good standing. Applicants must hold leadership positions on campus and must have significant contributions to their college campuses.
Target Student: College and Adult students.
Amount: Varies
Number of Awards: Varies
Based on Financial Need: No
Deadline: May
Applications are available online.

(732) NACOP Scholarship

National Association of Chiefs of Police
NACOP Scholarship Program
6350 Horizon Drive
Titusville, FL 32780

Phone: 321-264-0911
Email: kinc@aphf.org
URL: http://www.aphf.org/scholarships.html

Goal: To acknowledge law enforcement individuals.
Eligibility: Applicants must be disabled law enforcement officers wishing to get retrained or children of disabled officers. Applicants must maintain a 2.0 GPA and enroll in at least 6 credit hours.
Target Student: High school, College, Graduate and Adult students.
Amount: $500
Number of Awards: Varies
Based on Financial Need: No
Deadline: Varies
Applications are available by written request.

(733) NAMEPA Scholarship Program

National Association of Multicultural Engineering Program Advocates
341 N. Maitland Avenue
Suite 130

Maitland, FL 32751

Phone: 407-647-8839
Fax: 407-629-2502
Email: namepa@namepa.org
URL: http://www.namepa.org

Goal: To assist minority students in becoming engineers.
Eligibility: Applicants must be African-America, Latino, or American Indian high school seniors accepted at a college or university as an engineering major. Applicants must have a 2.7 GPA or higher, a minimum ACT score of 25 or a minimum SAT score of 1000 and attend an NAMEPA member school.
Target Student: High school students.
Amount: $1,000
Number of Awards: Varies
Based on Financial Need: No
Deadline: May
Applications are available online.

(734) NAMTA Foundation Visual Arts Major Scholarship

NAMTA Foundation for the Visual Arts
15806 Brookway Drive
Suite 300
Huntersville, NC 28078

Phone: 800-746-2682
Fax: 704-892-6247
Email: foundation@namta.org
URL: http://www.namtafoundation.org

Goal: To assist visual arts majors.
Eligibility: Applicants must be current undergradaute freshman, sophomores or juniors who are majoring in painting, drawing, sculpture, sketching or another type of visual art. The award is based on the artists talent, potential, extracurricular activities, GPA and financial need.
Target Student: College and Adult students.
Amount: Varies

Number of Awards: Varies
Based on Financial Need: Yes
Deadline: March
Applications are available online.

(735) Nancy Curry Scholarship

Child Nutrition Foundation
Scholarship Committee
700 S. Washington Street
Suite 300
Alexandria, VA 22314

Phone: 703-739-3900
Email: jcurtis@schoolnutrition.org
URL: http://www.schoolnutrition.org

Goal: To assist students who want to pursue a career in the food service industry.
Eligibility: Applicants or the parents of applicants must be School Nutrition Association members for at least one year and enrolled in a school foodservice related program at an educational institution.
Target Student: High school, College, Graduate and Adult students.
Amount: $500
Number of Awards: 1
Based on Financial Need: No
Deadline: April
Applications are available online.

(736) Nancy Reagan Pathfinder Scholarships

National Federation of Republican Women
124 N. Alfred Street
Alexandria, VA 22314

Phone: 703-548-9688
Fax: 703-548-9836
Email: mail@nfrw.org
URL:http://www.nfrw.org/programs/scholarships.htm

Goal: To honor former First Lady Nancy Reagan.
Eligibility: Applicants must be college sophomores or above, including master's degree students.
Target Student: College, Graduate and Adult students.
Amount: $2,500
Number of Awards: 3
Based on Financial Need: No
Deadline: June
Applications are available online. A completed application, three letters of recommendation, transcript, two essays and State Federation President Certification are required.

---

(737) Naomi Berber Memorial Scholarship

Print and Graphics Scholarship Foundation
Attn: Bernie Ecker
200 Deer Run Road
Sewickley, PA 15143

URL: http://www.gain.net

Goal: To assist students who are interested in careers in printing and graphic communications.
Eligibility: Applicants must be high school seniors, graduates or students at a two year or four year college. Applicants must be full-time students with a GPA of 3.0 or higher.
Target Student: High school, College and Adult students.
Amount: Varies
Number of Awards: Varies
Based on Financial Need: No
Deadline: March and April
Applications are available online. A completed application, transcript, course of study and two letters of recommendation are required to apply.

---

(738) Naomi Brack Student Scholarship

National Organization for Associate Degree Nursing
7794 Grow Drive
Pensacola, FL 32514

Phone: 850-484-6948
Fax: 850-484-8762
Email: richelle.torres@dancyamc.com
URL: http://www.noadn.org

Goal: To assist associates degree nursing students.
Eligibility: Applicants must be enrolled in an associate's degree program in nursing with a GPA of at least 3.0 and be active in their schools nursing association.
Target Student: College and Adult students.
Amount: $1,000
Number of Awards: Varies
Based on Financial Need: No
Deadline: September
Applications are available online. A completed application, statement, transcript, nomination form and two letters of recommendation are required to apply.

---

(739) NAPA Research and Education Foundation Scholarship

National Asphalt Pavement Association
5100 Forbes Boulevard
Lanham, MD 20706

Phone: 888-468-6499
Fax: 301-731-4621
URL: http://www.hotmix.org

Goal: To assist engineering and construction students interesting in hot mix asphalt technology.

Eligibility: Applicants must be U.S. citizens enrolled full-time in a construction management, civil engineering, or construction engineering program. The program must offer at least one hot mix asphalt course.
Target Student: College, Graduate and Adult students.
Amount: Varies
Number of Awards: Varies
Scholarship can be renewed.
Based on Financial Need: No
Deadline: Varies
Applications can be requested from the National Asphalt Pavement Association.

---

(740) NATA Scholarship

National Athletic Trainer's Association
National Athletic Trainer's Association
Research and Education Foundation
2952 Stemmons Freeway
Dallas, TX 75247

Phone: 214-637-6282
Fax: 214-637-2206
Email: barbaran@nata.org
URL: http://www.nata.org

Goal: To encourage the study of athletic training.
Eligibility: Applicants must be at least a junior in college. Scholarships are avialable for undergraduates as well as those purusing a masters degree and doctoral degree. Applicants must have a 3.2 GPA or higher and be sponsored by a certified athletic trainer in addition to being a member of the NATA.
Target Student: College, Graduate and Adult students.
Amount: $2,300
Number of Awards: 50-75
Based on Financial Need: No
Deadline: Varies
Applications are available online.

---

(741) Nation Institute/I.F. Stone Award for Student Journalism

Nation Institute
116 E. 16th Street
8th Floor
New York, NY 10003

Phone: 212-822-0250
Fax: 212-253-5356
URL: http://www.nationinstitute.org/blog/prizes/

Goal: To assist student journalists.
Eligibility: Applicants must be enrolled in a U.S. college or university and submit articles that were written outside of regular college coursework within the year prior to the application. Award selection is based on the article's demonstration of commitment to human rights, concern for the truth, investigative zeal, progressive politics and coverage of topics ignored by mainstream media.
Target Student: College and Adult students.
Amount: $1,000
Number of Awards: 1
Based on Financial Need: No
Deadline: Unknown
Application information is available online.

---

(742) National Aviation Explorer Scholarships

Explorers Learning for Life
P.O. Box 152079
Irving, TX 75015

Phone: 972-580-2433
Fax: 972-580-2137
Email: pchestnu@lflmail.org
URL: http://www.learningforlife.org/exploring

Goal: To assist students pursuing careers in aviation.

Eligibility: Applicants must be active members of an Aviation Explorer post.
Target Student: Junior high and younger, High school, College and Adult students.
Amount: $3,000 - $10,000
Number of Awards: Varies
Based on Financial Need: No
Deadline: March
Applications are available online.

---

(743) National College Match Program

QuestBridge
120 Hawthrone Avenue Suite 103
Palo Alto, CA 94301

Phone: 888-275-2054
Fax: 650-653-2516
Email: questions@questbridge.org
URL: http://www.questbridge.org

Goal: To help low income high school seniors with admission and full four year scholarships to top colleges.
Eligibility: Applicants must have demonstrated academic excellence and financial need. Students from all backgrounds and races are encouraged to apply.
Target Student: High school students.
Amount: Varies
Number of Awards: Varies
Scholarship can be renewable..
Based on Financial Need: Yes
Deadline: September
Applications are available online beginning in August. A completed application, two teacher recommendations, one counselor recommendation, a transcript and SAT and/or ACT score reports are required.

---

(745) National Dairy Shrine/Lager Dairy Scholarship

National Dairy Shrine
P.O. Box 1
Maribel, WI 54227

Phone: 920-863-6333
Fax: 920-863-8328
Email: info@dairyshrine.org
URL: http://www.dairyshrine.org

Goal: To assist students studying dairy and animal science who are planning on careers in the dairy industry.
Eligibility: Applicants must be beginning the second year of a two-year agricultural program in dairy or animal science and must have a 2.5 GPA or higher.
Target Student: College and Adult students.
Amount: $1,000
Number of Awards: 1
Based on Financial Need: No
Deadline: April
Applications are available online. A completed application, essay, transcript and two letters of recommendation are required to apply.

---

(744) National D-Day Museum Online Essay Contest

National D-Day Museum Foundation
945 Magazine Street
New Orleans, LA 70130

Phone: 504-527-6012
Fax: 504-527-6088
Email: info@nationalww2museum.org
URL: http://www.ddaymuseum.org

Goal: To increase knowledge of World War II by giving students the chance to compete in an essay contest.
Eligibility: Applicants must be high school students and write an essay of 1,000 or less on a topic selected by the sponsor. Only the first 500 essays will be accepted.
Target Student: High school students.
Amount: $250 - $1,000
Number of Awards: 6
Based on Financial Need: No
Deadline: March

Applications are available online.

(746) National Defense Transportation Association St. Louis Area Chapter Scholarship

National Defense Transportation
Association-Scott St. Louis Chapter
Attention: Scholarship Committee
P.O. Box 25486
Scott Air Force Base, IL 62225

URL: http://www.ndtascottstlouis.org

Goal: To promote careers in business, physical distribution and transportation logistics.
Eligibility: Award preference is given to those studying business, transportation logistics and physical distribution or a related field. High school students must live in Illinois or Missouri. College students must attend school in Colorado, Iowa, Illinois, Indiana, Kansas, Michigan, Minnesota, Missouri, Montana, North Dakota, Nebraska, South Dakota, Wisconsin and Wyoming.
Target Student: High school, College and Adult students.
Amount: $2,000 - $3,500
Number of Awards: 8
Based on Financial Need: No
Deadline: March
Applications are available online.

(748) National High School Poetry Contest/Easterday Poetry Award

Live Poets Society
P.O. Box 8841
Turnersville, NJ 08012

Email: lpsnj@comcast.net
URL:
http://www.highschoolpoetrycontest.com

Goal: To assist and recognize young poets.

Eligibility: Applicants must be U.S. high school students and must submit a poem that is 20 lines or less. The poem must be unpublished, in English and not submited to any other competition. Only one poem can be submitted in a 90 day period.
Target Student: High school students.
Amount: Up to $2,500
Number of Awards: Varies
Based on Financial Need: No
Deadline: March, June, September, December
To apply submit a self-addressed, stamped envelope with your poem or submit your poem online.

(749) National History Day Contest

National History Day
0119 Cecil Hall
University of Maryland
College Park, MD 20742

Phone: 301-314-9739
Fax: 301-314-9767
Email: info@nhd.org
URL: http://www.nationalhistoryday.org

Goal: To acknowledge students for their scholarship, initiative and cooperation.
Eligibility: Applicants must be in grades 6-12 and prepare history presentations throughout the year that are based on an annual theme. In February or March students compete in a district History Day contest. The winners then compete in a state contest usually in April or May. Those winners compete at the national level in June at the University of Maryland.
Target Student: Junior high and younger and High school students.
Amount: Varies
Number of Awards: Varies
Based on Financial Need: No
Deadline: Unknown
Applications are available online.

(750) National Italian American Foundation

National Italian American Foundation
1860 19th Street, NW
Washington, DC 20009

Phone: 202-387-0600
Fax: 202-387-0800
Email: scholarships@niaf.org
URL: http://www.niaf.org

Goal: To assist Italian American students as well as students of other backgrounds who are studying the Italian language or Italian studies.
Eligibility: Applicants must be Italian American studnets with an outstanding academic background or a student, from any ethnic background, who is majoring or minoring in Italian language or other Italian studies and have oustanding academic achievements. Applicants must be or plan to be enrolled in a college or university with a GPA of 3.5 or greater.
Target Student: High school, College and Adult students.
Amount: $2,000 - $12,000
Number of Awards: Varies
Based on Financial Need: No
Deadline: March
Applications are available online.

(751) National Junior Classical League Scholarships

National Junior Classical League
1122 Oak Street North
Fargo, ND 58102

Phone: 513-529-7741
Fax: 513-529-7742
Email: administration@njcl.org
URL: http://www.njcl.org

Goal: To assist students who are studying the classics.

Eligibility: Applicants must be NJCL members who are entering college in the upcoming year and plan to study the classics. The award is based on financial need, JCL service, academics and recommendtations with special consideration given to those who plan to teach classical humanities.
Target Student: High school students.
Amount: $1,200 - $2,500
Number of Awards: Varies
Based on Financial Need: Yes
Deadline: May
Applications are available online.

(747) National Junior Girls Scholarship

Ladies Auxiliary VFW
406 West 34th Street
10th Floor
Kansas City, MO 64111

Phone: 816-561-8655 x19
Fax: 816-931-4753
Email: jmillick@ladiesauxvfw.org
URL: http://www.ladiesauxvfw.org

Goal: To assist Junior Girls how are activily incolved in Junior Girls and have demonstrated leadership and academic excellence.
Eligibility: Applicants must be Junior Girls between the ages of 13 and 16 and active members of a Ladies Auxiliary VFW Junior Girls Unit for a minimum of one year and have held office.
Target Student: Junior high or younger, High school students.
Amount: $7,500
Number of Awards: 1
Based on Financial Need: No
Deadline: March
Applications are available online.

(752) National Latin Exam Scholarship

National Latin Exam

University of Mary Washington
1301 College Avenue
Fredericksburg, VA 22401

Phone: 888-378-7721
Email: nle@umw.edu
URL: http://ww.nle.org

Goal: To assist students with Latin proficiency.
Eligibility: Applicants must win the gold medal in Latin 3-4 Prose, 3-4 Poetry, or Latin 5-6 on the National Latin Exam. Applicants must take one latin or classical Greek course in each semester of their first year of college.
Target Student: High school students.
Amount: $1,000
Number of Awards: 21
Scholarship can be renewed.
Based on Financial Need: No
Deadline: September
Applications are automatically mailed to students who qualify.

---

(753) National Marbles Tournament Scholarship

National Marbles Tournament

URL:http://www.nationalmarblestournament.org

Goal: To assist marble shooters "mibsters."
Eligibility: Applicants must win first place in a local marble tournament and compete in a National Marbles Tournament. Applicants must be between 7 and 15 years old.
Target Student: Junior high or younger, High school students.
Amount: Varies
Number of Awards: Varies
Based on Financial Need: No
Deadline: Varies
Information on tournaments is available online.

---

(754) National Merit Scholarship Program and National Achievement Scholarship Program

National Merit Scholarship Corporation
1560 Sherman Avenue Suite 200
Evanston, IL 60201

Phone: 847-866-5100
Fax: 847-866-5113
URL: http://www.nationalmerit.org

Goal: To assist student with educational expenses through a merit based competition.
Eligibility: Applicants must be in high school and on the typical track towards completion and planning to enter college by the fall following graduation from high school. Applicants must be U.S. citizens, legal residents or in the process of becoming a U.S. citizen. Participation in the scholarship is based on the PSAT/NMSQT exam which must be taken by the 11th grade.
Target Student: High school students.
Amount: $2,500
Number of Awards: Varies
Scholarship can be renewed.
Based on Financial Need: No
Deadline: October, PSAT test date.
Application is made by taking the PSAT.

---

(755) National Oratorical Contest

American Legion
Attn: Americanism and Children and Youth Division
P.O. Box 1055
Indianapolis, IN 46206

Phone: 317-630-1249
Fax: 317-630-1369
Email: acy@legion.org
URL: http://www.legion.org

Goal: To acknowledge students for their knowledge of government and oral presentation skills.
Eligibility: Applicants must be high school students who are U.S. citizens or legal residents under age 20. Students give an oral presentation at the state level and winners compete at the national level. The topic of the presentation must be related to the Constitution and the duties and obligations citizens have to the goverment. The presentation must be between 8 and 10 minutes. The website also has an assigned topic that needs to be between 3 and 5 minutes.
Target Student: High school students.
Amount: $18,000
Number of Awards: Varies
Based on Financial Need: No
Deadline: Local American Legion departments must choose a winner by March 12.
Applications can be obtained from your local American Legion or from the state headquarters. Local competition deadlines are set by the local Posts.

(756) National Peace Contest

United States Institute of Peace
1200 17th Street, NW
Suite 200
Washington, DC 20036

Phone: 202-457-1700
URL: http://www.usip.org

Goal: To encourage high school students to explore peacebuilding.
Eligibility: Applicants must be in 9th to 12th grade and homeschooled or U.S. students in high school overseas. Applicants must be sponsored by a school club, community group o religious organization.
Target Student: High school students
Amount: $1,000 - $10,000
Number of Awards: 56

Based on Financial Need: No
Deadline: February
Applications are available online.

(757) National President's Scholarship

American Legion Auxiliary
8945 N. Meridian Street
Indianapolis, IN 46260

Phone: 317-569-4500
Fax: 317-569-4502
Email: alahq@legion-aux.org
URL: http://www.legion-aux.org

Goal: To assist the children of veterans who served the Armed Forces.
Eligibility: Applicants must be the children of veterans who served in the Armed Forces and members of The American Legion, high school seniors and 50 hours of community service.
Target Student: High school students.
Amount: $1,500 to $2,500
Number of Awards: 15
Based on Financial Need: Yes
Deadline: March
Applications can be obtained online. A completed application, four letters of recommendation, essays, proof of volunteering, transcripts, ACT/SAT scores and parents military service description are needed to apply.

(758) National Scholarship Program

American Board of Funeral Service Education
Scholarship Committee
3414 Ashland Avenue
Suite G
St. Joseph, MO 64506

Phone: 816-233-3747
URL: http://www.abfse.org

Goal: To assist students in funeral service and mortuary science programs with their educational expenses.

Eligibility: Applicants must be U.S. citizens, undergraduate students at an accredited school who have completed least one quarter or semester of a funeral service or mortuary science education program and have at least one term remaining in the program.

Target Student: College and Adult students.

Amount: $500 - $2,500

Number of Awards: Varies

Based on Financial Need: No

Deadline: March and September

Applications are available online.

---

(759) National Scholarship Program

National Scholastic Surfing Association
P.O. Box 495
Huntington Beach, CA 92648

Phone: 714-378-0899
Fax: 714-964-5232
Email: jaragon@nssa.org
URL: http://www.nssa.org

Goal: To assist NSSA members with their educational expenses.

Eligibility: Applicants must be competitive student NSSA members with a current year GPA of 3.0 or above. The award is based on leadership, academic achievement, service, career goals and recommendations.

Target Student: High school, College and Adult students.

Amount: Varies

Number of Awards: Varies

Based on Financial Need: No

Deadline: Varies

Applications are available with organization membership.

---

(760) National Sculpture Society Scholarship

National Sculpture Society
237 Park Avenue
Ground Floor
New York, NY 10017

Phone: 212-764-5645
Email: nss1893@aol.com
URL: http://www.nationalsculpture.org

Goal: To assist students of figurative or representational sculpture.

Eligibility: Applicants must provide a sculpture that represents their background. Appplicants must also submit a biography, two letters of recommendation and photos fo their work. Students must have financial need.

Target Student: College and Adult students

Amount: $2,000

Number of Awards: 4

Based on Financial Need: Yes

Deadline: June

Application information is available online.

---

(761) National Security Education Program David L. Boren Undergraduate Scholarships

Institute of International Education
1400 K Street NW
Washington, DC 20005

Phone: 202-326-7672
Fax: 202-326-7835
Email: boren@iie.org
URL: http://www.iie.org

Goal: To assist undergraduate students so they may study abroad in places that are vital to U.S. security interests.

Eligibility: Applicants must be undergraduate students in the U.S. who have an interest in working for the U.S. federal government after they graduate. Applicants must show how their study abroad would contribute to U.S. national security interests and preference is given to those willing to spend a full academic year abroad.
Target Student: College and Adult students.
Amount: Up to $20,000
Number of Awards: Varies
Based on Financial Need: No
Deadline: February
Applications are available online.

(762) National Society of Hispanic MBAs Scholarship

National Society of Hispanic MBAs
1303 Walnut Hill Lane
Suite 100
Irving, TX 75038

Phone: 877-467-4622
Fax: 214-596-9325
Email: scholarships@nshmba.org
URL: http://www.nshmba.org

Goal: To assist Hispanic students pursuing an MBA.
Eligibility: Applicants must be U.S. citizens or legal permanent residents of Hispanic heritage (must have at least one parent of full Hispanic heritage or both parents with half-Hispanic heritage.) Applicants must be member of the NSHMBA (applicants can become a member when they apply), and be enrolled or planning to enroll into master's of business or management programs. The award is based on financial need, community service, recommendations, work experience, academics, and a personal statement.
Target Student: College, Graduate and Adult students.

Amount: $2,500 - $10,000
Number of Awards: Varies
Based on Financial Need: Yes
Deadline: May
Applications are available online.

(763) National Ten Minute Play Contest

Actors Theatre of Louisville
National Ten Minute Play Contest
316 W. Main Street
Louisville, KY 40202

Phone: 502-584-1265
=
URL: http://www.actorstheatre.org

Goal: To assist emerging playwrights.
Eligibility: Applicants must submit one script that is not more than 10 pages in length.
Target Student: Junior high and younger, High school, College, Graduate and Adult students.
Amount: $1,000
Number of Awards: Varies
Based on Financial Need: No
Deadline: November
To apply simply submit the 10 page script.

(764) National Tour Association (NTA) Dr. Tom Anderson Graduate Scholarship

Tourism Cares
275 Turnpike Street
Suite 307
Canton, MA 02021

Phone: 781-821-5990
Fax: 781-821-8949
Email: scholarships@tourismcares.org
URL: http://www.tourismcares.org

Goal: To assist those studying travel, hospitality or tourism at the graduate level.

Eligibility: Applicants must be permanent residents of the U.S. or Canada and be entering or returning graduate students enrolled at an accredited U.S. or Canadian four-year school. Applicants must be studying hospitality, tourism or travel with a GPA of 3.0 or higher.
Target Student: College, Graduate and Adult students.
Amount: $1,000
Number of Awards: 1
Based on Financial Need: No
Deadline: April
Applications are available online. A completed application, resume, two letters of recommendation, essay, official transcripts and proof of residency are required to apply.

(765) National Tour Association (NTA) Eric Friedheim Graduate Scholarship

Tourism Cares
275 Turnpike Street
Suite 307
Canton, MA 02021

Phone: 781-821-5990
Fax: 781-821-8949
Email: scholarships@tourismcares.org
URL: http://www.tourismcares.org

Goal: To assist graduate students studying hospitality, travel and tourism.
Eligibility: Applicants must be U.S. permanent residents, entering or returning full time graduate students at an accredited four-year school. Applicants must be studying hospitality, travel, or tourism with a GPA of 3.0 or higher.
Target Student: Graduate and Adult students.
Amount: $1,000
Number of Awards: 1
Based on Financial Need: No
Deadline: April

Applications are available online. A completed application, two letters of recommendation, proof of residency, resume, essay and offical transcripts are required to apply.

(766) National Tour Association (NTA) Luray Caverns Graduate Research Scholarship

Tourism Cares
275 Turnpike Street
Suite 307
Canton, MA 02021

Phone: 781-821-5990
Fax: 781-821-8949
Email: scholarships@tourismcares.org
URL: http://www.tourismcares.org

Goal: To assist graduate students who are doing tourism related research.
Eligibility: Applicants can be residents of any country, however they must be enrolled at an accredited U.S. or Canadian four year school. Applicants must be entering or returning graduate students conducting research that focuses on tourism and have a proven commitment to the tourism industry with a GPA of 3.0 or higher.
Target Student: College, Graduate and Adult students.
Amount: $3,000
Number of Awards: 1
Based on Financial Need: No
Deadline: April
Applications are available online. A completed application, essay, resume, research proposal, proof of residency, transcript and letter of recommendation are required to apply.

(767) National Tour Association (NTA) New Horizons-Kathy LeTarte Undergraduate Scholarship

Tourism Cares
275 Turnpike Street
Suite 307
Canton, MA 02021

Phone: 781-821-5990
Fax: 781-821-8949
Email: scholarships@tourismcares.org
URL: http://www.tourismcares.org

Goal: To assist Michigan residents who are studying travel, tourism and hospitality at the undergraduate level.
Eligibility: Applicants must be permanent residents of Michigan and enrolled in an accredited U.S. or Canadian four-year school. Applicants must be undergraduate juniors or seniors studying travel, hospitality, and tourism with 60 or more credits completed by May of the year of application and a GPA of 3.0 or higher.
Target Student: College and Adult students.
Amount: $1,000
Number of Awards: 1
Based on Financial Need: No
Deadline: April
Applications are available online. A completed application, essay, transcript, resume, two letters of recommendation and proof of Michigan residency are required to apply.

---

(768) National Tour Association (NTA) Reno Campbell-Ruth McKinney Undergraduate Scholarship

Tourism Cares
275 Turnpike Street
Suite 307
Canton, MA 02021

Phone: 781-821-5990
Fax: 781-821-8949
Email: scholarships@tourismcares.org
URL: http://www.tourismcares.org

Goal: To assist North Carolina residents pursuing undergraduate degrees in tourism, travel or hospitality.
Eligibility: Applicants must be permanent residents of North Carolina and be full time undergraduate juniors or seniors at an accredited four-year school in the U.S. or Canada. Applicants must be studying hospitality, tourism or travel, have completed 60 credits or more by May of the application year and have a GPA of 3.0 or higher.
Target Student: College and Adult students.
Amount: $1,000
Number of Awards: 1
Based on Financial Need: No
Deadline: April
Applications are available online. A completed application, proof of residentcy, essay, resume, two lettes of recommendation and transcripts are required to apply.

---

(769) National Tour Association (NTA) Travel Leaders Graduate Scholarship

Tourism Cares
275 Turnpike Street
Suite 307
Canton, MA 02021

Phone: 781-821-5990
Fax: 781-821-8949
Email: scholarships@tourismcares.org
URL: http://www.tourismcares.org

Goal: To assist graduate students studying hospitality, tourism and travel.
Eligibility: Applicants can be residents of any country, but they must be entering or returning graduate students at an accredited U.S. or Canadian four-year school. Applicants must have a 3.0 or higher GPA and be studying hospitality, tourism or travel full time.
Target Student: College, Graduate and Adult students.

Amount: $1,000
Number of Awards: 3
Based on Financial Need: No
Deadline: April
Applications are available online. A completed application, essay, two letters of recommendation, transcripts, resume and proof of residency are required to apply.

(770) National Tour Association (NTA) Yellow Ribbon Undergraduate or Graduate Scholarship

Tourism Cares
275 Turnpike Street
Suite 307
Canton, MA 02021

Phone: 781-821-5990
Fax: 781-821-8949
Email: scholarships@tourismcares.org
URL: http://www.tourismcares.org

Goal: To assist hospitality, travel and tourism students with sensory and physical disabilities.
Eligibility: Applicants must be permanent residents of the U.S. or Canada, entering or returning undergraduate or graduate students enrolled at an accredited U.S. or Canadian school, have a sensory or physical disability, have a GPA of 2.5 or higher and be studying tourism, travel or hospitality full time.
Target Student: High school, College, Graduate and Adult students.
Amount: $5,000
Number of Awards: 1
Based on Financial Need: No
Deadline: April
Applications are available online. A completed application, resume, two letters of recommendation, transcript, essay, proof of residency and proof of disability are required to apply.

(771) National Washington Crossing Foundation Scholarship

Washington Crossing Foundation
P.O. Box 503
Levittown, PA 19058

Phone: 2150949-8841
Fax: 215-949-8843
Email: info@gwcf.org
URL: http://www.gwcf.org

Goal: To assist students planning careers in government service.
Eligibility: Applicants must be seniors in high school and submit an essay and letter of recommendation.
Target Student: High school seniors.
Amount: $500-$5,000
Number of Awards: Varies
Scholarship can be renewed.
Based on Financial Need: No
Deadline: January
Applications are available online.

(772) Naval Enlisted Reserve Association Scholarships

Naval Enlisted Reserve Association
6703 Farragut Avenue
Falls Church, VA 22042

Phone: 800-776-9020
Email: secretary@nera.org
URL: http://www.nera.org

Goal: To award the service and sacrifices made by Navy, Marine and Coast Guard members, retirees and their families.
Eligibility: Applicants must be members, in good standing, of the Navel Enlisted Reserve Association, or their spouses, children or grandchildren. Children and grandchildren must be under 23 and single on the application deadline. Applicants must be high school seniors or already working towards an undergraduate degree.

Target Student: High school, College and Adult students.
Amount: $2,500 to $3,000
Number of Awards: 6
Based on Financial Need: No
Deadline: June
Applications are available online.

(773) Naval Helicopter Association Scholarship

Naval Helicopter Association
P.O. Box 180578
Coronado, CA 82178

Phone: 619-435-7139
Fax: 619-435-7354
Email: nhascholars@hotmail.com
URL:http://www.nhascholarshipfund.org

Goal: To assit students who want to continue their education.
Eligibility: Applicants must be members or their dependents of the association or have an affiliation with naval aviation.
Target Student: High school, College and Adult students.
Amount: $2,000 to $3,000
Number of Awards: 9
Based on Financial Need: No
Deadline: January
Applications are available by mail.

(774) Navin Narayan Scholarship

American Red Cross Youth
2025 E. Street NW
Washington, DC 20006

Phone: 202-303-4498
URL: http://www.redcrossyouth.org

Goal: Named after Navin Narayan, a Red Cross volunteer who died at 23. The award is to recognize humanitarian contributions to the organization and achieved academic excellence.

Eligibility: Applicants must have volunteered a minimum of two years and must plan to attend a four-year college.
Target Student: High school students.
Amount: $2,500
Number of Awards: 1
Based on Financial Need: No
Deadline: February
Applications are available online.

(775) Navy College Fund

U.S. Navy Personnel
5720 Integrity Drive
Millington, TN 38055

Phone: 866-827-5672
Email: bupers_webmaster@navy.mil
URL: http://www.npc.navy.mil/channels

Goal: To encourage entry into critical specialities for the U.S. Navy.
Eligibility: Applicants must be non-prior service Navy recruits who must agree to serve three years on active duty. Applicants must have graduated from high school, between the ages of 17 and 30 and receive an "Honorable" character of service.
Target Student: High school, College and Adult students.
Amount: Varies
Number of Awards: Varies
Based on Financial Need: No
Deadline: Varies
Applications are available from Navy recruiters.

(776) Navy League Endowed Scholarship

Navy League Foundation
2300 Wilson Boulevard
Arlington, VA 22201

Phone: 800-356-5760
Fax: 703-528-2333
Email: lhuycke@navyleague.org

URL: http://www.navyleague.org

Goal: To assist military dependents with educational expenses.
Eligibility: Applicants must be dependents or direct descendants of active, reserve, retired, or honorably discharged members of the U.S. Navy, Coast Guard, U.S. Flag Merchant Marine, Marine Corps, or U.S. Naval Sea Cadet Corps. Applicants must also be high school seniors or equivalent and be entering an accredited college or university.
Target Student: High school, College and Adult students.
Amount: $2,500
Number of Awards: 4
Scholarship can be renewed.
Based on Financial Need: No
Deadline: March
Applications are availalbe online. A completed application, no more than two letters of recommendation, transcripts, FASFA information, SAT or ACT scores, list of academic and extracurriculiar activities and proof of qualifying sea service to apply.

---

(777) Navy Supply Corps Foundation Scholarship

Navy Supply Corps Foundation Inc.
1425 Prince Avenue
Athens, GA 30606

Phone: 706-354-4111
Fax: 706-354-0334
Email: evans@usnscf.com
URL: http://www.usnscf.com

Goal: To assist family members of Supply Corp members and enlisted Navy personnel with undergraduate educational expenses.
Eligibility: Applicants must be family members of Navy Supply Corps members (officer, enlisted, reserve, active duty and retired).

Target Student: College and Adult students.
Amount: $2,500 to $10,000
Number of Awards: 74
Based on Financial Need: Yes
Deadline: March
Applications are available online.

---

(778) Navy-Marine Corps ROTC College Program

U.S. Navy Reserve Officers Training Corps (NROTC)
Naval Service Training Comman Officer Development
NAS Pensacola
250 Dallas Street Suite A
Pensacola, FL 32508

Phone: 800-628-7682
Fax: 850-452-2486
Email: pnsc_nrotc.scholarship@navy.mil
URL: http://www.navy.com/navy/joining/education-opportunities/nrotc/

Goal: To assist NROTC students with educational expenses.
Eligibility: Applicants must be accepted or attending college with a NROTC program. Applicants must complete a summer training session and complete specified college courses throughout the year including naval science.
Target Student: College and Adult students.
Amount: Up to full tuition plus stipend and allowance.
Number of Awards: Varies
Scholarship can be renewed.
Based on Financial Need: No
Deadline: January
Applications are available online.

---

(779) Navy-Marine Corps ROTC Four-Year Scholarships

U.S. Navy Reserve Officers Training
Corps (NROTC)
Naval Service Training Comman Officer
Development
NAS Pensacola
250 Dallas Street Suite A
Pensacola, FL 32508

Phone: 800-628-7682
Fax: 850-452-2486
Email: pnsc_nrotc.scholarship@navy.mil
URL: http://www.navy.com/navy/joining/education-opportunities/nrotc/

Goal: To assist Navy ROTC students.
Eligibility: Applicants must plan to attend an eligible college or university program. Applicants must commit to eight years of military service with four of those as active duty.
Target Student: High school students.
Amount: Full tuition plus a stipend.
Number of Awards: Varies
Scholarship can be renewed.
Based on Financial Need: No
Deadline: January
Applications are available online.

(780) Navy-Marine Corps ROTC Two-Year Scholarships

U.S. Navy Reserve Officers Training
Corps (NROTC)
Naval Service Training Comman Officer
Development
NAS Pensacola
250 Dallas Street Suite A
Pensacola, FL 32508

Phone: 800-628-7682
Fax: 850-452-2486
Email: pnsc_nrotc.scholarship@navy.mil
URL: http://www.navy.com/navy/joining/education-opportunities/nrotc/

Goal: To assist NROTC students with educational expenses.

Eligibility: Applicants must be attending a college or university with an NROTC program and be in their freshman or sophomore year. They need to attend a summer session as well as completed specific courses in addition to Naval Science courses.
Target Student: College and Adult students.
Amount: Varies
Number of Awards: Varies
Scholarship can be renewed.
Based on Financial Need: No
Deadline: Varies
Applications are available online.

(781) Navy-Marine Corps/Coast Guard (NMCCG) Enlisted Dependent Spouse Scholarship

Navy Wives Clubs of America
P.O. Box 54022
NSA Mid-South
Millington, TN 38053

Phone: 866-511-6922
Email: scholarships@navywivesclubsofamerica.org
URL: http://www.navywivesclubsofamerica.org

Goal: To assist the spouses of specific military members with their educational expenses.
Eligibility: Applicants must be the spouse of enlisted Navy, Marine Corps or Coast Guard personnel. They must be accepted into college by May 30 in the year they apply.
Target Student: High school, College and Adult students.
Amount: Varies
Number of Awards: Varies
Based on Financial Need: No
Deadline: May
Applications are available online. To apply financial information and a transcript are required.

(782) NCAA Division I Degree Completion Award Program

National Collegiate Athletic Association
700 W. Washington Street
P.O. Box 6222
Indianapolis, IN 46206

Phone: 317-917-6222
Fax: 317-917-6888
Email: ahightower@ncaa.org
URL:http://www.ncaa.org/wps/wcm/connect/public/ncaa/academics/resources/scholarships+and+internships/di+degree+completion+awards

Goal: To assist athletes who have used all of their student aid.
Eligibility: Applicants must be student atheltes who have completed eligibility at an NCAA Division 1 school and received athletics-related aid. They must be within 30 semester units or 45 quarter units of completing their degrees and be entering their sixth year of college.
Target Student: College and Adult students.
Amount: Full tuition and fees
Number of Awards: Varies
Based on Financial Need: Yes
Deadline: May
Applications are available online. A completed application, tax forms transcripts, list of extracurricular activities, statement from the director of athletics and personal statement is requried to apply.

(783) NCAA Division II Degree Completion Award Program

National Collegiate Athletic Association
700 W. Washington Street
P.O. Box 6222
Indianapolis, IN 46206

Phone: 317-917-6222
Fax: 317-917-6888
Email: ahightower@ncaa.org
URL:http://www.ncaa.org/wps/wcm/connect/public/ncaa/academics/resources/scholarships+and+internships/dii+degree-completion+award

Goal: To assist athletes who have used all of their student aid.
Eligibility: Applicant shall be a student-athlete who has exhausted athletics eligibility at an active NCAA Division II institution within the past academic year. Awards are limited to student-athletes during their first 10 semesters or 15 quarters of full-time collegiate attendance. Applicant shall not be participating in another intercollegiate sport during the period of the award. Applicant must have received athletics-related financial aid from the NCAA Division II member institution. Applicant must be within 32 semester or 48 quarters hours of completion of his or her first undergraduate degree at the completion of the spring term. Applicant must have a 2.50 cumulative grade-point average.
Target Student: College and Adult students.
Amount: Up to $6,000
Number of Awards: Varies
Based on Financial Need: Yes
Deadline: April
Applications are available online. A completed application, personal statement, financial aid information, transcripts and endorsement from the director of athletics or coach are required.

(784) NCAA Postgraduate Scholarship

National Collegiate Athletic Association
700 W. Washington Street
P.O. Box 6222
Indianapolis, IN 46206

Phone: 317-917-6222

Fax: 317-917-6888
Email: ahightower@ncaa.org
URL: http://www.ncaa.org/

Goal: To assist student-athletes with high performance in both academics and sports.
Eligibility: Applicants must be in their final season of NCAA athletics eligibility or will not be using any remaining athletics eligibility and have an overall undergraduate minimum cumulative grade point average of 3.2 (based on 4.0 scale) or its equivalent. Have performed with distinction as members of the varsity team in the sport in which the student-athlete is being nominated. The degree of the student-athlete's athletics achievement will be weighed in conjunction with academic performance, university involvement and volunteer community service. Institutions should note participation in activities in which the student-athlete serves as an example to other students and demonstrates leadership qualities. Intend to continue academic work beyond the baccalaureate degree and enroll in a graduate degree program on a part- or full-time basis at an academically accredited graduate or degree-granting professional school. An academic professor of the college in which the student-athlete is currently enrolled must address the capability of the student-athlete for graduate study.
Target Student: College and Adult students.
Amount: $7,500
Number of Awards: 174
Based on Financial Need: No
Deadline: January, March, and May
Applications are available online.

(785) NCCPAP Scholarship

National Conference of CPA Practitioners
NCCPAP Scholarship
Attention: Scholarship Committee
22 Jericho Turnpike

Suite 110
Mineola, NY 11501

Phone: 888-488-5400
Email: lanak.nccpap@verizon.net
URL: http://www.nccpap.org

Goal: To assist future certified public accountants.
Eligibility: Applicants must be graduating high school seniors who are planning to become certified public accountants with a GPA of 3.3 or higher. Applicants must be applying to or accepted at a two or four year college as full time students.
Target Student: High school students.
Amount: $1,000
Number of Awards: Varies
Based on Financial Need: No
Deadline: December
Applications are available online.

(786) NCDXF Scholarship

American Radio Relay League Foundation
225 Main Street
Newington, CT 06111

Phone: 860-594-0397
Fax: 860-594-0259
Email: foundation@arrl.org
URL: http://www.arrlf.org

Goal: To assist amateur radio operators with interest in Dxing with educational expenses.
Eligibility: Applicants must have a Technicians Class Amateur Radio License or higher and who activity and interest in Dxing. Applicants must attend a junior college, trade school or four-year school in the U.S.
Target Student: High school, College and Adult students.
Amount: $1,500
Number of Awards: 2
Based on Financial Need: No
Deadline: February

Applciations are available online.

---

(787) NCGE and Nystrom Geography Award

National Council for Geographic Education
Jacksonville State University
206-A Martin Hall
700 Pelham Road North
Jacksonville, AL 36265

Phone: 256-782-5293
Fax: 256-782-5336
Email: ncge@jsu.edu
URL: http://www.ncge.org

Goal: To acknowledge K-12 teachers for excellent annual meeting presentations.
Eligibility: Applications must be K-12 teachers (or group of teachers) who submit a description of a classroom presentation they have created. The presentation must show current trends in geographic education and display an original teaching approach. Format for the lesson can be lessons, simulations, workshops, or other learning activites. Winners of the award are required to present their lesson at the NCGE meeting. To apply applicants must submit a Call for Proposal, NCGE application, abstract, three lettes of recommendation, lesson plan, proof of use of the lesson in the class, presenter registration form and registration.
Target Student: Graduate and Adult students.
Amount: $1,500
Number of Awards: Varies
Based on Financial Need: No
Deadline: April
Applications are available online.

---

(788) Nell Bryant Robinson Scholarship

Phi Upsilon Omicron Inc.

National Office
P.O. Box 329
Fairmont, WV 26555

Phone: 304-368-0612
Email: info@phiu.org
URL: http://www.phiu.org

Goal: To assist Phi Upsilon Omicron Members who are working towards a bachelor's degree in family and consumer sciences.
Eligibility: Preference for the award is given to applicants majoring in food and nutirtion or dietetics.
Target Student: College and Adult students.
Amount: $500 - $4,000
Number of Awards: Varies
Based on Financial Need: No
Deadline: February
Applications are available online. A completed application, transcript, personal statement, and three letters of recommendation.

---

(789) Nettie Dracup Memorial Scholarship

American Congress on Surveying and Mapping
6 Montgomery Village Avenue
Suite 403
Gaithersburg, MD 20879

Phone: 240-632-9716
Fax: 240-632-1321
Email: ilse.genovese@acsm.net
URL: http://www.acsm.net

Goal: To assist geodetic surveying students.
Eligibility: Applicants must be U.S. citizens, undergraduates and studying geodetic surveying at an accredited college. Applicants must be members of the American Congress on Surveying and Mapping.

Target Student: College and Adult students.
Amount: $2,000
Number of Awards: Varies
Based on Financial Need: No
Deadline: February
Applications are available online. A completed application, transcript, personal statement, proof of ACSM membership and three letters of recommendation are required to apply.

(790) New England FEMARA Scholarships

American Radio Relay League Foundation
225 Main Street
Newington, CT 06111

Phone: 860-594-0397
Fax: 860-594-0259
Email: foundation@arrl.org
URL: http://www.arrlf.org

Goal: To assist ham radio operators with educational expenses.
Eligibility: Applicants must have a technician ham radio license or higher and be residents of the New England States (Connecticut, Maine, Massachusetts, New Hampshire, Rhode Island or Vermont).
Target Student: High school, College, Graduate and Adult students.
Amount: $1,000
Number of Awards: Varies
Based on Financial Need: No
Deadline: February
Applications are available online.

(791) NFMC Claire Ulrich Whitehurst Piano Award

National Federation of Music Clubs Claire Ulrich Whitehurst Piano Award
Claire-Frances Whitehurst
3360 SW 18th Street
Miami, FL 33145

Phone: 305-445-2128
Fax: 317-638-0503
Email: info@nfmc-music.org
URL: http://www.nfmc-music.org

Goal: To assist young piano players.
Eligibility: Applicants must be high school sophomores, juniors or seniors who are under 18 years old and members of the National Federation of Music Clubs. Applicants must submit a tape of a piano solo performance. A $10 application fee is required. It is not recommended to apply to scholarships that require a fee.
Target Student: High school students.
Amount: $500
Number of Awards: 1
Based on Financial Need: No
Deadline: January in even numbered years
Applications are available online.

(792) NFMC Gretchen Van Roy Music Education

National Federation of Music Clubs
Rose M. Suggs
100 Applewood Drive
Apt. 188
Roswell, GA 30076

Phone: 678-997-8556
Fax: 317-638-0503
Email: rose331s@bellsouth.org
URL: http://www.nfmc-music.org

Goal: To assist students majoring in music education with their educational expenses.
Eligibility: Applicants must be college juniors who are majoring in music education and are affiliated with the National Federation of Music Clubs.
Target Student: College and Adult students.
Amount: $1,000
Number of Awards: 1
Based on Financial Need: No
Deadline: April

Applications are available online.

---

(793) NFMC Lynn Freeman Olson Competition Awards

National Federation of Music Clubs Olson Awards
James Schnars
6550 Shoreline Drive
Suite 7505
St. Petersburg, FL 33708

Phone: 317-638-4003
Fax: 317-638-0503
Email: info@nfmc-music.org
URL: http://www.nfmc-music.org

Goal: To assist student composers.
Eligibility: Applicants must be in grade 7 to age 25 and be members of the National Federation of Music Clubs.. There are three categories and one award is given to each. The categories are grade 7 to 9, grade 10 to 12, and high school graduates to age 25. The award is given on odd years and applicants must submit a piano composition for judging.
Target Student: Junior high or younger, High school and College students.
Amount: $1,000 - $1,500
Number of Awards: 3
Based on Financial Need: No
Deadline: March in odd numbered years
Applications are available online.

---

(794) NFMC Wendell Irish Viola Award

National Federation of Music Clubs
Dr. George Keck
421 Cherry Street
Akadelphia, AR 71923

Phone: 317-638-4003
Fax: 317-638-0503
Email: keckg@obu.edu
URL: http://www.nfmc-music.org

Goal: To acknowledge students with music talented.
Eligibility: Applicants must be between 12 and 18 years old and be Individual Junior Special members or Active Junior Club members of the National Federation of Music Club. A taped performance is required to apply.
Target Student: Junior high or younger and High school students.
Amount: $600
Number of Awards: 5
Based on Financial Need: No
Deadline: February
Applications are available online.

---

(795) Nido Qubein Scholarship

National Speakers Association
1500 S. Priest Drive
Attn: Scholarship Committee
Tempe, AZ 85281

Phone: 480-968-2552
Fax: 480-968-0911
URL: http://www.nsaspeaker.org

Goal: To encourage students to study professional speaking.
Eligibility: Applicants must be full-time students who are majoring or minoring in speech.
Target Student: College, Graduate and Adult students.
Amount: $5,000
Number of Awards: 4
Based on Financial Need: No
Deadline: June
Applications are available online or by written request.

---

(796) NLUS Stockholm Scholarship Fund

Naval Sea Cadet Corps
2300 Wilson Boulevard

Arlington, VA 22201

Phone: 800-356-5760
Email: alewis@scacadets.org
URL: http://www.seacadets.org

Goal: To assist selected cadets with educational expenses.
Eligibility: Applicants must be Sea Cadets for at least two years and be a member at the time of application. Applicants must be NSCC E-3 or higher and be recommended by their commanding officer, NSCC Committee Chairman and a high school principal or counselor. A 3.3 GPA or higher is required.
Target Student: High school students.
Amount: Varies
Number of Awards: Varies
Scholarship can be renewed.
Based on Financial Need: No
Deadline: May
Applications are available online. An application and proof of acceptance from a college or university is required.

(797) North American Rolex Scholarship

Our World-Underwater Scholarship Society
P.O. Box 4428
Chicago, IL 60680

Phone: 630-969-6690
Email: info@owuscholarship.org
URL: http://www.owuscholarship.org

Goal: To assist students who are certified rescue divers.

Eligibility: Applicants must be hold certification as a Rescue Diver or equivalent with a minimum of 25 dives logged in the past two years, has not yet earned a graduate degree by April 1st of the scholarship year and has not yet chosen a clearly defined career path, high academic standing, Submission of a completed diving medical examination form which is found in the application and between the ages of 21 and 26.
Target Student: College and Adult students.
Amount: $25,000
Number of Awards: 3
Based on Financial Need: No
Deadline: December
Applications are available online.

(798) Northwest Perspectives Essay Contest

Oregon Quarterly Magazine
204 Alder Building
5528 University of Oregon
Eugene, OR 97403

Phone: 541-346-5047
Email: quarterly@uoregon.edu
URL: http://www.oregonquarterly.com

Goal: To assist those with the best essay related to the Northwest region.
Eligibility: Applicants must be current undergraduate or graduate students or nonfiction writers who've never won first place in this contest, never had a featured article in Oregon Quarterly in the past year, are not employees of Oregon Quarterly or the University of Oregon and are not family members of employees.
Target Student: College, Graduate and Adult students.
Amount: Up to $750
Number of Awards: 6
Based on Financial Need: No
Deadline: January
Applications are available online.

(799) NPPF Television News Scholarship

National Press Photographers Foundation
Television News
Scholarship
Ed Dooks
5 Mohawk Dr.
Lexington, MA 02421

Phone: 781-861-6062
Email: dooks@verizon.net
URL: http://www.nppa.org

Goal: To assist students with potential in television news photojournalism, but with little opportunity and great need.
Eligibility: Applicants must be full time juniors or seniors at a four year school, submit a portfolio and show financial need. Applicants must be working towards a bachelor's degree in TV news photojournalism with courses taken in that subject. Applicants can apply to as many NPPA scholarships as they'd like, but they can only recieve one.
Target Student: College and Adult students.
Amount: $1,000
Number of Awards: 1
Based on Financial Need: No
Deadline: March
Applications are available online.

(800) NRA Outstanding Achievement Youth Award

National Rifle Association
11250 Waples Mill Road
Fairfax, VA 22030

Phone: 703-267-1505
Email: youth_programs@nrahq.org
URL: http://www.nrahq.org

Goal: To acknowledge NRA Junior Members who are active particpants in shooting sports.
Eligibility: Applicants must be NRA Junior Members (or Regular or Life Members that are under 18 years old) who have completed five core and five elective requirements. Core requirements include being current members of the NRA, attending and completing an NRA Basic Firearms Training, earning a rating in a shooting discipline, and submitting an essay.
Target Student: High school students.
Amount: $2,000 to $5,000
Number of Awards: 3
Based on Financial Need: No
Deadline: May
Applications are available online.

(801) NROTC Nurse Corps Scholarship

U.S. Naval Reserve Officers Training Corps
Naval Service Training Comman Officer Development
NAS Pensacola
250 Dallas Street Suite A
Pensacola, FL 32508

Phone: 800-628-7682
Fax: 850-452-2486
Email: pnsc_nrotc.scholarship@navy.mil
URL: http://www.navy.com/navy/joining/education-opportunities/nrotc/

Goal: To assist students who are planning to purse nursing degrees at an NROTC college or university.

Eligibility: Applicants must be in their second semester of high school and plan to enroll in an NROTC college or university to pursue a nursing degree. Applicants must be in the top 10% of their class, or have a combined SAT score (critical reading and math) of 1080 or a combined ACT (English and math) score of 43 or higher.
Target Student: High school students.
Amount: Varies
Number of Awards: Varies
Scholarship can be renewed.
Based on Financial Need: No
Deadline: January
Applications are available online. A completed application, transcripts, standardized test scores and three references are required to apply.

(802) NROTC Scholarship Program

Chief of Naval Education and Training/NROTC

Phone: 800-NAV-ROTC
URL: http://www.nrotc.navy.mil

Goal: To prepare future soliders for leadership positions in the Navy and Marine Corps.
Eligibility: Applicants must be U.S. citizens who are at least 17 years old as of Septermber 1 of their first year of college and no older than 23 on June 30 of their first year. They must be younger than 27 on their anticipated graduation date. Applicants must attend an NROTC college or university and be able to serve in the military. For the Navy option the applicant must have an SAT critical reading score of at least 530 and a math score of at least 520 or ACT score of at least 22 in English and 22 in math. The Marine Corps require a composite SAT score of 1000 or an ACT composite score of 22.
Target Student: High school and College students.

Amount: Full tuition including fees, books, uniforms and monthly stipend.
Number of Awards: Varies
Scholarship can be renewed.
Based on Financial Need: No
Deadline: January
Applications are available online.

(803) NSA Scholarship Foundation

National Society of Accountants
Scholarship Program
Scholarship America
One Scholarship Way
P.O. Box 297
Saint Peter, MN 56082

Phone: 507-931-1682
URL: http://www.nsacct.org

Goal: To assist students entering the accounting profession.
Eligibility: Applicants must be U.S. or Canadian citizen undergraduate students majoring in accounting and have a GPA of 3.0 or higher.
Target Student: College and Adult students.
Amount: $500 - $2,000
Number of Awards: 32
Based on Financial Need: No
Deadline: March
Applications are available online.

(804) NSCC Scholarship Funds

Naval Sea Cadet Corps
2300 Wilson Boulevard
Arlington, VA 22201

Phone: 800-356-5760
Email: alewis@seacadets.org
URL: http://www.seacadets.org

Goal: To assist Sea Cadets with educational expenses.

Eligibility: Applicants must be current Sea Cadets with at least two years of experience at the time of application. They be at the rate of NSCC E-3 or higher and be recommended by their commander., NSCC Committee Chairman, and principals and counselors. Applicants must have a GPA of 3.3 or higher and show a letter of acceptance from an accredited college or university. SAT and ACT scores are also considered.
Target Student: High school students.
Amount: Varies
Number of Awards: Varies
Based on Financial Need: No
Deadline: May
Applications are available online.

(805) NTA Arnold Rigby Graduate Scholarship

Tourism Cares
275 Turnpike Street
Suite 307
Canton, MA 02021

Phone: 781-821-5990
Fax: 781-821-8949
Email: scholarships@tourismcares.org
URL: http://www.tourismcares.org

Goal: To assist those studying travel, tourism and hospitality at the graduate level.
Eligibility: Applciants must be permanent residents of the U.S. or Canada attending a four-year postsecondary school in the U.S. or Canada. Applicants must be entering or continuing graduate students studying hospitality, tourims or tavel with a GPA of 3.0 or greater.
Target Student: College, Graduate and Adult students.
Amount: $1,000
Number of Awards: 1
Based on Financial Need: No
Deadline: April

Applications are available online. A completed application, resume, transcript, essay, proof of residency, and two letters of recommendation are required to apply.

(806) NTA Dave Herren Memorial Undergraduate or Graduate Scholarship

Tourism Cares
275 Turnpike Street
Suite 307
Canton, MA 02021

Phone: 781-821-5990
Fax: 781-821-8949
Email: scholarships@tourismcares.org
URL: http://www.tourismcares.org

Goal: To assist students studying travel, tourism and hospitality.
Eligibility: Applicants must be permanent residents of the U.S. and enrolled in an accredited U.S. four-year college/university. Applicants must be studying travel, hospitality or tourism and be entering or returning graduate or junior or senior undergraduate students with a GPA of 3.0 or higher. Undergraduate applicants must have 60 completed units by May of the application year.
Target Student: College, Graduate and Adult students.
Amount: $1,000
Number of Awards: 1
Based on Financial Need: No
Deadline: April
Applications are available online. A completed application, essay, resume, transcripts, two letters of recommendation and proof of residency are required to apply.

(807) NTA Mayflower Tours Patrick Murphy Undergraduate or Graduate Internship

Tourism Cares
275 Turnpike Street
Suite 307
Canton, MA 02021

Phone: 781-821-5990
Fax: 781-821-8949
Email: scholarships@tourismcares.org
URL: http://www.tourismcares.org

Goal: To assist travel and tourism students with an interest in political science.
Eligibility: Applicants can be a resident of any country, but they must be enrolled at an accredited U.S. school. Applicants must be entering or returning graduate students or undergraduate sophomores, juniors or seniors who are pursuing a degree in travel or tourism and have an interest in political science. Applicants must have a GPA of 3.0 or higher with strong interpersonal skills and strong oral and written communication skills.
Target Student: College, Graduate and Adult students.
Amount: $2,000
Number of Awards: 1
Based on Financial Need: No
Deadline: April
Applications are available online. A completed application, letter of recommendation, essay, transcrpts, rcsume and proof of residency are required to apply.

(808) Odenza Marketing Scholarship

Odenza Vacations
4664 Lougheed Highway Suite 230
Burnaby, BC V5C5T5

Phone: 877-297-2661
URL:http://www.odenzascholarships.com

Goal: To assist college students and future college students between the ages of 16 and 25 with their college expenses.

Eligibility: Applicants must be U.S. or Canadian citizens with at least one year of college remaining. Applicants must have a GPA of 2.5 or higher.
Target Student: High school, College and Graduate students.
Amount: $500
Number of Awards: Varies
Based on Financial Need: No
Deadline: March
Applications are avialable online. A completed application and two essays are required to apply.

(809) Off to College Scholarship Sweepstakes

Sun Trust
P.O. Box 27172
Richmond, VA 23261

Phone: 800-786-8787
URL: http://www.suntrusteducation.com

Goal: To assist students with their first year college expenses.
Eligibility: Applicants must be high school seniors (at least 13 years old) who are planning to attending a college or univerisity accredited by the U.S. Department fo Education in the fall following their graduation. Winners are chosen at random every two weeks.
Target Student: High school students.
Amount: $1,000
Number of Awards: 15
Based on Financial Need: No
Deadline: May
Applications are available online.

(810) OP Loftbed Scholarship Award

OP Loftbed
P.O. Box 573
Thomasville, NC 27361

Phone: 866-567-5638

Email: info@oploftbed.com
URL: http://www.oploftbed.com

Goal: To acknowledge students who show excellence in creative writing.
Eligibility: Applicants must be U.S. citizens who plan to attend an accredited college or university in the upcoming school year.
Target Student: High school, College and Adult students.
Amount: $500
Number of Awards: Varies
Based on Financial Need: No
Deadline: July
Applications are available online. A completed application and essay are required to apply.

(811) Optimist International Contest

Optimist International
4494 Lindell Boulevard
St. Louis, MO 63108

Phone: 314-371-6000
Fax: 314-371-6006
Email: programs@optimist.org
URL: http://www.optimist.org

Goal: To assist students for their writing skills.
Eligibility: Applicants must be under 18 on December 31 of the current school year. Applicants must write an essay on a sponsor specified topic and apply through a local Optimist Club. Students will compete at the local, district and international level.
Target Student: High school students.
Amount: $2,500
Number of Awards: Varies
Based on Financial Need: No
Deadline: February
Contact your local Optimist Club.

(812) Optimist International Oratorical Contest

Optimist International
4494 Lindell Boulevard
St. Louis, MO 63108

Phone: 314-371-6000
Fax: 314-371-6006
Email: program@optimist.org
URL: http://www.optimist.org

Goal: To assist students based on their oratorical skills.
Eligibility: Applicants must be students in the U.S. Canada or Caribbean who are under 16 years old on the last day of the year.
Target Student: Junior high and younger and High school students.
Amount: $1,000 - $2,500
Number of Awards: 3-Feb
Based on Financial Need: No
Deadline: March and June
Contact your local Optimist Club.

(813) Otto M. Stanfield Legal Scholarship

Unitarian Univeralist Association
25 Beacon Street
Boston, MA 02108

Phone: 617-742-2100
Email: info@uua.org
URL: http://www.uua.org

Goal: To assist Unitarian Universalist students starting or attending law school.
Eligibility: Applicants must be planning or attending law school at the graduate level. The award is based on financial need as well as activity with Unitarian Universalism.
Target Student: Graduate and Adult students.
Amount: Varies
Number of Awards: Varies

Based on Financial Need: Yes
Deadline: February
Applications are available online.

---

(814) Overseas Press Club Foundation Scholarships Internships

Overseas Press Club Foundation
40 W. 45 Street
New York, NY 10036

Phone: 202-493-9087
Fax: 201-612-9915
Email: foundation@opcofamerica.org
URL:http://ww.overseaspressclubfoundation.org

Goal: To encourage undergraduate and graduate students at U.S. colleges to pursure careers as foreign correspondents.
Eligibility: Applicants must be undergraduate and graduate students with an interest in a career as a foreign correspondent and be attending a U.S. college or university.
Target Student: College, Graduate and Adult students.
Amount: $2,000
Number of Awards: 12
Based on Financial Need: No
Deadline: December
Applications are available online.

---

(815) Parent Answer Scholarship Sweepstakes

Parent Answer Scholarship Sweepstakes
P.O. Box 9500
Wilkes-Barre, PA 18773

URL: http://www.collegeanswer.com

Goal: To assist the parents of college students.

Eligibility: Applicants must be U.S. residents and parents of undergraduate college students at a Title IV school. Applicants must sign up for the Sallie Mae Parent Anser e-Newsletter.
Target Student: College and Adult students.
Amount: $10,000
Number of Awards: 1
Based on Financial Need: No
Deadline: May
Applicants may enter the sweepstakes online or by mail.

---

(816) Parsons Brinckerhoff Golden Apple Scholarship

Conference of Minority Transportation Officials
818 18th Street NW
Suite 850
Washington, DC 20006

Phone: 202-530-0551
Fax: 202-530-0617
Email: comto@comto.org
URL: http://www.comto.org

Goal: To assist students planning careers in transportation in the fields of communications, marketing or finance.
Eligibility: Applicants must be graduating high school sensior who have been COMOTO members for at least one year with a GPA of 2.0 or higher and accepted into a college or technical program.
Target Student: High school students.
Amount: $2,500
Number of Awards: Varies
Based on Financial Need: No
Deadline: April
Applications are available online.

---

(817) Part-Time Student Scholarship

International Furnishings and Design Association

150 South Warner Road
Suite 156
King of Prussia, PA 19406

Phone: 610-535-6422
Fax: 610-535-6423
Email: merrymabbettinc@comcast.net
URL:http://www.ifdaef.org/scholarships.php

Goal: To assist part-time students majoring in interior design.
Eligibility: Applicants must undergraduate students attending school part-time at a U.S. school and majoring in interior design.
Target Student: College and Adult students.
Amount: $1,500
Number of Awards: 1
Based on Financial Need: No
Deadline: March
Applications are available online.

(818) Patriot's Pen Youth Essay Contest

Veterans of Foreign Wars
406 W. 34th Street
Kansas City, MO 64111

Phone: 816-968-1117
Fax: 816-968-1149
Email: kharmer@vfw.org
URL: http://www.vfw.org

Goal: To assist students grades 6 to 8.
Eligibility: Applicants must be in 6th - 8th grade in a public, home schooled or private school in the U.S. or its territories. To apply applicants must write an essay based on a topic that is determined by the sponsor.
Target Student: Junior high and younger.
Amount: Up to $10,000
Number of Awards: Varies
Based on Financial Need: No
Deadline: November

Applications are available online or at your local VFW post.

(819) Paul and Daisy Soros Felllowships for New Americans

Paul and Daisy Soros
400 W. 59th Street
New York, NY 10019

Phone: 212-547-6926
Fax: 212-548-4623
Email: pdsoros_fellows@sorosny.org
URL: http://www.pdsoros.org

Goal: To assist graduate students who are immigrants.
Eligibility: Applicants must be immigrants who are resident aliens, naturalized or children of two parents who have been naturalized. The winner must have already completed a bachelor's degree or be a college senior and over the age of 30 at the time of the application deadline.
Target Student: College, Graduate and Adult students.
Amount: $45,000
Number of Awards: 30
Scholarship can be renewed.
Based on Financial Need: No
Deadline: November
Applications are available online.

(820) Paul and Helen L. Grauer Scholarship

American Radio Relay League Foundation
225 Main Street
Newington, CT 06111

Phone: 860-594-0397
Fax: 860-594-0259
Email: foundation@arrl.org
URL: http://www.arrlf.org

Goal: To assist ham radio operators with their educational expenses.

Eligibility: Applicants must have a novice ham radio license or higher, must be a resident and attend school in ARRL Midwest Division (Iowa, Kansas, Missouri, or Nebraska)and be undergraduate or graduate students in electronics, communications or another related field.
Target Student: College, Graduate and Adult students.
Amount: $1,000
Number of Awards: 1
Based on Financial Need: No
Deadline: February
Applications are available online and must be mailed in.

(821) Pauline Langkamp Memorial Scholarship

Navy Wives Clubs of America
P.O. Box 54022
NSA Mid-South
Millington, TN 38053

Phone: 866-511-5922
Email: scholarships@navywivesclubsofamerica.org
URL: http://www.navywivesclubsofamerica.org

Goal: To assist college students who are the adult children of members of the Navy Wives Clubs of America.
Eligibility: Applicants must be the child of an NWCA member. They must not be holders of a military ID and must be enrolled or planning to enroll at a postsecondary school.
Target Student: High school, College and Adult students.
Amount: Varies
Number of Awards: Varies
Based on Financial Need: No
Deadline: May
Applications are available online.

(822) Pentagon Assistance Fund

Navy-Marine Corps Relief Society
875 North Randolph Street Suite 225
Arlington, VA 22203

Phone: 703-696-4960
Fax: 703-696-0144
Email: education@hq.nmcrs.org
URL: http://www.nmcrs.org

Goal: To assist the spouses of military personnel.
Eligibility: Applicants must be the spouse of a deceased victim of the 9/11/2001 terrorist attack on the Pentagon who have not remarried. They must be purusing an undergraduate degree and show financial need. They must maintain a 2.0 or higher GPA and have a Dependent's Uniformed Services Identification and Privilege Card.
Target Student: High school, College and Adult students.
Amount: Varies
Number of Awards: Varies
Based on Financial Need: Yes
Deadline: July
Applications are available online.

(823) Persina Scholarship for Diversity in Journalism

National Press Club
529 14th Street
13th Floor
Washington, DC 20045

Phone: 202-662-7500
URL: http://www.press.org

Goal: To assist promising future journalists.
Eligibility: Applicants must be high school seniors, have a 3.0 or higher GPA, and plan to start college the year after graduation.
Target Student: High school students.
Amount: $2,000 plus $500 for books
Number of Awards: 1

Based on Financial Need: No
Deadline: March
Applications are available online. A completed application, essay, transcripts, FASFA, letter of acceptance or proof of application, up to five work samples and three letters of recommendation are required to apply.

---

(824) PHD ARA Scholarship

American Radio Relay League Foundation
225 Main Street
Newington, CT 06111

Phone: 860-594-0397
Fax: 860-594-0259
Email: foundation@arrl.org
URL: http://www.arrlf.org

Goal: To assist ham radio operators in continuing their education.
Eligibility: Applicants must have a ham radio license of any class, be residents or attend school in the ARRL Midwest Division (Iowa, Kansas, Missouri, or Nebraska) and be studying journalism, computer science, or electronic engineering. Applicants can also be the children of deceased amateur radio operators.
Target Student: College, Graduate and Adult students.
Amount: $1,000
Number of Awards: 1
Based on Financial Need: No
Deadline: February
Applications are available online and submitted via mail.

---

(825) Phoenix Scholarship Program

Phoenix Scholarship Program
159 Concord Avenue Suite IC
Cambridge, MA 02138

Email: phoenixawards@gmail.com

Goal: To assist deserving high school seniors planning to pursue higher education.
Eligibility: Applicants must be U.S. high school seniors or high school graduates who have graduated within 13 months of the application deadline. Applicants must have a GPA of 2.75 or higher and have taken the SAT or ACT. Applicants must be in good standing at their high school and show good morals and enroll in an accredited college or university after high school graduation.
Target Student: High school students
Amount: Varies
Number of Awards: Up to 4
Based on Financial Need: No
Deadline: April
Applications are available via email.

---

(826) Pi Sigma Alpha Washington Internship Scholarships

Pi Sigma Alpha
The Washington Center
2301 M Street NW
5th Floor
Washington, DC 20037

Phone:
Email: info@twc.edu
URL: http://www.apsanet.org/-psa

Goal: To provide scholarships so Pi Sigma Alpha members can participate in internships during the summer and fall in Washington, DC.
Eligibility: Applicants must be Pi Sigma Alpha members and be nominated by their local chapter. The award is for a political science internship and is based on academics and service to the organization.
Target Student: College, Graduate and Adult students.
Amount: $2,000
Number of Awards: 4
Based on Financial Need: No

Deadline: May
Applications are available online.

---

(827) Pierre and Patricia Bikai Fellowship

American Center of Oriental Research
656 Beacon Street
5th Floor
Boston, MA 02215

Phone: 617-353-6571
Fax: 617-353-6575
Email: acor@bu.edu
URL: http://www.bu.edu/acor

Goal: To assist graduate students in an archaeological project at the American Center of Oriental Research.
Eligibility: Applicants must be graduate students. The award provides for room and board at ACOR with $600 per month of support. This award can be combined with the Harrell and Groot fellowships. This award does not support travel or field work.
Target Student: College and Adult students.
Amount: $600 - $1,200
Number of Awards: 2-Jan
Based on Financial Need: No
Deadline: February
Applications are available online.

---

(828) Platt Family Scholarship Prize Essay Contest

The Lincoln Forum
c/o Don McCue, Curator of the Lincoln Memorial Shrine
125 West Vine Street
Redlands, CA 92373

Phone: 909-798-7632
Email: archives@akspl.org
URL: http://www.thelincolnforum.org

Goal: To assist students who have written the best essay on Abraham Lincoln.
Eligibility: Applicants must be full-time undergraduate students enrolled in a U.S. college or university in the spring term and they must submt an essay on a sponsor determined topic.
Target Student: College and Adult students.
Amount: $500 - $1,500
Number of Awards: 3
Based on Financial Need: No
Deadline: July
Applications are available online. A completed application and essay are required to apply.

---

(829) Playwright Discovery Award

VSA Arts
518 Connecticut Avenue NW
Suite 600
Washington, DC 20006

Phone: 800-933-8721
Fax: 202-429-0868
Email: info@vsarts.org
URL: http://www.vsarts.org

Goal: To acknowledge promising young playwrights.
Eligibility: Applicants must be in 6th to 12th grade and submit a one-act script that is less than 40 pages in length that explores what it is like to live with a disability. First and second place winners will have their play performed at the JFK Performing Arts Center.
Target Student: Junior high and younger and High school students.
Amount: Varies
Number of Awards: Varies
Based on Financial Need: No
Deadline: Unknown
Applications are available online.

---

(830) PMI Founders Scholarship

Project Management Institute Educational
Foundation
14 Campus Boulevard
Newton Square, PA 19073

Phone: 610-356-4600
Fax: 610-356-0357
Email: pmief@pmi.org
URL: http://www.pmief.org

Goal: To assist project management
students.
Eligibility: Applicants must be
undergraduate students enrolled in
bachelor's degree programs in project
management or a related subject.
Target Student: College and Adult
students.
Amount: $2,000
Number of Awards: Varies
Based on Financial Need: No
Deadline: June
Applications are available online. A
completed application, two essays, resume,
and three letters of recommendation are
required to apply.

(831) Poster Contest for High School
Students

Christophers
12 E. 48th Street
New York, NY 10017

URL: http://www.christophers.org

Goal: To acknolwedge students for
exploring a theme in poster art.
Eligibility: Applicants must be high
school students and they must submit a
poster of orginal content that explores the
sponsors theme.
Target Student: High school students
Amount: $500 - $1,000
Number of Awards: Up to 8
Based on Financial Need: No
Deadline: February

Applications are available online.

(832) Predoctoral Fellowships for
Historian of American Art to Travel
Abroad

National Gallery of Art
2000B South Club Drive
Landover, MD 20785

Phone: 202-842-6482
Fax: 202-789-3026
URL:http://www.nga.gov/resources/casv
a.htm

Goal: To provide fellowships to doctoral
students in art history studying the art and
architecture of the U.S. including native
and pre-Revolutionary America.
Eligibility: Applicants must be nominated
by the chair of a graduate department in
art history or other appropriate
department. Each department is limited to
two nomines. Th award is for 8 weeks and
for travel to Africa, Asia, South American
or Europe. The travel fellowship is to
expand on the applicants knowledge not
advance their dissertation.
Target Student: Graduate and Adult
students.
Amount: Up to $4,500
Number of Awards: Up to 6
Based on Financial Need: No
Deadline: November
Application information is available online.
To apply applicants must submit
proposals, itineraries, curriculum vitae, two
letters from professors and a nomination
letter from the department chair.

(833) PricewaterhouseCoopers Ascend
Scholarship

Ascend: Pan-Asian Leaders in Finance and
Accounting
120 Wall Street
3rd Floor

New York, NY 10005

Phone: 212-248-4888
Email:scholarships@ascendleadership.org
URL: http://www.ascendleadership.org

Goal: To assist Ascend student members studying accounting.
Eligibility: Applicants must be active student members of Ascend who are undergraduate freshmen, sophomores or juniors studying accounting at an accredited U.S. postsecondary school. Applicants must not have worked for a Big 4 accounting firm and must have a GPA of 3.5 or higher.
Target Student: College and Adult students.
Amount: $3,000
Number of Awards: 4
Based on Financial Need: No
Deadline: July
Application infomration is available online. A completed application, essay, resume, transcript and talent profile is required.

(834) Princess Grace Awards

Princess Grace Awards
150 E. 58th Street
21st Floor
New York, NY 10155

Phone: 212-317-1470
Fax: 212-317-1473
Email: grants@pgfusa.org
URL: http://www.pgfusa.com

Goal: To assist young artists in theater, dance and film.
Eligibility: Applicants must submit an example of their work for the category in which they are applying. Applicants who are applying in theatre and dance need sponsorship from a professional school or company.
Target Student: High school, College and Adult students

Amount: $25,000
Number of Awards: Varies
Based on Financial Need: No
Deadline: Varies
Applications are available online.

(835) Principal's Leadership Award

Herff Jones
c/o National Association of Secondary School Principals
1904 Association Drive
Reston, VA 20191

Phone: 800-253-7746
Email: carrollw@principals.org
URL: http://www.principals.org/awards/

Goal: To acknowledge students for their leadership.
Eligibility: Applicants must be high school seniors who have been nominated by their high school principal. Each principal can nominate one student from their high school.
Target Student: High school students.
Amount: $1,000 to $12,000
Number of Awards: 100
Based on Financial Need: No
Deadline: December
Nomination forms are available online.

(836) Print and Graphics Scholarship

Graphic Arts Information Network
Print and Graphics Scholarship Foundation
Scholarship Competition
200 Deer Run Road
Sewickley, PA 15143

Phone: 412-741-6860
Fax: 412-741-2311
Email: pgsf@gatf.org
URL: http://www.gain.org

Goal: To assist students purusing careers in graphic communications.
Eligibility: Applicants must be high school seniors or high school graduates who have not yet begun college, or college students in two or four year college programs. Applicants are required to be full-time students, maintain a GPA of 3.0 or higher and interested in pursuing a career in graphic communications.
Target Student: High school, College and Adult students.
Amount: Varies
Number of Awards: 200+
Scholarship can be renewed.
Based on Financial Need: No
Deadline: April
Applications are available online.

---

(837) Prize in Ethics Essay Contest

Elie Wiesel Foundation for Humanity
55 Madison Foundation for Humanity
New York, NY 10022

Phone: 212-490-7788
Fax: 212-490-7788
Email: info@eliewieselfoundation.org
URL:http://www.eliewieselfoundation.org

Goal: To encourage the though and discussion of ethics and their role in education.
Eligibility: Applicants must be full time juniors or seniors at a U.S. accredited college or university and are required to write an essay on ethics. A faculty sponsor is required to review and sign the studdent's entry form.
Target Student: College and Adult students.
Amount: $2,500 - $5,000
Number of Awards: 5
Based on Financial Need: No
Deadline: December
Applications are available online.

(838) Prize in International Insolvency Studies

International Insolvency Institute
10332 Main Street
PMB 112
Fairfax, VA 20030

Phone: 703-591-6336
Fax: 703-802-0207
URL: http://www.iiiglobal.org

Goal: To acknowledge outstanding international insolvency researchers, analysts and commentators.
Eligibility: Applicants must be undergraduate or gradaute students, or practitioners of international insolvency studies for less than seven years.
Target Student: College, Graduate and Adult students.
Amount: Varies
Number of Awards: 1
Based on Financial Need: No
Deadline: Varies
Applications are available online. A completed application, original analysis, commentary or legal research is required to apply.

---

(839) Professional Scholarships

Insurance Scholarship Foundation of America
14286-19 Beach Boulevard
Suite 353
Jacksonville, FL 32250

Phone: 904-821-7188
Email: foundation@inssfa.org
URL: http://www.inssfa.org

Goal: To improve the insurance industry by assist education of its members.

Eligibility: Applications must be employed in the industry for a minimum of three years, be a NAIW member for at least three years, have the CPIW/M designation, must have active involvement in NAIW leadership activities and be engaged in a course of study to improve the skills and knowledge related to the applicants employment responsibilities.
Target Student: College, Graduate and Adult students.
Amount: $50 - $2,000
Number of Awards: Varies
Based on Financial Need: No
Deadline: August and January
Applicants are available online.

---

(840) Project on Nuclear Issues Essay Contest

Center for Strategic and International Studies
Project on Nuclear Issues
1800 K Street, NW
Washington, DC 20006

Phone: 202-887-0200
Fax: 202-775-3199
Email: jward@csis.org
URL: http://www.csis.org

Goal: To assist those who have written the best essay on nuclear weapons.
Eligibility: Applicants must be undergraduate, graduate or recent college graduate and submit an essay covering some aspect of nuclear weapons or strategy.
Target Student: College, Graduate and Adult students.
Amount: $1,500 - $5,000
Number of Awards: 4
Based on Financial Need: No
Deadline: Varies
Applications are available online.

(841) Project Vote Smart National Internship Program

Project Vote Smart
Internship Coordinator
1 Common Ground
Philipsburg, MT 59858

Phone: 406-859-8683
Fax: 406-859-8680
Email: intern@votesmart.org
URL: http://www.votesmart.org

Goal: To encourage college students and recent graduates to develop an interest in voter education.
Eligibility: Applicants must be current college students or recent college graduates who are able to willing to use a non-partisan attitude when doing voter education in a ten-week internship.
Target Student: Colege and Adult students.
Amount: All Living Costs
Number of Awards: Varies
Based on Financial Need: No
Deadline: Rolling
Applicatons are available online. A completed application, resume, essay and three references are required to apply.

---

(842) Proof-Reading.com Scholarship

Proof-Reading Inc.
12 Geary Street Suite 806
San Francisco, CA 94108

Phone: 866-433-4867
Email: support@proof-reading.com
URL: http://www.proof-reading.com

Goal: To acknowledge outstanding student essayists.

Eligibility: Applicants must be U.S. legal residents who are full time students at an accredited college or university with a 3.5 GPA or higher. Applicants must submit an essay on a topic determined by the sponsor.
Target Student: College and Adult students.
Amount: $1,500
Number of Awards: 1
Based on Financial Need: No
Deadline: June
Applications are available online. A completed application and essay are required.

(843) ProStart National Certificate of Achievement Scholarship

National Restaurant Assocation
Educational Foundation
175 W. Jackson Boulevard
Suite 1500
Chicago, IL 60604

Phone: 800-765-2122
Fax: 312-715-1010
Email: scholars@naref.org
URL: http://www.nraef.org

Goal: To assist students who have been recognized through the HBA/ProStart School to Career Initiative.
Eligibility: Applicants must be graduating high school sneiors who have received the ProStart School to Career Initiative.
Target Student: High school students.
Amount: At least $2,500
Number of Awards: Varies
Based on Financial Need: No
Deadline: August
Applications are available online. A completed application, copy of National Restaurant Association Educational Foundation ProStart National Certificate of Acheivement, copy of GPA and proof of acceptance into a culinary or restaurant/foodservice manageme

(844) Prudential Spirit of Community Awards

Prudential Spirit of Community Awards
Prudential Financial Inc.
751 Broad Street, 16th Floor
Newark, NJ 07102

Phone: 877-525-8491
Email: spirit@prudential.com
URL: http://spirit.comprudential.com

Goal: To acknowledge students for their volunteer work in their community.
Eligibility: Applicants must be students grades 5-12 and a legal U.S. resident participating in volunteer work that in part occurred in the year before the date of application.
Target Student: Junior high and younger and High school students.
Amount: $1,000 to $5,000
Number of Awards: 102
Based on Financial Need: No
Deadline: November
Applications are available online.

(845) Ray , NRP and Katie, WKTE Pautz Scholarship

American Radio Relay League Foundation
225 Main Street
Newington, CT 06111

Phone: 860-594-0397
Fax: 860-594-0259
Email: foundation@arrl.org
URL: http://www.arrlf.org

Goal: To asisst amateur radio operators from the ARRL Midwest Division.

Eligibility: Applicants must be ARRL members with a General Class Amateur Radio License or higher who are residents of Iowa, Kansas, Missouri, or Nebraska majoring in electronics, computer science or a related field.
Target Student: High school, College, or Adult students.
Amount: $500 - $1,000
Number of Awards: 1
Based on Financial Need: No
Deadline: February
Applications are available online.

(846) Ray and Gertrude Marshall Scholarship

American Culinary Federation
180 Center Place Way
St. Augustine, FL 32095

Phone: 800-624-9458
Fax: 904-825-4758
Email: acf@acfchefs.net
URL: http://www.achchefs.org

Goal: To assist students in culinary arts programs.
Eligibility: Applicants must be ACF junior members who are enrolled in a post-secondary culinary arts program or an ACF apprenticeship program and completed at least one grading period.
Target Student: College and Adult students.
Amount: Varies
Number of Awards: Varies
Based on Financial Need: Yes
Deadline: May and September
Applications are available online.

(847) Reid Blackburn Scholarship

National Press Photographers Foundation
Blackburn Scholarship
Fay Blackburn
The Columbian

P.O. Box 180
Vancouver, WA 98666

Phone: 360-759-8027
Fax: 919-383-7261
Email: fay.blackburn@columbian.com
URL: http://www.nppa.org

Goal: To assist photojournalism students.
Eligibility: Applicants must have completed at least one year as a full-time student at a four-year college or university, provide a portfolio, have demonstrated financial need, have completed courses in photojournalism and have at least half a year of undergradaute study remaining. Applicants can apply to any, but only win one NPPA award per year.
Target Student: College and Adult students.
Amount: Varies
Number of Awards: Varies
Based on Financial Need: Yes
Deadline: March
Applications are available online.

(848) Religious Liberty Essay Scholarship Contest

Baptist Joint Committee for Religious Liberty
Essay Contest
200 Maryland Avenue NE
Washington, DC 20002

Phone: 202-544-4226
Fax: 202-544-2094
Email: ccrowe@bjconline.org
URL: http://www.bjconline.org

Goal: To acknowledge students who have written outstanding essays about religious liberty.
Eligibility: Applicants must be high school juniors or seniors and must submit a 800 to 1,200 word essay on a topic that is related to religious freedom.
Target Student: High school students.

Amount: $100 to $1,000
Number of Awards: 3
Based on Financial Need: No
Deadline: March
Applications are available online. A registration form and essay are required to apply.

---

(849) Retiree's Association and the Bureau of Alcohol, Tobacco, Firearms and Explosives (ATFAR) Scholarship

Explorers Learning for Life
P.O. Box 152079
Irving, TX 75015

Phone: 972-580-2433
Fax: 972-580-2137
Email: pchestnu@lflmail.org
URL: http://www.learningforlife.org/exploring

Goal: To assist students pursuing a career in law enforcement.
Eligibility: Applicants must be in their senior year of high school or later and must be active Law Enforcement Explorers.
Target Student: High school, College and Adult students.
Amount: $1,000
Number of Awards: Varies
Based on Financial Need: No
Deadline: March
Applications are available online. A completed application, three letters of recommendation and an essy are required to apply.

---

(850) Return 2 College Scholarship

R2C Scholarship Program

URL: http://www.return2college.com/awardprogram.cfm

Goal: To assist college and adult students with educational expenses.
Eligibility: Applicants must be college or adult students who are attending or planning to attend a two or four-year college or graduate school in the next 12 months. Applicants must be at least 17 years old and U.S citizens or permanent residents.
Target Student: High school, College and Adult students.
Amount: $1,500
Number of Awards: Varies
Based on Financial Need: No
Deadline: March, August, December
Applications are available online.

---

(851) Rhodes Scholar

Rhodes Scholarship Trust
Attn: Elliot F. Gerson
8229 Boone Boulevard Suite 240
Vienna, VA 22182

Email: amsec@rhodesscholar.org
URL: http://www.rhodesscholar.org

Goal: To provide full tuition to 32 American students with outstanding achievements.
Eligibility: Applicants must be U.S. citizens between 18 and 24 who will complete their bachelors degree by the time of the award. The award covers two or three years of study at the University of Oxford. The award selection is based on scholastic, literary, and atheltic achievements as well as character.m
Target Student: College students.
Amount: Full tuition plus stipend.
Number of Awards: 32
Based on Financial Need: No
Deadline: October
Applications are available online.

---

(852) Richard W. Bendicksen Memorial Scholarship

American Radio Relay League Foundation
225 Main Street
Newington, CT 06111

Phone: 860-594-0397
Fax: 860-594-0259
Email: foundation@arrl.org
URL: http://www.arrlf.org

Goal: To assist amateur radio operators
with educational expenses.
Eligibility: Applicants must have an active
amateur radio operators of any class and
be attending a four-year institution of
higher learning.
Target Student: High school, College and
Adult students.
Amount: $2,000
Number of Awards: 1
Based on Financial Need: No
Deadline: February
Applications are available online.

(853) Ritchie-Jennings Memorial Scholarship

Association of Certified Fraud Examiners
Scholarships Program Coordinator
The Gregor Building
716 West Avenue
Austin, TX 78701

Phone: 512-478-9000
Fax: 512-478-9297
Email: memberservices@acfe.com
URL: http://www.acfe.com

Goal: To assist accounting, business,
finance, and criminal justice students
working to become Certified Fraud
Examiners.
Eligibility: Applicants must be full-time
undergraduate and graduate students with
a major or minor in criminal justice,
finance, business or accounting.
Target Student: College, Graduate and
Adult students.

Amount: $1,000 - $10,000
Number of Awards: 30
Based on Financial Need: No
Deadline: February
Applications are available online.   A
completed application, three letters of
recommendation, with at least one coming
from a Certified Fraud Examiner or local
CFE Chapter, and essay are required to
apply.

(854) Robert J. Yourzak Scholarship

Project Management Institute Educational
Foundation
14 Campus Boulevard
Newton Square, PA 19073

Phone: 610-356-4600
Fax: 610-356-0357
Email: pmief@pmi.org
URL: http://www.pmief.org

Goal: To assist project management
students.
Eligibility: Applicants must be project
management majors enrolled in degree
program at a college or university.
Target Student: College and Adult
students.
Amount: $2,000
Number of Awards: Varies
Based on Financial Need: No
Deadline: June
Applications are available online. A
completed application, two essays, resume,
and three letters of recommendation are
required to apply.

(855) Roller Skating Foundation Scholarship, Current College Student Category

Roller Skating Foundation
6905 Corporate Drive
Indianapolis, IN 46278

Phone: 317-347-2626
Fax: 317-347-2636
Email: foundation@rollerskating.com
URL: http://www.rollerskating.org

Goal: To assist sports, hotel and food and beverage management.
Eligibility: Applicants must be undergraduate seniors majoring insports, hotel or food and beverage managemen with a 3.4 or higher GPA and demonstrated leadership ability.
Target Student: College and Adult students.
Amount: $1,000
Number of Awards: 1
Based on Financial Need: Yes
Deadline: April
Applications are available online. A completed application, transcripts, essay, income tax information and three letters of recommendation are required to apply.

(856) Roller Skating Foundation Scholarship, High School Student Category

Roller Skating Foundation
6905 Corporate Drive
Indianapolis, IN 46278

Phone: 317-347-2626
Fax: 317-347-2636
Email: foundation@rollerskating.com
URL: http://www.rollerskating.org

Goal: To assist high school students who are headed for college.
Eligibility: Applicants must be high school seniors who plan to enroll in an accredited university by the fall following their graduation from high school. Applicants must have a 3.4 GPA or higher and be certified as a regular patron by a Roller Skating Association member skating center. Applicants must have composite standardized test scores that are at least in the 85th percentile.

Target Student: High school students.
Amount: $4,000
Number of Awards: 1
Based on Financial Need: Yes
Deadline: April
Applications are available online. A completed application, transcript, personal essay, three letters of recommendation and income tax informaton is requried to apply.

(857) Ron Culp Scholarsip for Mentorship

Public Relations Student Society of America
33 Maiden Lane
11th Floor
New York, NY 10038

Phone: 212-460-1474
Fax: 212-995-0757
Email: prssa@prsa.org
URL: http://www.prssa.org

Goal: To assist public relations and journalism students who have mentored others who were pursuing careers in public relations.
Eligibility: Applicants must be members of the Public Relations Student Society of America in good standing. They must be undergraduate seniors majoring in journalism, public relations or a related field at an accredited college or university who are preparing for careers in the field of public relations.
Target Student: College and Adult students.
Amount: $1,000
Number of Awards: 1
Based on Financial Need: No
Deadline: June
Applications are available online. A nomination from someone who knows about the applicant's mentoring is required to apply.

(858) Ronald McDonald House Charities U.S. Scholarships

Ronald McDonald House Charities
1321 Murfreesboro Road Suite 800
Nashville, TN 37217

Phone: 855-670-ISTS
Email: contactus@applyists.com
URL: http://www.rmhc.org

Goal: To assist high school seniors with educational expenses.
Eligibility: Applicants must be high school seniors younger than 21 years oldwith a GPA of 2.7 or higher. Applicants must reside in a Ronald McDonald House Charities chapter area. Four scholarships are available RMHC/Scholars, RMHC/Asia, RMHC/African-American Future Achievers and RMHC/HACER.
Target Student: High school students.
Amount: $1,000
Number of Awards: Varies
Based on Financial Need: Yes
Deadline: December
Applications are available online. A completed application, transcripts, parents tax forms, letter of recommendation and personal statement are required to apply.

(859) Ruth Clark Furniture Design Scholarship

International Furnishings and Design Association
150 South Warner Road
Suite 156
King of Prussia, PA 19406

Phone: 610-535-6422
Fax: 610-535-6423
Email: merrymabbettinc@comcast.net
URL: http://www.ifdaef.org/scholarships.php

Goal: To assist students interested in residential furniture design.
Eligibility: Applicants must be studying interior design or a related subject full time at the undergraduate or graduate level with a concentration in residential upholstered or wood furniture design.
Target Student: College, Graduate and Adult students.
Amount: $3,000
Number of Awards: 1
Based on Financial Need: No
Deadline: March
Applications are available online. A completed application, essay, transcript, letter of recommendation and five furniture designs arerequired to apply.

(860) Ruth Lillly Poetry Fellowship

Poetry Magazine
444 N. Michigan Avenue
Suite 1850
Chicago, IL 60611

Phone: 312-787-7070
Fax: 312-787-6650
Email: mail@poetryfoundation.org
URL: http://www.poetryfoundation.org/foundation/prizes_fellowship.html

Goal: To encourage students to study writing and poetry.
Eligibility: Applicants must be U.S. residents between the age of 21 and 31 who are currently enrolled undergraduate or graduate students with a major in English or creative writing.
Target Student: College, Graduate and Adult students.
Amount: $15,000
Number of Awards: 5
Based on Financial Need: No
Deadline: March
Applications are available online. A completed application, essay, and poetry sample are required to apply.

(861) Ruth Stanton Community Grant

Action Volunteering
Ruth Stanton Community Grant
P.O. Box 1013
Calimesa, CA 92320

Email: painter5@ipsemail.com
URL: http://www.actionvolunteering.com

Goal: To assist students in performing community service activities.
Eligibility: Applicants must be active in performing community service work.
Target Student: High school, College, Graduate and Adult students.
Amount: $500
Number of Awards: Varies
Based on Financial Need: No
Deadline: May
Applications are available online. A completed application, essay and letter of recommendation are required to apply.

(862) Sadler's Wells Global Dance Contest

Sadler's Wells

Phone: 020 7863 8198
Fax: 020 7863 8199
Email: info@globaldancecontest.com
URL: http://www.globaldancecontest.com

Goal: To assist dancers and choreographers.
Eligibility: Applicants must be the age of majority or older in their country (18 years old in the U.S.) and submit a dance video to YouTube and register to enter the contest.
Target Student: High school, College, Graduate and Adult students.
Amount: $2,980 plus travel expenses to London
Number of Awards: 1
Based on Financial Need: No

Deadline: June
Applications are available online. A completed registration from and YouTube video are required to enter.

(863) Sally Strain Memorial Scholarship

The Online Degree Advisor
P.O. Box 2790
Turlock, CA 95380

Email: scholarship@theonlinedegreeadvisor.com
URL: http://www.theonlinedegreeadvisor.com

Goal: To assist students with their edcuational expenses.
Eligibility: Applicants must be 17 years old or older and planning to attend school in the next 12 months. Students can be majoring in any field and can be attending online or in person.
Target Student: High school, College, Graduate and Adult students.
Amount: $100
Number of Awards: 1
Based on Financial Need: No
Deadline: August
Applications are available online.

(864) Salvatore J. Natoli Dissertation Award in Geographic Education

National Council for Geographic Education
Jacksonville State University
206-A Martin Hall
700 Pelham Road North
Jacksonville, AL 36265

Phone: 256-782-5293
Fax: 256-782-5336
Email: ncge@jsu.edu
URL: http://www.ncge.org

Goal: To acknowledge doctoral research.

Eligibility: Applicants must have received their doctoral degree in the past two years and are expected to present their research at a meeting. Applicants must submit a paper that is based on their dissertation, including abstracts, cover letter that states the title of the dissertation, date of the degree conferal, the names of major professors, institution where degree was earned, verification letters from the professors, application for program participation at the annual meeting and applicants social security number.
Target Student: Graduate and Adult students.
Amount: $500
Number of Awards: 1
Based on Financial Need: No
Deadline: April
Applications are available online.

(865) Samuel H. Kress Foundation Paired Fellowship for Research in Conservation and the History of Art

Kress Foundation
174 East 80th Street
New York, NY 10075

Phone: 212-861-4993
URL: http://www.kressfoundation.org

Goal: To provide fellowships for research in conservation and the history of art.
Eligibility: Applicants must be teams of two with the appropriate terminal degree for five years or more, one being in art history, archaeology or a related field and the other in conservation or materials science. Applications will be considered in the area of history and conservation of the visual arts in Europe before the early nineteenth century.
Target Student: Graduate and Adult students.
Amount: $12,000
Number of Awards: Varies
Based on Financial Need: No

Deadline: March for Conservation and November for History of Art Applications are available online. To apply submit a completed application, proposal, travel schedule, collections or institutions for the research, two publications and two letters of recommendation.

(866) Samuel Huntington Public Service Award

National Grid
25 Research Drive
Westborough, MA 01582

Phone: 508-389-2000
URL: http://www.nationalgridus.com

Goal: To assist students who are willing to perform one year of humanitarian service after graduation.
Eligibility: Applicants must be graduating college seniors and willing to perform one year of humanitarian service in the U.S. or abroad. The service can be through a charity, religious group, education or government organization.
Target Student: College and Adult students.
Amount: $10,000
Number of Awards: Varies
Based on Financial Need: No
Deadline: January
Applications are available online.

(867) SanDisk Foundation Scholarship Program

SanDisk Foundation Scholarship Program c/o International Scholarship and Tuition Service Inc
1321 Murfreesboro Road Suite 800
Nashville, TN 37217

Phone: 855-670-ISTS
Email: contactus@applyists.com

URL: http://www.sandisk.com/about-sandisk/corporate-social-responsibility/community-engagement/sandisk-scholars-fund

Goal: To assist students with demonstrated leadership and entrepreneurial interests.

Eligibility: Applicants must be high school seniors or college junior or below and must attend or be planning to attend a full-time undergraduate degree program with demonstarted financial need. As many as 27 $2,500 renewable scholarships are available to the public. as many as 3 $2,500 scholarships are available for dependents of SanDisk employees and two applicants will be chosen as "SanDisk Scholars" and will be awarded full tuition scholarships for up to four years.

Target Student: High school, College and Adult students.

Amount: $2,500 to Full tuition.

Number of Awards: Up to 30 Scholarship can be renewed.

Based on Financial Need: Yes

Deadline: March

Applications are available online. A completed application and essay are required to apply.

---

(868) Scholar Athlete Milk Mustache of the Year Award

National Fluid Milk Processor Promotion Board
Scholar Athlete Milk Mustache of the Year
P.O. Box 9249
Medford, NY 11763

URL: http://www.bodybymilk.com

Goal: To assist outstanding student athletes.

Eligibility: Applicants must be high school seniors with a GPA of 3.2 GPA or higher, participate in a high school club or sport and be a legal resident of the 48 contiguous states. Applicants are asked to describe themselves in 75 words or less in regards to how drinking milk has been a part of their life and training.

Target Student: High school students.

Amount: $7,500

Number of Awards: 25

Based on Financial Need: No

Deadline: March

Applications are available online.

---

(869) Scholarship Drawing for $1,000

Edsouth
eCampusTours
P.O. Box 36014
Knoxville, TN 37930

Phone: 865-342-0670

Email: info@ecampustours.com

URL: http://www.ecampustours.com

Goal: To help students pay for college.

Eligibility: Applicants must be U.S. citizens or legal residents enrolled in a higher education institution. The winner must be enrolled in an eligible institution within one year of the award.

Target Student: High school, College, Graduate and Adult students.

Amount: $1,000

Number of Awards: 2

Based on Financial Need: No

Deadline: March

Applications are available online.

---

(870) Scholarship in Book Production and Publishing

Bookbuilders West
1032 Irving Street #602
San Francisco, CA 94122

URL: http://www.bookbuilders.org

Goal: To assist students pursuing careers in publishing.
Eligibility: Applicants must be enrolled in a college, university or tech school in Alaska, Arizona, California, Colorado, Hawaii or Wyoming with a GPA of 2.0 or higher.
Target Student: College or Adult students.
Amount: $1,000
Number of Awards: Varies
Based on Financial Need: No
Deadline: May
Applications are available from the colleges publishing department. A completed application, letter from a faculty member and student book project are required to apply.

---

(871) Scholarship Program for Young Pianists

Chopin Foundation of the United States Inc.
1440 79th Street Causeway
Suite 117
Miami, FL 33141

Phone: 305-868-0624
Fax: 305-865-5150
Email: info@chopin.org
URL: http://www.chopin.org

Goal: To assist pianists in preparing and qualifying for the American National Chopin Piano Competition.
Eligibility: Applicants must be 14 to 17 years old and full-time students studying music and majoring in piano. A completed application, references, audio tapes and career goals are needed to apply. They also charge a $25 application fee. As mentioned, it is not recommended to apply to scholarships that charge a fee.
Target Student: High school and College students.

Amount: $1,000
Number of Awards: Up to 10
Scholarship can be renwed.
Based on Financial Need: No
Deadline: April
Applications are available online.

---

(872) Scholarship Slam

Power Poetry
295 E. 8th Street Suite 3W
New York, NY 10009

Email: help@powerpoetry.org
URL: http://powerpoetry.org/poetry-slams/scholarship

Goal: To acknowledge students who write a slam poem.
Eligibility: Applicants must be 25 years old or younger and U.S. citizens.
Target Student: High school, College and Graduate students.
Amount: $1,000
Number of Awards: 1
Based on Financial Need: No
Deadline: November
Applicants must join the website and submit their poem.

---

(873) Scholarships for Military Children

Defense Commissary Agency
Attn: OC
1300 E. Avenue
Fort Lee, VA 23801

Phone: 804-734-8860
Email: info@militaryscholar.org
URL: http://www.militaryscholar.org

Goal: To assist the children of military personnel.

Eligibility: Applicants must be the unmarried dependents of military personnel (active duty, reserve, retired or deceased) who are under 21 (23 if they are full time students) and enrolled in the Defense Enrollment Eligibility Reporting System Database. Applicants must be enrolled or plan to enroll in a full time undergraduate degree program with a GPA of 3.0 or higher. If the applicants is in a 2-year college the program they are enrolled in must allow for direct transfers into four year programs. Applicants must also not be recipients of full scholarships or be accepted into the U.S. Military Academy.
Target Student: High school and College students.
Amount: $1,500
Number of Awards: Varies
Based on Financial Need: No
Deadline: February
Applications are available online.

---

(874) Scholarships for Student Leaders

National Association for Campus Activities
13 Harbison Way
Columbia, SC 29212

Phone: 803-732-6222
Fax: 803-749-1047
Email: info@naca.org
URL: http://www.naca.org

Goal: To help develop professionals in campus activiites.
Eligibility: Applicants must be current undergraduate students involved in campus leadership and they must have made significant contributions to their campus community and shown leadership skills.
Target Student: College and Adult students.
Amount: Varies
Number of Awards: Varies
Based on Financial Need: No

Deadline: November
Applications are available online.

---

(875) Scholarships to Oslo International Summer School

Sons of Norway Foundation
1455 West Lake Street
Minneapolis, MN 55408

Phone: 800-945-8851
Fax: 612-827-0658
Email: foundation@sofn.com
URL: http://www.sofn.com

Goal: To assist students who attend Oslo International Summer School.
Eligibility: Applicants must be admitted to Oslo International Summer School and be Sons of Norway members or children or grandchildren of members (must be members for one year prior to application). Application is based on the essay, GPA, letters of recommendation and financial need.
Target Student: College, Graduate and Adult students.
Amount: $1,500
Number of Awards: 2
Based on Financial Need: Yes
Deadline: March
Applications are available online.

---

(876) Scholastic Art and Writing Awards

Scholastic
557 Broadway
New York, NY 10012

Phone: 212-343-6100
Fax: 212-389-3939
Email: a&wgeneralinfo@scholastic.com
URL: http://www.artandwriting.org

Goal: To assist creative young writers and artists.

Eligibility: Applicants must be in grades 7 to 12 in a U.S. or Canadian school. Applicants must submit writing or art to one of the following categories: dramatic scripts, general writing, humor, journalism, nonfiction, novel, personal essay, poetry, science fiction, short story and short short story.
Target Student: Junior high and younger, High school students.
Amount: Up to $10,000
Number of Awards: Varies
Based on Financial Need: No
Deadline: December
Applications are available online.

---

(877) Schwan's Food Service Scholarship

Child Nutrition Foundation
Scholarship Committee
700 S. Washington Street
Suite 300
Alexandria, VA 22314

Phone: 703-739-3900
Email: jcurtis@schoolnutrition.org
URL: http://www.schoolnutrition.org

Goal: To assist those entering the foodservice industry.
Eligibility: Applicants or the parents of applicants must be School Nutrition Association members for a minimum of one year and working towards a career in school foodservice.
Target Student: High school, College, Graduate and Adult students.
Amount: Up to $2,500
Number of Awards: Varies
Scholarship can be renewed.
Based on Financial Need: No
Deadline: April
Applications are available online.

---

(878) Seabee Memorial Scholarship

Seabee Memorial Scholarship Association
P.O. Box 6574
Silver Spring, MD 20916

Phone: 301-570-2850
Email: smsa@erols.com
URL: http://www.seabee.org

Goal: To assist the children of past, present, active, reserve or retired Seabees.
Eligibility: Applicants must be the children or grandchildren of regular, reserve, retired or deceased officers or enlisted personnel who have or are now serving with the Navel Construction Force or Naval Civil Engineer Corps. This scholarship is specifically for bachelors degrees.
Target Student: High school, College or Adult students.
Amount: Varies
Number of Awards: Varies
Based on Financial Need: No
Deadline: April
Applications are available online or by written request.

---

(879) Second Chance Scholarship Contest

American Fire Sprinkler Association
12750 Merit Drive
Suite 350
Dallas, TX 75251

Phone: 214-349-5965
Fax: 214-343-8898
Email: acampbell@firesprinkler.org
URL: http://www.afsascholarship.org

Goal: To assist students in paying for educational costs.
Eligibility: Applicants must be U.S citizens or legal residents, high school graduates or GED recipients who are enrolled at a college or university by the spring of the upcoming academic year. The award is determined by random drawing.

Target Student: College, Graduate and Adult students.
Amount: $1,000
Number of Awards: 5
Based on Financial Need: No
Deadline: August
Applicants must read an article on fire sprinklers and take a ten question test. The number of correct responses is the number of entries that are made.

---

(880) Senior Fellowship Program

National Gallery of Art
2000B South Club Drive
Landover, MD 20785

Phone: 202-842-6482
Fax: 202-789-3026
URL:http://www.nga.gov/resources/casva.htm

Goal: To assist scholars of visual arts with fellowships.
Eligibility: Applicants should have their Ph.D. for at least five years, or have an equivalent record of accomplishments at the time of the application. Applicants must submit an application, proposal, copies of publications and three letters of recommendation. All fellowships are for full-time research in Washington and winners are expected to participate in activities. The following fellowships are awarded each year: Paul Mellow Fellowship, Frese Senior Fellowship, 4 to 6 Ailsa Mellow Bruce and Samuel H. Kress Senior Fellowships. Bot the Paul Mellon and Ailsa Mellon Bruce Senior Fellowships are for study in history, theory and criticism of viual arts of any geographical area from any period. The Frese Senior Fellowship is for history, theory and critiscism of sculpture, prints, drawings or decorative arts from any area or period.
Target Student: Graduate and Adult students.
Amount: Up to $50,000

Number of Awards: 5-7
Based on Financial Need: No
Deadline: October
Applications are available online.

---

(881) Sergeant Major Douglas R. Drum Memorial Scholarship Fund

American Military Association
5436 Peru Street
Suite 1
Plattsburgh, NY 12901

Phone: 800-424-2969
Fax: 518-324-5204
Email: info@amra1973.org
URL: http://www.amra1973.org

Goal: To assist AMRA members, their spouses, children and grandchildren with educational expenses.
Eligibility: Applicants must be full time students who are pursuing or planning to pursue an undergraduate degree at a two year or four year college or university.
Target Student: High school, College or Adult students.
Amount: Varies
Number of Awards: Varies
Based on Financial Need: No
Deadline: March
Applications are available online.

---

(882) Shawn Carter Foundation Scholarship

Shawn Carter Foundation

Email: scsfapplicant@shawncartersf.com
URL: http://www.shawncartersf.com

Goal: To assist students enrolled at vocational trade schools.
Eligibility: Applicants must be high school seniors or college students who are between 18 and 25 years old with a GPA of 2.5 of higher.

Target Student: High school or College students.
Amount: $1,500 - $2,500
Number of Awards: Varies
Based on Financial Need: No
Deadline: May
Applications are available online.

---

(883) Shell/CAPT Process Technology Scholarship

Center for the Advancement of Process Technology
1200 Aubrun Road
Texas City, CA 94122

Phone: 409-938-1211
Fax: 409-938-1285
Email: sturnbough@com.edu
URL: http://www.captech.org

Goal: To assist students who are working towards a career in chemical, mechanicla or physical process technology.
Eligibility: Applicants mus tbe U.S. citizens or authorized to work full-time in the U.S. Applicants must be enrolled or planning to enroll in a two-year degree in electrical technology, mechanical technology, process technology, compression technology or instrumentation technology with a 2.5 GPA or higher.
Target Student: High school, College and Adult students.
Amount: Up to $2,500
Number of Awards: Varies
Scholarship can be renewed.
Based on Financial Need: No
Deadline: May
Applications are available online. A completed application, transcript and two letters of recommendation are required to apply.

---

(884) Shepherd Scholarship

Ancient and Accepted Scottish Rite of Freemansonry Southern Jurisdiction
1733 16th Street NW
Washington, DC 20009

Phone: 202-232-3579
Fax: 202-464-0487
URL: http://www.srmason-sj.org

Goal: To assist students pursuing degrees related to serving the country.
Eligibility: Applicants need to have accepted enrollment in a college or university. The award is based on dedication, ambition, academic preparation, financial need and promise of outstanding performace. Applicants do not need to be Masons or related to Masons.
Target Student: High school, College and Adult students.
Amount: $1,500
Number of Awards: Varies
Scholarship can be renewed.
Based on Financial Need: Yes
Deadline: April
Applications are available online. A completed application, transcripts and a maximum of four letters of recommendation are required.

---

(885) Sheryl A. Horak Memorial Scholarship

Explorers Learning for Life
P.O. Box 152079
Irving, TX 75015

Phone: 972-580-2433
Fax: 972-580-2137
Email: pchestnu@lflmail.org
URL:http://www.learningforlife.org/exploring

Goal: To assist students who are pursuing careers in law enforcement.

Eligibility: Applicants must be in their senior year of high school and members of a Law Enforcement Explorer post.
Target Student: High school students.
Amount: $1,000
Number of Awards: 1
Based on Financial Need: No
Deadline: March
Applications are available online. A completed application, three letters of recommendation and an essy are required to apply.

---

(886) Shields-Gillespie Scholarship

American Orff-Schulwerk Association
P.O. Box 391089
Cleveland, OH 44139

Phone: 440-543-5366
Email: info@aosa.org
URL: http://www.aosa.org

Goal: To assist teachers (pre-K and kindergarten) with program funding, instruments and training.
Eligibility: Applicants must be a member of AOSA and be U.S. citizens or have lived in the U.S. for the past five years.
Target Student: College, Graduate and Adult students.
Amount: Varies
Number of Awards: Varies
Based on Financial Need: No
Deadline: January
Applications are available for AOSA members online.

---

(887) Short-Term Travel Grants

International Research and Exchanges Board
2121 K Street NW
Suite 700
Washington, DC 20037

Phone: 202-628-8188

Fax: 202-628-8189
Email: irex@irex.org
URL: http://www.irex.org

Goal: To assist U.S. postdoctoral students and those with other graduate degrees with expenses to travel to Europe and Eurasia.
Eligibility: Applicants must have a Ph.D. or terminal degree and be U.S. citizens or legal residents for a minimum of three years prior to applying for the grant. The grant provides for eight weeks of independent research on projects that contriute to the knowledge of political, economic and cultural development in the area being studied.
Target Student: Graduate and Adult students.
Amount: Unknown
Number of Awards: Varies
Based on Financial Need: No
Deadline: February
Applications are available online.

---

(888) Shut Up and Sweat Athletic Gear Student Athlete Annual Scholarship

No Excuses Wear
c/o Student Athlete Scholarship Committee
976 Lake Isabella Way
San Jose, CA 95123

Phone: 408-927-7027
Email: noexcuseswear@yahoo.com
URL: http://www.noexcuseswear.com

Goal: To assist college bound high school students.
Eligibility: Applicants must be high school seniors who are athletes with a GPA of 3.0 or higher.
Target Student: High school students.
Amount: Varies
Number of Awards: Varies
Based on Financial Need: No
Deadline: August

Application instructions are available online. A nomination letter, transcripts and a list of extracurricular activities are required.

(889) Siemens Awards for Advanced Placement

Siemens Foundation
170 Wood Avenue South
Iselin, NJ 8330

Phone: 877-822-5233
Fax: 732-603-5890
Email: foundation.us@siemens.com
URL: http://www.siemens-foundation.org

Goal: To assist outstanding Advanced Placement students.
Eligibility: Students do not apply for this award but are chosen by the College Board based on their AP test scores. The award is given to those with the greatest number of scores of 5 on eight AP science and math exams.
Target Student: High school students.
Amount: $2,000-$5,000
Number of Awards: 102
Based on Financial Need: No
Deadline: Varies
Applications are not requried for this award.

(890) Signet Classic Student Scholarship Essay Contest

Penguin Group
Academic Marketing Department
Signet Classic Student Scholarship
375 Hudson Street
New York, NY 10014

URL:http://us.penguingroup.com/static/html/services-academic/essayhome.html

Goal: To aknowledge high school students for their essays on literature.
Eligibility: Applicants must be high school juniors or seniors and submit an essay on one of five topics that are selected by the sponsor regarding a piece of literature. Each English teacher may submit one junior and one senior essay.
Target Student: High school students.
Amount: $1,000
Number of Awards: 5
Based on Financial Need: No
Deadline: April
English teachers or the parent of a home schooled student may submit essays.

(891) Simon Youth Foundation Community Scholarship

Simon Youth Foundation
225 W. Washington Street
Indianapolis, IN 46204

Phone: 800-509-3676
Fax: 317-263-2371
Email: syf@simon.com
URL: http://www.syf.org

Goal: To assist students who live in communities with Simon properties.
Eligibility: Applicants must be high school seniors who are planning to attend a two year or four year college or university or tech/vocational school full time. The award is based on financial need, academic performance, potential, participation in school and community activities, honors and awards.
Target Student: High school students.
Amount: $1,400 - $28,000
Number of Awards: Varies
Based on Financial Need: Yes
Deadline: March
Applications are available online. Only the first 3,000 applications received will be considered.

(892) Sinfonia Foundation Scholarship

Sinfonia Foundation
Scholarship Committee
10600 Old State Road
Evansville, IN 47711

Phone: 800-473-2649 x110
Fax:
Email: sef@sinfonia.org
URL: http://www.sinfonia.org/sef/

Goal: To assist collegiate members and chapters of Sinfonia.
Eligibility: Applicants must have completed two semesters of college and be in good academic standing.
Target Student: College and Adult students.
Amount: $1,000 - $5,000
Number of Awards: 3
Based on Financial Need: No
Deadline: February
Applications are available online. A completed application, references and an essay are required to apply.

(893) SOAR Scholarship

Students Overcoming Adversity
Responsibly
P.O. Box 481030
Charlotte, NC 28269

Email: emergedevelopment2@yahoo.com
URL:http://www.adriannemccauley.com/scholarship.html

Goal: To assist students who have overcome adversity.
Eligibility: Applciants must be U.S. citizens who are high school seniors who will graduate in the year of their application.
Target Student: High school students.
Amount: $1,000
Number of Awards: 1
Based on Financial Need: No

Deadline: April
Applications are available online. An completed application and essay are required to apply.

(894) Sons of Union Veterans of the Civil War Scholarships

Sons of Union Veterans of the Civil War
John R. Ertell, Chair
634 Grace Avenue
Spring City, PA 19475

Phone: 610-948-1278
Email: jertell@verizon.net
URL: http://www.suvcw.org

Goal: To assist students who are associated with the Sons of Union Veterans of the Civil War with educational expenses.
Eligibility: Male applicants must be members or associates of the Sons of Union Veterans of the Civil War. Females applicants must be daughters or granddaughters of members or associates and current members of the Women's Relief corps, Ladies of the Grand Army Republic, Daughters of the Union Veterans of the Civil War 1861-1865 or Auxiliary to the Sons of Union Veterans of the Civil War. Applicants must rank in the top 25% of their graduating class and completed school and community service.
Target Student: High school, College and Adult students.
Amount: $1,000
Number of Awards: 2
Based on Financial Need: No
Deadline: March
Applications are available online.

(895) Sorantin Competition

San Angelo Symphony
Sorantin Award
P.O. Box 5922

San Angelo, TX 76902

Phone: 325-658-5877
Fax: 325-653-1045
Email: assistant@sanangelosymphony.org
URL:http://www.sanangelosymphony.org

Goal: To assist musical performers.
Eligibility: There are two divisions in which you can compete strings and piano. A winner and runner up are selected from each division and the winner recieves and extra $3,000 and performs at the San Angelo Symphony. A $75 application fee is required to apply, as as mentioned it is not recommened to apply to scholarships that cost money.
Target Student: Junior high and younger, High school, College, Graduate and Adult students.
Amount: $1,000 - $3,000
Number of Awards: Varies
Based on Financial Need: No
Deadline: October
Applications are available online.

---

(896) Specialty Equipment Market Association (SEMA) Memorial Scholarship

Specialty Equipment Market Association
1575 S. Valley Vista Drive
Diamond Bar, CA 91765

Phone: 909-396-0289
Fax: 909-860-0184
Email: education@sema.org
URL: http://www.sema.org

Goal: To assist students working towards careers in automotive aftermarket.
Eligibility: Applicants must have demonstrated financial need, a GPA of 2.5 or higher and be pursuing a career in the automotive aftermarket or a related field.
Target Student: College and Adult students.
Amount: $1,000 - $4,000

Number of Awards: Varies
Based on Financial Need: No
Deadline: April
Applications are available online.

---

(897) Sportquest All-American Scholarships for Females

Sportquest All-American Program
P.O. Box 53433
Indianapolis, IN 46253

Phone: 317-270-9495
Fax: 317-244-0495
Email: info@allamericanaward.org
URL: http://www.allamericanaward.org

Goal: To assist Christian athletes.
Eligibility: Applicants must be one of the top three female Christian atheltes in their high school graduating class and be nominated by their schools. Applicants must have a GPA of 3.0 or higher and be current high school sophomores or above.
Target Student: High school students.
Amount: $1,500
Number of Awards: 6
Based on Financial Need: No
Deadline: March
Applications are available online.

---

(898) Sportquest All-American Scholarships for Females

Sportquest All-American Program
P.O. Box 53433
Indianapolis, IN 46253

Phone: 317-270-9495
Fax: 317-244-0495
Email: info@allamericanaward.org
URL: http://www.allamericanaward.org

Goal: To assist Chirstian athletes.

Eligibility: Applicants must be one of the top male female Christian atheltes in their high school graduating class and be nominated by their schools. Applicants must have a GPA of 3.0 or higher and be current high school sophomores or above.
Target Student: High school students.
Amount: $1,500
Number of Awards: 6
Based on Financial Need: No
Deadline: March
Applications are available online.

---

(899) SPS Future Teacher Scholarship

Society of Physics Students
One Physics Ellipse
College Park, MD 20740

Phone: 301-209-3007
Fax: 301-209-0839
Email: sps@aip.org
URL:http://www.spsnational.org/programs/scholarships

Goal: To assist students majoring in physics who are participating in a teacher education program and intend to pursue a career in physics education.
Eligibility: Applicants must be members of SPS and intend to become physics teachers. Applicants must be undergraduate physics majors in their junior or senior year at the time of application.
Target Student: College and Adult students.
Amount: $2,000
Number of Awards: 1
Based on Financial Need: No
Deadline: February
Applications are available online or from SPS chapter advisors.

---

(900) SSPI Scholarship Program

Society of Satellite Professionals International
Tamara Bond
55 Broad Street
14th Floor
New York, NY 10004

Phone: 212-809-5199
Fax: 212-825-0075
Email: rbell@sspi.org
URL: http://www.sspi.org

Goal: To assist high school, undergraduates and graduate students in satellite-related disciplines.
Eligibility: Applicants must be high school seniors, undergraduate or graduate students, members of SSPI, and studying satellite-related technologies, policies or appliations. There are a number of scholarships with different requierments such as financial need, race, gender and GPA.
Target Student: High school, College, Graduate and Adult students.
Amount: $2,500 - $3,500
Number of Awards: Varies
Based on Financial Need: Some
Deadline: May
Applications are available online.

---

(901) STA Travel Inc. Scholarship

Foundation for Global Scholars
12050 North Pecos Street
Suite 320
Westminster, CO 80234

Phone: 303-502-7256
Email:kbrockwell@foundationforglobalscholars.org
URL:http://www.foundationforglobalscholars.org

Goal: To assist students who want to study abroad.

Eligibility: Applciants must be U.S. or Canadian citizens who are currently attending a North American college or university. Applicants must be able to apply transfer credits from studying abroad to their degree program. Applicants must be majoring in foreign language, international business, travel, tourism, international studies, film art or photography.
Target Student: College and Adult students.
Amount: Varies
Number of Awards: Varies
Based on Financial Need: No
Deadline: Varies
Applications are available online. A completed application, transcripts and essay are required to apply.

---

(902) Standout Student College Scholarship

College Peas LLC
1210 Forest Avenue
Highland Park, IL 60035

Phone: 847-681-0698
URL: http://www.collegepeas.com

Goal: To assist college bound high school students whose interests make them stand out from their peers.
Eligibility: Appicants must be current high school students with a GPA of 2.0 or higher and plan to enroll in a four year college or university full time.
Target Student: High school students.
Amount: $500
Number of Awards: Varies
Based on Financial Need: No
Deadline: January
Applications are available online. A completed application a and essay are required to apply.

---

(903) Stella Blum Research Grant

Costume Society of America
Ann Wass
5903 60th Avenue
Riverdale, MD 20737

Phone: 800-272-9447
Fax: 908-359-7619
Email:national.office@costumesocietyamerica.com
URL:http://www.costumesocietyamerica.com

Goal: To assist CSA members working in the North American costume field.
Eligibility: Applicants must be accepted into an undergraduate or graduate program at an accredited college or university, be members of the Costume Society of America and be performing a research project related to North American costume. Applications are evaluated based on topic, feasibility, time frame, methodology, bibliography, budget, applicant's qualifications and how the research will impact the costume field.
Target Student: High school, College, Graduate and Adult students.
Amount: $2,000 and a $500 travel stipend.
Number of Awards: 1
Based on Financial Need: No
Deadline: May
Applications are available online.

---

(904) Stephen D. Pisinski Memorial Scholarship

Public Relations Student Society of America
33 Maiden Lane
11th Floor
New York, NY 10038

Phone: 212-460-1474
Fax: 212-995-0757
Email: prssa@prsa.org
URL: http://www.prssa.org

Goal: To assist students majoring in journalism, public relations and communications.
Eligibility: Applicants must be members of the Public Relations Student Society of America and be undergraduate juniors or seniors majoring in journalism, public relations or communications with a GPA of 3.3 or higher.
Target Student: College and Adult students.
Amount: $1,500
Number of Awards: 1
Based on Financial Need: No
Deadline: June
Applications are available online. A completed application, transcript, resume, essay, two letters of recommendation and two writing samples are required to apply.

---

(905) Stephen J. Brady STOP Hunger Scholarship

Sodexo Foundation
9801 Washingtonian Boulevard
Gaithersburg, MD 20878

Phone: 800-763-3946
stophunger@sodexofoundation.org
URL: http://www.sodexofoundation.org

Goal: To assist students who have been active in the movement to end hunger.
Eligibility: Applicants must be U.S. citizens or permanent residents who are in kindergarten to graduate school enrolled at an accredited U.S. institution. Applicants must have been active in at least one unpaid volunteer effort to end hunger within the past 12 months. Previous recipients and Sodexo employees are not eligible for the award.
Target Student: Junior high students or younger, High school, College, Graduate and Adult students.
Amount: $5,000
Number of Awards: Varies

Based on Financial Need: No
Deadline: December
Applications are available online. A completed application and supporting documents are required to apply.

---

(906) Steven Hymans Extended Stay Scholarship

American Hotel and Lodging Educational Foundation
1201 New York Avenue NW
Suite 600
Washington, DC 20005

Phone: 202-289-3188
Fax: 202-289-3199
Email: chammond@ahlef.org
URL: http://www.ahlef.org

Goal: To provide educational funds to help teach students about the needs of extended stay visitors in the lodging industry.
Eligibility: Applicants must be undergraduate students with experience working at an extended stay facility and interested in pursuing a career in that segment of the lodging industry.
Target Student: College and Adult students.
Amount: $1,000 - $3,000
Number of Awards: Varies
Based on Financial Need: No
Deadline: May
Applications are available online.

---

(907) Still Photographer Scholarship

National Press Photographers Association
Still Photographer Scholarship
Bill Sanders
Photo Editor, Asheville Citizen-Times
P.O. Box 2090
Asheville, NC 28802

Email: wsanders@citizen-times.com

URL: http://www.nppa.org

Goal: To honor the photojournalism profession.
Eligibility: Applicants must have completed one year as a full-time student at a four-year college or university with completed courses in photojournalism. Applicants can apply to as many NPPA scholarships as they wish but they can only win one.
Target Student: College and Adult students.
Amount: $2,000
Number of Awards: Varies
Based on Financial Need: Yes
Deadline: March
Applications are available online.

---

(908) Stillman-Kelley Awards

National Federation of Music Clubs
Stillman-Kelley Award
Sue Breuer
4404 Travis Country
Cicle B4
Austin, TX 78735

Phone: 512-892-5633
URL: http://www.nfmc-music.org

Goal: To assist young musicians and composers.
Eligibility: Applicants must be under the age of 17, members of the National Federation of Music Clubs and instrumentalists. The award is given in the Northeastern and Southeastern in even years and Central and Western in odd years.
Target Student: High school students.
Amount: $500 - $1,000
Number of Awards: 8
Based on Financial Need: No
Deadline: February
Applications are available online.

---

(909) Stokes Educational Scholarship Program

National Security Agency
9800 Savage Road, Suite 6779
Ft. George G. Meade, MD 20755

Phone: 410-854-4725
URL: http://www.nsa.gov

Goal: To recruit individuals, especially minority high school seniors, with skills that are useful to the NSA.
Eligibility: Applicants must be high school seniors at the time of the application, be U.S. citizens, have a GPA of 3.0 or higher, with a minimum ACT score or 25 or SAT score of 1600. Applicants must have demonstrated leadership skills and planning to major in computer science or computer electrical engineering.
Target Student: High school students.
Amount: Full tuition, fees, salary and summer employment.
Number of Awards: Varies
Scholarship can be renewed.
Based on Financial Need: No
Deadline: November
Applications are available online.

---

(910) Stuart Cameron and Margaret McLeod Memorial Scholarship

Institute of Management Accountants
10 Paragon Drive
Montvale, NJ 7645

Phone: 800-638-4427
Email: students@imanet.org
URL: http://www.imanet.org

Goal: To assist students of management accounting.

Eligibility: Applicants must be full-time or part-time or graduate students, IMA student members and have declared a four or five year program in management accounting, financial management or information technology in which they plan to pursue as a career.
Target Student: College, Graduate and Adult students.
Amount: $5,000
Number of Awards: 1
Based on Financial Need: No
Deadline: February
Applications are available online. A completed application, resume, transcripts, two letters of recommendations and statement is required to apply.

(911) Stuck at Prom Scholarship

Henkel Consumer Adhesives
32150 Just Imagine Drive
Avon, OH 44011

URL: http://www.stuckatprom.com

Goal: To acknowledge students for their creative use of duct tape.
Eligibility: Applicants must attend high school prom as a couple wearing attire made of duct tape. The award is given to the most original attire.
Target Student: High school students.
Amount: $500 - $3,000
Number of Awards: Varies
Based on Financial Need: No
Deadline: June
Applications are available online. A prom picture and contact information are required ot apply.

(912) Student Academy Awards

Academy of Motion Picture Arts and Sciences
8949 Wilshire Boulevard
Beverly Hills, CA 90211

Phone: 310-247-3000
Email: rmiller@oscars.org
URL: http://www.oscars.org

Goal: To assist filmmakers without professional experience.
Eligibility: Applicants must be full time students at a U.S. college, university, fill or art school. The films for this award must be made as part of a course curriculum and can be in the categories of alternative, animation, documentary or narrative. The slection of the award is based on the films production quality, originality, entertainment and resourcefulness.
Target Student: College, Graduate and Adult students.
Amount: Varies
Number of Awards: Varies
Based on Financial Need: No
Deadline: April
Applications are available online.

(913) Student Achievement Grants

NEA Foundation
1201 16th Street NW
Suite 416
Washington, DC 20036

Phone: 202-822-7840
Fax: 202-822-7779
Email: info-neafoundation@list.nea.org
URL: http://www.neafoundation.org

Goal: To encourage the academic achievement of U.S. students by providing money for teachers.
Eligibility: Applicants must be current public K-12 teachers or support professionals or faculty or staff at a public higher ed school. Grant preference is given

to those working with economically disadvantaged students. Money can be used for materials, supplies, equipment, transportation, software or scholars-in-residence. Professional developmetn can be covered in some situations.
Target Student: Graduate and Adult students.
Amount: $2,000 - $5,000
Number of Awards: Varies
Based on Financial Need: No
Deadline: February, June and October. Applications are available online.

(914) Student Activist Awards

Freedom from Religion Foundation
P.O. Box 750
Madison, WI 53701

Phone: 608-256-5800
Email: info@ffrf.org
URL: http://www.ffrf.org

Goal: To assist high school and college activists.
Eligibility: The selection of the award is based on activism for free thought and/or separation of church and state.
Target Student: High school, College and Adult students.
Amount: $1,000
Number of Awards: Varies
Based on Financial Need: No
Deadline: Varies
Contact the organization for more information.

(915) Student Design Competition

International Housewares Association
6400 Shafer Court
Suite 650
Rosemont, IL 60018

Phone: 847-292-4200
Fax: 847-292-4211

URL: http://www.housewares.org

Goal: To acknolwedge and encourage young and promising designers in the housewares industry.
Eligibility: Applicants must be enrolled undergraduate or graduate students in an IDSA-affiliated college or university.
Target Student: College, Graduate and Adult students.
Amount: Varies
Number of Awards: Varies
Based on Financial Need: No
Deadline: December
Applications are available online.

(916) Student Paper Competition

American Criminal Justice Association
P.O. Box 601047
Sacramento, CA 95860

Phone: 916-484-6553
Fax: 916-488-227
Email: acjalae@aol.com
URL: http://www.acjalae.org

Goal: To encourage students to study criminal justice.
Eligibility: Applicants must be undergraduate or graduate members of the American Criminal Justice Association - Lambda Alpha Epsilon and submit an original paper on the topic of criminal justice, law enforcement, criminology, juvenile justice, courts, corrections, prevention, planning and evaluation or career development and education in criminal justice. Students may apply for membership along with their paper submission.
Target Student: College, Graduate and Adult students.
Amount: $50 - $150
Number of Awards: 9
Based on Financial Need: No
Deadline: January

Applications are available online or by written request.

---

(917) Student Translation Award

American Translators Association
225 Reinekers Lane
Suite 590
Alexandria, VA 22314

Phone: 703-683-6100
Fax: 703-683-6122
Email: ata@atanet.org
URL: http://www.atanet.org

Goal: To encourage translation projects by students.
Eligibility: Applicants must be graduate students or a student group that is attending an accredited college or university in the U.S. Applicants must not be published translators and computer-assisted translations are not eligible. Translations should be froma foreign language into English and the project must have post-grant goals such as publication or teaching material.
Target Student: College, Graduate and Adult students.
Amount: $500
Number of Awards: 1
Based on Financial Need: No
Deadline: June
Applications are available online. To apply applicants must submit a completed entry form, statement of purpose, letter of recommendation, translation sample along with the source language text, proof of permission to publish from the copyright holder and

---

(918) Student with a Disability Scholarship

Americna Speech-Language-Hearing Foundation
2200 Research Boulevard
Rockville, MD 20850

Phone: 301-296-8700
Email: foundation@asha.org
URL: http://www.ashfoundation.org

Goal: To assist graduate students with a disability studying communication sciences and disorders.
Eligibility: Applicants must be full-time graduate students. Master's degree students in a program that is accredited by the Council on Academic Accreditation for Audiology and Speech Pathology. Applicants in doctoral programs do not need to be in an accredited program.
Target Student: Graduate and Adult students.
Amount: $5,000
Number of Awards: 1
Based on Financial Need: No
Deadline: Unknown
Applications are available online. A completed application, transcript, essay, recommendation from a faculty member or workplace committee, reference form and statement of good standing are required to apply.

---

(919) Study Abroad Grants

Honor Society of Phi Kappa Phi
7576 Goodwood Boulevard
Baton Rouge, LA 70806

Phone: 800-804-9880
Fax: 225-388-4900
Email: awards@phikappaphi.org
URL: http://www.phikappaphi.org

Goal: To assist undergraduate students who will study abroad.

Eligibility: Applicants do not need to be Phi Kappa Phi members, but must attend an insitution that has a Phi Kappa Phi chapter. Applicants must have between 30 and 90 credits hours and at least two semesters remaining after their return from their study abroad. Applicants must have already been accepted into a study abroad program and have a GPA of 3.5 of higher.
Target Student: College and Adult students.
Amount: $1,000
Number of Awards: 50
Based on Financial Need: No
Deadline: April
Aplicants are available online. A completed application, personal statement, transcripts, letter of acceptance and two letters of recommendation are required.

(920) Summer Fellowship Program

American Institute for Economic Research
P.O. Box 1000
Attn: Susan Gillette, Assistant to the President
Great Barrington, MA 01230

Phone: 413-528-1216
Fax: 413-528-0103
Email: fellowships@aier.org
URL: http://www.aier.org

Goal: To assist college eniors entering doctoral programs in economics or a related field with summer fellowships.
Eligibility: Applicants must be college seniors who are going to enter a doctoral program in economics or related field.
Target Student: College and Adult students.
Amount: Room and Board in addition to a $500 stipend.
Number of Awards: Varies
Based on Financial Need: No
Deadline: March
Applications are available online.

(921) Summer Graduate Research Fellowships

Institute for Humane Studies at George Mason University
331 N. Fairfax Drive
Suite 440
Arlington, VA 22201

Phone: 800-697-8799
Fax: 703-993-4890
Email: his@gmu.edu
URL: http://www.theihs.org

Goal: To assist graduate students interested in research in the classical liberal tradition.
Eligibility: Applicants must be graduate students in areas related to the classical liberal tradition and should be focusing on a discrete writing transcripts. The award is based on the applicants resume, GRE or LSAT scores and graduate transcripts, writing sample, and research proposal and bibliography for a thesis chapter or publishable paper.
Target Student: Graduate and Adult students.
Amount: $5,000 + travel and housing
Number of Awards: Varies
Based on Financial Need: No
Deadline: Unknown
Applications are available online.

(922) SuperCollege Scholarship

SuperCollege.com
Scholarship Dept. 673
2713 Newlands Avenue
Belmont, CA 94002

Email: supercollege@supercollege.com
URL:
http://www.supercollege.com/scholarship

Goal: To assist high school, college and graduate students with their educational expenses.

Eligibility: Applicants must be high school, college or graduate students in the U.S. who are planning or attending a college or university within the next 12 months. The scholarship can be used of tuition, books, room and board, computers or other educational expenses.

Target Student: High school, College, Graduate and Adult students.

Amount: $1,500

Number of Awards: 1

Based on Financial Need: No

Deadline: March, July, October, December

Applications are available online.

---

(923) Swackhamer Disarmament Video Contest

Nuclear Age Peace Foundation
1187 Coast Village Road
PMB 121, Suite 1
Santa Barabara, CA 93108

Phone: 805-965-3443
Fax: 805-568-0466
URL: http://www.wagingpeace.org

Goal: To assist high school students who create a video about world peace.

Eligibility: Applicants must be high school students from anywhere and submit a video on the sponsor specified topic. The video should be to to three minutes and the award is based on originality, development of point of view, insight, clarity of expression, organization and grammar.

Target Student: High school students.

Amount: $1,000

Number of Awards: Up to 8

Based on Financial Need: No

Deadline: April

Applications are available online.

---

(924) Tackle Hunger Scholarship

Do Something Inc.
24-32 Union Square East
4th Floor
New York, NY 10003

Phone: 212-254-2390
Email: tacklehunger@dosomething.org
URL: http://www.dosomething.org

Goal: To assist students who have organized food drives.

Eligibility: Applicants must be students or a group of students who have organized a food drive in their community. Applicants must have collect at least ten pounds of food and the award is determine by random drawing.

Target Student: High school, College, Graduate and Adult students.

Amount: Up to $1,000

Number of Awards: 1

Based on Financial Need: No

Deadline: December

Application information is available online. A completed food drive and and entry form are required.

---

(925) TACTYC Accounting Scholarship

Teachers of Accounting at Two-Year Colleges
Aims Community College
c/o Lori Hatchell
5401 West 20th Street
Greeley, CO 80632

Email: scholarship@tactyc.org
URL: http://www.tactyc.org

Goal: To assist accounting students working towards a two-year undergraduate degree or are moving to a four year school after completing a two-year degree in accounting.

Eligibility: Applicants must be undergraduate accouting students working towards a two-year degree or pursuing a bachelors degree ater completing a two-year degree in accounting.
Target Student: College and Adult students.
Amount: $1,000
Number of Awards: 4
Based on Financial Need: No
Deadline: March
Applications are available online.

(926) Talbots Scholarship Foundation

Talbots
Scholarship Management Services, Scholarship America
One Scholarship Way
P.O. Box 297
Saint Peter, MN 56082

Phone: 507-931-1682
URL:http://www.talbots.com/scholarship

Goal: To assist women who are returning to college.
Eligibility: Applicants must be female U.S. residents who earned their high school diploma or GED at least 10 years ago and are now enrolling or planning to enroll in an undergraduate four year college or university or vocational or tech school. Only the first 1,000 applicants are considered.
Target Student: College and Adult students.
Amount: $15,000 - $30,000
Number of Awards: 11
Based on Financial Need: No
Deadline: January
Applications are available online.

(927) Taylor/Blakeslee University Fellowships

Council for the Advancement of Science Writing
P.O. Box 910
Hedgesville, WV 25427

Phone: 304-754-6786
Email: diane@nasw.org
URL: http://www.casw.org

Goal: To assist graduate students in science writing.
Eligibility: Applicants must be U.S. citizens enrolled in a U.S. graduate level writing program.
Target Student: Graduate and Adult students.
Amount: $5,000
Number of Awards: Varies
Based on Financial Need: No
Deadline: July
Information is avaiable by contacting the sponsor.

(928) Teacher Education Scholarship Fund

American Montessori Society
281 Park Avenue South
New York, NY 10010

Phone: 212-358-1250
Fax: 212-358-1256
Email: info@amshq.org
URL: http://www.amshq.org

Goal: To assist aspiring Montessori teachers.
Eligibility: Applicants must be accepted, yet not attending an AMS teacher education program.
Target Student: High school, College and Adult students.
Amount: Varies
Number of Awards: Varies
Scholarship can be renewed.
Based on Financial Need: Yes
Deadline: May

Application information is available online. A completed application, personal statement, evidence of financial need and letters of recommendation are required to apply.

(929) Teacher of the Year Award

Veterans of Foreign Wars Teacher of the Year Award
406 W. 34th Street
Kansas City, MO 64111

Phone: 816-968-1117
Fax: 816-968-1149
Email: tbeauchamp@vfw.org
URL: http://www.vfw.org

Goal: To honor the countries best elementary, junior high and high school teachers who teach their student's about citizenship and American history.
Eligibility: Applicants must be current teachers that teach at least half of the school day in the classroom grades K-12.
Target Student: Graduate and Adult students.
Amount: $1,000
Number of Awards: 3
Based on Financial Need: No
Deadline: November
Application information is available online. Initial nominations must be sent to the local VFW.

(930) Telluride Association Summer Programs

Telluride Association
217 West Avenue
Ithaca, NY 14850

Phone: 607-273-5011
Fax: 607-272-2667
Email: telluride@cornell.edu
URL: http://www.tellurideassociation.org

Goal: To provide high school students with a college level summer experience.
Eligibility: Applicants must be juniors in high school. A applicants from a variety of socio-economic backgrounds. The award covers tuition and room and board during summer programs in New York, Texas and Michigan. Students apply by taking the PSAT/NMSQT test and scoring in the top 1 percent or by being nominated by a teacher or counselor.
Target Student: High school students.
Amount: Tuition for a summer program.
Number of Awards: 64
Based on Financial Need: No
Deadline: January
Applications are sent to students that have been nominated.

(931) The Lowe's Scholarship

Lowe's Company
1000 Lowe's Boulevard
Mooreseville, NC 28117

Phone: 800-44-LOWES
URL: http://www.careers.lowes.com/college_recruiting_scholarship.aspx

Goal: To assist high school students in communities where Lowe's opperates stores to pay for educational expenses.
Eligibility: Applicants must be high school seniors planning to enroll in an accredited two or four year college or university in the U.S. Selection of the award is based on leadership abilties, community involvement and academic acheivement.
Target Student: High school students.
Amount: $2,500
Number of Awards: 140
Scholarship can be renewed.
Based on Financial Need: No
Deadline: February
Applications are available online.

(932) Thelma A. Robinson Award in Ballet

National Federation of Music Clubs
Anne Cruxent
5530 Lajeune Road
Coral Gables, FL 33146

Phone: 330-638-4003
Fax: 317-638-0503
Email: acruxent@bellsouth.net
URL: http://www.nfmc-music.org

Goal: To assist students who are also ballet dancers.
Eligibility: Applicants must be 13 to 16 years old and members of the NFMC.
Target Student: Junior high and younger and High school students.
Amount: $2,500
Number of Awards: 1
Based on Financial Need: No
Deadline: October
Applications are available online.

(933) Thespian Scholarships

Educational Theatre Association
2343 Auburn Avenue
Cincinati, OH 45219

Phone: 513-421-3900
URL: http://www.edta.org

Goal: To support student thespians.
Eligibility: Applicants must be seniors in high school and a member of the International Thespian Society and planning to major or minor in communivative arts in college.
Target Student: High school students.
Amount: Up to $4,500
Number of Awards: Varies
Based on Financial Need: No
Deadline: May
Applications are available online.

(934) Thomas H. Steel Fellowship Fund

Pride Law Fund
P.O. Box 2602
San Francisco, CA 94104

Email: info@pridelawfund.org
URL: http://www.pridelawfund.org

Goal: To assist law students with a project serving the lesbian, gay, bisexual and transgender community.
Eligibility: Applicants must be students in their final year of law school or law school graduates who finished school in the past three years. The award is based on the quality and scope of the project, the applicants public service activities and their relation to the LGBT community.
Target Student: Graduate and Adult students.
Amount: Up to $35,000
Number of Awards: 1
Based on Financial Need: No
Deadline: April
Applications are available online. A completed application, resume, project description, two reference letters, transcript, timetable and budget are required to apply.

(935) TLMI Four Year Colleges/Full-Time Students Scholarship

Tag and Label Manufacturers Institute Inc.
1 Blackburn Center
Cloucester, MA 01930

Phone: 978-282-1400
Fax: 978-282-3238
Email: office@tlmi.com
URL: http://www.tlmi.com

Goal: To assist students planning to pursue a career in tag and label manufacturing.

Eligibility: Applicants must have a demonstrated interest in the tag and label manufacturing industry and be taking the correct courses for this career at an accredited four-year college. Applicants must be full-time sophomores or juniors with a 3.0 or higher GPA.
Target Student: College and Adult students.
Amount: $5,000
Number of Awards: Up to 6
Based on Financial Need: No
Deadline: March
Applications are available online. A completed application, personal statement, and three letters of recommendation are required to apply.

(936) TLMI Two-Year College or Technical Degree Program Scholarship

Tag and Label Manufacturers Institute Inc.
1 Blackburn Center
Cloucester, MA 1930

Phone: 978-282-1400
Fax: 978-282-3238
Email: office@tlmi.com
URL: http://www.tlmi.com

Goal: To assist students enrolled in a flexographic printing program of study.
Eligibility: Applicants must be full-time students a flexographic printing program at a two-year college or a degree-granting technical school with a GPA of 3.0 or higher with demonstrated interest in pursuing a career in the tag and label industry.
Target Student: College and Adult students.
Amount: $1,000
Number of Awards: 4
Based on Financial Need: No
Deadline: March
Applications are available online. A completed application, transcript and personal statement are required to apply.

(937) Tobin Sorenson Physical Education Scholarship

Pi Lambda Theta
P.O. Box 6626
Bloomington, IN 47407

Phone: 800-487-3411
Fax: 812-339-3462
Email: office@pilambda.org
URL: http://www.pilambda.org

Goal: To assist future K-12 physical education teacher.
Eligibility: Applicants must be working towards a career as a physical education teacher, adapted physical education teacher, coach, recreational therapist, dance therapist or realted profession at the K-12 level, have 3.5 GPA or higher and have demonstrated leadership abilities and involvement in extracurricular activities.
Target Student: College and Adult students.
Amount: $1,000
Number of Awards: 1
Based on Financial Need: No
Deadline: April
Applications are available online.

(938) Tom and Judith Comstock Scholarship

American Radio Relay League Foundation
225 Main Street
Newington, CT 6111

Phone: 860-594-0397
Fax: 860-594-0259
Email: foundation@arrl.org
URL: http://www.arrlf.org

Goal: To asisst ham radio operators with their educational expenses.

Eligibility: Applicants must have any class of ham radio license, be residents of Texas or Okalahoma and be high school seniors that have been accepted at a two or four-year college or univeristy.
Target Student: High school students.
Amount: $2,000
Number of Awards: 1
Based on Financial Need: No
Deadline: February
Applications are available online but must be submitted via mail.

---

(939) Tourism Cares Academic Scholarship Program

Tourism Cares
275 Turnpike Street
Suite 307
Canton, MA 02021

Phone: 781-821-5990
Fax: 781-821-8949
Email: scholarships@tourismcares.org
URL: http://www.tourismcares.org

Goal: To assist undergraduate and graduate students who are studying hospitality, tourism, travel or a realted field at an accredited school.
Eligibility: Applicants must be U.S. citizens enrolled as part-time or full-time students in the upcoming fall semester. There are many scholarship opportunties available and specific criteria for each can be found online.
Target Student: College and Adult students.
Amount: $1,000 - $5,000
Number of Awards: 59
Based on Financial Need: No
Deadline: April
Applications are available online.

---

(940) Tourism Cares Sustainable Tourism Scholarship

Tourism Cares
275 Turnpike Street
Suite 307
Canton, MA 02021

Phone: 781-821-5990
Fax: 781-821-8949
Email: scholarships@tourismcares.org
URL: http://www.tourismcares.org

Goal: To encourage sustainable tourism and to assist graduate students studying tourism with educational expenses.
Eligibility: Applicants must be enrolled in a graduate tourism program with a GPA of 3.0 or higher. Those in developing countries are encouraged to apply.
Target Student: Graduate and Adult students.
Amount: $1,000
Number of Awards: Varies
Based on Financial Need: No
Deadline: April
Applications are available online.

---

(941) Transatlantic Fellows Program

German Marshall Fund of the United States
1744 R Street NW
Washington, DC 20009

Phone: 202-683-2650
Fax: 202-265-1662
Email: info@gmfus.org
URL: http://www.gmfus.org

Goal: To develop research in foreign policy, international security, trade, and economic development and immigration.
Eligibility: Fellowships are by invitation from GMF and given to policy-practitioners, journalists, academics and businesspeople. The fellowship provides for work in Washington, DC, Brussels and Belgium.
Target Student: Graduate and Adult students.

Amount: Varies
Number of Awards: Varies
Based on Financial Need: No
Deadline: Varies
Contact John K. Glenn at the GMF organization for more information.

---

(942) Translation Prize

American-Scandinavian Foundation
58 Park Avenue
New York, NY 10016

Phone: 212-879-9779
Email: grants@amscan.org
URL: http://www.amscan.org

Goal: To encourage Scandinavian literature to be translated to English.
Eligibility: The award is to the applicant with the best translation of poetry, fiction, drama, or literary prose written by a Scandinavian author in Danish, Finnish, Icelandic, Norwegian or Swedish after 1800. The applicants translation cannot have previously been published in the English language.
Target Student: Junior high or younger, High school, College, Graduate and Adult students.
Amount: $2,000
Number of Awards: 1
Scholarship can be renewed.
Based on Financial Need: No
Deadline: June
Applications are available online.

---

(943) Tri State Surveying and Photogrammetry Kits M. Kunze Memorial Scholarship

American Congress on Surveying and Mapping
6 Montgomery Village Avenue
Suite 403
Gaithersburg, MD 20879

Phone: 240-632-9716
Fax: 240-632-1321
Email: ilse.genovese@acsm.net
URL: http://www.acsm.net

Goal: To assist current and future land surveors who are taking courses in business.
Eligibility: Applicants must be member of the American Congress on Surveying and Mapping, licensed professional land surveyors, certified photogrammetrists, land surveying interns or current full-time land surveying students taking courses in business adminsitration and management.
Target Student: College and Adult students.
Amount: $1,000
Number of Awards: Varies
Based on Financial Need: No
Deadline: February
Applications are available online. A completed application, transcript, personal statement, three letters of recommendation and proof of ACSM are required to apply.

---

(944) TruFit Good Citizenship Scholarship

Citizens Bank

URL:http://www.citizensbank.com/scholarship/

Goal: To assist high school seniors and college students who have volunteered their time.
Eligibility: Applicants must be at least 16 years old and attended or have been accepted into a nationally accredited four year college, university or graduate program.
Target Student: High school, College, Graduate and Adult students.
Amount: $1,000 - $5,000
Number of Awards: 40
Based on Financial Need: No
Deadline: April

Applications are available online. An essay or video are required to apply.

---

(945) Truman Scholar

Truman Scholarship Foundation
712 Jackson Place NW
Washington, DC 20006

Phone: 202-395-4831
Fax: 202-395-6995
Email: office@truman.gov
URL: http://www.truman.gov

Goal: To assist college junior leaders who are planning to pursue a career in government, non-profits, education or other public service with educational expenses.
Eligibility: Applicants must be juniors who are attending an accredited U.S. college or university and be nominated by the school. Applicants must be U.S. citizens or legal residents.
Target Student: College and Adult students.
Amount: Up to $30,000
Number of Awards: Up to 68
Based on Financial Need: No
Deadline: February
Contact the foundation or your school's Truman Faculty Rep.

---

(946) Tuitiion Scholarship Program

Thomas Pniewski, Director of Cultural Affairs
Kosciuszko Foundation
15 East 65th Street
New York, NY 10021

Phone: 212-734-2130 x214
Fax: 212-628-4552
Email: tompkf@aol.com
URL:http://www.thekf.org/kf/about/about_us/

Goal: To assist full-time graduate students in the U.S. and in specified graduate programs in Poland.
Eligibility: Applicants must be U.S. citizens or permanent residents of Polish descent who are starting or continuing their graduate education with a GPA of 3.0 or higher. The award is based on the students achievements, academics, interest in Polish studies or their involvement in the Polish community as well as financial need.
Target Student: College, Graduate and Adult students.
Amount: $1,000 - $7,000
Number of Awards: Varies
Scholarship can be renewed.
Based on Financial Need: Yes
Deadline: January
Applications are available online.

---

(949) U.S JCI Senate Scholarship Grants

U.S. JCI Senate
106 Wedgewood Drive
Carrollton, GA 30117

Email: tom@smipc.net
URL: http://www.usjcisenate.org

Goal: To assist high school students who want to continue their education.
Eligibility: Applicants must be high school seniors who are planning to attend college full time, U.S. ctizens and graduating from a U.S. high school, approved home school or GED test.
Target Student: High school students.
Amount: $1,000
Number of Awards: Varies
Based on Financial Need: No
Deadline: December -January
Applications are available from the guidance office.

---

(948) U.S. Bank Scholarship Program

U.S. Bank
U.S. Bancorp Center
800 Nicollet Mall
Minneapolis, MN 55402

Phone: 800-242-1200
URL: http://www.usbank.com/student-lending/scholarship.html

Goal: To assist high school seniors who plan to attend college.
Eligibility: Applicants must be high school seniors who are planning to attend a college or university or current college freshman, sophomores or juniors who are currently attending full-time an accredited two year or four year college or university and be U.S. citizens or permanent residents. The award is determined by a random drawing.
Target Student: High school, College and Adult students.
Amount: $1,000
Number of Awards: 40
Based on Financial Need: No
Deadline: March
Applications are available online.

(950) UDT-SEAL Scholarship

Naval Special Warfare Foundation
P.O. Box 5965
Virginia Beach, VA 23471

Phone: 757-363-7490
Email: info@nswfoundation.org
URL: http://www.nswfoundation.org

Goal: To assist the dependents of UDT-SEAL Association members.
Eligibility: Applicants must be single dependents of a UDT-SEAL Association member who has served or is serving in the U.S. Armed Forces.
Target Student: High school and College students.
Amount: Varies

Number of Awards: Varies
Based on Financial Need: No
Deadline: March
Applications are available by contacting the NWSF.

(947) Ukulele Festival Hawaii's College Scholarship Program

Ukulele Festival Hawaii
c/o Roy Sakuma Productions Inc.
3555 Harding Avenue, Suite 1
Honolulu, HI 96816

Phone: 808-732-3739
Email: info@roysakuma.net
URL: http://www.roysakuma.net/ukulelefestival

Goal: To assist students who play the ukulele.
Eligibility: Appicants must be Hawaii high school students and plan to attend a four-year college or university in the fall after their graduation.
Target Student: High school students.
Amount: $1,000
Number of Awards: Varies
Based on Financial Need: No
Deadline: March
Applications are available from Roy Sakuma Productions.

(951) Undergraduate Scholarship

International Technology and Enginerring Educators Association
Foundation for Technology and Engineering Educators
1914 Association Drive, Suite 201
Reston, VA 20191

Phone: 703-860-2100
Fax: 703-860-0353
Email: info@iteea.org
URL: http://www.iteaconnect.org

Goal: To assist undergraduate students who are majoring in technology education teacher preparation.
Eligibility: Applicants must be ITEA members with a GPA of 2.5 or higher and full-time undergraduate students.
Target Student: College and Adult students.
Amount: $1,000
Number of Awards: 1
Based on Financial Need: No
Deadline: December
Application information is available online.

---

(952) Undergraduate Scholarships

Radio Television Digital News Association
4121 Plank Road #512
Fredericksburg, VA 22407

Phone: 202-659-6510
Fax: 202-223-4007
Email: stacey@rtdna.org
URL: http://www.rtdna.org

Goal: To acknowledge achievements in electronic journalism.
Eligibility: Applicants must be full-time sophomores or higher in any major with the career goal of working in television or radio news. Applicants can only apply to one RTNDA scholarship.
Target Student: College and Adult students.
Amount: Varies
Number of Awards: Varies
Based on Financial Need: No
Deadline: May
Applications are available online.

---

(953) Undergraduate Scholarships

Sigma Alpha Lota Philanthropies
Director, Undergraduate Scholarships
One Tunnel Road
Asheville, NC 28805

Phone: 828-251-0606
Fax: 825-251-0644
Email: jkpete@cox.net
URL: http://www.sai-national.org

Goal: To assist Sigma Alpha Lota members with demonstrated leadership, academic and musical skills.
Eligibility: Applicants must be active SALP members for at least one year and demonstrate financial need.
Target Student: College and Adult students.
Amount: $1,500- $2,000
Number of Awards: 15
Based on Financial Need: Yes
Deadline: March
Applications are available online.

---

(954) Undergraduate Transfer Scholarship

Jack Kent Cooke Foundation
Undergraduate Transfer Scholarship
44325 Woodridge Parkway
Lansdowne, VA 20176

Phone: 800-498-6478
Fax: 319-337-1204
Email: jkc-u@act.org
URL: http://www.jkcf.org

Goal: To assist community college students so that they may attend a four-year university.
Eligibility: Applicants must be students or recent alumni from an accredited U.S. community or junior college who are planning to pursue a bachelors degree at a four year college or university. Applicants must be nominated by the Jack Kent Cooke Foundation faculty rep at their school. Applicants must have a GPA of 3.5 or higher.
Target Student: College or Adult students.
Amount: Up to $30,000
Number of Awards: 50

Scholarship can be renewed.
Based on Financial Need: No
Deadline: December
Applications are available online and mailed in.

(955) United Daughters of the Confederacy Scholarship

United Daughters of the Confederacy
328 North Boulevard
Richmond, VA 23220

Phone: 804-355-1636
Fax: 804-353-1396
Email: hqud@rcn.com
URL: http://www.hqudc.org

Goal: To assist the descendants of Confederates.
Eligibility: Applicants must be "lineal descendants" of Confederates or other eligible descendants and have a GPA of 3.0 or higher.
Target Student: College, Graduate and Adult students.
Amount: Varies
Number of Awards: Varies
Scholarship can be renewed.
Based on Financial Need: No
Deadline: Varies
Contact the Division Second VP that is listed on the website.

(956) United States Senate Youth Program

William Randolph Hearst Foundation
90 New Montgomery Street
Suite 1212
San Francisco, CA 94105

Phone: 800-841-7048 x4540
Fax: 415-243-0760
Email: ussyp@hearstfdn.org
URL: http://www.hearstfdn.org/ussyp/

Goal: To give students exposure to their government in action.
Eligibility: Applicants must be juniors or seniors in high school who hold an elected position at school or in a civic club. USSYP brings 104 high school delegates together with high level officials from each branch of government for a week long program.
Target Student: High school students.
Amount: $5,000
Number of Awards: 104
Based on Financial Need: No
Deadline: Varies
To apply contact your school principal, counselor or state selection contact.

(957) University Language Services College Scholarship

University Language Services
15 Maiden Lane Suite 300
New York, NY 10038

Phone: 800-419-4601
Fax: 866-662-8048
Email: service@universitylanguage.com
URL: http://www.universitylanguage.com

Goal: To assist college bound high school students.
Eligibility: Applicants must be high school students at an accredited high school. Applicants must submit a photo that they have taken while visiting a college campus along with a description of how the photo shows college life.
Target Student: High school students.
Amount: $100- $500
Number of Awards: 3
Based on Financial Need: No
Deadline: October
Applications information is available online.

(958) University of California Public Policy and International Affairs Law Fellowship

Univeristy of California at Berkeley
UCPPIA Summer Institute
Goldman School of Public Policy
2607 Hearst Avenue #7320
Berkeley, CA 94720

Phone: 510-643-9170
Fax: 510-643-6274
Email: nadine.spingola@berkeley.edu
URL: http://gspp.berkeley.edu/ppia

Goal: To encourage prosepective graduate students to pursue a degree in law and public policy.
Eligibility: Applicants must be permanent residents or U.S. citizens who are undergraduate seniors with at least one semester or two quarters of coursework left before graduating. Applicants must be interested in careers in law and public service with a demonstrated interest in policy issues that affect underserved populations and applicants must have overcome obstacles to purusing their college education.
Target Student: College and Adult students.
Amount: At least $5,000
Number of Awards: 10
Based on Financial Need: No
Deadline: Varies
Applications are available online. A completed application and personal statement are required to apply.

(959) University of California Public Policy and International Affairs Summer Institute

Univeristy of California at Berkeley
UCPPIA Summer Institute
Goldman School of Public Policy
2607 Hearst Avenue #7320
Berkeley, CA 94720

Phone: 510-643-9170
Fax: 510-643-6274
Email: nadine.spingola@berkeley.edu
URL: http://gspp.berkeley.edu/ppia

Goal: To assist students interested in pursuing a graduate education in public policy.
Eligibility: Applicants must be permanent residents or U.S. citizens who are undergraduate seniors with one semester/two quarters or more remaining before graduating. Applicants must be interested in careers in public service and have demonstrated interest in policy issues that affect underserved populations. Applicants must also have overcome an obstacle in pursuit of their college degree.
Target Student: College and Adult students.
Amount: At least $5,000
Number of Awards: 30
Based on Financial Need: No
Deadline: Varies
Applications are available online. A completed application with a personal statement are required to apply.

(960) USBC Annual Zeb Scholarship

United States Bowling Congress
5301 S. 76th Street
Greendale, WI 53129

Phone: 800-514-2695 x3168
Email: smart@bowl.com
URL: http://www.bowl.com

Goal: To acknowledge USBC Youth members who have high academic achievement and have participated in community service.

Eligibility: Applicants must be members and have competed in certified events with the United States Bowling Congress. Applicants must be 22 years old or younger and are high school seniors or college students with a GPA of 2.5 or greater. Applicants must not have particpated in a professional bowling tournament except for Pro-AM's and have a bowling average of 175.
Target Student: High school and College students.
Amount: $6,000
Number of Awards: 1
Scholarship can be renewable.
Based on Financial Need: No
Deadline: Varies
Applications are available online.

---

(961) USBC Youth Ambassador of the Year

United States Bowling Congress
5301 S. 76th Street
Greendale, WI 53129

Phone: 800-514-2695 x3168
Email: smart@bowl.com
URL: http://www.bowl.com

Goal: To acknowledge contributions made to the sport of bowling, academic achievement and community service.
Eligibility: Applicants must be USBC Youth members who are high school seniors and are going to be 18 or older by August 1 of the year of their selection. They must be nominated by a USBC member.
Target Student: High school students.
Amount: $1,500
Number of Awards: 2
Based on Financial Need: No
Deadline: Varies
Applications are available online.

---

(962) USGIF Scholarship Program

United States Geospatial Intelligence Foundation
2325 Dulles Corner Boulevard
Suite 450
Herndon, VA 20171

Email: scholarships@usgif.org
URL: http://www.usgif.org/education/scholarships

Goal: To assist students studying geospatial sciences with their educational expenses.
Eligibility: Applicants must be high school seniors, college or graduate studetns. The award is based on the applicants achievements in a field that is related to geospatial intelligence.
Target Student: High school, College, Graduate and Adult students.
Amount: $2,000 - $5,000
Number of Awards: 20
Based on Financial Need: No
Deadline: April
Application information is available online.

---

(963) Vercille Voss IFDA Graduate Student Scholarship

International Furnishings and Design Association
150 South Warner Road
Suite 156
King of Prussia, PA 19406

Phone: 610-535-6422
Fax: 610-535-6423
Email: merrymabbettinc@comcast.net
URL: http://www.ifdaef.org/scholarships.php

Goal: To assist interior design graduate students.
Eligibility: Applicants must be graduate students who are interior design majors (or closely related) at a U.S. school.

Target Student: College, Graduate and Adult students.
Amount: $2,000
Number of Awards: 1
Based on Financial Need: No
Deadline: March
Applications are available online. A completed application, transcript, essay, two original design examples, letter of recommendation, and proof of graduate school acceptance (for new students) are required to apply.

(964) Veterans Caucus Scholarship

Veterans Caucus of the American Academy of Physician Assistants

Email: shanley@veteranscaucus.org
URL: http://www.veteranscaucus.org

Goal: To assist U.S. military veterans who are enrolled in a physician assistant program.
Eligibility: Applicants must be U.S. military veterans who are enrolled in an accredited physician assistant training program.
Target Student: College, Graduate and Adult students.
Amount: Varies
Number of Awards: 1
Based on Financial Need: No
Deadline: March
Applications are available online. A completed application and personal statement are required.

(965) Vincent Chin Scholarship

Asian American Journalists Association
5 Third Street
Suite 1108
San Francisco, CA 94103

Phone: 415-346-2051
Fax: 415-346-6343

Email: naova@aaja.org
URL: http://www.aaja.org

Goal: To assist college students interested in careers in journalism.
Eligibility: Applicants must be graduating high school seniors or full-time undergraduate or graduate students who support the mission of the AAJA and are committed to working within the community, however they are not required to be Asian Americans. Award selection is based on the applicants potential to support journalism as it relates to issues faced by Pacific Islanders and Asian Americans.
Target Student: High school, College, Graduate and Adult students.
Amount: $500
Number of Awards: 1
Based on Financial Need: Yes
Deadline: May
Applications are available online. A completed application, resume, two letters of recommendation, work samples and essay are required to apply.

(966) Violet Richardson Award

Soroptimist International of the Americans
1709 Spruce Street
Philadelphia, PA 19103

Phone: 215-893-9000
Fax: 215-893-5200
Email: siahq@soroptimist.org
URL: http://www.soroptmist.org

Goal: To acknowledge young women who have contributed to their community through volunteer efforts.
Eligibility: Applicants must be women between the ages of 14 and 17 who have made outstanding contributions through their volunteer efforts. Work that benefits women or girls is of specific interest. This is a local award and is not available in all communities.

Target Student: High school students.
Amount: $2,500
Number of Awards: Varies
Based on Financial Need: No
Deadline: December
To get more information contact your local Soroptimist club.

(967) Visine Students with Vision Scholarship Program

Johnson and Johnson Healthcare Products
c/o International Scholarship and Tuition Service Inc
1321 Murfreesboro Road Suite 800
Nashville, TN 37217

Phone: 855-670-ISTS
Email: contactus@applyists.com
URL: http://www.visine.com/scholarship

Goal: To assist students who have a vision that is effectivily communicated through essay or video.
Eligibility: Applicants must be high school seniors or college freshman, sophomore or juniors and show involvment in school and community. Students must show financial need and be able to demonstrate their vision through an essay or video. A GPA of 2.8 or above is required.
Target Student: High school, College and Adult students.
Amount: $5,000
Number of Awards: Up to 10
Based on Financial Need: No
Deadline: March
Applications are available online.

(968) Visiting Senior Fellowship Program

National Gallery of Art
2000B South Club Drive
Landover, MD 20785

Phone: 202-842-6482
Fax: 202-789-3026
URL:http://www.nga.gov/resources/casva.htm

Goal: To provide fellowships to visual arts students.
Eligibility: Applicants have had their Ph.D. for at least 5 years or an equivalent level of professional accomplishments. Applications are considered for: history, theory and criticism of the visual arts of any geographical area or period. Fellowships are for full-time research in Washington. The awards are for up to twelve short-term Paul Mellon and Ailsa Mellon Bruce Visiting Senior Fellowships.
Target Student: Graduate and Adult students.
Amount: $6,000 - $8,000
Number of Awards: Up to 12
Scholarship can be renewed.
Based on Financial Need: No
Deadline: September and March
Applications are available online. A completed application, two letters of recommendation, and copies of publications.

(969) Voice of Democracy Audio Essay Contests

Veterans of Foreign Wars
406 W. 34th Street
Kansas City, MO 64111

Phone: 816-968-1117
Fax: 816-968-1149
Email: kharmer@vfw.org
URL: http://www.vfw.org

Goal: To encourage patriotism with students with audio essays.
Eligibility: Applicants must submit a 3 to 5 minute audio essay based on the yearly theme. Applicants must be in the 9th to 12th grade in high school or home school program.

Target Student: High school students.
Amount: Up to $30,000
Number of Awards: Varies
Based on Financial Need: No
Deadline: November
Applications are available online, but submission must be made to the local VFW post.

---

(970) VRG Scholarship

Vegetarian Resource Group
P.O. Box 1463
Baltimore, MD 21203

Phone: 410-366-8343
Fax: 410-366-8804
Email: vrg@vrg.org
URL: http://www.vrg.org

Goal: To acknowledge high school seniors who promote vegetarianism.
Eligibility: Applicants must be graduating from a U.S. high school who have promoted vegetarianism in their community and school. Selection of the award based on compassion, courage, and commitment to help promote a "peaceful world through a vegetarian diet or lifestyle."
Target Student: High school students.
Amount: $5,000
Number of Awards: 2
Based on Financial Need: No
Deadline: February
Applications are available online, mail, phone or email.

---

(971) W.H. Howie McClennan Scholarship

International Association of Fire Fighters
1750 New York Avenue NW
Washington, DC 20006

Phone: 202-737-8484
Fax: 202-737-8418

URL: http://www.iaff.org

Goal: To assist the children of firefighters who have died in the line of duty.
Eligibility: Applicants must be the children of firefighters who have died in the line of duty. The applicant's parent must have been a member in good standing of the International Association of Fire Fighters (AFL-CIO/CLC) at the time of their death. The award is based on financial need, academics and promise.
Target Student: High school, College and Adult students.
Amount: $2,500
Number of Awards: 1
Scholarship can be renewed.
Based on Financial Need: Yes
Deadline: February
Applications are available by written request.

---

(972) Watson Travel Fellowship

Thomas J. Watson Fellowship
11 Park Place
Suite 1503
New York, NY 10007

Phone: 212-245-8859
Fax: 212-245-8860
Email: tjw@watsonfellowship.org
URL: http://www.watsonfellowship.org

Goal: To award a one year grant for independent study and travel outside of the U.S.
Eligibility: Applicants must be graduating seniors from a participating college who are nominated by their college. A list of participating colleges is available online.
Target Student: College and Adult students.
Amount: Up to $35,000
Number of Awards: Varies
Based on Financial Need: No
Deadline: November

Applicants who are interested in applying should contact their local Watson liaison to start the process.

(973) Wendy's High School Helsman Award

Wendy's Restaurants

Phone: 800-205-6367
Email: wendys@act.org
URL:http://www.wendyshighschoolheisman.com

Goal: To acknowledge high school students who have excelled in academics, athletics and student leadership.
Eligibility: Applicants must be beginning their high school senior year and have participated in one o fthe 27 sanctioned sports. Students must have a GPA of 3.0 or higher. Award selection is based on academics, community service and athletic accomplishments.
Target Student: High school students.
Amount: Varies
Number of Awards: Varies
Based on Financial Need: No
Deadline: October
Applications are available online.

(974) Werner B. Thiele Memorial Scholarship

Gravure Education Foundation
1200-A Scottsville Road
Rochester, NY 14624

Phone: 315-589-8879
Fax: 585-436-7689
Email: lwshatch@gaa.org
URL: http://www.gaa.org

Goal: To assist college juniors and seniors who are majoring in printing, graphic arts or graphic communications.

Eligibility: Applicants must be enrolled full-time at one of the GEF Learning Resource Centers: Arizona State University, California Polytechnic State University, Clemson University, Murray State, Rochester Institute of Technology, University of Wisconsin-Stout or Western Michigan University.
Target Student: College and Adult students.
Amount: $1,000
Number of Awards: 1
Based on Financial Need: No
Deadline: April
Applications are available online.

(975) Wesley-Logan Prize

American Historical Association
400 A Street SE
Washington, DC 20003

Phone: 202-544-2422
Fax: 202-544-8307
Email: info@historians.org
URL: http://www.historians.org

Goal: To select a scholarly/literary book for the award that focuses on the history of dispersion, relocation, settlement, or adjustment of people from Africa or on their return to that continent.
Eligibility: Eligible books must have been published between May 1 of the preceeding year and April 30 of the year of application.
Target Student: Junior high students or younger, High school students, College, Graduate and Adult students.
Amount: Varies
Number of Awards: Varies
Based on Financial Need: No
Deadline: May
Application information is available online.

(976) Where's FRANKIE the Diploma Frame? Scholarship Photo Contest

Church Hill Classics
594 Pepper Street
Monroe, CT 6468

Phone: 800-447-9005
Fax: 203-268-2468
Email: info@diplomaframe.com
URL: http://www.framemyfuture.com

Goal: To assist college students with the costs of textbooks.
Eligibility: Applicants must be legal U.S. residents who are 18 years old or above and full-time college students or the family member of full-time college students. Applicants must submit a photo showing the sponsor's mascot participating in a summer activity. Award selection is based on the creativity and popularity of the photo.
Target Student: College, Graduate and Adult students.
Amount: $500 Gift Card
Number of Awards: 3
Based on Financial Need: No
Deadline: August
Applications are available online.

(977) William B. Ruggles Right to Work Scholarship

National Institute for Labor Relations Research
William B. Ruggles Scholarship Selection Committee
5211 Port Royal Road
Suite 510
Springfield, VA 22151

Phone: 703-321-9606
Fax: 703-321-7342
Email: research@nilrr.org
URL: http://www.nilrr.org

Goal: To assist students devoted to high standards in journalism.

Eligibility: Applicants must be undergraduate or graduate students who are majoring in journalism with demonstrated understanding of the principles of unionism and the problems that are associated with compulsory unionism.
Target Student: College, Graduate and Adult students.
Amount: $2,000
Number of Awards: 1
Based on Financial Need: No
Deadline: December
Applications are available online.

(978) William E. Simon Fellowship for Noble Purpose

Intercollegiate Studies Institute
3901 Centerville Road
Wilmington, DE 19807

Phone: 800-526-7022
Fax: 302-652-1760
Email: simon@isi.org
URL: http://www.isi.org

Goal: To assist graduating college seniors who are committed to strengthening civil society.
Eligibility: Applicants must be graduating college seniors with self directed plans to improve society. Award selection is based on academics, recommendations, extracurricular activities and project goals.
Target Student: College and Adult students.
Amount: $40,000
Number of Awards: 1
Based on Financial Need: No
Deadline: January
Applications are available online. A completed application, essay, transcript, recommendation letters, and outline of educational achievements are required.

(979) William L. Hastie Award

National Association of Blacks in Criminal Justice
North Carolina Central University
P.O. Box 19788
Durham, NC 27707

Phone: 919-683-1801
Fax: 919-683-1903
Email: office@nabcj.org
URL: http://www.nabcj.org

Goal: To acknowledge the demonstration of national leadership in criminal justice and the pursuit of policy change in the field.
Eligibility: Be nominated by a member of the NABCJ.
Target Student: College, Graduate and Adult students.
Amount: Varies
Number of Awards: 1
Based on Financial Need: No
Deadline: May
Nomination applications are available online.

---

(980) William R. Goldfarb Memorial Scholarship

American Radio Relay League Foundation
225 Main Street
Newington, CT 06111

Phone: 860-594-0397
Fax: 860-594-0259
Email: foundation@arrl.org
URL: http://www.arrlf.org

Goal: To assist high school seniors, who are amateur radio operators, pursuing bachelor's degrees in business, computers, medical, nursing, engineering or science.
Eligibility: Applicants must have demonstrated financial need and plan on attending a regionally accredited college or university.
Target Student: High school students.

Amount: $10,000
Number of Awards: 1
Based on Financial Need: Yes
Deadline: February
Applications are available online.

---

(981) William S. Bullinger Scholarship

Federal Circuit Bar Association
1620 I Street NW
Suite 900
Washington, DC 20006

Phone: 202-466-3923
Fax: 202-833-1061
URL: http://www.fedcirbar.org

Goal: To assist law students with fianncial need who have academic promise.
Eligibility: Applicants must be undergraduate aor graduate law students who show academic promise and have demonstrated financial need.
Target Student: College, Graduate and Adult students.
Amount: $5,000
Number of Awards: 1
Based on Financial Need: Yes
Deadline: April
To apply applicants must submit one page that discusses their financial need, their qualifications for the scholarship and their interest in law, transcripts and a curriculm vitae.

---

(982) Win Free Tuition Giveaway

Next Step Magazine
86 W. Main Street
Victor, NY 14565

Phone: 800-771-3117
Email: webcopy@nextstepmag.com
URL:http://www.nextstepmagazine.com/winfreetuition

Goal: To support higher education.

Eligibility: Applicants must be legal U.S. or Canadian residents who are 14 or older who are planning to enroll in college by September 30th, 3 years after the application date. The award is an annual sweepstakes for one year's tuition up to $10,000 and 11 monthy $1,000 drawings.
Target Student: High school, College, Graduate and Adult students.
Amount: $1,000 - $10,000
Number of Awards: 12
Based on Financial Need: No
Deadline: June
Applications are available online.

---

(983) Women Band Directors International College Scholarships

Women Band Director International
Nicole Rubis Aakre
WBDI Scholarship Chair
7424 Whistlestop Drive
Austin, TX 78749

Email: nrubis1@gmail.com
URL:
http://www.womenbanddirectors.org

Goal: To assist future female band directors.
Eligibility: Applicants must be studying music with the goal of becoming a band director.
Target Student: College, Graduate and Adult students.
Amount: Varies
Number of Awards: 10
Based on Financial Need: No
Deadline: December
Applications are available online.

---

(984) Women In Geographic Education Scholarship

National Council for Geographic Education
Jacksonville State University

206-A Martin Hall
700 Pelham Road North
Jacksonville, AL 36265

Phone: 256-782-5293
Fax: 256-782-5336
Email: ncge@jsu.edu
URL: http://www.ncge.org

Goal: To assist undergraduate and graduate women who are planning a career in geography education.
Eligibility: Applicants must be enrolled in a degree program that leads to a career in geographic education, have a 3.0 GPA with a 3.5 GPA in geography courses.
Target Student: College, Graduate and Adult students.
Amount: $500
Number of Awards: 1
Based on Financial Need: No
Deadline: April
Applications are available online. A completed application, and essay are required to apply.

---

(985) Women In Need Scholarship

Educational Foundation for Women in Accounting
P.O. Box 1925
Southeastern, PA 19399

Phone: 610-407-9229
Fax: 610-644-3713
Email: info@efwa.org
URL: http://www.efwa.org

Goal: To assist female re-entry students purusing degrees in accounting with educational expenses.
Eligibility: Applicants must be female students who are working towards a degree in accounting.
Target Student: College and Adult students.
Amount: $2,000
Number of Awards: 1

Scholarship can be renewed.
Based on Financial Need: Yes
Deadline: April
Applications are available online.

---

(986) Women In Transition Scholarship

Edcuational Foundation for Women in
Accounting
P.O. Box 1925
Southeastern, PA 19399

Phone: 610-407-9229
Fax: 610-644-3713
Email: info@efwa.org
URL: http://www.efwa.org

Goal: To assist female re-entry students
working towards a degree in accounting.
Eligibility: Applicants must be female
students who are working towards a degree
in accounting.
Target Student: High school, College and
Adult students.
Amount: Up to $4,000
Number of Awards: 1
Scholarship can be renewed.
Based on Financial Need: Yes
Deadline: April
Applications are available online.

---

(987) Women Marines Association Scholarship Program

Woman Marines Association
P.O. Box 8405
Falls Church, VA 22041

Phone: 888-525-1943
Email: wma@womenmarines.org
URL: http://www.womenmarines.org

Goal: To assist Marines and their families.

Eligibility: Applicants must be sponsored
by a Women Marines Association member.
Applicants must have served or be serving
in the Marine Corps or Reserve, be a direct
descendant, sibling or descendant of a
sibling of a member of the Marines or have
completed two years in a ROTC program.
Applicants must have a GPA of 3.5 or
above. High school graduates must have a
SAT score of 1100 or above or a ACT
score of 25 or greater.
Target Student: High school, College and
Adult students.
Amount: $1,500
Number of Awards: 8
Based on Financial Need: No
Deadline: January
Applications are available online. A
completed application, copy of sponsor's
membership card, photo, three letters of
recommendation, proof of Marine, or
ROTC status or relationship to a Marine
and proof of draft registration.

---

(988) Women's Overseas Service League Scholarships for Women

Women's Overseas Service League
Scholarship Committee
P.O. Box 7124
Washington, DC 20044

Email: kelsey@openix.com
URL: http://www.wosl.org/scholarships.htm

Goal: To assist women in the military and
other public service careers.
Eligibility: Applicants must show a
commitment to advancing their career and
must have completed a minimum of 12
semester or 18 quarter hours of study at a
college or university and working towards
a degree. Applicants must agree to
enrolling for six semester or nine quarter
units each academic period and have a
GPA of 2.5 or higher.

Target Student: College and Adult students.
Amount: $500 - $1,000
Number of Awards: Varies
Scholarship can be renewed.
Based on Financial Need: Yes
Deadline: March
Applications are available online. A completed application, statement of financial need, resume, three letters of reference, essay and official transcripts are required to apply.

(989) Women's Western Gold Foundation Scholarship

Women's Western Golf Foundation
393 Ramsay Road
Deerfield, IL 60015

Phone: 608-274-0173
Email: cocomc2000@comcast.net
URL: http://www.wwga.org

Goal: To assist female students involved in golf.
Eligibility: Applicants must be seniors in high school, demonstrate financial need, show academic excellence, and good character. Applicants must maintain a 3.0 GPA of above to renew the scholarship.
Target Student: High school students.
Amount: $2,000
Number of Awards: Varies
Scholarship can be renewed.
Based on Financial Need: Yes
Deadline: March
Applications are available online.

(990) Working Abroad Grant

InterExchange Inc.
161 Sixth Avenue
New York, NY 10013

Phone: 212-924-0446
Fax: 212-924-0575

Email: grants@interexchange.org
URL:http://www.interexchange.org/content/1/en/home.html

Goal: To develop an international understanding and develop cutlural awareness by assisting Americans working abroad.
Eligibility: Applicants must be U.S. citizens between age 18 and 28 and accepted into an InterExchange Working Abroad program aside from the language school.
Target Student: High school, College, Graduate and Adult students.
Amount: $1,500
Number of Awards: Vaires
Based on Financial Need: No
Deadline: 8 Weeks before the program start date.
Applications are available online.

(991) Worldstudio Foundation Scholarship Program

Worldstudio Foundation
200 Varick Street
Suite 507
New York, NY 10014

Phone: 212-807-1990
Fax: 212-807-1799
Email:scholarshipcorrdinator@worldstudio.org
URL: http://www.worldstudio.org

Goal: To assist art and design students with financial need.
Eligibility: Applicants must be full-time undergraduate or graduate students studying fine art, commerical art, design or architecture.
Target Student: High school, College, Graduate or Adult students.
Amount: $200 - $6,000
Number of Awards: Varies
Based on Financial Need: Yes
Deadline: April

Applications are available online.

---

(993) Yashiyama Young Entrepreneurs Program

Hitachi Foundation
1215 17th Street NW
Washington, DC 20036

Phone: 202-457-0588
Fax: 202-296-1098
URL: http://www.hitachifoundation.org

Goal: To acknowledge student entrepreneurs.
Eligibility: Applicants must be at least 18 years old and 29 years old or younger when their business began to generate revenue. The business must be one to five years old, generated revenue for a minimum of one year and be helping to create opportunties for low-income Americans.
Target Student: College, Graduate and Adult students.
Amount: Up to $40,000 over two years
Number of Awards: Varies
Based on Financial Need: No
Deadline: March
Applications are available online.

---

(992) Yasme Foundation Scholarship

American Radio Relay League Foundation
225 Main Street
Newington, CT 06111

Phone: 860-594-0397
Fax: 860-594-0259
Email: foundation@arrl.org
URL: http://www.arrlf.org

Goal: To asisst students involved in amateur radio who are majoring in science and engineering.

Eligibility: Applicants must have an amateur radio license and be enrolled in a college or university. Preference for the award is given to those with demonstrated community service, participation in amateur radio clubs and in the top 10 percent of their class.
Target Student: High school, College and Adult students.
Amount: $2,000
Number of Awards: Varies
Scholarship can be renewed.
Based on Financial Need: No
Deadline: February
Applications are available online.

---

(994) Young American Creative Patriotic Art Awards Program

Ladies Auxiliary VFW
406 West 34th Street
10th Floor
Kansas City, MO 64111

Phone: 816-561-8655 x19
Fax: 816-931-4753
Email: jmillick@ladiesauxvfw.org
URL: http://www.ladiesauxvfw.org

Goal: To encourage patriotic art.
Eligibility: Applicants must be high school students from the state of the sponsoring Ladies Auxiliary. Applicants must submit one piece of partiotic art that was completed during the current school year and signed by a teacher.
Target Student: High school students.
Amount: $5,000 - $10,000
Number of Awards: 8
Based on Financial Need: No
Deadline: March
Applications are available online.

---

(995) Young Jazz Composer Award

ASCAP Foundation
One Lincoln Plaza

New York, NY 10023

Phone: 212-621-6219
URL: http://www.ascapfoundation.org

Goal: To acknowledge talented young jazz composers.
Eligibility: Applicants must be under 30 years old and U.S. citizens or permanent residents and must submit one original composition, including a score and performance.
Target Student: Junior high and younger, High school, College, Graduate and Adult students.
Amount: Varies
Number of Awards: Varies
Based on Financial Need: No
Deadline: December
Applications are available online.

(996) Young People for Fellowship

Young People For
2000 M Street NW
Suite 400
Washington, DC 20036

Phone: 202-467-4999
Fax:
Email: zdryden@fpaw.org
URL: http://www.youngpeoplefor.org

Goal: To assist and cultivate young progressive leaders.
Eligibility: Applicants must be undergraduate students who are interesting in encouraging social change on their campus and in their communities.
Target Student: College and Adult students.
Amount: Varies
Number of Awards: 150
Based on Financial Need: No
Deadline: January
Applications are available online.

(997) Young Scholars Program

Jack Kent Cooke Foundation Young
Scholars Program
301 ACT Drive
P.O. Box 4030
Iowa City, IA 52243

Phone: 800-498-6478
Fax: 703-723-8030
Email: jkc@jackkentcookefoundation.org
URL: http://www.jkcf.org

Goal: To assist high achieving students with financial need with educational opportunities throughout high school.
Eligibility: Applicants must be in the 7th grade who are planning to attend a high school in the U.S. and have financial need. Applicants must show academic achievement through academic records, academic awards, letters of recommendation and a GPA of 3.5 or higher, although some exceptions can be made. Over two summers recipients must participate in a Young Scholars Week and Young Scholars Reunion in Washington DC.
Target Student: Junior high students and younger.
Amount: Varies
Number of Awards: 60
Scholarship can be renewed.
Based on Financial Need: Yes
Deadline: April
Applications are available online as well as at regional talent centers. A completed application, personal release, financial aid forms, tax forms, school report, teacher recommendation, personal recommendation and survey form are required to apply.

(998) YoungArts Program

National Foundatoin for Advancement in the Arts
444 Brickell Avenue

P-14
Miami, FL 33131

Phone: 800-970-ARTS
Fax: 305-377-1149
Email: info@nfaa.org
URL: http://www.nfaa.org

Goal: To assist young individuals in the arts.
Eligibility: Applicants must be high school seniors or 17 or 18 years old by December 1 in the year of their application and be U.S. citizens or permanent residents. There is a fee for this scholarship and as mentioned, it is not advisable to apply for a scholarship with a fee.
Target Student: High school students.
Amount: $10,000
Number of Awards: Varies
Based on Financial Need: No
Deadline: October
Applications are available online.

---

(999) Youth Free Expression Network Film Contest

National Coalition Against Censorship
275 Seventh Avenue
15th Floor
New York, NY 10001

Phone: 212-807-6222
Fax: 212-807-6245
Email: ncac@ncac.org
URL: http://www.ncac.org

Goal: To acknowledge students who have created films on a topic related to censorship.
Eligibility: Applicants must be 19 years old or younger and create a film that is 4 minutes or less that is a documentary, music video, or experimental.
Target Student: Junior high and younger, High school and College students.
Amount: Up to $5,000

Number of Awards: 3
Based on Financial Need: No
Deadline: October
Applications are available online.

(1000) Youth Scholarship

Society of Broadcast Engineers
9102 N. Meridian Street
Suite 150
Indianapolis, IN 46260

Phone: 317-846-9000
Fax: 317-846-9120
Email: mclappe@sbe.org
URL: http://www.sbe.org

Goal: To assist students planning a career in the technical aspects of broadcasting.
Eligibility: Applicants must be graduating high school seniors who are planning to enroll in a college, university or technical school in a field of study that leads to a career in broadcast engineering or a related field.
Target Student: High school students.
Amount: $1,000 - $3,000
Number of Awards: Up to 3
Based on Financial Need: No
Deadline: July
Applications are available online. A completed application, transcript, biography and essay are required to apply.

(1001) Zachary Taylor Stevens Memorial Scholarship

American Radio Relay League Foundation
225 Main Street
Newington, CT 6111

Phone: 860-594-0397
Fax: 860-594-0259
Email: foundation@arrl.org
URL: http://www.arrlf.org

Goal: To assist students involved in amateur radio.

Eligibility: Applicants muat have a Technician Class radio license or higher enrolled in a two- or four-year college, university or technical school. Preference is given to those living in Michigan, Ohio and West Virgina.

Target Student: High school, College and Adult students.

Amount: $750

Number of Awards: 1

Based on Financial Need: No

Deadline: February

Applications are available online.

Scholarship Name Index:

Air Force ROTC Professional Officer Course Early Release Program - 63

Air Force ROTC SOAR Program - 64

Air Force Spouse Scholarship - 65

Air Traffic Control Association Scholarship Program - 66

Airman Memorial Foundation Scholarship Program - 67

AISI/AIST Foundation Premier Scholarship - 68

AIST Benjamin F. Fairless Scholarship - 69

AIST Ronald E. Lincoln Memorial Scholarship - 70

AIST Smith Graduate Scholarship - 71

AIST William E. Schwabe Memorial Scholarship - 72

AIST Willy Korf Memorial Fund - 73

Akash Kuruvilla Memorial Scholarship - 74

Al Neuharth Free Spirit Scholarship and Conference Program - 75

Alice T. Schafer Prize - 76

Alice W. Rooke Scholarship - 77

Allied Dental Health Scholarships - 78

Alpha Kappa Alpha Financial Need Scholars - 79

Alpha Kappa Alpha Merit Scholarship - 80

Alpha Mu Tau Fraternity Undergraduate Scholarships - 81

Alphonso Deal Scholarship Award - 82

AMBUCS Scholars - 83

AMCA Music Scholarship - 84

Amelia Earhart Fellowships - 85

American Architectural Foundation and Sir John Soane's Museum Foundation Traveling Fellowship - 86

American Bar Association Essay and Writing Competition - 87

American Bar Association-Bar/Bri Scholarshisp - 88

American Darts Organization Memorial Scholarships - 89

American Essay Contest - 90

American Express Scholarship Competition - 91

American Legion Baseball Scholarship - 92

American Legion Junior Air Rifle National Championship Scholarships - 93

American Legion Legacy Scholarship - 94

American Police Hall of Fame Educational Scholarship Fund - 95

American Quarter Horse Foundation Scholarship - 96

American Society of Crime Laboratory Directors Scholarship Program - 97

American Society of Travel Agents American Express Travel Undergraduate Scholarship - 98

American Society of Travel Agents Arnold Rigby Graduate Scholarship - 99

American Society of Travel Agents Avis Budget Group Graduate Scholarship - 100

American Society of Travel Agents David J. Hallissey Memorial Undergraduate or Graduate Internship - 101

American Society of Travel Agents Healy Graduate Scholarship - 102

American Society of Travel Agents Holland America Line Graduate Research Scholarship - 103

American Society of Travel Agents Joseph R. Stone Graduate Scholarship - 104

American String Teachers Association National Solo Competition - Senior Division - 105

American Theatre Organ Society Scholarships - 106

America's First Freedom Student Competition - 107

Americoprs Vista - 108

Americorps National Civilian Community Corps - 109

AMS Graduate Fellowship in the History of Science - 110

AMS Undergraduate Scholarships - 111

AMS/Industry Minority Scholarships - 112

AMS/Industry/Government Graduate Fellowships - 113

AMT Student Scholarship - 114

Amtrol Inc. Scholarship - 115

AMVETS National Scholarship for Entering College Freshman - 116

AMVETS National Scholarship for Veterans - 117

Amy Lowell Poetry Travelling Scholarship - 118

Anchor Scholarship Foundation Scholarship - 119

Angus Foundation Scholarship - 120
Annie's Sustainable Agriculture
Scholarships - 121
Annual Logistics Scholarship Competition
- 122
Annual Music Student Scholarships - 123
Annual NBNA Scholarships - 124
ANS Graduate Scholarship - 125
ANS Incoming Freshman Scholarships -
126
ANS Undergraduate Scholarships - 127
Antoinette Lierman Medlin Scholarship -
128
AOC Scholarships - 129
AORN Foundation Scholarship Program -
130
AOS Master's Scholarship Program - 131
APF/COGDOP Graduate Research
Scholarships - 132
APF/TOPSS Scholars Essay Competition
- 133
Appaloosa Youth Association Art Contest
- 134
Appaloosa Youth Association Essay
Contest - 135
Appaloosa Youth Association Speech
Contest - 136
Apprentice Ecologist Initiative Youth
Scholarship Program - 137
APS Minority Scholarship - 138
ARC Welding Awards - 139
ARIT Fellowships for Research in Turkey
- 140
Armed Services YMCA Annual Essay
Contest - 141
Army College Fund - 142
Army Nurse Corps Association
Scholarships - 143
Army ROTC Advanced Course - 144
Army ROTC Four-Year Scholarship
Program - 145
Army ROTC Green to Gold Scholarship
Program - 146
Arnold Sobel Endowment Fund
Scholarships - 147
ARRL Scholarship Honoring Senator
Barry Goldwater, K7UGA - 148
Art Awards - 149

ASABE Foundation Engineering
Scholarship Foundation - 150
ASCA/AISC Student Design Competition
- 151
ASDSO Dam Safety Scholarships - 152
ASEV Scholarships - 153
ASF Olin Fellowship - 154
ASHA Youth Scholarships - 155
ASHRAE Scholarship Program - 156
ASLA Council of Fellows Scholarships -
157
ASM Outstanding Scholars Awards - 158
ASME Foundation - ASME Auxiliary
FIRST Clarke Scholarship - 159
ASME Foundation Scholarships - 160
ASNE Scholarship Program - 161
ASNT Fellowship - 162
Aspiring Police Officer Scholarship - 163
Association for Women in Science
Educational Awards - 164
Association of Equipment Management
Professionls Foundation Scholarship - 165
Association of Federal Communications
Consulting Engineers Scholarships - 166
Association of Food and Drug Officials
Scholarship Award - 167
ASTM International Katherine and Bryant
Mather Scholarship - 168
Astronaut Scholarship - 169
Atlas Shrugged Essay Contest - 170
AUA Foundation Research Scholars
Program - 171
Automotive Hall of Fame Scholarships -
172
Aviation Distributors and Manufacturers
Association Scholarship Program - 173
Aviation Insurance Association Education
Foundation Scholarship - 174
AWSEF Scholarship - 175
AXA Achievement Community
Scholarship - 176
AXA Achievement Scholarships - 177
Babe Ruth League Scholarships - 178
Bachelor's Scholarships - 179
Banks Family Scholarship - 180
Barold Scholarship - 181
Barry M. Goldwater Scholarship and
Excellence in Education Program - 182

Engineering Undergraduate Award - 373
EOD Memorial Scholarship - 374
Esther R. Sawyer Research Award - 375
Ethnic Minority and Women's Enhancement Scholarship - 376
Eugene Gene Sallee, W4YFR Memorial Scholarship - 377
Eugene S. Kropf Scholarship - 378
Excellence in Engineering, Mathematics or the Sciences Scholarship - 379
Excellence of Scholarship Award - 380
Executive Women International Scholarship Program - 381
F.W. "Belch" Beichley Scholarship - 382
FA Davis Student Awad - 383
FALCON - Full Year Asian Language Concentration - 384
Families of Freedom Scholarship Fund - 385
Federal Junior Duck Stamp Program and Scholarship Competition - 386
Fellowship Award - 387
Fellowship in Aerospace History - 388
Fellowships for Regular Program in Greece - 389
Fellowships/Grants to Study in Scandinavia - 390
Ferrous Metallurgy Education Today - 391
FFTA Scholarship Competition - 392
Finlandia Foundation National Student Scholarships Program - 393
First Cavalry Division Association Scholarship - 394
FiSCA Scholarship - 395
Fisher Broadcasting Scholarships for Minorities - 396
Florence C. and Robert H. Lister Fellowship - 397
Foundation for Global Scholars General Scholarship - 398
Foundation for Neonatal Research and Education Scholarships - 399
Foundation for Surgical Technology Advanced Education/Medical Mission Scholarship - 400
Foundation for Surgical Technology Scholarships - 401
Foundation of the National Student Nurses' Association Career Mobility Scholarships - 402
Foundation of the National Student Nurses' Association Specialty Scholarship - 403
Fountainhead Essay Contest - 404
FOWA Scholarship for Outdoor Communications - 405
Frances M. Schwartz Fellowship - 406
Francis Walton Memorial Scholarship - 407
Francis X. Crowley Scholarship - 408
Frank and Brennie Morgan Prize for Outstanding Research in Mathematics by an Undergraduate Student - 409
Frank and Dorothy Miller ASME Auxiliary Scholarships - 410
Frank Lanza Memorial Scholarship - 411
Frank M. Coda Scholarship - 412
Frank Newman Leadership Award - 413
Frank Sarli Memorial Scholarship - 414
Fraternal Order of Eagles Memorial Foundation - 415
Fred M. Young, Sr./SAE Engineering Scholarship - 416
Fred R. McDaniel Memorial Scholarship - 417
Frederic G. Melcher Scholarship - 418
Frederick Burkhardt Residential Fellowships for Recently Tenured Scholars - 419
Freedom of Speech PSA Contest - 420
Freshman and Sophmore Scholarships - 421
Freshman Undergraduate Scholarship - 422
From Failure to Promise Essay Contest - 423
FSF Scholarship Program - 424
Fulbright Grants - 425
Fund for American Studies Internships - 426
Future Engineers Scholarship - 427
Future Teacher Scholarship - 428
Gabe A. Harti Scholarship - 429
Gaige Fund Award - 430
Gamma Theta Upsilon-Geographical Honor Society - 431

Garland Duncan Scholarships - 432
Garmin Scholarship - 433
Gary Wagner, K3OMI Scholarship - 434
Gary Yoshimura Scholarship - 435
GAT Wings to the Future Management Scholarship - 436
GBT Student Support Program - 437
GCSAA Scholars Competition - 438
GCSAA Student Essay Contest - 439
GED Jump Start Scholarship - 440
GEF Resource Center Scholarships - 441
Gen and Kelly Tanabe Student Scholarship - 442
Gene Carte Student Paper Competition - 443
Gene Haas Foundation Machining Technology Scholarship - 444
General Fund Scholarships - 445
General Henry H. Arnold Edcuation Grant Program - 446
General Heritage and Culture Grants - 447
General James H. Doolittle Scholarship - 448
GeoEye Foundation Award for the Application of High Resolution Digital Satellite Imagery - 449
George A. Hall / Harold F. Mayfield Award - 450
George A. Roberts Scholarships - 451
George A. Strait Minority Scholarship - 452
George and Viola Hoffman Award - 453
GE-Reagan Foundation Scholarship Program - 454
German Studies Research Grant - 455
Gertrude Cox Scholarship For Women in Statistics - 456
Gift for Life Scholarship - 457
Gilbreth Memorial Fellowship - 458
Giles Sutherland Rich Memorial Scholarship - 459
Gilman International Scholarship - 460
Giuliano Mazzetti Scholarship - 461
Gladys Anderson Emerson Scholarship - 462
Glenn Miller Scholarship Competition - 463
Global Citizen Awards - 464
GNC Nutritional Research Grant - 465

Go! Study Abroad Scholarship - 466
Go! Volunteer Abroad Scholarship - 467
Golden Gate Restaurant Association Scholarship - 468
Graduate Fellowships - 469
Graduate Research Award - 470
Graduate Research Fellowship Program - 471
Graduate Research Grant - Master and Doctoral - 472
Graduate Scholarship - 473
Graduate Scholarships Program - 474
Graduate Student Research Grants - 475
Graduate Student Scholarship - 476
Graduate Summer Student Research Assistantship - 477
Gravure Publishing Council Scholarship - 478
Green Mountain Water Environment Association Scholarship - 479
Green/Sustainable Design Scholarship - 480
Grotto Scholarships - 481
H.P. Milligan Aviation Scholarship - 482
Hanscom Air Force Base Spouses' Club Scholarship - 483
Hansen Scholarship - 484
Harlequin Dance Scholarship - 485
Harness Racing Scholarship - 486
Harness Tracks of America Scholarship Fund - 487
Harold and Inge Marcus Scholarship - 488
Harold Bettinger Scholarship - 489
Harrell Family Fellowship - 490
Harry A. Applegate Scholarship - 491
Harry J. Harwick Scholarship - 492
Harry S. Truman Research Grant - 493
HAS Research Grants - 494
Hawaii Association of Broadcasters Scholarship - 495
Hayek Fund for Scholars - 496
Health Careers Scholarships - 497
Health Resources and Services Administration-Bureau of Health Professions Scholarships for Disadvantaged Students - 498
Health Sciences Student Fellowship - 499
Henry Adams Scholarship - 500

Joe Francis Haircare Scholarship Program - 567

Joe Perdue Scholarship - 568

Joel Polsky Academic Achievement Award - 569

Johansen International Competition for Young String Players - 570

John and Elsa Gracik Scholarships - 571

John and Muriel Landis Scholarship - 572

John Bayliss Radio Scholarship - 573

John D. Graham Scholarship - 574

John F. and Anna Lee Stacey Scholarship Fund for Art Education - 575

John F. Duffy Scholarship - 576

John F. Kennedy Profile in Courage Essay Contest - 577

John Foster Memorial College Scholarship - 578

John Henry Comstock Graduate Student Awards - 579

John J. McKetta Scholarship - 580

John Jowdy Scholarship - 581

John L. Imhoff Scholarship - 582

John Lennon Scholarship Competition - 583

John M. Haniak Scholarship - 584

John Mabry Forestry Scholarship - 585

John O. Crane Memorial Fellowship - 586

John R. Johnson Memorial Scholarship Endowment - 587

John S. Marshall Memorial Scholarship - 588

John S.W. Fargher Scholarship - 589

John V. Wehausen Graduate Scholarship - 590

John Wright Memorial Scholarship - 591

Johnny Davis Memorial Scholarship - 592

Jolly Green Meomorial Scholarship - 593

Jon C Ladda Memorial Foundation Scholarship - 594

Jonathan Jasper Wright Award - 595

Joseph C. Johnson Memorial Grant - 596

Joseph Frasca Excellence in Aviation Scholarship - 597

Joseph M. Parish Memorial Grant - 598

Joseph P. and Helen T. Cribbins Scholarship - 599

Joseph S. Rumbaugh Historical Oration Contest - 600

Josephine De Karman Fellowship - 601

JTG Scholarship in Scientific and Technical Translation or Interpretation - 602

Judith Haupt Member's Child Scholarship - 603

Julius and Esther Stulberg International String Competition - 604

Junior and Senior Scholarships - 605

Junior Composers Award - 606

Junior Fellowships - 607

Junior Felowships - 608

Junior Scholarship Program - 609

K.K. Wang Scholarship - 610

K2TEO Martin J. Green, Sr. Memorial Scholarship - 611

Karen O'Neil Memorial Scholarship - 612

Karla Girts Memorial Community Outreach Scholarship - 613

Kathem F. Gruber Scholarship Program - 614

Kenneth Andrew Roe Scholarship - 615

King Olav V Norwegian-American Heritage Fund - 616

Kit C. King Graduate Scholarship Fund - 617

Klussendorf Scholarship - 618

Kohl's Kids Who Care Scholarship - 619

KOR Memorial Scholarship - 620

Kymanox's James J. Davis Memorial Scholarship for Students Studying Abroad - 621

L. Phil Wicker Scholarship - 622

La Fra Scholarship - 623

Landscape Forms Design for People Scholarship - 624

Larry Williams Photography and AYA Photo Contest - 625

Larson Aquatic Research Support - 626

Laurel Fund - 627

Lawrence E. and Thelma J. Norrie Memorial Scholarship - 628

Lawrence G. Foster Award for Excellence in Public Relations - 629

Lawrence Ginocchio Aviation Scholarship - 630

Leaders and Achievers Scholarship Program - 631

Learning and Leadership Grants - 632

Lee S. Evans Scholarship - 633
Lee Tarbox Memorial Scholarship - 634
Legal Opportunity Scholarship Fund - 635
Len Assante Scholarship Fund - 636
Letters About Literature Contest - 637
Lewis A. Kingsley Foundation Scholarship - 638
Lewis C. Hoffman Scholarship - 639
Liberty Mutual Safety Research Fellowship - 640
Life Lessons Essay Contest - 641
Light Metals Division Scholarship - 642
Lions International Peace Poster Contest - 643
Lisa Zaken Award for Excellence - 644
Litherland Scholarship - 645
Lockheed Martin/HENAAC Scholars Program - 646
Lois Britt Park Industry Memorial Scholarship Program - 647
Long-Term Member Sponsored Scholarship - 648
Lotte Lenya Competition for Singers - 649
Lou and Carole Prato Sports Reporting Scholarship - 650
Lou Hochberg Awards - 651
Louis Agassiz Fuertes Award - 652
Love Your Body Poster Contest - 653
Lowell Gaylor Memorial Scholarship - 654
Lowell H. and Dorothy Loving Undergraduate Scholarship - 655
LTG and Mrs. Joseph M. Heiser Scholarship - 656
LTK Engineering Services Scholarship - 657
Luci S. Williams Houston Scholarship - 658
Lucille and Charles A. Wert Scholarship - 659
LULAC General Awards - 660
LULAC Honors Awards - 661
LULAC National Scholastic Achievement Awards - 662
Lyndon B. Johnson Foundation Grants-in-Aid Research - 663
Madeline Pickett Cogswell Nursing Scholarship - 664
Maley/FTE Scholarship - 665

Mandell and Lester Rosenblatt Undergraduate Scholarship - 666
Marine Corps League Scholarships - 667
Marine Corps League Scholarships - 668
Markley Scholarship - 669
Marliave Fund - 670
Marsh College Scholarship - 671
Marsh Scholarship Fund - 672
Marshall E. McCullough Scholarship - 673
Marshall Memorial Fellowship - 674
Marshall Scholar - 675
Marvin Mundel Memorial Scholarship - 676
Mary Church Terrell Award - 677
Mary Lou Brown Scholarship - 678
Mary Opal Walanin Scholarship - 679
Mary Paolozzi Member's Scholarship - 680
Mary Rhein Memorial Scholarship - 681
Masonic-Range Science Scholarship - 682
Materials Processing and Manufacturing Division Scholarship - 683
Matthew H. Parry Memorial Scholarship - 684
Mattie J.T. Stepanek Caregiving Scholarship - 685
Maurice B. Cohill, Jr. Young Investigator Award - 686
McNeil Consumer Health Rural and Underserved Scholarship - 687
Medal of Honor AFCEA ROTC Scholarships - 688
Medger Evers Award - 689
Media Fellows Program - 690
Mediacom World Class Scholarship Program - 691
Medical Student Summer Research Training in Aging Program - 692
Medtronic Physio-Control Advanced Nursing Practice Scholarship - 693
Melvin R. Green Scholarships - 694
Members-at-Large Reentry Award - 695
Memorial Scholarship Fund - 696
Mensa Education and Research Foundation Scholarship Program - 697
Metro Scholarship - 698
Metro Youth Football Association Scholarship - 699
Metropolitan Opera National Council Auditions - 700

MG James Ursano Scholarship Fund - 701
MGMA Midwest Section Scholarship - 702
MGMA Western Section Scholarship - 703
Michael Kidger Memorial Scholarship - 704
Microsoft Tuition Scholarships - 705
Mid-Continent Instrument Scholarship - 706
Mike Carr Student Paper Competition - 707
Mike Nash Memorial Scholarship Fund - 708
Military Award Program - 709
Military Officers' Benevolent Corporation Scholarships - 710
Military Order of the Purple Heart Scholarship - 711
Milton F. Lunch Research Fellowship - 712
Minorities and Women Educational Scholarship - 713
Minority Dental Student Scholarship - 714
Minority Fellowship Program - 715
Minority Scholarship Program - 716
Minority Student Scholarship - 717
MLA Scholarship - 718
MLA Scholarship for Minority Students - 719
MLA/NLM Spectrum Scholarship - 720
MOAA Base/Post Scholarships - 721
Montgomery GI Bill - Active Duty - 722
Montgomery GI Bill - Selected Reserve - 723
Montgomery GI Bill - Tuition Assistance Top-Up - 724
Morton B. Duggan, Jr. Memorial Education Recognition Award - 725
Morton Gould Young Composer Award - 726
Most Valuable Student Scholarships - 727
Myrtle and Earl Walker Scholarship - 728
NABF Scholarship Program - 729
NACA East Coast Graduate Student Scholarship - 730
NACA Regional Council Student Leader Scholarships - 731
NACOP Scholarship - 732
NAMEPA Scholarship Program - 733
NAMTA Foundation Visual Arts Major Scholarship - 734
Nancy Curry Scholarship - 735
Nancy Reagan Pathfinder Scholarships - 736
Naomi Berber Memorial Scholarship - 737
Naomi Brack Student Scholarship - 738
NAPA Research and Education Foundation Scholarship - 739
NATA Scholarship - 740
Nation Institute/I.F. Stone Award for Student Journalism - 741
National Aviation Explorer Scholarships - 742
National College Match Program - 743
National Dairy Shrine/Lager Dairy Scholarship - 744
National D-Day Museum Online Essay Contest - 745
National Defense Transportation Association St. Louis Area Chapter Scholarship - 746
National High School Poetry Contest/Easterday Poetry Award - 747
National History Day Contest - 748
National Italian American Foundation - 749
National Junior Classical League Scholarships - 750
National Junior Girls Scholarship - 751
National Latin Exam Scholarship - 752
National Marbles Tournament Scholarship - 753
National Merit Scholarship Program and National Achievement Scholarship Program - 754
National Oratorical Contest - 755
National Peace Contest - 756
National President's Scholarship - 757
National Scholarship Program - 758
National Scholarship Program - 759
National Sculpture Society Scholarship - 760
National Security Education Program David L. Boren Undergraduate Scholarships - 761
National Society of Hispanic MBAs Scholarship - 762
National Ten Minute Play Contest - 763

National Tour Association (NTA) Dr. Tom Anderson Graduate Scholarship - 764

National Tour Association (NTA) Eric Friedheim Graduate Scholarship - 765

National Tour Association (NTA) Luray Caverns Graduate Research Scholarship - 766

National Tour Association (NTA) New Horizons-Kathy LeTarte Undergraduate Scholarship - 767

National Tour Association (NTA) Reno Campbell-Ruth McKinney Undergraduate Scholarship - 768

National Tour Association (NTA) Travel Leaders Graduate Scholarship - 769

National Tour Association (NTA) Yellow Ribbon Undergraduate or Graduate Scholarship - 770

National Washington Crossing Foundation Scholarship - 771

Naval Enlisted Reserve Association Scholarships - 772

Naval Helicopter Association Scholarship - 773

Navin Narayan Scholarship - 774

Navy College Fund - 775

Navy League Endowed Scholarship - 776

Navy Supply Corps Foundation Scholarship - 777

Navy-Marine Corps ROTC College Program - 778

Navy-Marine Corps ROTC Four-Year Scholarships - 779

Navy-Marine Corps ROTC Two-Year Scholarships - 780

Navy-Marine Corps/Coast Guard (NMCCG) Enlisted Dependent Spouse Scholarship - 781

NCAA Division I Degree Completion Award Program - 782

NCAA Division II Degree Completion Award Program - 783

NCAA Postgraduate Scholarship - 784

NCCPAP Scholarship - 785

NCDXF Scholarship - 786

NCGE and Nystrom Geography Award - 787

Nell Bryant Robinson Scholarship - 788

Nettie Dracup Memorial Scholarship - 789

New England FEMARA Scholarships - 790

NFMC Claire Ulrich Whitehurst Piano Award - 791

NFMC Gretchen Van Roy Music Education - 792

NFMC Lynn Freeman Olson Competition Awards - 793

NFMC Wendell Irish Viola Award - 794

Nido Qubein Scholarship - 795

NLUS Stockholm Scholarship Fund - 796

North American Rolex Scholarship - 797

Northwest Perspectives Essay Contest - 798

NPPF Television News Scholarship - 799

NRA Outstanding Achievement Youth Award - 800

NROTC Nurse Corps Scholarship - 801

NROTC Scholarship Program - 802

NSA Scholarship Foundation - 803

NSCC Scholarship Funds - 804

NTA Arnold Rigby Graduate Scholarship - 805

NTA Dave Herren Memorial Undergraduate or Graduate Scholarship - 806

NTA Mayflower Tours Patrick Murphy Undergraduate or Graduate Internship - 807

Odenza Marketing Scholarship - 808

Off to College Scholarship Sweepstakes - 809

OP Loftbed Scholarship Award - 810

Optimist International Contest - 811

Optimist International Oratorical Contest - 812

Otto M. Stanfield Legal Scholarship - 813

Overseas Press Club Foundation Scholarships Internships - 814

Parent Answer Scholarship Sweepstakes - 815

Parsons Brinckerhoff Golden Apple Scholarship - 816

Part-Time Student Scholarship - 817

Patriot's Pen Youth Essay Contest - 818

Paul and Daisy Soros Felllowships for New Americans - 819

Paul and Helen L. Grauer Scholarship - 820

Pauline Langkamp Memorial Scholarship - 821

Pentagon Assistance Fund - 822

Persina Scholarship for Diversity in Journalism - 823

PHD ARA Scholarship - 824

Phoenix Scholarship Program - 825

Pi Sigma Alpha Washington Internship Scholarships - 826

Pierre and Patricia Bikai Fellowship - 827

Platt Family Scholarship Prize Essay Contest - 828

Playwright Discovery Award - 829

PMI Founders Scholarship - 830

Poster Contest for High School Students - 831

Predoctoral Fellowships for Historian of American Art to Travel Abroad - 832

PricewaterhouseCoopers Ascend Scholarship - 833

Princess Grace Awards - 834

Principal's Leadership Award - 835

Print and Graphics Scholarship - 836

Prize in Ethics Essay Contest - 837

Prize in International Insolvency Studies - 838

Professional Scholarships - 839

Project on Nuclear Issues Essay Contest - 840

Project Vote Smart National Internship Program - 841

Proof-Reading.com Scholarship - 842

ProStart National Certificate of Achievement Scholarship - 843

Prudential Spirit of Community Awards - 844

Ray , NRP and Katie, WKTE Pautz Scholarship - 845

Ray and Gertrude Marshall Scholarship - 846

Reid Blackburn Scholarship - 847

Religious Liberty Essay Scholarship Contest - 848

Retiree's Association and the Bureau of Alcohol, Tobacco, Firearms and Explosives (ATFAR) Scholarship - 849

Return 2 College Scholarship - 850

Rhodes Scholar - 851

Richard W. Bendicksen Memorial Scholarship - 852

Ritchie-Jennings Memorial Scholarship - 853

Robert J. Yourzak Scholarship - 854

Roller Skating Foundation Scholarship, Current College Student Category - 855

Roller Skating Foundation Scholarship, High School Student Category - 856

Ron Culp Scholarsip for Mentorship - 857

Ronald McDonald House Charities U.S. Scholarships - 858

Ruth Clark Furniture Design Scholarship - 859

Ruth Lillly Poetry Fellowship - 860

Ruth Stanton Community Grant - 861

Sadler's Wells Global Dance Contest - 862

Sally Strain Memorial Scholarship - 863

Salvatore J. Natoli Dissertation Award in Geographic Education - 864

Samuel H. Kress Foundation Paired Fellowship for Research in Conservation and the History of Art - 865

Samuel Huntington Public Service Award - 866

SanDisk Foundation Scholarship Program - 867

Scholar Athlete Milk Mustache of the Year Award - 868

Scholarship Drawing for $1,000 - 869

Scholarship in Book Production and Publishing - 870

Scholarship Program for Young Pianists - 871

Scholarship Slam - 872

Scholarships for Military Children - 873

Scholarships for Student Leaders - 874

Scholarships to Oslo International Summer School - 875

Scholastic Art and Writing Awards - 876

Schwan's Food Service Scholarship - 877

Seabee Memorial Scholarship - 878

Second Chance Scholarship Contest - 879

Senior Fellowship Program - 880

Sergeant Major Douglas R. Drum Memorial Scholarship Fund - 881

Shawn Carter Foundation Scholarship - 882

Undergraduate Scholarships - 953
Undergraduate Transfer Scholarship - 954
United Daughters of the Confederacy
Scholarship - 955
United States Senate Youth Program - 956
University Language Services College
Scholarship - 957
University of California Public Policy and
International Affairs Law Fellowship - 958
University of California Public Policy and
International Affairs Summer Institute -
959
USBC Annual Zeb Scholarship - 960
USBC Youth Ambassador of the Year -
961
USGIF Scholarship Program - 962
Vercille Voss IFDA Graduate Student
Scholarship - 963
Veterans Caucus Scholarship - 964
Vincent Chin Scholarship - 965
Violet Richardson Award - 966
Visine Students with Vision Scholarship
Program - 967
Visiting Senior Fellowship Program - 968
Voice of Democracy Audio Essay
Contests - 969
VRG Scholarship - 970
W.H. Howie McClennan Scholarship - 971
Watson Travel Fellowship - 972
Wendy's High School Helsman Award -
973
Werner B. Thiele Memorial Scholarship -
974
Wesley-Logan Prize - 975
Where's FRANKIE the Diploma Frame?
Scholarship Photo Contest - 976
William B. Ruggles Right to Work
Scholarship - 977
William E. Simon Fellowship for Noble
Purpose - 978
William L. Hastie Award - 979
William R. Goldfarb Memorial Scholarship
- 980
William S. Bullinger Scholarship - 981
Win Free Tuition Giveaway - 982
Women Band Directors International
College Scholarships - 983
Women In Geographic Education
Scholarship - 984

Women In Need Scholarship - 985
Women In Transition Scholarship - 986
Women Marines Association Scholarship
Program - 987
Women's Overseas Service League
Scholarships for Women - 988
Women's Western Gold Foundation
Scholarship - 989
Working Abroad Grant - 990
Worldstudio Foundation Scholarship
Program - 991
Yashiyama Young Entrepreneurs Program
- 992
Yasme Foundation Scholarship - 993
Young American Creative Patriotic Art
Awards Program - 994
Young Jazz Composer Award - 995
Young People for Fellowship - 996
Young Scholars Program - 997
YoungArts Program - 998
Youth Free Expression Network Film
Contest - 999
Youth Scholarship - 1000
Zachary Taylor Stevens Memorial
Scholarship – 1001

Scholarship Sponsor Index:

American Concrete Insitute Student
Fellowship Program - 27
American Concrete Insitute ACI James
Instruments Student Award - 25
American Congress on Surveying and
Mapping - 14
American Congress on Surveying and
Mapping - 35
American Congress on Surveying and
Mapping - 223
American Congress on Surveying and
Mapping - 789
American Congress on Surveying and
Mapping - 943
American Congress on Surveying and
Mapping - 655
American Copy Editor's Society - 24
American Council of Engineering
Companies of New York - 23
American Council of Independent
Laboratories - 28
American Council of Learned Societies -
32
American Council of Learned Societies -
33
American Council of Learned Societies -
242
American Council of Learned Societies -
419
American Council of Learned Societies
(ACLS) - 502
American Criminal Justice Association - 29
American Criminal Justice Association -
916
American Culinary Federation - 846
American Darts Organization - 89
American Dental Association Foundation -
78
American Dental Association Foundation -
317
American Dental Association Foundation -
714
American Dental Education Association -
39
American Dental Hygienists' Assocaition
(ADHA) Institute for Oral Health - 271
American Dental Hygienists' Association
Insitute for Oral Health - 547

American Dental Hygienists' Association
Institute for Oral Health - 41
American Dental Hygienists' Association
Institute for Oral Health - 222
American Dental Hygienists' Association
Institute for Oral Health - 294
American Dental Hygienists' Association
Institute for Oral Health - 343
American Dental Hygienists' Association
Institute for Oral Health - 613
American Dietetic Association Foundation
- 37
American Federation for Aging Research -
692
American Fire Sprinkler Association - 879
American Floral Endowment - 489
American Foreign Service Association
(AFSA) - 50
American Foreign Service Association
(AFSA) - 51
American Foundation - 120
American Foundation for Urologic
Disease Inc. - 171
American Ground Water Trust - 115
American Ground Water Trust - 181
American Harlequin Corporation - 485
American Health Information
Management Association Foundation - 56
American Historical Association - 388
American Historical Association - 551
American Historical Association - 975
American Holistic Nurses' Association -
249
American Hotel and Lodging Educational
Foundation - 91
American Hotel and Lodging Educational
Foundation - 906
American Hotel and Lodging Educational
Foundation (AH&LEF) - 358
American Hotle and Lodging Educational
Foundation - 534
American Institute for Contemporary
German Studies - 298
American Institute for Economic Research
- 920
American Institute for Foreign Study - 541
American Institute of Aeronautics and
Astronautics - 58

American Institute of Certified Public Accountants - 59
American Institute of Chemical Engineers - 334
American Institute of Chemical Engineers - 580
American Institute of Indian Studies - 608
American Institute of Mining, Metallurgical and Petroleum Engineers - 588
American Jersey Cattle Association - 238
American Kennel Club - 609
American Legion - 93
American Legion - 94
American Legion - 367
American Legion - 755
American Legion Auxiliary - 757
American Legion Baseball - 92
American Mathematical Society and Mathematical Association of America - 409
American Medical Technologists - 114
American Meteorlogical Society - 110
American Meteorlogical Society - 111
American Meteorlogical Society - 112
American Meteorlogical Society - 113
American Meteorological Society - 422
American Military Association - 881
American Montessori Society - 928
American Nuclear Society - 125
American Nuclear Society - 126
American Nuclear Society - 127
American Nuclear Society - 572
American Numismatic Society - 335
American Numismatic Society - 406
American Nursery and Landscape Association - 235
American Nurses Association - 266
American Orchid Society - 131
American Orff-Schulwerk Association - 886
American Physical Society - 138
American Physiological Society - 308
American Police Hall of Fame and Museum - 95
American Psychological Association Foundation - 132
American Psychological Association Foundation - 133
American Psychological Association Foundation - 190

American Quarter Horse Foundation - 96
American Radio Relay League Foundation - 148
American Radio Relay League Foundation - 199
American Radio Relay League Foundation - 231
American Radio Relay League Foundation - 244
American Radio Relay League Foundation - 245
American Radio Relay League Foundation - 252
American Radio Relay League Foundation - 311
American Radio Relay League Foundation - 336
American Radio Relay League Foundation - 345
American Radio Relay League Foundation - 355
American Radio Relay League Foundation - 360
American Radio Relay League Foundation - 377
American Radio Relay League Foundation - 407
American Radio Relay League Foundation - 417
American Radio Relay League Foundation - 434
American Radio Relay League Foundation - 445
American Radio Relay League Foundation - 544
American Radio Relay League Foundation - 559
American Radio Relay League Foundation - 611
American Radio Relay League Foundation - 622
American Radio Relay League Foundation - 678
American Radio Relay League Foundation - 786
American Radio Relay League Foundation - 790
American Radio Relay League Foundation - 820

NAMTA Foundation for the Visual Arts - 734

Nation Institute - 741

National Air Transportation Foundation Meisinger Scholarship - 301

National Amateur Baseball Federation - 729

National Asphalt Pavement Association - 739

National Association for Campus Activities - 669

National Association for Campus Activities - 730

National Association for Campus Activities - 731

National Association for Campus Activities - 874

National Association for Gifted Children - 8

National Association of Blacks in Criminal Justice - 595

National Association of Blacks in Criminal Justice - 677

National Association of Blacks in Criminal Justice - 689

National Association of Blacks in Criminal Justice - 979

National Association of Broadcasters - 420

National Association of Chiefs of Police - 732

National Association of Multicultural Engineering Program Advocates - 733

National Association of Pediatric Nurse Practitioners - 687

National Athletic Trainer's Association - 740

National Bicylce League (NBL) - 207

National Black Nurses Association - 124

National Black Police Association - 82

National Business Aviation Association - 630

National Cattlemen's Foundation - 186

National Center for Juvenile Justice - 686

National Coalition Against Censorship - 999

National Collegiate Athletic Association - 376

National Collegiate Athletic Association - 782

National Collegiate Athletic Association - 783

National Collegiate Athletic Association - 784

National Conference of CPA Practitioners NCCPAP Scholarship - 785

National Council for Geographic Education - 276

National Council for Geographic Education - 380

National Council for Geographic Education - 787

National Council for Geographic Education - 864

National Council for Geographic Education - 984

National Court Reporters Association - 414

National Dairy Shrine - 300

National Dairy Shrine - 328

National Dairy Shrine - 618

National Dairy Shrine - 673

National Dairy Shrine - 744

National D-Day Museum Foundation - 745

National Defense Transportation Association-Scott St. Louis Chapter - 746

National Education Association - 553

National Federation of Music Clubs - 792

National Federation of Music Clubs - 794

National Federation of Music Clubs - 932

National Federation of Music Clubs Claire Ulrich Whitehurst Piano Award - 791

National Federation of Music Clubs Junior Composers Award - 606

National Federation of Music Clubs Olson Awards - 793

National Federation of Music Clubs Stillman-Kelley Award - 908

National Federation of Republican Women - 736

National Federation of State Poetry Societies - 361

National FFA Organizations - 302

National Fluid Milk Processor Promotion Board - 868

National Foundatoin for Advancement in the Arts - 998

National Gallery of Art - 832

Ronald Reagan Presiential Foundation - 454

Rosalynn Carter Institute for Caregiving - 685

Sadler's Wells - 862

San Angelo Symphony - 895

SanDisk Foundation Scholarship Program - 867

Scholarship Detective - 3

Scholastic - 149

Scholastic - 876

School Band and Orchestra Magazine - 123

Seabee Memorial Scholarship Association - 878

Seafarers International Union of North American - 247

Second Indianhead Division Association - 535

Shawn Carter Foundation - 882

Siemens Foundation - 889

Sigma Alpha Lota Philanthropies - 953

Simon Youth Foundation - 891

Sinfonia Foundation - 892

Society for Range Management - 682

Society for Technical Communication - 322

Society of Automotive Engineers International - 205

Society of Automotive Engineers International - 330

Society of Automotive Engineers International - 416

Society of Automotive Engineers International - 648

Society of Broadcast Engineers - 1000

Society of Manufacturing Engineers Education Foundation - 444

Society of Manufacturing Engineers Education Foundation - 461

Society of Manufacturing Engineers Education Foundation - 728

Society of Naval Architects and Marine Engineers - 474

Society of Naval Architects and Marine Engineers - 590

Society of Naval Architects and Marine Engineers - 666

Society of Physics Students - 504

Society of Physics Students - 899

Society of Plastics Engineers - 280

Society of Plastics Engineers - 610

Society of Satellite Professionals International - 900

Sodexo Foundation - 905

Sons of Norway Foundation - 447

Sons of Norway Foundation - 616

Sons of Norway Foundation - 875

Sons of Union Veterans of the Civil War - 894

Soroptimist International of the Americans - 966

Specialty Equipment Market Association - 896

Sportquest All-American Program - 897

Sportquest All-American Program - 898

Students Overcoming Adversity Responsibly - 893

Sun Trust - 809

SuperCollege.com - 922

Tag and Label Manufacturers Institute Inc. - 935

Tag and Label Manufacturers Institute Inc. - 936

Talbots - 926

Teachers of Accounting at Two-Year Colleges - 925

Telluride Association - 930

The Lincoln Forum - 828

The Minerals, Metals and Materials Society - 642

The Minerals, Metals and Materials Society - 683

The Online Degree Advisor - 863

Third Marine Division Association - 696

Thomas J. Watson Fellowship - 972

Thomas Pniewski, Director of Cultural Affairs - 946

Tourims Cares - 100

Tourims Cares - 101

Tourims Cares - 102

Tourims Cares - 103

Tourims Cares - 104

Tourism Cares - 98

Tourism Cares - 99

Tourism Cares - 764

Tourism Cares - 765

Tourism Cares - 766

General Category –

ACADEMICS/GENERAL

MoolahSpot Scholarship - 2
$,1500 College JumpStart Scholarship - 3
$1,500 Scholarship Detective Launch Scholarship - 4
Advancing Aspirations Global Scholarship - 44
Akash Kuruvilla Memorial Scholarship - 74
Alpha Kappa Alpha Financial Need Scholars - 79
American Essay Contest - 91
AXA Achievement Community Scholarship - 176
AXA Achievement Scholarships - 177
Best Buy @ 15 Scholarship Program - 192
Big Dig Scholarship - 196
Blogging Scholarship - 204
Burger King Scholars Program - 219
C.I.P. Scholarship - 221
Carson Scholars - 234
Castle Ink's Green Scholarship - 236
Charles Shafae' Scholarship - 246
Church Hill Classics "Frame My Future" Scholarship - 258
CIA Undergraduate Scholarship Program - 259
CKSF Scholarships - 260
Coca-Cola All-State Community College Academic Team - 269
Coca-Cola Scholars Program - 270
College Answer $1,000 Scholarship - 272
College Prep Scholarship for High School Juniors - 274
CollegeNET Scholarship - 276
Congress Bundestag Youth Exchange Program - 281
Congressional Black Caucus Spouses Education Scholarship - 283
Create Real Impact Contest - 293
CrossLites Scholarship Contest - 295
Davidson Fellows Award - 309
Davis-Putter Scholarship Fund - 310
Dell Scholars Program - 313
Direction.com College Scholarship - 319
Discus Awards College Scholarships - 320
Dollars for Scholars Scholarship - 331
Dr. Arnita Young Boswell Scholarship - 341
Dr. Wynetta A. Frazier Sister to Sister Scholarship - 347
Dream Deferred Essay Contest on Civil Rights in the Mideast - 348
Educational Advacement Foundation Merit Scholarship - 362
Families of Freedom Scholarship Fund - 385
FiSCA Scholarship - 395
Foundation for Global Scholars General Scholarship - 398
Freedom of Speech PSA Contest - 420
From Failure to Promise Essay Contest - 423
Fulbright Grants - 425
GE-Reagan Foundation Scholarship Program - 441
Gen and Kelly Tanabe Student Scholarship - 443
Global Citizen Awards - 464
Go! Study Abroad Scholarship - 466
Graduate Scholarship - 474
Hayek Fund for Scholars - 495
Holocaust Remembrance Project Essay Contest - 508
Horatio Alger Association Scholarship Program - 511
Humane Studies Fellowships - 516
Imagine America Promise - 532
Joe Foss Institute Essay Scholarship Program - 566
John F. Kennedy Profile in Courage Essay Contest - 577
Josephine De Karman Fellowship - 601
Kymanox's James J. Davis Memorial Scholarship for Students Studying Abroad - 621
Letters About Literature Contest - 637
Life Lessons Essay Contest - 641
LULAC General Awards - 660
LULAC Honors Awards - 661
LULAC National Scholastic Achievement Awards - 662
Marshall Memorial Fellowship - 674
Marshall Scholar - 675

ACCOUNTING/FINANCE

AEROSPACE AND AVIATION

AGRICULTURE/HORTICULTURE /ANIMALS

BUSINESS AND MANAGEMENT

CHEMISTRY

COMMUNICATIONS

Naomi Berber Memorial Scholarship 737
NCDXF Scholarship 786
New England FEMARA Scholarships 790
Nido Qubein Scholarship 795
Optimist International Contest 811
Optimist International Oratorical Contest 812
Parsons Brinckerhoff Golden Apple Scholarship 816
Paul and Helen L. Grauer Scholarship 820
PHD ARA Scholarship 824
Print and Graphics Scholarship 836
Ray , NRP and Katie, WKTE Pautz Scholarship 846
Richard W. Bendicksen Memorial Scholarship 852
Scholarship in Book Production and Publishing 870
SSPI Scholarship Program 900
Student with a Disability Scholarship 918
TLMI Four Year Colleges/Full-Time Students Scholarship 935
Tom and Judith Comstock Scholarship 938
Transatlantic Fellows Program 941
William R. Goldfarb Memorial Scholarship 980
Yasme Foundation Scholarship 992
Zachary Taylor Stevens Memorial Scholarship 1001

COMPUTER RELATED
AFCEA General Emmett Paige Scholarships 45
AFCEA General John A. Wickham Scholarships 46
AFCEA Ralph W. Shrader Diversity Scholarships 47
AFCEA ROTC Scholarships 48
AFCEA Scholarship for Working Professionals 49
AGA Scholarships 53
AOC Scholarships 129
Astronaut Scholarship 169
Davidson Fellows Award 309
Graduate Research Fellowship Program 471
HIMSS Foundation Scholarship 506

HORIZONS Foundation Scholarship 513
IEEE President's Scholarship 522
Intel Science Talent Search 537
Lockheed Martin/HENAAC Scholars Program 646
Microsoft Tuition Scholarships 705
Stokes Educational Scholarship Program 909

CONSTRUCTION
AAGS Joseph F. Dracup Scholarship Award 15
ACI James Instruments Student Award for Research on NDT on Concrete 25
AGC Graduate Scholarships 54
AGC Undergraduate Scholarships 55
Centex Homes "Build Your Future" Scholarship 239
Delta Faucet Company Scholarships 315
IRF Fellowship Program 548
Lee S. Evans Scholarship 633
Milton F. Lunch Research Fellowship 712

CULINARY ARTS
Academic Scholarship for High School Seniors 20
Academic Scholarship for Undergraduate ProStart Alumni and ManageFirst Students 21
Chain des Rotisseurs Scholarship 240
Golden Gate Restaurant Association Scholarship 468
IFEC Scholarships Award 526
IFSEA Worthy Goal Scholarship 527
ProStart National Certificate of Achievement Scholarship 843
Ray and Gertrude Marshall Scholarship 845

DENTISTRY
ADHA Institute Scholarship Program 41
Allied Dental Health Scholarships 78
Cadbury Adams Community Outreach Scholarships 222
Colgate "Bright Smiles, Bright Futures" Minority Scholarships 271
Crest Oral-B Laboratories Dental Hygiene Scholarships 294

ENGLISH AND WRITING

ETHNIC STUDIES

Fellowships/Grants to Study in Scandinavia 390
Finlandia Foundation National Student Scholarships Program 393
Fulbright Grants 425
General Heritage and Culture Grants 447
German Studies Research Grant 455
Gilman International Scholarship 460
IACI/NUI Visting Fellowship in Irish Studies 519
International Scholarships 541
John O. Crane Memorial Fellowship 586
Junior Fellowships 607
King Olav V Norwegian-American Heritage Fund 616
Marshall Memorial Fellowship 674
Marshall Scholar 675
National Italian American Foundation 749
National Security Education Program David L. Boren Undergraduate Scholarships 761
Scholarships to Oslo International Summer School 875
Short-Term Travel Grants 887
Tuitiion Scholarship Program 946
Working Abroad Grant 990

FOOD SERVICE
Academic Scholarship for High School Seniors 20
Academic Scholarship for Undergraduate ProStart Alumni and ManageFirst Students 21
CNF Professional Growth Scholarship 267
GED Jump Start Scholarship 440
Golden Gate Restaurant Association Scholarship 468
IFEC Scholarships Award 526
IFSEA Worthy Goal Scholarship 527
Nancy Curry Scholarship 735
ProStart National Certificate of Achievement Scholarship 843
Schwan's Food Service Scholarship 877

FOREIGN LANGUAGE
ACL/NJCL National Greek Examination Scholarship 30
ACL/NJCL National Latin Examination Scholarships 31

Bridging Scholarships for Study Abroad in Japan 213
Council on International Educational Exchange Scholarships 290
FALCON - Full Year Asian Language Concentration 384
Fellowships for Regular Program in Greece 389
JTG Scholarship in Scientific and Technical Translation or Interpretation 602
KOR Memorial Scholarship 620
National Italian American Foundation 749
National Junior Classical League Scholarships 750
National Latin Exam Scholarship 752
National Security Education Program David L. Boren Undergraduate Scholarships 761
Stokes Educational Scholarship Program 909
Student Translation Award 917
Translation Prize 942

FORESTRY AND OUTDOORS
Apprentice Ecologist Initiative Youth Scholarship Program 137
ASF Olin Fellowship 154
Association for Women in Science Educational Awards 164
Campus Safety Health and Environmental Management Association Scholarship 225
Federal Junior Duck Stamp Program and Scholarship Competition 386
George A. Hall / Harold F. Mayfield Award 450
Green Mountain Water Environment Association Scholarship 479
John Mabry Forestry Scholarship 585
John Wright Memorial Scholarship 591
Louis Agassiz Fuertes Award 652
Masonic-Range Science Scholarship 682

GRAPHIC ART
Art Awards 149
FFTA Scholarship Competition 392
Lions International Peace Poster Contest 643
Print and Graphics Scholarship 836

MILITARY, FIRE AND POLICE

ORGANIZATIONS AND CLUBS

PERFORMING ARTS, MUSIC AND DRAMA

PSYCHOLOGY

PUBLIC ADMINISTRATION AND SOCIAL WORK

PUBLIC AND COMMUNITY SERVICE

SOCIAL SCIENCE AND HISTORY

UNION RELATED

VOCATIONAL

Montgomery GI Bill - Active Duty 722
Nell Bryant Robinson Scholarship 788
Shawn Carter Foundation Scholarship 882
Shell/CAPT Process Technology
Scholarship 883
Specialty Equipment Market Association
(SEMA) Memorial Scholarship 896
Werner B. Thiele Memorial Scholarship
974

CPSIA information can be obtained
at www.ICGtesting.com
Printed in the USA
BVOW03s0533010517
482792BV00004BA/53/P